Money
1988

Money
1988

By the Editors of MONEY Magazine

Oxmoor House®

ISBN: 0-8487-0724-9
ISSN: 0891-172X

Manufactured in the United States of America
First Printing 1988

Published by arrangement with Oxmoor House, Inc.
Book Division of Southern Progress Corporation
P.O. Box 2463, Birmingham, Alabama 35201

Executive Editor: Ann H. Harvey
Production Manager: Jerry Higdon
Associate Production Manager: Rick Litton
Art Director: Bob Nance

Money 1988
Compiled and Edited by Junius Ellis

Editor: Vicki L. Ingham
Editorial Assistant: D. Lynne Hopkins
Designer: Cynthia R. Cooper

Photograph opposite title page by Jim Bathie

To order *Money* magazine, write to: *Money*, P.O. Box 54429, Boulder, CO 80322-4429.

Money Staff
Managing Editor: Landon Y. Jones
Executive Editor: Frank Lalli
Assistant Managing Editors: Richard A. Burgheim, Frank B. Merrick
Senior Editors: Joseph S. Coyle, Caroline Donnelly, Augustin Hedberg, Robert J. Klein, Tyler Mathisen, Kevin S. McKean, Michael Sivy
Art Director: Eric Seidman
Picture Editor: Deborah Pierce
Editor, Investor's Scorecard: Pauline Tai
Senior Writers: Jerry Edgerton, Richard Eisenberg, Marlys Harris
Staff Writers: Greg Anrig Jr. (Washington), William C. Banks, Diane Harris, Robert McNatt, Robin Micheli, Andrea Rock, Eric Schurenberg, Suzanne Seixas, John Stickney, Candace E. Trunzo, Walter L. Updegrave, Leslie N. Vreeland
Chief of Reporters: Katharine B. Drake
Senior Reporters: Jordan E. Goodman, Lani Luciano
Reporters: Martha J. Mader (deputy chief), Jan Alexander, Debra Wishik Englander, Carla A. Fried, Beth M. Gilbert, Jersey Gilbert, J. Howard Green, Bruce Hager, Daphne D. Mosher (letters), Jeanne L. Reid, D. Jacqueline Smith, Caren M. Weiner, Holly Wheelwright
Design and Picture Departments: Dan Lloyd Taylor (assistant design director), Donna Ingram, Karen Oeff
Miriam Hsia (assistant picture editor), Leslie Yoo (picture researcher)
Copy Chief: Sukey Rosenbaum
Copy Desk: Patricia A. Feimster, Andrew Schwartz (deputy chiefs), Eve Sennett, Suzanne Justin Riggio, Mark Hudson Giles, Margaret J. Stefanowicz, Kathleen Beakley, Bill O'Connor, Judith Ryan, Edward M. Gay Jr., Ricki Tarlow, Keith E. Johnson, Sarah Plant
Editorial Production Manager: Barbara A. Hersch
Editorial Production: Karen Harper Diaz, Gary S. Costello

Editor's Note

Congratulations! In the past 12 months you have survived some of the most turbulent events ever experienced in the financial lives of Americans. It was a wild ride. The year 1987 began benignly with the introduction of a new tax law giving you the lowest tax brackets you are likely to see in your lifetime. But financial markets gyrated unpredictably as the Dow Jones Industrial Average leaped past 2000, pirouetted all the way to 2700—and then tumbled nearly 1000 points in six frightening weeks last fall.

How are you doing now? You may feel relieved but not relaxed. A quick checkup will most likely show that your vital signs are healthy. This book will help you do just that. If your finances are in good order, you might be wondering about where to invest in 1988 and beyond. This book will help you do that, too. Perhaps you are considering tapping the equity in your home. Then, too, you might have other ideas about boosting your insurance coverage or planning your retirement or building an estate to pass on to your heirs.

If those are your concerns, you will find *Money 1988* a uniquely valuable publication. These 61 articles summarize in one convenient place the most useful information published by *Money* magazine over the past year. Here you will find tax tips for homeowners and mutual fund investors. You will learn about investments ranging from single-state municipal bonds to bonds sold in foreign countries. Your family can gather here insights about the best life insurance policies and the best ways to buy a new house. We will help you manage all your finances with a sharp eye on building your assets while reducing your debts.

The Editors of *Money* are delighted to join with Oxmoor House in offering you this annual sourcebook. We are convinced that you have the opportunity to build a wonderful financial future for you and your family. We trust that *Money 1988* will help you achieve it successfully.

LANDON Y. JONES
Managing Editor, *Money*

Contents

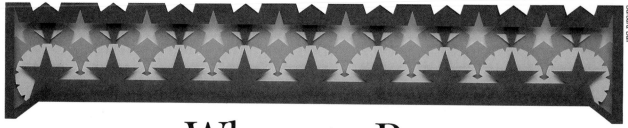

Where to Put Your Money in 1988

In the long run, October's unprecedented stock market collapse could prove to be a perverse blessing. A number of respected economists, including former Federal Reserve Board chief Paul Volcker, argue that the stunning loss of some $500 billion in stock values in a single day may expunge speculative excess from the overblown markets, thereby paving the way for more realistic gains this year. Interest and inflation rates, which had been rising, suddenly reversed course to provide another long-term plus for the financial markets. And politicians, shocked by the looming threat of recession, are finally taking steps to cut the massive budget and trade deficits—the twin problems that have long threatened to topple the prosperous-looking house of cards that Reaganomics built.

That said, the cloud cast by that blackest of Mondays is still awfully dark. The historic 26% two-day drop in stock prices in mid-October and the wild market gyrations that followed raise profound questions about your personal finances. Among them: Will you have to revamp investment strategies and re-allocate assets? Should you alter your plans for retirement? Will the crash affect your spending and saving? Where should you put your money in the months ahead?

First, the Big Question

The magnitude of the market crash makes accurate predictions about its repercussions nearly impossible. Of past declines, only the 23% two-day fall in October 1929 came close in size. And everybody knows what followed that one. Most forecasters do not envision a repeat of the Great Depression—slower economic growth certainly, as anxious consumers cut their spending; recession possibly, but not outright financial catastrophe. Yet with economists confessing lack of faith in their own forecasts, the consensus view is not terribly reassuring.

A few lonely bulls insist that the primary trend in stock prices is up and that the October massacre was nothing more than a dramatic correction in the most powerful advance in postwar history. But by the widely accepted definition of a bear market—a drop of more than 20%—this one growled like a genuine grizzly. Despite the partial comeback in prices since mid-October, the momentum of the market, a broad measure of the direction of stock prices, still shows declining issues outpacing advancing ones by nearly two to one.

Just how long it will be before stocks can

mount a lasting recovery depends on the economy. In agreement with most other forecasters, Allen Sinai, chief economist at Shearson Lehman Brothers, estimates that the gross national product will grow by a sluggish 1.5% to 2% in 1988, one and one-half percentage points less than had been expected before the crash. He also expects inflation to run 3.5% to 4% this year, down one percentage point from pre-crash forecasts. Interest rates, which were expected to rise modestly in 1988, are now more likely to fall by one percentage point, as consumer spending and borrowing moderate. With U.S. officials no longer trying to prop up the dollar through higher interest rates, the trade deficit may begin to shrink as the weakening greenback increases demand for American goods abroad by lowering their cost.

But economists cannot rule out the possibility that the downturn could deepen into a recession—two or more consecutive quarters of negative economic growth. The odds on Wall Street of recession next year are as high as three to one. And even though the stock market is sometimes overly nervous, it is considered a reasonably reliable leading economic indicator. Of the thirteen major declines in stock prices in the postwar period, eight have been followed by a recession. Moreover, market declines as large as the one from August through October have always resulted in recession.

Severe bear markets always accompany the first stages of recession. During the 1973-74 economic slump, for example, the Dow Jones Industrial Average dropped 45% over a period of 23 months. If the current market follows that pattern, within the next 12 months or so the Dow would hit bottom around 1500—13.7% below Black Monday levels. The average record of postwar bear markets: a 31% decline over a 15-month period. Even after the bear retreats, the suffering is not over. According to a study by Yale professor of finance Roger Ibbotson, investors who held on to their stocks in bear markets since World War II have had to wait from 14 to 42 months just to break even.

Indicators to Watch

Forecasters' lack of faith in their current economic predictions suggests that you may want to do your own sleuthing in the coming months to determine the direction of the economy and the financial markets. Here are some of the indicators to watch for in the press.

Retail sales. Consumer spending is crucial to economic growth. Reports on retail sales, released in the middle of every month by the U.S. Commerce Department, will flash early warnings of consumer retrenchment. A decline of about 1% for at least two to three months running would indicate a significant slowdown in consumer purchasing; repeated drops of 2% or more over the same period could signal recession.

Orders for business plant and equipment. Corporate planners anxious about a downturn tend to cut back on capital spending to shore up the bottom line. In fact, business investment fell by one-half of one percentage point in the third quarter of 1987, according to the Commerce Department's quarterly reports on orders for plant and equipment. Progressively larger declines could be a clue that corporate executives smell recession in the air. If so, you should too.

The federal funds and discount rates. The federal funds rate (the interest rate charged by Federal Reserve banks to banks borrowing funds overnight) is the most sensitive indicator of the future direction of interest rates because it is set daily according to market conditions. The federal funds rate has been falling since Black Monday, indicating less fear of inflation. Announcement of a cut in the discount rate (the rate the Fed charges member banks for longer-term loans) would confirm a downward rate trend.

The financial markets. Lower interest rates and reduced risk of inflation are good news for stock and bond prices. While percentage changes in major market indexes such as the Dow reflect the general direction of stock prices, they can sometimes be misleading because of the limited number of companies represented. For the big picture, turn to two measures of market breadth—the number of advancing stocks versus declining issues and the number of shares hitting new highs versus those dropping to new lows. Successive weeks of contraction in the number of issues rising in price and reaching new highs relative to the number that are declining or falling to new lows is a sign of basic market weakness.

Be prepared for a blurry picture. Harbingers of recession or resurgence, while useful tools, nearly always flash confusing signals at first. Some forecasters believe that months may pass before consumers respond fully to the stock market's decline. Retail sales during the 1929 Christmas season, they point out, were robust—hardly a prescient warning of the tight money, failed banks, and 25% unemployment that followed.

You need not—indeed, should not—wait until you are sure where the evidence is pointing before making some cautious, reasoned adjustments to your portfolio. Whether the economy tumbles into recession or rebounds smartly, one underlying investment theme is clear: the very uncertainty of the outlook combined with the recent violent market moves dictates a shift from aggressive strategies that strive for maximum gains to defensive maneuvers that protect your capital. What happened in October is the financial equivalent of an earthquake, and what the aftershocks will be is still unknown. This is no time to compromise on safety.

What to Do Next

Leading investment strategists recommend several specific moves:
● Regard market rallies as opportunities to dump your riskiest stocks. Even analysts who were super-bullish before the crash now say

Where to Make the Most Money in 1988

Many of Wall Street's premier forecasters were as surprised as the smallest investor by the severity of the stock market's October plunge. Still, two dozen of the bravest market gurus agreed to forecast the current prospects for investments in their areas of expertise for *Money*. Their advice, which is tempered with a new, cautious wisdom gained from Black Monday, is meant to help you invest your money profitably over the coming year. In each category, we highlight the range of the experts' predictions, which were often widely disparate, for total return over the next 12 months. In some categories, we also include estimates of levels of price indexes at the end of 1988.

STOCKS

Blue chips
-10% to +18%
Best prospects include food and beverage companies, banks, casualty insurers, pharmaceuticals, and paper manufacturers. The Dow Jones Industrial Average at year-end: 1700 to 2300.

Small growth stocks
-27% to +5%
Warns Charles Allmon, editor of *Growth Stock Outlook*: "There's no way around it, these stocks are going down." The Value Line Composite Index at year-end: 130 to 190, compared with a 1987 high of 289.

Utilities
+8% to +27%
Robert Farrell, chief investment strategist at Merrill Lynch, says the group will outperform the market in the next six months, with dividends representing about a third of the total return. Dow Jones Utility Average at year-end: 76 versus its recent level of 70.

Oil stocks
+5% to +11%
Expected to lag the market but dividend yields

are high. Standard & Poor's oil index at year-end: 475 versus its recent 490.

European stocks
+20% to +40%

A weaker dollar will again produce double-digit gains for American investors. Most promising: the German, French, and British stock markets.

Pacific Basin stocks
+15% to +30%

Bullish forecasters see Japanese stocks ending the year with the Nikkei Dow at 27,000, while bears expect the index to settle at its current 22,000 level. The Singapore market could rebound 30%, while the Hong Kong market is likely to be Asia's laggard.

BONDS

Long-term T-bonds
0% to +18%

Increased odds of a recession raise the likelihood of capital gains on issues with 30-year maturities, but the dollar's fall could result in flatter values.

Medium-term T-bonds
+3% to +16%

Best choices: five- to seven-year maturities. The latter offer 97% of the 8.9% yield on a 30-year bond but will suffer only half the decline if rates rise.

Short-term T-bonds
+6% to +10%

Two- to four-year bonds provide maximum price protection and a 7% yield if they are held to maturity.

Medium-term corporates
+8% to +20%

Maturities of five to seven years offer the best hedge against rising rates.

Ginnie Maes
+7% to +15%

Falling rates could prompt early mortgage paybacks, keeping returns near the low end of the range.

20-year tax-exempts
+1% to +20%

Attractive for people in the 28% and 33% brackets.

PRECIOUS METALS

Gold
-28% to +20%

Continued market uncertainties could push the price of gold to $550, up from its recent $450. But contrarian analyst John Dessauer warns that gold may hit lows of $330 an ounce as inflation and interest rates both plummet.

Silver
-15% to +40%

Slower economic growth would keep prices flat, at best. Silver's price is more volatile than gold's, so it will gain more if inflation fears spread.

REAL ESTATE

Single-family homes
+6% to +7%

Appreciation is expected to be strongest in the Northeast, weakest in the Southeast.

REITs
+5% to +27%

Mortgage REITs are likely to outperform REITs that aim primarily for capital gains from property sales.

that the prospects are slim for a sustained surge. For example, Prudential-Bache analyst Joseph Feshbach, who predicted that "it's clear sailing to a 3500 Dow" last September, now agrees with consensus forecasts suggesting that the index will trade between the low 1700s and 2200 in early 1988. The prime candidates for sale are volatile stocks that typically rise or fall more than the market average and issues with lofty price-to-earnings ratios of 20 or higher, versus a recent P/E of 14 for the market overall. From October 1 through October 19, when the market P/E averaged 18, the 20% of stocks with the highest multiple—27 and above—fell 15% more than the average issue.

● Park 50% to 75% of the cash you get from selling stock. If there is a recession, cash investments, such as certificates of deposit or money-market accounts, may give you the safest and greatest return on your money. And if both the economy and stock prices confound the experts by recovering quickly, you will have the cash on hand to move swiftly back into the market.

● Invest the rest of the cash from stock sales in high-quality bonds. If interest rates continue to fall, as experts expect, your bonds will increase in value. And if rates reverse course, the interest from top-grade issues will provide you with a safe income. You might also consider putting 5% to 10% of your money into gold as a hedge against inflation, though that investment is becoming increasingly risky.

● Do not sell stocks that are fundamentally sound unless you must. It is only human to panic when all those around you are stampeding for the exits. But fight the urge. The time to sell shares is when prices are rising; selling into a decline only turns your paper losses into real ones. View your high-quality stocks as long-term holdings. Do not be panicked into selling good companies at bad prices.

● Reassess the way your retirement funds are invested. Start with the money that you and your employer contribute jointly to company-sponsored retirement accounts, such as a profit-sharing, thrift, or 401(k) plan. Typically these plans allow you to choose the mix of investments in your account periodically from among a stock fund, fixed-income fund, money-market fund, or shares in your company's stock. How much you may already have been hurt by falling stock prices depends on the choice you made. Overall, these plans fell about 15% in value from the August market peak to early November, according to the non-profit Employee Benefit Research Institute in Washington, D.C. Accounts that were fully invested in stocks, however, suffered losses that averaged 26%.

If you have sustained losses of that magnitude, your first instinct may be to run for cover by shifting all your money to fixed-income investments as soon as you can. But do not rush to that decision. If you are at least a decade away from retirement, you are better off sticking mainly with stocks, advises Paul Westbrook, a financial planner in Watchung, New Jersey. Over a 10-year period, stocks will usually outperform fixed-income funds by an average of 6% to 7% a year, and thus allow you to recoup your current losses. If you have fewer than 10 years until retirement, focus on preserving your capital by shifting 40% to 80% of your money into your plan's fixed-income or money-market fund. And if you are within two to four years of retirement, put the entire amount into cash as soon as you can. For the short term, Westbrook says, the chances of making back what you have already lost in stocks in a bear market is about zero.

The lasting lesson of the worst week in financial history could well be a renewed appreciation of the risks inherent in investing—and a greater respect for the long-term strategies that help to reduce them. On the pages that follow, *Money*'s editors offer specific suggestions for defensive investing.

Safe Places to Park Your Cash

In the immediate wake of the stock market crash, money-market fund assets rose sharply to a new high of $303 billion. Many banks and brokerages were overwhelmed with demand for certificates of deposit as investors joined traditional savers in a rush to safe cash havens. Stock market refugees were switching the remnants of their holdings into cash—some resolving never again to go near Wall Street, others standing by for an opportune moment to get back in and scoop up bargains in shares or bonds. Whether you joined the fleeing mobs or are just coming into a bundle of money, preserving your wealth against jumpy markets and a cloudy economic outlook is, understandably, of greater concern to you now than ever before.

Nonetheless, you would certainly like to earn more than the 5% or so available in the sanctuary of a passbook savings account. And you can. If you are willing to bank by mail, for example, you can get around 7.5% in federally insured money-market deposit accounts at savings and loans with solid balance sheets. If you are willing to tie up money in a CD for one year, yields recently ranged up to 8.5% at financially sound thrifts accepting out-of-state deposits that are federally insured up to $100,000.

Which alternative you choose may depend on how long you plan to leave your money untouched. Ask yourself as well whether you agree with the interest-rate consensus, which says rates will decline over the coming year, or with the minority view that resurging inflation will push rates up. If you cannot decide between those clashing forecasts, split your cash equally between a money-market fund (recently yielding an average of 6.5%), which quickly catches up with current rates, and a one-year CD, which will lock in the current yield, recently an average of 7.6%.

Pick a Guardian You Trust

Safety depends partly on the type of institution to which you entrust your money. The choices include the following:

Bank deposits. Despite the highest number of bank failures in U.S. history (156 through October 1987), federally insured deposits are generally considered to be as safe as U.S. Treasuries, which remain a worldwide symbol of invulnerability. If a thriving bank or S&L merges with an insolvent institution, depositors feel little impact. For nearly a third of the banks that failed last year, however, no rescuer came forth. That can prove costly. Depositors who do not file claims with the proper authorities in the first few days after the bank failure might have to wait several weeks to retrieve their money. And during that time, they earn no interest on it.

Brokerage accounts. The collapse of a few small brokerage firms following Black Monday alarmed millions of investors, causing some to question the safety of even their brokerage firm money-market funds. On that count, at least, they seem to have worried needlessly. Assets of brokerage clients are guaranteed by the Securities Investor Protection Corporation

(SIPC), a $390 million fund maintained by its 11,305 member brokerage firms and supplemented by a $500 million credit line with a consortium of banks, plus a $1 billion credit line with the U.S. Treasury. If a brokerage firm should happen to go under, the assets in clients' accounts will be replaced.

SIPC's guarantee is limited, however, to $500,000 worth of securities held in the broker's "street name" and $100,000 of uninvested cash balances. The higher limit takes in money-market fund shares and CDs held by the brokerage firm (many brokers deal in bank CDs). SIPC guarantees only that the number of money-market fund shares you hold will be replaced; no protection is promised against fluctuations in the value of those shares. Thus shares in a brokerage money-market fund are no more and no less safe than shares of any other money fund.

Nonbrokerage money-market funds. Unless they include the word *insured* in their title, most money-market funds have no formal safety net. You are relying on the nature of the investment portfolio to secure the liquidity and value of your assets. Money funds achieve safety and a constant $1 share value by restricting their portfolios to short-term, high-quality debt issues, such as Treasury bills, CDs, and prime commercial paper—debt obligations of blue-chip corporations. Your risk therefore is nearly nil.

Insured money funds yield less than uninsured ones, so unless you cannot bear even the slightest uncertainty, skip the insurance. Money-market funds designed for individual investors have an almost unblemished record for preserving shareholders' principal.

Weigh Yields and Risks

Outside the shelter of bank deposits and the money market, you must confront the risk that your cash investment may lose market value or yield less than the going interest rate. Most investment advisers and economists think that slower economic growth as a result of anxiety created by the crash will cause rates to stabilize or even gently decline through most of this year. Another analytical camp, however, believes that a resurgence of inflation will drive interest rates up later this year. These pessimists advocate maintaining flexibility by sticking with money-market funds or fixed-rate investments with maturities no longer than six months. The best places for your cash hinge on your plans for the money and your guess about rates. Your specific choices, which follow, cover a range of yields and risks.

Treasury bills: 6% to 6.9%. Starting at the low end of the yield spectrum, Treasury bills offer two major attractions: government-guaranteed safety of principal, and interest that is exempt from state and local taxes. Recent returns have been 6% for three-month bills, 6.5% for six-month bills, and 6.9% for twelve-month bills. T-bills require a minimum investment of $10,000. If that amount is more than you want to invest, you can get into T-bills for $2,000 or less through money-market funds that invest in them exclusively. Two examples include Capital Preservation Fund, recently yielding 6.1%, and Neuberger & Berman Government Money Fund, at 5.8%.

Then there is the best known of all Treasuries: U.S. savings bonds. You can still buy them at $25 and up at banks and through payroll savings plans. Series EE bonds, the current version, pay rates adjusted every six months to equal 85% of the average return on five-year Treasury notes, with a guaranteed five-year yield of 6%. Last November the rate rose from 5.84% to 7.17%.

Like other Treasuries, EE bonds are exempt from state and local taxes. Federal income taxes are deferred until redemption unless you wish to pay them currently. There is one catch: you earn the full rate only by holding the bond for five years. Your money is locked up for the first six months. After that, early withdrawals result in reduced yields. You can get a much better return at present—8.4%—from a five-year bank CD.

Money-market bank accounts: 4.9% to 7.8%. Returns on money-market deposit accounts at banks change from week to week, but not in lockstep with the money market. Bankers pay only as much as they must to retain deposits, and they have found most customers willing to sacrifice a bit of yield for the convenience of banking locally. Thus yields recently averaged from 5.2% in Los Angeles to 6.5% in Houston, with a national average of 5.8%.

On deposits of $2,500 or more, however, you can get yields as much as a third higher than the national average at several federally insured banks that accept out-of-state deposits. Two such institutions to which Glen King Parker, publisher of the monthly *Income & Safety* newsletter, has assigned his highest safety rating of A are Empire of America in Houston (800-872-2443), yielding 7.8% in late 1987, and Brookside Savings Bank in Kansas City, Missouri (816-361-7070), yielding 7.25% at the end of the year.

Money-market funds: 5.7% to 7.3%. Among the money funds that have been paying more than average while maintaining top safety rates are Vanguard Prime, yielding 7.3%; Cardinal Government, 7.1%; and Kemper Money Market, 7.2%. But if your 1988 income tax bracket is 33% (see page 28), you may get a better after-tax return from a tax-free money fund. Among the funds with the highest tax-free yields: Calvert Tax-Free Reserve and Vanguard Municipal, both yielding around 4.9%. To beat those returns, someone in the 33% bracket would have to earn more than 7.4%—higher than any taxable money fund was paying recently.

Certificates of deposit: 5.7% to 9%. If you go along with the consensus that interest rates are headed down, consider locking in rates on a one-year or 18-month CD early this year. That is the advice of James Christian, chief economist for the U.S. League of Savings Institutions, and John Charlesworth, manager of portfolio services at Merrill Lynch. Their rationale: since any recovery in stocks appears at least two quarters away, a lot of money is going to be parked in maturities of six months or less, putting downward pressure on those short-term rates.

Near the top of the rate range for one-year CDs lately was Bay Loan & Investment in East Greenwich, Rhode Island, (800-233-5411), rated A for safety by *Income & Safety* and yielding 8.5%. Two thrifts with B ratings (meaning capital resources meet but do not exceed federal guidelines) that were recently offering above-average yields of 8.8% are Virginia Beach Savings & Loan (800-368-3090) and Bay View Federal Savings in Corpus Christi, Texas, (512-887-6971).

Here and there, banks and thrifts are promoting CDs that purport to give you penalty-free access to your money. Examine such offers carefully. You may find that they let you withdraw only a small fraction of your principal without penalty, or that they do not compound your interest and therefore produce below-average effective yields. Another strategy for those who would rather not gamble on the direction interest rates are headed: spread your cash equally among six-month, one-year and two-year CDs. In the staggering markets we have seen recently, a staggered approach keeps you covered no matter what happens.

The Game Is Not Over for Stocks

Months after the crash of 1987, investors are still assessing the damage to their portfolios and wondering how they should proceed. The best advice: it is too late to sell stocks to avoid heavy losses, but too early for a buying spree. No one knows when the market will begin a sustained recovery, or whether it will take another sickening dive first. The time, however, is right, to begin laying the foundation for the portfolio you want in place before the next upturn—beginning with defensive blue chips and utilities that you would not mind owning for the next three to ten years.

Extreme caution is advised, however. Historically, in the wake of a drop like the one on Black Monday there has been a rally followed by a new low (see the graphs opposite). Trading volume is usually far more subdued on the second drop than it is on the first (605 million shares changed hands on October 19).

In general, analysts counsel investors who have not sold their holdings already to hang on until the market has recovered a substantial portion of its falloff, thereby reducing initial paper losses. While you wait, you will continue to earn the same dividends you did before the crash. Analysts expect no cuts in payouts, unless there is a severe recession. Then the dividends of retail and cyclical businesses would be reduced first.

There are several exceptions to the don't-sell rule: if a further decline in the market will cause too much psychic or financial pain, investors should get out now—otherwise they are apt to panic and sell at the bottom, says Prudential-Bache portfolio strategist Greg Smith. Smith would also use rallies "to weed out the really speculative issues that somebody's Uncle Harry recommended." But investors who decide to stay with their holdings should not remain glued to a Quotron machine if the market heads down again. People who follow prices that closely tend to become upset and liquidate their positions anyway. Rather, Smith suggests that they simply ignore their stocks until the market turns up again.

When to Begin Buying

It is not too soon for buyers to begin tiptoeing back into stocks, especially if they have a lot of spare cash. That does not mean getting 100% invested, however; investors could still get clobbered by price drops. Commit only money that you can afford to be without for a number of years.

It is difficult to say when it will again be safe for full-scale buying of stocks. Most investors are as bad at timing market bottoms as they are at judging market tops. Certainly one indication that stocks have entered a stabilizing period will be when the market story disappears from the TV evening news and from newspaper front pages.

In the meantime, there are strategies that will help you buy shares in a volatile market. One is dollar-cost averaging, investing a set number of dollars at regular intervals. That way your average cost per share becomes less than the stock's average price, because you buy more shares when the price is low and fewer when the price is high.

Another way to protect yourself is to enter

buy orders with your broker at prices 20% below current levels. For example, if you have $20,000 to put into stocks, John Templeton of Templeton Funds suggests placing buy orders of $5,000 apiece on 20 stocks. When you get four, cancel the rest. This bottom fishing will not necessarily get you in at the absolute bottom, says Templeton, "but you'll do all right." If the market goes into a tailspin, though, you may want to cancel all but four of the orders; otherwise you could end up with too many orders filled.

What to Buy

As for what to buy, depressed markets have one redeeming feature: they allow you to upgrade your portfolio at reasonable prices. Here is a shopping list of stocks to consider.

Blue chips. One place to begin is with all those blue chips that you have longed to own but could not afford. These stocks also add security to your portfolio in uncertain times; they tend to lose less in a market sell-off than do secondary issues—and they are likely to be the first to recover.

Utilities. Another area of promise is interest-sensitive stocks, such as those of utilities. When interest rates fall—as many analysts predict for the coming year—dividends paid by utilities

become increasingly attractive and help put a floor under stock prices. For example, while the Standard & Poor's 500-stock index was down 24.7% from October 13 through October 20, the electric utilities dropped 12.3% and regional telephones were off 14.2%. Such companies also benefit from stable demand, says Dean Witter Reynolds investment strategist John Connolly, who is recommending Baltimore Gas & Electric, FPL Group, Dominion Resources, and Southern California Edison. Eric Miller, a Donaldson Lufkin & Jenrette portfolio strategist, likes telephone utilities as well, such as Southwestern Bell, Bell Atlantic, and Contel.

Even better than a company with a secure dividend is one with a rising dividend, which tends to pull a stock's price up with it. William Lippman, president of L.F. Rothschild Management, favors Wisconsin Energy, which recently yielded 6% and has increased its payout for the past 27 years straight. He is also enthusiastic about Exxon (yielding 4.8%) and Atlanta Gas & Light (yielding 7.2%), the biggest gas distributor in the Southeast.

Banks. Lower interest rates also increase the appeal of bank stocks by lowering the cost of their raw product: money. Some banks are further improving their earnings outlook by writing off problem loans. The stocks of such institutions are selling at very inviting prices now, having been particularly hard hit by the

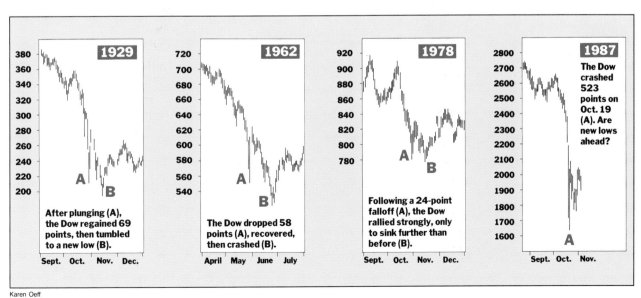

1929 — After plunging (A), the Dow regained 69 points, then tumbled to a new low (B).

1962 — The Dow dropped 58 points (A), recovered, then crashed (B).

1978 — Following a 24-point falloff (A), the Dow rallied strongly, only to sink further than before (B).

1987 — The Dow crashed 523 points on Oct. 19 (A). Are new lows ahead?

Karen Oeff

market's crash. Miller suggests J.P. Morgan, Citicorp, and Norwest, a regional in Minneapolis that he considers a turnaround play.

Insurance companies. Casualty insurers benefit from lower interest rates because they hold large bond portfolios that increase in value as rates come down. Moreover, constant demand for their product tends to make these companies somewhat immune to recession, says Marshall Acuff, portfolio strategist at Smith Barney Harris Upham. He particularly likes American International Group and General Re Corporation.

Paper and pharmaceuticals. As interest rates drop, the dollar is likely to decline as well, and that would benefit businesses receiving a substantial portion of their revenues from exports, including paper and pharmaceutical companies. It would also help domestic producers that face tough competition from importers. Consequently, Robert Nurock, editor of the *Astute Investor*, is looking for significant capital gains in paper stocks such as Great Northern Nekoosa, International Paper, and Federal Paperboard; pharmaceuticals such as Eli Lilly and Johnson & Johnson; and computer manufacturers, including Compaq, Apple, and NCR.

Consumer nondurables. Should there be a full-blown recession, consumer nondurables—food, beverages, and tobacco, for example—can offer protection. These businesses sell products that people continue to buy even in an economic slump. Multinationals, including giants such as Coca-Cola, PepsiCo, and RJR Nabisco, are also helped by a lower dollar. And they are substantial cash generators whose dividends are more likely to increase than to decrease. Here investors should focus on leading American brand names, says Prudential-Bache's Smith, who would also buy Anheuser-Busch, Campbell Soup, and Hershey Foods.

Foreign stocks. Investors can find exciting buying opportunities as well in foreign stocks, which are relatively cheaper than U.S. ones. Even though the October crash hit all world markets, undercutting to some extent the argument that global diversification helps protect a portfolio against losses, for the period of January 1 to November 5 the World Index was up 11.2% versus only 2.2% for the U.S. market. Because of the difficulty of assessing foreign companies, most investors are better off buying an international or global fund rather than individual stocks. (For more on foreign investing, see pages 87-95.)

You can also buy closed-end single-country funds, shares of which trade on one of the stock exchanges or over the counter. The Scandinavia Fund, Germany Fund, France Fund, and Helvetia Fund (Switzerland) offer U.S. investors the double benefit of depressed market prices on top of deep discounts in the price of the funds themselves; many are selling at 4% to 26% below their net asset value. But investors should be aware that share prices for closed-end funds were hit much harder than most other issues when the stock market fell, tumbling 31% versus 26% for the Dow.

Money Sources

To subscribe to *Astute Investor* newsletter, write to P.O. Box 988, Paoli, PA 19301. It is published every three weeks and costs $197 a year.

All Eyes Are Again on Bonds

Suddenly bonds are back. While stocks were tumbling around shareholders' ears, bonds soared, returning to bondholders nearly half of what they had taken away in losses during their mid-1987 slump. Now bonds continue to hold out hope of capital gains, although the times call for caution and selectivity. As the economic outlook has changed drastically, so have the kinds of bonds that constitute the best choice.

Anyone who had money in long-term Treasuries or bond funds for all of 1987 lost about 23% of the value of his or her portfolio as interest rates on 30-year bonds rose from 7.5% in March to 10.2% in mid-October. (When rates rise, the value of existing bonds falls, and vice versa.) Those ballooning rates were a potent ingredient in the economic mix that set off the stock crash. But as stocks fell, billions flowed out of the stock market and over to bonds. Interest rates on long-term Treasury bonds dropped back to 8.9%. T-bond values increased 13%, and somewhat smaller rallies occurred in corporate and municipal issues.

A majority of forecasters believe that still lower rates lie ahead. The shock to consumer and business confidence from the stock crash, they say, will weaken economic growth and increase the chance of a recession this year. A softer economy lowers demand for credit and thus tends to reduce interest rates. Furthermore, the Federal Reserve Board is not likely to tighten monetary policy soon. Economists such as Henry Kaufman of Salomon Brothers foresee long-term Treasury rates falling as low as 8% by early 1988. That would translate into a 9% gain in the value of a bond bought to yield 8.9% recently.

Stay with Quality

While prospects for price appreciation in bonds have improved, the risks of default have increased. With hard times in the economy possibly ahead, investors should stick with high-quality bonds. At the top of the quality ladder are Treasury securities, whose principal and interest are guaranteed by the U.S. government. Highly rated municipal bonds and the bonds of some blue-chip corporations also qualify as high quality. The top-rated corporates, recently yielding about 9.8%, include such solid companies as Procter & Gamble, Eastman Kodak, and General Electric.

Almost as well secured as Treasuries are GNMA (Government National Mortgage Association) certificates, more popularly known as Ginnie Maes, and those of other alphabet-soup federal agencies. These instruments, which are shares in pools of government-guaranteed mortgages, pay a yield that is about one percentage point higher than that on comparable Treasury securities. The interest is not exempt from most state and local taxes, however, as is Treasury interest. Moreover, GNMA yields fall sharply when rates decline and homeowners refinance their mortgages. Since the minimum for buying new mortgage-backed certificates directly is $25,000, most individuals invest in them through mutual funds.

Investors who own so-called junk bonds of lower-rated companies or who have invested in junk bonds through mutual funds should especially heed the call to quality. The days right after Black Monday in the stock market showed what can happen when investors start worrying about a recession. Even as prices of other bonds rallied, the average high-yield bond fund dropped 4% and some individual junk bonds fell as much as 20%.

No matter how much you have enjoyed the returns, it is time to consider moving out of high-yield bonds. Many junk bonds were issued as part of leveraged buy-outs and thus involve companies with very substantial debt. If a recession cuts revenues, such companies could have trouble keeping up the payments on their junk bonds. Your extra annual yield could be wiped out easily in a few days by falling values.

Municipal bonds, on the other hand, are more attractive now than they were before the crash. During the collapse, municipal bond prices rallied less than Treasuries because foreign and other investors moving out of stocks mostly switched to government securities. As a result, municipal yields are inflated compared with those on taxable investments. At current yield levels, tax-exempts make sense for investors in the 28% and 33%—but not the 15%—bracket. (To estimate your tax bracket, see page 28.) Twelve-year AA-rated municipal bonds were recently paying 7.1%. That is the equivalent of a 10.6% taxable yield to an investor in the 33% bracket and of a 9.9% taxable yield to someone in the 28% bracket. Taxable yields that fat are available only on lower-rated corporate bonds.

Steven J. Hueglin of the bond firm Gabriele Hueglin & Cashman in New York City suggests that investors stick to general-obligation bonds issued by states and backed by their full taxing power, as opposed to bonds that are paid off with revenues from specific projects. For many investors, home-state bonds will be preferable in order to escape state and local as well as federal taxes.

While most forecasters expect interest rates to fall, a significant minority argue that long-term rates could rise back above 10% during the first half of this year before eventually declining as a recession gets under way. The Fed, they say, has to worry about foreign investors, who in recent years have financed the deficit through massive purchases of Treasury issues. Foreigners were spooked by the crash; they may well demand higher rates to keep the money coming. But rates were not bid up in the early November sale of Treasury bonds—the first since the crash—largely because German interest rates were lowered the same day. Foreign demand for increased U.S. rates could materialize, however, if the decline of the dollar accelerates. A weaker dollar devalues foreign investors' holdings of U.S. securities in terms of their home currencies.

When in Doubt, Hedge

Traditional bond strategy dictates that you buy long-term bonds with maturities of ten to thirty years if you believe interest rates will fall, and short-term issues of three years or less if you believe interest rates will rise. Long-term bonds fall the most in price if rates rise because the investor is locked into a below-market yield for a longer time. Conversely, if rates fall, long-term bonds provide the greatest capital gains. In a climate of rising rates, short-term bonds suffer fewer capital losses and, as they expire, offer the chance to reinvest at better rates. By staying in very short-term fixed-income investments such as money-market funds, you get almost immediate adjustment to higher rates.

Bond investors who are basically optimistic—but who want to hedge against the possibility of rising rates—should compromise with medium-length maturities. Not only do such bonds reduce risk, but at current yield levels, they pay out almost as much as longer-term securities. Economist David Jones of Aubrey G. Lanston & Company suggests that investors buy five-year Treasury instruments, noting that they were yielding 8.3% recently, compared with just 8.7% for ten-year Treasuries. Even for unhesitantly bullish bond investors looking to lock in high yields, Treasury maturities beyond 10 years and munis beyond 15 make no sense now, since the additional yield is insignificant compared with the risks in tying up your money for a decade or more.

Match Strategies to Goals

Here is a look at some strategies designed to meet specific investment objectives.

A long-range goal. If you have a specific target, such as providing for retirement, you might consider bonds that will mature near when the money will be needed, even if that requires maturities beyond 10 years. With yields higher than ordinary Treasuries, 20-year zero-coupon T-bonds were recently yielding about 9.1%. They look especially attractive at 10% and above, where your money doubles in about seven years. To produce that compounding effect, however, all interest must be reinvested at 10%, and only with zero-coupon bonds do you get an assured rate of reinvestment. Zeros are sold at a discount and paid off at full face value at maturity, setting the reinvestment rate from the start.

Even though you do not collect annual interest on zeros, the IRS does collect annual tax on the implied interest. So zeros work best in an Individual Retirement Account or other tax-deferred account or in a child's custodial account.

Income. If you are retired or for other reasons want to collect the income from bonds, consider putting a third of your capital into five-year Treasuries or seven-year municipals to get a reasonably high return with little risk. For higher yield, put a third of your money into 10-year Treasuries or 15-year municipals. The 8.7% Treasury yield or 7.25% municipal rate will keep you ahead of inflation, currently projected at about 4% a year. Keep the final third of your cash in a money-market fund, and if rates do rise above 10% for long-term Treasuries or 9% for municipals, consider locking in that unusually high yield with 15-year Treasuries or 20-year municipals that offer protection against early refunding.

If income is your chief goal, but you still worry about possible drops in the value of your portfolio, you might stagger your maturities even more—a technique known as laddering. For example, you might buy bonds with two-, four-, six-, eight-, and ten-year maturities if you have sufficient capital. If rates rise, you could reinvest the short-term bonds at the higher rates as they mature. On the other hand, if rates fall, your longer-term bonds will appreciate in value.

Total return. If you are using bonds as one element in a long-term strategy to build up your assets, you want the highest possible combination of yield and capital gains. Thus, like an income investor, you might want to put a third of your funds in five-year Treasuries or seven-year municipals, a third in ten-year Treasuries, and keep a third in liquid investments. If rates rise above 10%, however, shift the money from your medium-term bonds as well as from your money-market fund into 20-year Treasuries, where you will have greater potential for capital gains if rates fall later. If long-term rates should go as low as 6% before the end of the 1980s because of a weak economy and continuing low inflation—as some forecasters expect—you could realize a capital gain of about 50% on 20-year Treasury bonds bought with a 10.5% interest rate. Treasury bonds are more suitable than municipals for this strategy because you have surer call protection as rates fall and because capital gains on municipal bonds are taxable just as on all other bonds.

With a weaker dollar the chief threat to bond prices, several advisers suggest one additional hedge. They would have you invest about 10% of your bond portfolio in a foreign bond fund. If the dollar falls, a fund denominated in a foreign currency would be worth more in dollars and would make up for the loss in your domestic bond fund.

Such a hedge is one way a bond investor can protect himself these days. But the bond investor's best defense is flexibility. Put at least some of your bond portfolio in short-term investments. Then be patient, know what you plan to do if rates reach levels high enough to buy long-term bonds, and do not waste time if you see your opportunity.

The End of Innocence in Mutual Funds

The pain of October was spread around all too liberally, but the shock may have been most keen among mutual fund investors. Roughly two out of every three stock fund shareholders at the August 1987 peak had opened their accounts since the bull market took off five years before. As a result, many had never previously had to contemplate serious losses, even if just on paper. Now they do: of the $1 trillion in wealth that vaporized between late August and the closing bell on Black Monday, more than $54 billion belonged to mutual fund shareholders.

Regardless of when you entered the game, if you owned a stock fund through the October massacre, you are now a seasoned investor. Yet as every market veteran has learned, you gain little dwelling on past losses. You have now had time to catch your breath and assess the damage. It is time to focus again on the future—to re-evaluate your fund strategies in light of the lessons of the crash and a new, and suddenly uncertain, economic outlook.

Lessons from the Crash

The chaos of the crash only reaffirms the basic principles of investing and managing risk. They bear repeating here.

Stock funds do not shield you from stock market risk. Among the few things that devalued faster than stocks on Black Monday was the illusion that mutual funds' much vaunted selling points—diversification, professional management, and the ability to switch funds or redeem shares by telephone—would spare investors the worst of a bear market. In the main, they did not. Thousands of shareholders who tried to switch from stock funds into the safety of money-market funds on October 19 were stymied by clogged switchboards. But as it happened, the truly unlucky ones were those who got through. They were cashed out at the day's closing price—which, as of early November, was the lowest point so far in the bear market (as measured by the Dow Jones Industrial Average). As for diversification—diluting the risk by spreading a portfolio among dozens of different securities—its virtues simply became irrelevant when virtually every stock in the world plopped.

Perhaps the greatest disappointment lay in how poorly most professional fund managers defended their shareholders from the crash. Last September 30, the average stock fund had only 9.5% of its portfolio in cash, a full percentage point less than its position 12 months earlier. Consequently, when the storm hit, funds got blasted nearly as hard as the market as a whole: during October the average diversified stock fund plunged 20.9%, compared with the 21.5% drop in the Standard & Poor's 500-stock index. In fairness, one month is a meaninglessly short period in which to judge a fund manager. Moreover, many managers make no pretense of trying to bail out of the market when stocks appear too high priced; they stay invested at all times. But the lesson is clear: if you invest in stock funds, you must accept risk—and the responsibility for avoiding more risk than you can accept is yours alone.

Fund categories that trail the averages during a bull market tend to outperform them in a bear. The wallflowers of last year's bull market were balanced and equity income funds, two kinds that tend to invest conservatively in high-dividend stocks and bonds. Yet these funds fell 25% to 40% less, on average, than the typical stock fund. By contrast, the growth-oriented stock funds that had been the champions for the 12 months through September 30 were utterly routed.

The crash thus underscores the folly of simply projecting a fund's recent past performance indefinitely into the future. You will form a far more realistic expectation of how a fund will behave in any given market by sizing up the fund's investment style and level of risk. Before you commit to any fund, check the kinds of securities it holds and whether the manager stays fully invested in stocks or leavens the mix with cash or bonds. To find out, see the statement of investment policy in the fund's prospectus and the listing of holdings in its most recent annual report. Your best clue to a fund's risk level is its performance in past bear markets; the heavy bleeders in October were also the big losers in past massacres. (To check fund performances in the last major down cycle, which lasted from June 1983 to July 1984, see the mutual fund rankings and alphabetical listing beginning on page 197.)

You will lower your risk if you hold several funds with different investment strategies. If you owned bond funds and money-market funds as well as stock funds during the crash, you probably were stung but not ruined. Most advisers recommend a portfolio comprising five to seven funds, including a money-market fund, bond funds, and stock funds drawn from various categories as detailed below.

Since most funds require a minimum investment of $1,000, assembling a diversified port-folio would probably require a stake of $10,000 to $15,000. If you cannot invest that much, you can still diversify by buying into a so-called asset allocation fund. The managers of these funds apportion their money among stocks, bonds, cash, and sometimes precious metals, foreign currencies, and international equities. Predictably, all but one of the eight asset allocators held up better than the averages during October. The most solid performer, Paine Webber Asset Allocation, actually gained 2.8%. One of four such funds that periodically change the mix, the Paine Webber fund entered October 83% in bonds, 11% in cash, and only 6% in stocks. Blanchard Strategic also has a flexible portfolio. Three other funds—Permanent Portfolio, Vanguard STAR, and USAA Cornerstone—keep a more or less fixed allocation.

Adjusting to the Post-Crash Era

No one can predict the economic aftershocks of Black October, but a majority of fund advisers believe that the outlook points to slower growth or even a recession—a bearish prognosis indeed for stock funds. A *Money* survey of more than two dozen mutual fund investment pros turned up these cautionary themes.

Increase your holdings in bond and money-market funds. But if you are a long-term investor, you should continue to keep a portion of your portfolio in equity funds. Most fund watchers' readings of the near-term outlook, however, indicate that short-term bond funds and money-market funds should have a key position in most portfolios now. For example, Gerald Perritt, editor of the monthly *Mutual Fund Letter*, recommends keeping 50% in stock funds, 30% in bond funds, and 20% in money-market funds. Be sure to make any adjustments in your portfolio over a period of a few months. Doing so eliminates the chance that you will sell all at a temporary bottom in the market.

Favor stock funds with higher than average yields. Funds that emphasize income as well as growth—such as equity income, balanced, and growth and income funds—should have an edge over purer growth funds in the volatile market that many advisers see ahead. The reliable stream of income from the high-dividend stocks and convertibles that these funds hold will partially offset stock market risk. Meanwhile, the equity component of the portfolio still allows the fund to participate in upswings. Funds that emphasize conservative, dividend-paying stocks and convertibles include Decatur I, T. Rowe Price Equity Income, and Pilgrim MagnaCap.

Favor stock funds with high cash positions. Funds that currently keep a portion of their portfolio outside the stock market in short-term investments such as Treasury bills or corporate paper—called cash because they fluctuate only minimally in value and are readily sold—should be relatively insulated from further tumbles in the stock market. Having cash on hand also gives a manager the freedom to pick up stocks at bargain prices, and in the event of another rout, the fund will be able to meet redemptions without having to sell stocks into the slide. Impressive long-term performers with current cash positions greater than 25% include Strong Total Return, Nicholas Fund, and Founders Growth.

Confine your bond choices to high-quality funds with relatively short or intermediate average maturities. October's flight from stocks into Treasury bonds and high-quality corporates ignited a bond market rally that all but erased the effect of the prolonged decline in bond funds. Many market observers point out, however, that the problem that bedeviled bonds throughout much of 1987—the threat that a weakening dollar would drive foreign investors away from American issues—has not disappeared. Consequently, unless the dollar strengthens, the bond market bust could resume. If that happens, funds that hold long-term bonds will be hit hardest. Also be wary of funds specializing in the high-yielding, low-quality instruments known as junk bonds. The prospect of an economic slowdown is nearly as bearish for them as for stocks because of the risk that junk issuers could be swept under by hard times and default. Two high-quality, short-term bond funds are Vanguard Fixed Income Short-Term, recently yielding 7.4%, and Twentieth Century U.S. Governments, yielding 8.3%.

Focus on the long term. More than anything else, your investment goals will determine whether the crash of 1987 was an irredeemable disaster or a temporary setback. If your goal is less than one to three years away, the prospects of completely recouping your losses are not encouraging. On the other hand, if your goal is three to five years away or more, the odds of eventually seeing your shares back at their peak levels improve. Between now and the time you need the money, there will doubtless be more vertiginous swings in the market, perhaps under the shadow of a bear. But painful as they may be, market slumps do not last forever—the longest postwar losing streak, for example, was 21 months. What is more, the stock market's tendency to rise over the long run has always worked to the advantage of patient investors.

Of course, there is always the possibility that all this caution is unnecessary. Perhaps the economy will shrug off Bloody Monday and go on to boom, carrying stock mutual funds with it. But the most prudent course at present seems to be to reserve your optimism for the long term.

Money **Sources**

To subscribe to *Mutual Fund Letter*, write to 205 W. Wacker Dr., Chicago, IL 60606. Cost: $115 a year.

How to Make Getting Out Easier

Thousands of investors tried to parachute out of their mutual funds last October, only to find their lines tangled. Phone lines, that is. Fidelity alone reported that its 1,400 telephone representatives received more than a million phone calls between October 19 and October 23. Meanwhile, another million-plus calls came in over an automated system that lets shareholders check account balances and make switches using touch-tone phones. The Securities and Exchange Commission's Office of Consumer Affairs reported that investor complaints rose 200% on October 21 and October 22, with telephone problems the most frequently cited annoyance. Load-fund shareholders were less likely than no-load investors to get itchy dialing fingers. Calmed by their brokers, they were also perhaps inclined to stay in a fund for which they had recently paid a sales charge.

Mercifully short-lived were the most chilling crash-related service troubles—the activation by Fidelity, T. Rowe Price, and Financial Programs, among others, of prospectus rules that allow funds to delay payouts on redemptions for five business days. Price lifted the stricture after 24 hours for all but one of its funds, T. Rowe Price International Stock. Because of market volatility, the rule was still being enforced in early November for that fund. Fidelity eased after 48 hours, and Financial Programs after a similar span, except for sector funds. Redemptions from them were held up for the full five days. Although the damage from the tightened withdrawal rules was controlled—amounting to a few days of lost interest or a missed opportunity to jump back into the market on the double-quick—investors were reminded to pay closer attention to prospectus fine print and, henceforth, to arrange bailout procedures in advance. Many such precautionary steps are best taken when you open your account. Among them:

● Sign up simultaneously for telephone switching and redemption privileges.

● Open a money-market account in the fund family if you have the minimum at your disposal. A haven for your stock fund flight capital can save you time and, therefore, money in a diving market. You also will not face the costly frustration of being reminded, as some investors were in October, that an account cannot be opened until you read the prospectus.

● Have transfer-by-wire privileges in place. If your stock or bond fund has no money-market sibling, arrange to have the cash wired to your bank account.

● Keep a written redemption request handy for funds such as Vanguard Index Trust, Babson Value, and Hartwell Growth, which forbid phone switches. In those cases, you should keep at home a letter (with signature guarantee, if required) authorizing the fund to shift your cash into a money market or send it to you. When the time comes, simply dispatch the missive to your fund by overnight courier. You will receive the next day's closing price, just as you would with a late-night phone call.

● When making a switch, strike before the New York markets close. A call at any time during trading hours guarantees redemption at that day's closing net asset value. If you call after 4 p.m. in the East (1 p.m. on the West Coast), you will receive the following day's closing price. A tip from Vanguard insiders to avoid being put on hold: ring up at 2:30 ET (when service reps are all back from lunch).

● Avoid touch-tone switching, especially in a crunch. To ensure that your transaction does not get mis-executed in the shuffle, Eric Kobren, president of the Mutual Fund Investors Association, urges you to talk to a sales rep and note his or her name, the time of your call, and the transaction number. That way no one—not even you—can blame a blooper on a faceless computer.

Your Taxes

The Tax Reform Act of 1986—the most radical new tax law in a half century—has proved to be a mixed blessing for most people. While there are mercifully fewer tax brackets and much lower rates, more of your income is now taxable because many venerable deductions have vanished or are being phased out.

Although Congress will undoubtedly tinker with the freshly retooled tax code to increase revenues before long, you can save more than enough in taxes in the interim to justify prompt action. Last year the top marginal tax rate of 38.5% for individuals was the lowest since 1931. This year, barring major changes in the law, the federal government will be even more accommodating, claiming no more than 33¢ out of every dollar you earn. (See page 28.) That maximum rate is a full 37 percentage points lower than the top levy just seven years ago and the lowest it is likely to be in your lifetime.

In return, lawmakers pulled out or drastically cut back many of taxpayers' most cherished perennials. Say so long, for example, to the two-earner deduction, the sales tax write-off, income averaging, the dividend exclusion, traditional tax shelters, and—beginning this year—the preferential rates afforded long-term capital gains on assets held longer than six months. Consider yourself fortunate if you can still find comfort in IRAs, miscellaneous deductions, and the medical expense write-off, all of which are only shadows of their former selves. Meanwhile, make the most of the sacrosanct mortgage interest deduction and what is left of the consumer interest deduction, which disappears completely by 1991.

The disorientation caused by the demise of these tax breaks afflicts everybody. This chapter will help you cut through the confusion with advice on how to update and adjust your tax planning to ensure that you pay no more taxes than the law prescribes. Doing so will give you the confidence to take the offensive—almost always the best tax-saving strategy—in this and subsequent years.

TAX TABLES: SINGLE FILERS				MARRIED COUPLES FILING JOINTLY		
If your taxable income* exceeds	You will pay	Plus this percentage of your taxable income that exceeds the amount in the first column		If your taxable income* exceeds	You will pay	Plus this percentage of your taxable income that exceeds the amount in the first column
1987				**1987**		
$0	$0	11.0%		$0	$0	11.0%
1,800	198	15.0		3,000	330	15.0
16,800	2,448	28.0		28,000	4,080	28.0
27,000	5,304	35.0		45,000	8,840	35.0
54,000	14,754	38.5		90,000	24,590	38.5
1988				**1988**		
$0	$0	15.0%		$0	$0	15.0%
17,850	2,678	28.0		29,750	4,463	28.0
43,150	9,762	33.0		71,900	16,265	33.0
100,480	28,681	28.0		171,090†	48,997	28.0

†If you have dependent children and your taxable income exceeds $171,090, the 33% rate applies to earnings of up to $171,090 plus $10,920 per child. A couple with two children, for example, would be taxed at 33% on income up to $192,930 and then 28% on income above that amount.
*Taxable income is adjusted gross income minus deductions and exemptions.

Is Your Return Audit Bait?

How to avoid getting swept into the IRS's ever-widening net.

Few encounters in life are more harrowing than an Internal Revenue Service audit. Your chances of experiencing this trauma have been fairly remote in the past: the IRS scrutinizes a mere 1.3% of the 96 million or so individual returns filed each year. The bad news is that the IRS is trying harder to tilt those odds more heavily against you.

Last year the IRS began a three-year plan that eventually will add 7,500 auditors to its payroll—an almost 50% increase that will expand the audit force to 24,500. In addition, the IRS is working its way quickly through a massive backlog of tax-shelter audits. Thus IRS revenue officers who formerly ferreted out shelter-hungry investors in abusive tax-avoidance schemes may soon shift their sights to middle-income taxpayers who stretch an itemized deduction or two. As a result, your chances of being audited could be as much as 60% greater within the next few years. That is a frightening possibility, considering the IRS collects roughly $4,000 an audit.

Some factors that determine who gets audited are beyond your control. If you earn more than $50,000, for example, you are eight to ten times more likely to get an audit notice than someone earning less than $10,000. And if you are self-employed, the odds are even higher that the IRS will call you in for a chat. The IRS has found that self-employed people are more likely than salaried workers to understate their income and overstate their expenses.

Still, by understanding how the IRS audit-selection system works and knowing which deductions are most likely to touch off alarms, you can reduce the likelihood of sending in a tax return loaded with audit bait. Most returns are singled out for an audit via the IRS's discriminant function system, or DIF, a computer program that gives numerical values to such key items on your tax return as deductions, adjustments to income, and the number of credits and exemptions you claim. If a deduction is disproportionate to your income, the computer will flag it.

A score is based on two things: how much the IRS believes you are likely to err, or cheat, when taking a particular deduction—casualty and theft deductions are natural high scorers—and how much your deductions vary from certain statistical standards. (The IRS derives these norms through exhaustive line-by-line Taxpayer Compliance Measurement Program, or TCMP, audits conducted on 50,000 randomly selected taxpayers every three years.) The computer then tallies the scores of the individual items on the return and assigns each return an overall DIF score.

The higher this number, the more likely you are to be audited. The surest way to avoid an audit is to post a low DIF score. How low a score? The IRS is not saying. The DIF program is the most closely guarded secret in the IRS. Outsiders do not know the relative weights the IRS assigns to specific deductions, nor will the IRS divulge the deduction norms from the TCMP audits. The IRS does publish average deductions for several income brackets, though they are not used to compute the DIF scores. Exceed these averages by more than 10% and your chances of an audit grow substantially. (See the table on page 30.) Former IRS employees and numerous tax accountants agree, however, that disproportionate deductions in the following areas will almost certainly win you an audit.

Employee business expenses. Labeled the "kiss of death" by IRS tax examiners, deductions for a home office, business travel and entertainment, and business use of an automobile that are disproportionate to your income almost certainly result in an audit invitation. Most people do not document these expenses correctly, and the IRS knows it can assess additional tax by challenging these deductions.

Charitable contributions. Cash contributions are not likely to draw attention, but large donations of property will. If you donate property, be sure to attach an independent appraisal of its market value to your return.

Casualty and theft losses. Again, the IRS knows people frequently overstate an item's value or simply miscalculate the allowable deduction. A casualty or theft loss is deductible only to the extent an individual loss exceeds $100 and all losses for the year exceed 10% of your adjusted gross income. The new tax law stipulates that if an item was insured, you must seek reimbursement from your insurance company. You may then deduct the difference, if any, between the item's fair market value and the reimbursement.

Bad debts. The IRS jumps on this deduction because people attempt to claim it for what essentially amounts to a gift to a family member or friend. To qualify for this deduction, you must show the loan is a legal obligation—a contract or loan note suffices—and that you made a bona fide effort to collect the debt. Hiring a lawyer, writing dunning letters, or filing a claim in small-claims court can usually establish this effort.

Hobby losses. Deducting losses for such activities as horse breeding, yachting, car racing, and other activities that seem more pleasure than profit motivated are definitely audit bait. The chief giveaway: a huge loss, say $50,000, versus only $5,000 or so of income.

Interest expense. Because of the spate of refinancing in recent years, the IRS will be looking for taxpayers taking an illegal deduction for mortgage loan points. Points are deductible in the year paid only in proportion to that part of the loan used to renovate or purchase a house.

Medical expenses. Capital expenses for such special items as swimming pools and elevators for invalids or heart patients tend to trigger audits. The cost minus the amount by which such items raise the fair market value of your home is deductible. The IRS will scrutinize medical deductions even more closely now, on the theory that the tougher new threshold on medical expenses of 7.5% of adjusted gross income, up from 5%, will tempt taxpayers to inflate medical expenses so they can get over that hump.

Although these deductions do increase your odds for an audit, do not let that discourage you from taking your fair share. But if you do take these deductions, make sure you can substantiate them. Proper documentation can sometimes stave off an audit even after you have been flagged for one. After the computer singles out your return, it goes to a tax classifier who decides who will handle the audit. But if a high medical deduction, for example, is the problem and you have attached receipts of doctor bills and copies of medical insurance reimbursements, the classifier might decide that the deduction is warranted and remove your return from the audit pile.

Tax shelters are the single largest audit trigger, accounting for roughly a third of all audits. The types of shelters most likely to raise the ire of the IRS—and be disallowed as deductions—are those where write-offs exceed two times the amount you have invested. Although the new tax bill has done away with many abusive tax shelters, the IRS will still be auditing tax shelters for at least the next three to five years. In fact, the agency has made it clear that it will pursue pre-1987 returns with deductions for tax shelters.

Finally, you also flirt dangerously with the possibility of an audit by failing to report income such as interest, dividends, and capital gains. In the past few years, the IRS has become much more adept at matching, via computer and optical scanning equipment, the income information you give on your tax return against information supplied by banks and brokerage houses.

In 1985, for example, some 3.6 million people received notices that the income they reported did not jibe with IRS records. Moreover, real estate brokers must now report real estate sales to the IRS, making it more difficult to hide real estate profits.

The IRS also plans to match the records of those who pay alimony versus those who claim to receive it. In 1985, about 500,000 individuals took an alimony deduction, while only 350,000 claimed alimony as income.

The consequences for cheating are also more unpleasant. Previously, if you did not report interest or dividend income, you simply paid the tax plus interest. But now the IRS presumes you were negligent in not reporting the income and automatically assesses, on top

Exceed These Averages at Your Own Risk

This table shows average deductions in six categories for several income groups, based on statistics compiled by the Internal Revenue Service from 1984 tax returns. Tax specialists agree that your chances of being audited increase significantly if your deductions exceed these averages by more than 10%.

Adjusted gross income	Employee business expense	Medical	Interest	Alimony	Gift	Casualty theft loss
$20,000-24,999	$2,054	$1,468	$3,076	$3,223	$767	$2,621
25,000-29,999	2,150	1,421	3,476	4,513	802	5,968
30,000-39,999	2,190	1,749	4,032	5,267	874	3,256
40,000-49,999	2,227	1,876	4,796	4,685	1,104	4,340
50,000-74,999	3,030	3,127	6,492	6,880	1,545	3,964
75,000-99,999	4,062	6,315	9,589	9,958	2,420	2,965
100,000-200,999	6,662	9,494	13,703	14,293	4,234	11,319

of the tax and interest you owe, a negligence penalty equal to 5% of the tax due plus 50% of the accrued interest. And if you understate your tax liability by the greater of $5,000 or 10% of the tax you actually paid, the IRS now slaps you with a 20% penalty instead of the old 10% levy.

In the opinion of Gerald Padwe, national director of tax practice at the accounting firm Touche Ross, Congress sees these penalties as a revenue-raising device in an era of high budget deficits. You can expect to see agents imposing more harsh penalties. In short, not only are the odds of getting caught going up, so is the price.

Money Basics

Adjusted gross income (AGI). Your gross income minus nonitemized deductions such as those for IRA contributions and alimony payments.

Tax credit. A dollar-for-dollar reduction of your income taxes, such as the child care credit. A credit is more valuable than a tax deduction, which reduces only taxable income, thereby cutting taxes by only the percentage of your tax bracket.

How to Get Wiser about Tax Advisers

You may need a professional to guide you through the fine print of reform.

Tax reform has compounded the complexities of filing individual returns. Aside from the mind-numbing exercise of determining how much your employer should withhold in light of the fewer brackets and deductions, you also must adjust your strategies for borrowing, investing, and saving. You can make this transition less confusing and costly if you can afford to hire an astute tax practitioner. A tax pro can not only fill out your forms but also help you find ways to cut your tax bill even though write-offs are sparser under the new rules.

A tax practitioner's fee may not be justified if your return is fairly straightforward. For example, you should be able to complete your forms accurately yourself if your income was mostly from salary, your deductions are relatively easy to compute, and you did not own any limited partnerships or sell your home or other investments last year.

For filers with more multifaceted returns, the best time to begin your search for a tax adviser is in May or June, when most generally shift into low gear and have free time to meet with prospective clients. Both the services offered and the fees charged by tax practitioners vary tremendously. You can hire someone just to prepare your return or to give you sophisticated tax planning advice throughout the year. The cost can be as little as $50 annually or upwards of $1,000. Because the term tax practitioner is all encompassing, it is critical to select the right type of adviser for your needs.

Do not confuse a financial planner with a tax practitioner. Certainly a financial planner should be knowledgeable about the tax laws and provide you with savvy tax planning advice. But a planner's role is that of quarterback for your team of financial advisers; he or she is the strategist watching over your cash flow and debts while making suggestions about investments, insurance, retirement, and estate planning as well as your taxes. He or she is not the person you want to prepare your tax return. For that assignment, you should line up someone who completes returns routinely.

You rarely need to hire the ultimate tax practitioner: a tax lawyer. This high-priced specialist—who charges anywhere from $75 to $250 an hour—gets the nod only when you are facing, say, a divorce or estate planning that requires both tax and legal advice.

You should instead choose among three other types of tax pros—storefront preparers, certified public accountants, and enrolled agents. In general, look for advisers who have been in the business at least four years; you cannot afford to turn your taxes over to a neophyte. Here are some other points to consider.

Storefront Preparers

A tax preparer from a storefront chain is best if you plan to file a 1040A, 1040EZ, or a 1040 that comprises mostly salary income and routine deductions such as mortgage interest and property taxes. You can expect to get your tax forms completed accurately and professionally from a reputable storefront preparer. But do not count on receiving any tax planning advice. Storefront preparers are usually part-timers who handle returns only during tax season. Should you have tax questions after April 15, you may have to go to one of the chains' regional offices, which are staffed with full-time employees.

The price you pay a storefront preparer depends on the complexity of your tax return and the type of service you desire. The average fee at H&R Block for completing federal and state tax returns is around $50. At a typical Block office, you generally sit across from a part-time preparer at a table in an airy room without privacy. But at Block's Executive Tax Service offices, where you work with a full-time preparer in a private room, the average fee is about $100.

Use a local, independent storefront tax preparer only if he comes recommended from people you trust. Otherwise, you could be easy prey for a fly-by-night operator who vanishes after April 15. If you are audited by the Internal Revenue Service and cannot find your tax preparer, you might be unable to explain one of the write-offs that you claimed on your tax return. And just the fact of your using some here-today-gone-tomorrow preparer could provoke an audit. The IRS has a hit list of tax preparers that the agency thinks are dishonest or show signs of intentional misconduct, warns Jack Warren Wade, Jr., an ex-IRS revenue officer and author of *Audit-Proofing Your Return*. The IRS does not release the names of these preparers or even say how many there are, but few such miscreants work for reputable firms, says Wade.

C.P.A.'s and Enrolled Agents

These pros provide tax planning advice and prepare returns. You should certainly consider hiring a certified public accountant or an enrolled agent if you invest regularly or are self-employed. Generally, C.P.A.'s and enrolled agents are of equal caliber. Caution: not all C.P.A.'s specialize in taxes, so be sure you talk only with ones who do. All enrolled agents have worked for the IRS as revenue agents (a fancy name for auditors) for at least five years or have passed a tough two-day IRS test. Some enrolled agents are also C.P.A.'s.

Both types of advisers charge hourly fees ranging between $50 and $150. Enrolled agents sometimes charge as much as 25% less than C.P.A.'s do, to drum up business, because enrolled agents are less familiar to the public than C.P.A.'s. As a rule, the bigger the C.P.A. firm, the more you will be charged. If your family's income is about $50,000, you can figure on paying either one—C.P.A. or enrolled agent—between $300 and $500 for your federal and state tax returns.

Start looking for a C.P.A. or enrolled agent by asking for a referral from someone you trust who has family income and investments that are comparable to yours. That way, you will be dealing with professionals whose clients are people like yourself. You can get several names and phone numbers of members of the National Association of Enrolled Agents by calling 800-424-4339.

Plan to meet with two or three potential advisers for an hour or so each. These tête-à-têtes are generally free. The purpose of the session is to match you up with someone who has a tax temperament like yours. You might be quite conservative about taxes and want to claim only deductions such as mortgage interest that are considered by the IRS to be unquestionably legitimate. Or you might instead take an aggressive stance toward the IRS and be willing to claim iffy write-offs. Neither approach is necessarily wrong or right, but problems arise when client and adviser do not share the same outlook. Enrolled agents tend to be more conservative than accountants because many of the agents formerly worked for the IRS.

When you are feeling out pros, see how much they know about the subjects that bear on your particular case. You might ask such tough but fair questions as: How will my mutual fund earnings be taxed? Which home-office expenses are deductible? Should I worry about the alternative minimum tax?

If you are told that you will not understand something, exit politely. Why work with someone who condescends to you? Worse yet, he may be covering up his own ignorance. But do not dismiss an adviser just because he does not know the answer to one of your questions. After all, the tax law, which was immense and complicated before tax reform, is even more so now. When the adviser does not know an answer, ask for one within a week or two. If he does not act on your request in time, you may not want to hire him.

You should talk with your C.P.A. or enrolled agent at least three times a year. Such sessions usually cost about $100 an hour. In the fall, discuss your tax bill due in April, year-end tax planning ideas, and ways to reduce next year's taxes. In January or February, meet with your adviser to turn over your records for preparing your tax return. After your tax practitioner has completed your tax return, get together with him or her to discuss the results and ways to reduce your bill for next year.

Other occasions call for a chat with your adviser too. Meet with him before making investment decisions with tax implications such as buying or selling real estate; before an important change in your life such as marriage, divorce, the birth of a child, or a job switch; and after passage of major federal or state income tax legislation.

Ideally, your financial planner and tax pro will complement each other. Your planner might, for example, suggest you cut your taxes by setting up a home office. Then your tax adviser will estimate the actual amount you would save on taxes and explain how to manage the office without running afoul of the IRS. Conversely, your tax adviser might recommend that you invest in tax-free municipal bonds, and your planner could then select the best muni bond mutual fund for you.

Sooner or later, you might need to dump your tax practitioner. Deciding when to call it quits is difficult because performance is hard to measure. Do not fire your adviser immediately just because your tax return is audited. You will need his help to get through the ordeal. But you should think about replacing your tax practitioner if:

● You wind up owing the IRS money on disallowed write-offs that your adviser had said were legitimate.

● You expected, but did not receive, much useful tax planning advice all year round.

● You get unrealistic promises. For example, your tax preparer might guarantee your return will not be audited. Only the IRS knows for sure who will be audited.

● You discover that your adviser filed your return after April 15 without telling you he would miss the deadline.

● You cannot reach him. If he does not return phone calls or routinely puts you off, he is not doing his job.

● You detect technical incompetence. Any tax preparer is entitled to make a minor mistake on a tax return. But if your preparer bungles the job year after year, the error is certainly yours for staying with him so long.

Meet the New Tax Forms

The Internal Revenue Service has decided that its contribution to simplicity in tax filing will consist of not complicating matters by unveiling any revolutionary new tax forms. In triumph, the 1040 redrafting committee has produced this familiar old camel (plus 10 new schedules.) If you look hard, however, you can zero in on important alterations. Here some of the subtle and potentially costly changes are highlighted.

Form 1040 Department of the Treasury—Internal Revenue Service **1987** U.S. Individual Income Tax Return

REGISTER THE CHILDREN
Children five and over can be claimed as exemptions only if they have Social Security numbers. Go to the post office now for forms to register them.

REPORT TAX-FREE INCOME
You have to report it even though you do not have to pay taxes on it.

SIC TRANSIT MOVING COSTS
Unreimbursed moving expenses were declared here, where they reduced your adjusted gross income. Now they are an item-ized deduction on Schedule A.

TOUGHER IRA
To see if you can claim an IRA deduction, you must fill out a worksheet in the instruction booklet.

UNEMPLOYMENT TAX
No matter how small your earnings, all your unemploy-ment benefits are now subject to taxation.

LOST GAINS
These entries look innocently familiar. But on the schedules referred to, you can no longer exclude 60% of long-term capital gains, nor can you write off all losses from limited partnerships.

DEPENDENT CLAUSE
If your parents claim you as an exemption, you cannot take an exemption on your own return this year.

SIGHTLESS OR OLD
People who are blind or over 65 can no longer claim extra exemptions. Instead of deducting $1,900 for either condition, they get a much smaller additional standard deduction: $600 if they are married, $750 if single.

BUILT-IN DEDUCTION
Standard deductions are no longer built into the tax tables. Claim these unless you can grab larger deductions by itemizing.

PAY AS YOU GO
If too little tax is being withheld from your pay or you are underpaying your quarterly estimated tax, you are risking a penalty.

MISSING TAX SCHEDULE
Schedule G, income averaging, is gone from the tax code.

Form 1040 (1987)   Page 2

Tax Computation (See Instructions on page 13.)

31 Amount from line 30 (adjusted gross income) 31

Caution: If you can be claimed as a dependent on another person's return, check here and see page 13. Also see page 13 if you are married filing a separate return and your spouse itemizes, or you are a dual-status alien.

32 If you itemize, attach Schedule A (Form 1040). Enter the amount from Schedule A, line 26, skip lines 33a and 33b, and go to line 34 32
   If you do NOT itemize, complete lines 33a and 33b.

33a Check if: You were 65 or over Blind; Spouse was 65 or over Blind.
   Add the number of boxes checked. Enter the total here . . . ▶ 33a

b Standard deduction. If on page 1, you checked Filing Status box: { 1 or 4, enter $2,540 / 2 or 5, enter $3,760 / 3, enter $1,880 } Caution: If you completed line 33a, enter amount from chart on page 14 . . . 33b

34 Subtract line 32 or 33b, whichever applies, from line 31. Enter the result . . . 34

35 Multiply $1,900 by the total number of exemptions claimed on line 6e (see page 14) . 35

36 Taxable income. Subtract line 35 from line 34. Enter the result (but not less than zero) 36
   Caution: If under age 14 and you have more than $1,000 of unearned income, check here ▶ and see page 14.

37 Enter tax here. Check if from Tax Table, Tax Rate Schedule X, Y, or Z, Schedule D or Form 8615 (Computation of tax for children under age 14 who have more than $1,000 of unearned income) 37

38 Additional taxes (see page 14). Check if from Form 4970, Form 4972, or Form 5544 . 38

39 Add lines 37 and 38. Enter the total tax . . . . ▶ 39

Credits (See Instructions on page 14.)

40 Credit for child and dependent care expenses (attach Form 2441) 40

41 Credit for the elderly or for the permanently and totally disabled (attach Schedule R) 41

42 Add lines 40 and 41. Enter the total 42

43 Subtract line 42 from line 39. Enter the result (but not less than zero) . . . 43

44 Foreign tax credit (attach Form 1116) . . 44

45 General business credit. Check if from Form 3800, Form 3468, Form 5884, Form 6478, Form 6765, or Form 8586 . 45

46 Add lines 44 and 45. Enter the total 46

47 Subtract line 46 from line 43. Enter the result (but not less than zero) . . . ▶ 47

Other Taxes (Including Advance EIC Payments)

48 Self-employment tax (attach Schedule SE) 48

49 Alternative minimum tax (attach Form 6251) 49

50 Tax from recapture of investment credit (attach Form 4255) 50

51 Social security tax on tip income not reported to employer (attach Form 4137) . 51

52 Tax on retirement plans (attach Form 5329) 52

53 Add lines 47 through 52. This is your total tax . . . . . . ▶ 53

Payments Attach Forms W-2, W-2G, and W-2P to front.

54 Federal income tax withheld 54

55 1987 estimated tax payments and amount applied from 1986 return 55

56 Earned income credit (see page 16) 56

57 Amount paid with Form 4868 57

58 Excess social security tax and RRTA tax withheld (see page 17) 58

59 Credit for Federal tax on gasoline and special fuels (attach Form 4136) 59

60 Regulated investment company credit (attach Form 2439) . 60

61 Add lines 54 through 60. These are your total payments . . . ▶ 61

Refund or Amount You Owe

62 If line 61 is larger than line 53, enter amount OVERPAID . . . ▶ 62

63 Amount of line 62 to be REFUNDED TO YOU . . . . . . ▶ 63

64 Amount of line 62 to be applied to your 1988 estimated tax ▶ 64

65 If line 53 is larger than line 61, enter AMOUNT YOU OWE. Attach check or money order for full amount payable to "Internal Revenue Service." Write your social security number, daytime phone number, and "1987 Form 1040" on it 65
   Check ▶ if Form 2210 (2210F) is attached. See page 17. Penalty: $

Please Sign Here
Under penalties of perjury, I declare that I have examined this return and accompanying schedules and statements, and to the best of my knowledge and belief, they are true, correct, and complete. Declaration of preparer (other than taxpayer) is based on all information of which preparer has any knowledge.

Your signature   Date   Your occupation

Spouse's signature (if joint return, BOTH must sign)   Date   Spouse's occupation

Paid Preparer's Use Only
Preparer's signature   Date   Check if self-employed
Firm's name (or yours if self-employed) and address   E.I. No.
                                                                 ZIP code

MEDICAL THRESHOLD
You must spend 50% more than last year, in proportion to your adjusted gross income, before you can claim medical deductions.

DEAD DEDUCTION
Here is one place the IRS editors remind us that something important is missing: the sales tax deduction.

HOUSES DIVIDED
These instructions may lead to the bad news that some of your mortgage interest can no longer be written off.

FIRST-YEAR BITE
The calculation here takes away 35% of your deduction for interest on credit cards, car loans, and other consumer loans. Final phaseout: 1990.

MISCELLANEOUS HURDLE
Odds and ends, such as union dues, investment expenses, and tax preparer fees, are not deductible anymore until they exceed 2% of your AGI.

UNCHARITABLE OMISSION
Last year, nonitemizers could deduct their contributions. Now charity begins (line 14a) and ends (line 17) on Schedule A.

SCHEDULES A&B
(Form 1040)
Department of the Treasury
Internal Revenue Service

Schedule A—Itemized Deductions
(Schedule B is on back)
▶ Attach to Form 1040. ▶ See Instructions for Schedules A and B (Form 1040).

OMB No. 1545-0074
1987
Attachment Sequence No. 07

Name(s) as shown on Form 1040 — Your social security number

Medical and Dental Expenses
(Do not include expenses reimbursed or paid by others.)
(See Instructions on page 19.)

1a Prescription medicines and drugs, insulin, doctors, dentists, nurses, hospitals, insurance premiums you paid for medical and dental care, etc. — 1a
b Transportation and lodging — 1b
c Other (list—include hearing aids, dentures, eyeglasses, etc.) ▶ — 1c
2 Add lines 1a through 1c, and enter the total here — 2
3 Multiply the amount on Form 1040, line 31, by 7.5% (.075) — 3
4 Subtract line 3 from line 2. If zero or less, enter -0-. **Total** medical and dental ▶ 4

Taxes You Paid
(See Instructions on page 20.)

Note: General sales taxes are no longer deductible.
5 State and local income taxes — 5
6 Real estate taxes — 6
7 Other taxes (list—include personal property taxes) ▶ — 7
8 Add the amounts on lines 5 through 7. Enter the total here. **Total** taxes ▶ 8

Interest You Paid
(See Instructions on page 20.)

Caution: If you paid interest on a loan incurred after August 16, 1986, that is secured by your home OR if you paid mortgage interest on more than two homes, see page 20 of the Instructions.

9a Deductible home mortgage interest you paid to financial institutions (report deductible points on line 10) — 9a
b Deductible home mortgage interest you paid to individuals (show that person's name and address) ▶ — 9b
10 Deductible points — 10
11 Deductible investment interest — 11
12a Personal interest you paid (see page 20) — 12a
b Multiply the amount on line 12a by 65% (.65). Enter the result — 12b
13 Add the amounts on lines 9a through 11, and 12b. Enter the total here. **Total interest** ▶ 13

Contributions You Made
(See Instructions on page 21.)

14a Cash contributions. (If you gave $3,000 or more to any one organization, report those contributions on line 14b.) — 14a
b Cash contributions totaling $3,000 or more to any one organization. (Show to whom you gave and how much you gave.) ▶ — 14b
15 Other than cash (You must attach Form 8283 if over $500.) — 15
16 Carryover from prior year — 16
17 Add the amounts on lines 14a through 16. Enter the total here. **Total contributions** ▶ 17

Casualty and Theft Losses
18 Casualty or theft loss(es) (attach Form 4684). (See page 21 of the Instructions.) ▶ 18

Moving Expenses
19 Moving expenses (attach Form 3903 or 3903F). (See page 22 of the Instructions.) ▶ 19

Miscellaneous Deductions Subject to 2% AGI Limit
(See Instructions on page 22.)

20 Unreimbursed employee business expenses (attach Form 2106) — 20
21 Other expenses (list type and amount) ▶ — 21
22 Add the amounts on lines 20 and 21. Enter the total. — 22
23 Multiply the amount on Form 1040, line 31, by 2% (.02). Enter the result here — 23
24 Subtract line 23 from line 22. Enter the result (but not less than zero) ▶ 24

Other Miscellaneous Deductions
25 Miscellaneous deductions not subject to 2% AGI limit (see page 22). (List type and amount.) ▶ 25

Total Itemized Deductions
26 Add the amounts on lines 4, 8, 13, 17, 18, 19, 24, and 25. Enter your answer here and on Form 1040, line 32. ▶ 26

For Paperwork Reduction Act Notice, see Form 1040 Instructions.
Schedule A (Form 1040) 1987

Leveling the Playing Field

Loss of the two-income deduction puts working couples on a more even footing with other groups.

Tax reform means compromise. But the new code puts some taxpayers at a greater disadvantage than others. Working couples and many singles, for example, have seen precious deductions slip away. For most heads of household, on the other hand, hefty gains will help to shield more of their dollars from the IRS. Following are the most important changes affecting these three classes of taxpayers.

Working couples. With only three tax rates—15%, 28%, and 33%—pooling incomes no longer pushes most two-earner couples into higher brackets. For this reason, Congress saw fit to repeal the two-earner deduction, which was an attempt to offset the jump into a higher bracket by allowing working couples to write off up to $3,000. Yet despite the lawmakers' reasoning, the marriage penalty—or the additional tax you pay as joint filers over what you would owe if you filed as singles—persists under the new law. There are significant exceptions, however. Couples with combined incomes between $50,000 and $60,000 generally will be hardest hit by the revised marriage penalty. A husband and wife who each earn $30,000, for example, may face as much as a 6% tax increase. Their marriage penalty in 1987 and 1988 will average around $1,365, compared with $547 under the old law.

The two-earner deduction also provided working couples the opportunity to recover job-related costs, such as transportation, clothing, and meals, which are usually greater for

them than for one-earner couples. Now the only tax break remaining for dual earners is the child-care credit. Working couples with no children and one-earner childless couples are the same in the tax man's eyes, despite the difference in their daily expenses. In many cases, a working couple's newly limited ability to deduct IRA contributions will further expose such a household to taxes. Until now, each worker was entitled to a full $2,000 IRA deduction, resulting in a $4,000 maximum for working couples. With reform, the deduction is off limits for both spouses if only one of them is covered by a pension and their adjusted gross income tops $50,000.

Singles. Like many other taxpayers, singles may see their rates, but not their taxes, go down. Although the loss of favored provisions, such as the deductions for consumer interest and sales tax, affects everyone, tax reform makes it particularly difficult for singles to itemize. The reason: singles tend to be renters and thus cannot take advantage of the major surviving deductions—mortgage interest payments and property taxes. Thus many tax specialists advise singles to buy a home for themselves or a house to rent out. Under the new law, single owners of rental property have a relative advantage over working couples: if you make less than $100,000 and actively manage your own property, you can write off up to $25,000 of real estate losses annually against your regular earnings. The income limit for joint filers is also $100,000. Singles are less likely to exceed this cap than married couples who combine their salaries.

Head of household. To qualify for this filing status you must be unmarried and pay more than half the cost of your parents' household, even if they live apart from you, or your own household, which must include a child, grandchild, or any of a number of other qualifying relatives, such as siblings or in-laws. An exception: a married person may qualify if he or she has dependent children and pays more than half the costs of a household of which his or her spouse has not been a member during the last six months of the year.

Two reforms in the new law especially reduce the tax burden for household heads who do not itemize: the increased standard deduction and the higher personal exemption. Before tax reform, the standard deduction for heads of household was the same as for single filers, 68% of that of a married couple. By 1988, however, a household head's standard deduction will have jumped by 77%. At a high of $4,400 it will be 88% of that of a married joint filer. Between now and 1989, the personal exemption will also rise, from $1,950 this year to $2,000; thereafter it will increase with the cost of living. Taken together, these changes raise the level of income at which most heads of household must begin to pay taxes, letting single parents and other taxpayers with dependents keep more of their cash for living expenses.

How Tax Reform Affects Your Mutual Funds

Loopholes are lost, but opportunities are gained.

In the case of mutual funds, the Tax Reform Act of 1986 has both given and taken away. The most notable losses are two obscure tax breaks you might never have missed—until you filed your returns. One allowed funds to defer income for you by paying it out the year after it was earned. The other, in effect, let you automatically write off the fund's investment expenses. Now you could wind up owing taxes this year on earnings that went to pay the fund's bills.

On the bright side, the law leaves intact provisions that give fund investors special latitude in calculating capital gains—the difference between what you paid for your shares and what you receive when you redeem them. For most fund shareholders, however, the key changes are not the ones aimed specifically at funds but those that affect all investors: the reduction in tax brackets and the repeal of the preferential treatment for long-term capital gains.

The New Rules for Investors

The new tax code shifts its affection from racy growth-stock funds to their traditionally stodgy income-oriented cousins, which invest in bonds or in high-dividend stocks. The reason is the phase-out of the distinction, as far as taxes are concerned, between income and long-term capital gains. Before January 1, 1987, if you owned any security longer than six months and sold it at a profit, only 40% of the gain was taxable. Now all capital gains—not just 40%—are taxable.

For 1987 only, there was a transition rule: the maximum long-term gains rate was 28%, even for investors paying rates of 35% or 38.5% on other income. In subsequent years, capital gains and other income such as your salary, interest, and dividends will be taxed at the same rate, up to the maximum 33% for single filers with taxable incomes over $43,150 and for married couples filing jointly with taxable incomes over $71,900.

Thus, other investment considerations aside, income-producing funds look more attractive than they did formerly, relative to low-yielding growth funds. Take, for example, a married couple with a taxable income of $37,980 to $49,420, which put them in the 33% tax bracket in 1986. Now the rate they pay on long-term gains has more than doubled, from 13.2% in 1986 to 28% in 1987 and thereafter. But the tax they face on their interest and dividends has dropped from 33% to 28%. As a result, the couple will net 17% less after taxes from a growth fund that appreciates exactly as much as it did in 1986. But they earn 7.5% more from an income fund that paid identical dividends in 1986.

While market analysts still expect growth funds to outperform income funds over the long haul, the after-tax advantage will narrow. Because the tax code no longer rewards you for taking the risk of investing in stock funds, you have a strong incentive to look into income funds. Moreover, what is good for income funds may be even better for total-return funds, which aim for a mix of capital gains and income.

What about losses? The new law makes the chore of weeding out your losing funds a lot less onerous. In the past, there was a tax incentive to hold on to losing funds in hopes that they would turn around: you could deduct only 50% of losses on the sale of assets held for more than six months. What is more, deductible losses were limited to $3,000 a year, although losses in excess of that amount could be carried over into future years. The new law lets you deduct 100% of your long-term losses, up to $3,000 annually, and carry forward excess losses. So the tax penalty for selling at a long-term loss is gone.

New Wrinkles for Funds

In addition to these changes, which affect all investments, the tax code introduces a number of provisions specifically aimed at mutual funds. Here are the changes that are most likely to affect fund shareholders.

Inflexible dividend distributions. A fund can generate income in either of two ways: by taking profits on appreciated stocks or bonds in its portfolio or by receiving interest or dividends from the securities it owns. The Internal Revenue Service requires most funds to pay the income to shareholders after subtracting expenses. You owe tax on these distributions in the year you receive them, as you would on interest or dividends paid by a company in which you owned stocks or bonds. If a fund has realized any capital gains, they will be included in the distributions along with interest and dividends.

Under the old law, most funds had to pass on to shareholders all the income generated during their fiscal year, within 12 months of the fiscal year-end. That often meant that shareholders automatically deferred taxes on at least some of the income until many months after the fund had received it. For instance, the Nicholas Fund, a growth fund with a fiscal year ending on March 31, did not pay out any of the income it earned between April 1985 and March 1986 until April 1986. Shareholders paid no tax on income the fund earned in the last nine months of 1985 until they filed their 1986 tax returns.

The new law slams that loophole shut. Now funds must distribute all of the income and profits they earn during the calendar year. This change delivered a double whammy in 1987 because a fund had to pay out not only all the income it earned during the year but also whatever it still owed you from that part of 1986 that fell during the fund's fiscal 1987. In the Nicholas Fund, for example, you would have ended up owing taxes on 21 months' worth of income on your 1987 return. Take consolation that in 1988 and subsequent years you pay tax on only one year's worth of dividends at a time.

Deductionless expenses. In the process of investing your money, a fund incurs costs; on average, administrative expenses and advisory fees absorb about 1% of a fund's total assets annually. Previously the fund deducted those expenses from its investment earnings before making distributions—in effect, you automatically received a deduction for investment expenses. Now such expenses may be deductible only if your total miscellaneous deductions exceed 2% of your adjusted gross income.

To make sure that mutual fund investors do not automatically receive a deduction that other investors might not get, the new law changes how funds report their distributions. For example, in its 1986 fiscal year, the Nicholas Fund yielded $1.07 a share before expenses. If you owned 300 shares—about $9,000 worth—your portion of the gross income would have been $321. Your share of fund expenses would have been $57, and so your net income would have been $264. The fund would have distributed that amount to you in April 1986, and you would pay taxes on it when you filed your 1986 taxes.

In 1988 and thereafter, you would still receive only $264 but would have to report all $321 as income. You could include the $57 of expenses with your miscellaneous deductions. Unless the total figure for those deductions exceeds 2% of your income, however, you lose all $57 of the deduction, and you would owe tax on all $321. The revamped Form 1099 your fund sends you next January will list both the gross dividends you must report and the expenses you can deduct.

The provision hits some funds harder than others. Dividends paid by municipal bond funds get off scot-free; their shareholders need to report only the interest they receive (and, of course, they still pay no federal taxes on it). But growth funds, which tend to run up relatively high expenses and earn little interest or dividend income, get stung. Shareholders in some of these funds may find they owe more in taxes than they receive in dividends.

Income from short-term hedges. The old tax code permitted a fund to earn no more than 30% of its total income from investments held less than three months. That limited a fund manager's freedom to protect his portfolio by hedging—using short-term defensive transactions to offset possible losses. Now, however, a gain on a short-term transaction undertaken specifically as a hedge can be offset by a loss in the part of the portfolio being hedged. For example, a fund manager, concerned that a stock in his portfolio might decline, could buy an option that will increase in value if the price of his stock drops within the next three months. If the loss on the stock and the gain on the option are equal, then none of the income from that transaction counts toward the 30% limit, and the fund manager can continue hedging against portfolio losses without going over his limit.

Several funds, including Dreyfus Strategic Income and Dreyfus Strategic Investing, are designed to take advantage of the revamped rule. They trade options on the securities in their portfolios to boost income and help hold share prices steady.

Ways to Figure Your Capital Gains

When you take your profits on shares of a mutual fund, you must pay tax on your capital gain. The tax code lets you use any of four methods to calculate the shares' cost, so you can choose the one that results in the smallest tax. Whichever you choose, remember to subtract from your gain the value of shares purchased with reinvested dividends or distributions of capital gains. You paid taxes on them in the year they were made.

Once you decide on a method, you must use it every time you sell shares from that fund. Note that if you sell all your shares in the same year, the total gain you report will be the same no matter what method you use to calculate it. But if you sell over a period of years, the different methods let you control when you will recognize different parts of the gain. Here are the four methods and how they work.

Specific identification method. This one gives you the most control over the results, but as a practical matter it is the most difficult to apply.

When instructing a fund to sell, you must identify the shares in your sell order by the date you bought them and the price you paid for them. For example, to minimize your gain you could simply instruct the fund to sell the shares you paid the most for. To stand up to IRS scrutiny, however, you need confirmation that the specified shares were indeed sold, and few funds' transaction statements describe which shares were redeemed. If you bought the shares through a broker, he or she can generally confirm that the order was filled as you requested. But if you bought shares directly from a fund, you run the risk that your calculation will be disallowed in an IRS audit.

FIFO method. If you do not specifically identify the shares you redeem, the IRS assumes that you sell shares in the order you purchased them. If your fund's shares have risen fairly steadily, this first-in, first-out (or FIFO) method will generally give you the largest gain—and a heftier tax bill. Normally you would want to report as small a gain as possible. But if you sold shares in 1987 that you held longer than six months, you might prefer to use FIFO when you file your 1987 return, to make sure

the ones you sold qualify for the transition-year rate of 28% on long-term gains.

Single-category and double-category methods. Instead of calculating a different gain for each block of shares you bought, you can figure an average cost for shares you sell. You can use either of two averaging methods. With *single category* you simply calculate an average cost for all the shares you own, which can result in a bigger tax bill than the previously cited methods.

Or you can choose *double category*, in which you calculate one average for shares you have held longer than six months and a separate average for shares you bought more recently. Then when you file your taxes, you designate the shares you have sold as coming from one category or the other. The double category method may be advantageous in figuring your 1987 tax bill if you are in the 35% bracket or higher and sold shares from the long-term category last year, because you benefit from the favorable rates on long-term gains. From now on, the sole rationale for committing to the double category is the hope that the next round of tax reforms will reinstate the preferential rates on long-term gains.

Your House Still Boasts the Best Breaks

Mortgage interest deductions are worth less than before, but no other shelter stands as tall as your home.

Although weathered a bit by the new tax rules, your home remains one of the few solid tax shelters left—and it is still the best investment most people can make.

While mortgage interest and other sacrosanct housing write-offs survived the reform

storm, they probably are not worth as much to you now as they were before. If you are like most people, your tax rate has dropped under reform, and that automatically lessens the value of any deductions you may take. If, for example, you were previously in the 50% tax bracket, a mortgage deduction of $15,000 used to be worth $7,500; with your rate at 33% this year, the same deduction shaves only $4,950 off your tax bill.

Therefore owning a home now becomes more expensive, claiming a bigger slice of your after-tax income. This fundamental change may not leave you in worse financial shape overall, particularly if your after-tax income goes up. But you might have to allocate your budget differently to pay for a current mortgage or settle for a less costly house if you are looking to buy. To determine your best strategies, you need to re-examine the economics of home ownership in light of the new tax rules and rates, following these guidelines.

Mortgage interest. In the past, all mortgage interest was deductible. From now on, however, you can write off only the mortgage interest on first and second homes. And the write-off is limited to the interest on mortgage principal up to the amount of the original purchase price of the home plus the cost of any improvements.

This cap comes into play if you want to refinance your house or take out a home-equity loan. As long as your house serves as collateral on the loan, you can deduct the interest but only up to the prescribed limits, even if your equity in the house exceeds that amount. Take, for example, a house you bought for $100,000 with a $20,000 down payment. All the interest on the $80,000 mortgage would be deductible. Say you later added $20,000 of improvements and paid off the mortgage, and the house is now appraised at $200,000. If you take out a second mortgage, you will be able to deduct only the interest on a loan of up to $120,000—the original purchase price ($100,000) plus the cost of improvements ($20,000)—regardless of the house's current appraised value of $200,000.

There are, of course, some exceptions. You can borrow more than the rules allow and still deduct your interest in full if you use the extra money for medical or educational expenses for yourself, your spouse, or a dependent. And no matter how you spend the extra money, you can continue to write off part of the excess

interest through 1990. The excess interest is treated the same way as interest on consumer debt: you can deduct 65% in 1987, 40% in 1988, 20% in 1989, and 10% in 1990. The deduction disappears in 1991.

What if you refinanced your home long ago and already carry mortgage debt that exceeds the new limits? Do not worry. Congress made a special exception for you. If you took out your mortgage on or before August 16, 1986, interest on the entire loan amount is deductible. If you established a home-equity line of credit before the cutoff date, however, only the money you actually borrowed by that time falls under this exemption. Any money borrowed after that date is subject to the new restriction.

Two major warnings about deducting mortgage interest apply if you expect to be subject to the alternative minimum tax (AMT), which is intended to make wealthy taxpayers pay their fair share. If you refinance your mortgage, only the interest on loan amounts up to the existing balance will be considered deductible for the purposes of the AMT. You will have to add back into your income any excess interest when you compute your AMT tax, even if the money is used for medical or educational expenses. Also, if you take out a home-equity loan or second mortgage, to deduct the interest for purposes of the AMT, you must have used the money to make substantial home improvements or to pay down your existing mortgage.

The sum of all these rule changes is that the mortgage deduction is still a significant tax break that can add up to sizable savings, not least of all because it provides a unique source of tax-advantaged credit. You can borrow against the equity in your house within the new limits for whatever purpose you wish—for example, to buy a car—and still write off your interest in full.

In case you ever decide to use a home-equity loan or second mortgage, you should begin now to keep thorough records of all expenses related to improvements you make on your home. The bigger the tally, the greater the pool of funds you can tap later and still get a tax break on the interest.

Points. Up-front fees, or points that you pay in advance for a mortgage, are still deductible for a primary residence. Points and other closing fees have always had to be amortized, and they still must. On a first mortgage, you can deduct in the first year all the points that you paid in advance. But on a second mortgage or any type of refinancing, the Internal Revenue Service requires you to spread out the deduction for points over the life of the loan unless you spend the money to make substantial home improvements.

Not all accountants agree with the IRS interpretation. Some have advised their clients to challenge the IRS and deduct their points in full, with the expectation that the issue will be settled favorably either through litigation or legislation. Others have recommended taking a deduction in the first year for points that apply to the original purchase price of the home and amortizing the rest. Members of the Senate and the House of Representatives have introduced legislation that would make points paid for refinancing deductible, but the measures were still pending in late 1987.

Property taxes. The new tax law preserves the deduction for property taxes.

Deferral of gain. Under current rules, as under the old ones, you can defer taxes on any profit from the sale of a primary residence if you buy another of equal or greater value within two years. And, as before, if the new house costs less, you are liable for taxes only on the amount of gain that exceeds the purchase price of the new home. Of course, long-term profits from the sale of real estate, as with those from other kinds of assets, no longer receive favorable tax treatment after 1987, when the maximum tax rate on capital gains was 28%. In 1988 and thereafter you must pay taxes on any gain at your regular income tax rate.

One-time exclusion. Unchanged in the revised rules is the provision that allows taxpayers 55 years of age and older a one-time exclusion from taxes of $125,000 in profits on the sale of their primary residence.

Money Basics

Alternative minimum tax (AMT). A tax designed to make high-income earners pay their fair share of taxes. If you make less than $150,000 a year, you probably need not fear the AMT.

Amortization. The reduction of debt through regular payments of principal and interest. Payments must be large enough to satisfy the loan by its maturity date.

Exclusion. An item that must be reported on your return but is not taxed, such as profits of up to $125,000 on the sale of your home.

Points. A lender's fee. One point equals 1% of the mortgage.

Money Tips

Consider investing in real estate that needs rehabilitation. The tax reform law retains the so-called rehab tax credit. To claim the credit, which reduces your tax dollar for dollar, you must spend for rehabilitation purposes at least $5,000 or the amount you paid for the building, whichever is more.

Take your time when you buy a new house. You can wait two years to buy a principal residence after selling your house and defer taxes on any profit you received until you sell the new house. Just be sure the new house costs as much or more than the sales price of your former residence.

Think about staying in your vacation house for more than 14 days or 10% of the time the house is in use. That way, you will be able to call it your second residence, which will entitle you to deduct 100% of the mortgage interest and property taxes.

Tough New Rules for Rental Real Estate

No more easy depreciation, no more lovable losses: those tax shelters-by-the-sea are mostly a fond memory.

If you own a vacation home or a property that you rent out, it is time to reappraise your investment. Tax reform has weakened many of the write-offs that made owning such properties worthwhile.

In the past, tax breaks often allowed investors to profit from even money-losing properties. But the new tax law razes that built-in support by restricting the deductibility of rental losses against other income. It also lengthens the time you must take to depreciate your property and no longer lets you speed up depreciation write-offs in the early years. The result is that you are going to have to look at property apart from tax considerations now.

Whether you are planning to buy or already own rental property, calculating your after-tax cash flow is more crucial than ever. The numbers may tell you that you need to shop for something different, rearrange the financing on existing units, convert a vacation home rental to a residence by spending more time in it yourself, or even sell your holdings. But before you do any of the calculations, you must understand the new rules of rental real estate, which can be complex and confusing. Here are the most important.

Vacation Homes

If you own just one vacation home—it can be a house, an apartment, a condo, a live-aboard boat, or a mobile home—and reserve it solely for your own use, you can avoid the trickiest sections of the revamped rules. The new law allows you to deduct interest on a mortgage up to the original purchase price plus the cost of improvements. So if you do not rent out your hideaway, you can simply take deductions on it as a second home.

Your tax situation is not so simple if you rent out your retreat for part of the year. The deductions you can take—and the total tax benefit you will reap—will depend mostly on whether the property is classified as a residence or a rental. For example, if your second home is a rental under the new law, you may no longer be able to deduct all of your mortgage interest.

Your property is considered a residence if you use it for personal purposes more than 14 days a year or more than 10% of the time you rent it out at a fair market rate, whichever is greater. You can include days when it is used by a spouse, relatives, part-owners of the property, a person with whom you have an arrangement to swap vacation homes for a comparable period of time, or anyone who rents it at less than the fair market rate. Days spent solely on repair and maintenance of the property do not count toward personal or rental use.

Deductions you can take for rental expenses on a residence are basically limited to the income you receive from it. Thus, in any year you use your vacation home yourself and rent it out, you must allocate your expenses between personal and rental use. The calculation is further complicated by an IRS rule that prescribes the order in which you must write off the rental expenses. For example, if you occupy your home for 20 days and rent it out 60 days, rental use accounts for three-fourths of the total usage and expenses. After you allocate your expenses, you must deduct rental expenses, up to the amount of your rental income, in this order: mortgage interest and property taxes, operating expenses such as utilities and insurance, and, finally, depreciation. Then, because the property is technically a second residence, you can deduct any remaining mortgage interest. You can also deduct any leftover property taxes since they are deductible for both residences and rentals.

If you rent out your second home for no more than 14 days a year, the rental income is tax-free—you do not even have to report it. If you rent it out for longer than that, any income left after you have deducted your expenses is taxed at the same rate as your regular earnings.

What if you own more than one vacation home? Each year you may designate any one of them as your second residence.

Rental Property

For taxpayers interested in qualifying a house as a rental so they can take advantage of rental losses, the guidelines get tough. Once you have satisfied the basic occupancy standard—you cannot use the house more than 14 days or 10% of the time it is rented—the property is subject to the same rules and restrictions that affect all real estate investments.

First, if the property is newly purchased, you must use the new 27½-year, straight-line depreciation method. (Even if your house is considered a residence rather than a rental, the new schedule applies to any deductions you take for depreciation.) But if you bought your property and placed it in service before January 1, 1987, you can still take advantage of the old 19-year, accelerated depreciation

schedule, which lets you take bigger write-offs in the early years.

Second, rental expenses cannot be used to offset your regular income. They are considered passive losses, and the new tax law allows you to deduct them only against passive income from other rental properties or limited partnerships—not against active income, such as wages and salary, or against portfolio income, such as dividends or interest.

The old rules, which let you use rental losses to offset any kind of income, gave real estate quite a power punch. High-bracket taxpayers could shelter taxable income by writing off their rental losses. Even cash-hemorrhaging properties became healthy investments once the tax benefits were factored in.

While the new passive-loss restrictions may be crippling to some real estate investors, other owners get a break. The new law makes an exception for investors who fall within certain income limitations. If your adjusted gross income is $100,000 or less, you can deduct as much as $25,000 in passive losses, as long as you own at least 10% of the property and are actively involved in managing it. (You can use a rental agent, but your contract with him or her should show that you make such decisions as approving tenants and authorizing repairs.)

If your income is above $100,000, you lose 50¢ of the active rental allowance for every dollar your income exceeds that amount. The deduction is disallowed entirely for incomes of $150,000 or more.

Remember also that you must still allocate your real estate expenses between personal and rental uses, which is particularly important if your property qualifies as a rental. That is because under the new rules, with the sole exception of property taxes, you cannot fully deduct any expenses that are allocated to personal use—including mortgage interest. All of the mortgage interest on any home used to be deductible, even if you took rental losses on the property.

Now, however, mortgage interest allocated to personal use is considered personal interest and is subject to the same four-year phaseout as interest on consumer debt. On the other hand, you can take advantage of the gradual phaseout of the passive-loss deduction that is similar to the consumer interest phaseout, as long as your rental property was in service by October 22, 1986. You can deduct 65% of your excess passive losses on such holdings in 1987, 40% in 1988, 20% in 1989, and 10% in 1990, but none thereafter. If your rental losses exceed $25,000, or your income exceeds $150,000, you can carry forward your losses. You can then use them in later years to a) offset passive income, b) take active rental allowances in years when your income eventually drops below the $150,000 limit, or c) reduce your taxable gain dollar for dollar when you sell the property.

Because of the new rules, if you own a vacation home that qualifies as a rental, you might want to consider converting it to a second home. In general, you should look at how much you are using it for rental and personal purposes and see whether a minor change would provide a tax benefit. If your rental losses are substantial, and to some extent deductible, you may be best off continuing to treat the property as a rental and writing off the losses. But some high-income taxpayers who cannot benefit from any of the $25,000 active rental allowance may find that they come out ahead by changing the status of the property to a residence and writing off mortgage interest in full.

You might also consider refinancing your principal residence to pay off any debt—with full deductibility—on your rental properties. By shifting the interest deduction entirely to the first house, you can reduce your losses on the rentals and increase their income. But you should evaluate the cost of refinancing, including closing costs and interest expenses, before you take out a new loan. And, of course, you must be careful not to exceed the new restrictions on deductibility of mortgage interest.

If you think you may be better off selling, be sure to consider another provision of reform: the abolition of the favorable tax treatment of capital gains. When you sell your property, any profit is taxed at your regular rate after 1987. If your state taxes capital gains, do not underestimate the impact. Because of the way that many states link their tax systems to the federal code, capital-gains taxes will claim a bigger share of your profits than in the past unless legislatures amend the state laws.

Money Basics

Active income. Earnings are divided into three parts by the new tax law: active, passive, and portfolio. Active income includes wages, salaries, tips, and commissions.

Active rental loss allowance. A write-off of up to $25,000 of rental losses that can offset all types of income as long as the owner actively manages the property and has an adjusted gross income of $100,000 or less. The allowance is reduced by 50¢ for every dollar above that amount until it is phased out entirely for incomes of $150,000 or more.

Carryovers. Tax losses not taken in the year they are incurred that can be used to offset capital gains or income in later years.

Depreciation. The allocation of an asset's cost over a certain period of time. Newly purchased residential real estate, for example, must be depreciated over 27½ years, so deductions for depreciation in any one year are limited to two-fifty-fifths of the cost.

Passive income. Rents and other money you receive from activities in which you do not actively participate—for example, a real estate limited partnership in whose operations you are not involved on a regular, continuous, and substantial basis.

Portfolio income. Interest, dividends, mortgage income, royalties, and capital gains.

Taxable income. That portion of your income on which you owe federal tax. Taxable income equals adjusted gross income minus itemized deductions or the standard deduction if you do not itemize, and personal exemptions.

Being Generous Will Cost You More

Lower rates and stricter rules for charitable gifts made 1987 the first year of giving dangerously.

The cost of giving has gone up under tax reform. Beginning last year, nonitemizers can no longer write off charitable contributions. If you itemize, you can still deduct your cash donations and the fair market value of most gifts of property, even if you paid much less. But lower overall income tax rates reduce the value of the deduction.

If you itemize and give property such as stocks and real estate to a charity, you may be in for an unpleasant surprise. That is because the appreciation in property gifts must now be added back to your income to compute the alternative minimum tax, a flat 21% levy that ensures the well-to-do will pay their fair share. And the appreciation in gifts of tangible personal property such as art, antiques, and collectibles will be disallowed entirely unless the gift is used for the charity's tax-exempt purpose. Say you donate to the local museum a painting that cost you $10,000 and is now worth $20,000. If the museum auctions off the painting instead of displaying it, you will get a deduction equal only to the $10,000 you paid for the painting, even if the museum buys another one with the proceeds. Previously, the value of such donations was reduced by 40%, representing your taxable gain if you had sold the property yourself. Now the deduction must be decreased by the entire amount of the appreciation. So it is important to know how your gift will be used.

Before giving appreciated property, com-pute both your regular tax and your alternative minimum tax, advisably at year-end when you can best estimate your tax bill. If you fall under the AMT, identify any items in your regular tax subject to the AMT and postpone donating them until the following year. You may put off taking your real estate shelter losses, for example. You could also try to accelerate income into an AMT year. If you are contributing stock, give some of it in December and the rest the following year. A well-timed gift may enable you to keep the full value of your charitable deduction.

If the AMT is unavoidable, you could still benefit by giving appreciated property along with property on which you have suffered a loss. Your AMT liability that is attributable to your gift of appreciated property will be reduced dollar for dollar by your loss. You also avoid the brokerage fees of selling the loss property. This is in contrast to the standard advice, which is to sell the loss property, realize the loss, and donate the proceeds to charity or give appreciated property so that you do not have to recognize the gain.

Concern over the increase in capital-gains rates has some big givers considering more elaborate strategies. One of them is the charitable remainder trust, which lets you avoid capital gains and estate tax while providing current income. Such trusts are not for everybody because the legal costs involved in setting one up can run to $2,500 or more, making the practical minimum size about $100,000. Whenever you give something away, it costs you, but the charitable remainder trust allows you to increase your income and accomplish your charitable goals at the same time.

When you put income-producing assets in such a trust, you name yourself as the beneficiary of a specific annual percentage of the income. Whatever remains in the trust when you die goes to the charity you have designated as trustee. A one-time deduction in the year you establish the trust is based on a calculation involving your age, the amount of the trust's principal, and the payout rate. Assuming a 28% tax bracket for a couple in their

mid-fifties, for example, a $100,000 trust that gives them an 8.5% interest payout will yield an $11,564 deduction; a 10% payout delivers an $8,270 deduction.

You can realize additional tax benefits over the years by continuing to donate appreciated property to the trust. Its assets are, in effect, owned by the tax-exempt charitable organization. As trustee, it can sell the property and invest the proceeds without ever paying capital gains tax. With greater tax-free sums to invest, the trust permits assets to appreciate faster than they could in your own portfolio. As they do, both your income and your bequest to charity rise accordingly.

Compromise Can Help Both Divorce Parties Win

Shifts in tax rates are creating a new math for divorce settlements.

If breaking up is hard to do, tax reform has not made it any easier. The drop in tax rates makes alimony costlier to the payer, and the rise in capital-gains taxes makes settlements of appreciated property less attractive to the receiver. So negotiating a divorce agreement will be trickier—and more important—than ever. The principal points follow.

Alimony. It is still deductible by the one who pays it, but the write-off is worth less with the top rate capped at 33%. Meanwhile, the nearly 6% of women who receive alimony are taxed on payments received. The likely outcome: a divorcing husband will be even less willing to make alimony settlements than before.

On a more conciliatory note, couples who are divorcing now have added flexibility in planning their settlements, thanks to a rule in

the new law that allows larger alimony payments over a shorter period of time. A 1984 tax ruling took away the payer's deductions on payments in excess of $10,000 a year if they were not continued for at least six years. This ruling was designed to prevent property settlements—which are nondeductible—from being disguised as alimony. Under the new law, annual payments of more than $15,000 are fully deductible as alimony if they are made for three consecutive years. This period can be shortened to 13 months if an ex-spouse makes the payments on December 31 of the first year, December 31 of the second, and January 1 of the third.

Property. Since capital gains are taxed at the same rate as ordinary income beginning this year, the spouse who gets the house will wind up with less after selling it. As with the old law, the spouse who receives appreciated property will have to pay tax on the full amount of appreciation from the time the property was bought. For 1988, the effect on this taxpayer would be a rise in the maximum federal tax on the capital gain from 28% to 33%. So the spouse left with the property might want to hold out for additional assets or alimony in a settlement.

The children. Although tax reform increases exemptions for dependents from $1,080 to $1,900 in 1987, $1,950 in 1988, and $2,000 in 1989, the spouse who gets the children is not ahead much. That is because the lowered tax rates diminish the value of the exemption, so the tax benefit for someone in the 28% bracket is less than $600. Moreover, beginning this year personal exemptions are phased out for taxpayers with incomes above $89,560, so a custodial parent with income above that amount will not be able to claim exemptions for dependents.

A warning to those inclined to cheat: both of the divorced or separated parents cannot get away with claiming the same child as an exemption. Reason: the new law requires all parents taking this write-off to obtain a Social Security number for each dependent and report it on their returns.

Child support is still nondeductible by the parent who pays it, and nontaxable to the one who receives it. Some fathers, however, may become less willing to assume responsibility for their children's educations since they will no longer be able to deduct the interest from tuition loans.

Negotiating. With many husbands no longer in higher brackets than their wives—partly because of fewer brackets, partly because of women's job advances—some traditional negotiating concerns will intensify as others diminish. Because of the lower rates in general, there will be less quibbling over what is alimony and what is child support, and the incentive to disguise settlements as alimony will diminish. In the past, it was usually taken for granted that the husband would receive any tax shelters the couple owned since his need for them was greater. Now that assumption is no longer valid, and because rates are lower and tax shelters are a shambles, expect to see these wrecks turning up on bargaining tables as assets. To determine whether a partnership has any value, you will have to hire an appraiser.

One kind of asset that shines more brightly is pensions. Shorter vesting schedules under tax reform will make them more valuable. The nonpensioned divorcing spouse might ask for 50% of the value of the plan. But because of the fees charged for dividing a plan, if the benefits are small, he or she might be better off trading it for other assets.

Money Tip

Donate strategically to your child's education. Each parent can still give as much as $10,000 a year, free of tax, to each child. The easiest way to make the gift is by opening a Uniform Gifts to Minors Act custodial account at a bank or brokerage. Under the new rules, however, your child's net unearned income above $1,000 is taxed at your rate—until the child turns 14. Then all income is taxed at the child's rate. So give your child assets timed to pay off after that 14th birthday, such as tax-deferred U.S. savings bonds. Or invest for your child in zero-coupon municipal bonds, which usually furnish no taxable income, or growth stocks, which usually provide little. Be aware, however, that divorce courts in several states, including California, have ruled that some parents are obliged to support their children's college educations and pay taxes on accounts and trusts earmarked for schooling. The IRS might cite those cases and disallow the advantages of income shifting in those states.

Your Benefits May Never Be the Same

Rule changes are prompting reappraisals of early retirement, company savings plans, and pensions.

Everyone from your broker to your barber has probably given you a post-tax-reform prognosis for your investment portfolio. Chances are, though, that you have heard little about how the new tax rules will affect your employee-benefits package. Buried in the new law are some startling provisions.

Tighter limits on contributions to pension and company-sponsored savings plans. The aim in Congress was to make such plans more equitable for lower-paid workers by trimming benefits of big earners. But in some cases the new rules will hurt middle managers as well as tycoons.

New restrictions and a 10% penalty on withdrawals you make from your company savings plan before reaching age 59½. Congress has limited the use of such plans to retirement savings by discouraging short-term investment.

Greatly reduced pension benefits if you call it quits early. To discourage early retirement and thereby save Social Security costs, Congress slashed the maximum you can now receive. The new maximum benefit for early retirees depends on your year of birth and age at retirement.

A 15% tax penalty on extra-large retirement nest eggs. It was just one of many moves that Congress made to raise revenue.

As a result of all the new rules, employees must chart a fresh course for their savings. Following are the most important changes—along with advice on how to cope with them—from employee-benefits consultants and retirement advisers. Unless otherwise noted, all provisions took effect January 1, 1987.

Contributions

Congress has restricted contributions that you and your employer can make to company-sponsored savings and pension plans, but the limits are still generous. Money that you and your employer contribute to tax-sheltered annuities, 401(k) salary-reduction, profit-sharing, stock-ownership, and other savings plans still grows tax-free until you withdraw it. You put after-tax dollars in all such plans except for 401(k)s and annuities, which are also known as 403(b) plans and are available only to employees of tax-exempt organizations. As under prior law, annual contributions that you and your employer make to all such savings plans combined cannot exceed 25% of your pay or $30,000, whichever is less.

Under the old law, however, your annual after-tax contributions never counted against those limits unless they exceeded 6% of your pay. Now all of your after-tax contributions count. In addition, you cannot squirrel away more than $7,000 a year in a 401(k) or more than $9,500 annually in a 403(b) annuity. That $9,500 limit is reduced by each dollar you put into other salary-reduction plans such as 401(k)s. Starting in 1988, the cap on 401(k) contributions will increase with inflation; after it reaches $9,500, the same limit will apply to 401(k)s and 403(b)s.

Yet another new provision will hurt big earners. The amount of your annual compensation that your company can count when calculating its contributions to your savings and pension plans will drop to $200,000 in 1989 and be adjusted for the cost of living thereafter. Currently there is no limit.

Though limits on contributions to company plans still seem ample for most employees, other provisions of the tax act may further trim allowable contributions for middle managers whom the Internal Revenue Service and Congress consider highly paid. The law mandates a smaller spread between the average percentage of pay that a company's higher- and lower-paid workers may contribute to tax-sheltered savings plans. Employees are considered higher paid if they earn more than $75,000 a year; earn more than $50,000 and are among the top 20% highest-paid employees; own more than 5% of the company; or are officers of the company and earn more than $45,000.

Here is how these nondiscrimination tests work: assume that a corporation's lower-paid employees, as a group, contribute on average 5% of their pay to a 401(k) plan while their higher-paid colleagues put away 8% on average. All would have been well under the old rules, but the reform act reduces the allowable gap between the two groups' average contributions to two percentage points. So in this case, the employer must return to the higher-paid group an amount equal to 1% of their pay plus any earnings they have accumulated; it must be returned to them within two months from the end of the year in which the contributions were made. The employees will owe tax on any pretax contributions and earnings returned to them.

Benefits consultants predict that most companies will limit contributions from highly paid employees to avoid the administrative night-

mare of kicking excess contributions back to those employees. Based on how much its employees have contributed to a plan in the past, an employer can announce a ball-park estimate of the percentage of pay that higher-paid workers will be able to contribute. The nondiscrimination provisions took effect January 1, 1987—except for the new rules on 403(b) annuities, which are the same as for 401(k)s but come into play in 1989. Annuities held by church employees are exempt from these provisions.

Lower limits on contributions to company plans can cause other mischief. If a company maintains both a pension plan to which it contributes on behalf of employees as well as savings plans funded by employer and employee contributions, the IRS uses a complex formula to determine an overall limit on benefits that can be accrued in both types of plans. If an employee hits the limit because too much money has been contributed to his or her savings accounts, employers will generally cut back the employee's pension benefits because there is a chance that the employee will not stay long enough to collect a pension. In many cases, a company makes up such losses by establishing a supplemental pension plan that is not regulated by the IRS.

Withdrawals

Determined to discourage the use of tax-deferred savings plans for short-term investment, Congress wrote into the tax law new restrictions and a 10% tax penalty on withdrawals you make from such plans before reaching age 59½.

Particularly hard hit were 401(k)s. Under the old law, you could withdraw your contributions, earnings, and, in some plans, even your employer's contributions if you retired, left the company, became disabled, or could prove hardship, which was loosely interpreted to include buying a house.

If you plead hardship starting in 1989, however, you will be able to withdraw only your own contributions from a 401(k), on which you must pay income taxes. Also, effective in 1987, if you are under age 59½, a 10% tax penalty is levied on the withdrawal. The same rules apply to early withdrawals from 403(b)s.

The 10% penalty is imposed on early withdrawals of taxable sums from savings plans to which you contribute after-tax dollars. The penalty is waived for early withdrawals from any type of plan under certain conditions: if you become disabled; if you die and your beneficiaries receive the money; if you leave the company and take your cash as an annuity payable over the rest of your life; if you are at least 55 and take early retirement; or if you need the money to pay medical bills that exceed 7.5% of your adjusted gross income.

The income tax treatment of withdrawals from savings plans to which you contribute after-tax dollars is also less favorable under the new tax law. In the past, you could withdraw only your after-tax contributions, but now every withdrawal you make must consist of a prorated share of your contributions and their earnings. The rule does not apply to contributions you made before 1987, no matter when you withdraw those funds. Your company may require that each withdrawal you make include prorated shares of its contributions and their earnings, earnings attributable to your pre-1987 contributions, or both. Most companies will allow you to withdraw your pre-1987 contributions first.

Assume, for example, that you have in your profit-sharing account $20,000: $2,000 in contributions that you made after 1986 and $18,000 attributable to earnings and your employer's contributions. If you withdraw $2,000, $200 is considered a nontaxable withdrawal of your after-tax contributions while $1,800 is a taxable withdrawal of your earnings, your employer's contributions, and earnings on them. Unless you are exempt from the penalty for early withdrawal, the 10% tax also applies to the $1,800.

Given all of these new restrictions on savings plans, you may wonder whether you would be better off foregoing your company's plans and investing outside of your company instead. But before you start tossing memorandums from your company's benefits department in the trash, answer these questions:

- How likely is it that you will need your money before retirement? If you do not think that you will need it until after you reach age 59½, the magic of tax-deferred accumulation in a company savings plan is hard to beat.
- How valuable are your company's matching contributions? Remember that you make an automatic profit if your employer chips in, say, 50¢ for every dollar you invest. To entice younger workers to make a long-term commitment, companies may try to offer the financial incentive of increased matching contributions.
- Would you miss the tax write-off for contributions to a 401(k) or 403(b)? Chances are you would, especially if you can no longer deduct IRA contributions.
- How does a company plan's rate of return compare with outside alternatives?
- Can you avoid the tax on early withdrawals by borrowing against your company plan?

Borrowing

More companies will sweeten their savings plans by adding loan provisions, predicts Henry Von Wodtke, director of loans consulting for Buck Consultants, a benefits consulting firm in New York City. Of 104 companies surveyed by Buck last year, 62 let employees borrow against their 401(k)s.

Alas, tax reform also imposes some restrictions on loans from company plans. The maximum amount that you could borrow at any one time was the lesser of a) $50,000, or b) one-half of your vested balance or $10,000, whichever is greater. Under the new law, the $50,000 limit is reduced by your highest outstanding loan balance over the past 12 months. You must also repay such loans within five years, making payments at least quarterly. Your employer can waive the five-year rule and set its own repayment schedule only if you borrow in order to buy a principal residence for yourself.

Of course, borrowing has become less appealing under the new tax code because the deduction for consumer loan interest is being phased out. Worse yet, the interest deduction has already been completely eliminated for loans secured by your contributions to a 401(k) plan or an annuity; the same rule applies to loans from any type of company plan if the borrower is a company owner or an officer earning $45,000 a year or more.

Reduced Pension Benefits

Tax reformers took a machete to maximum pension benefits that early retirees can collect. Under the old rules, the most you could receive was $90,000 a year. The limit was reduced if you retired before age 62, but it was never lower than $75,000 a year at age 55. Under the new law, the maximum pension benefit remains $90,000, but the $75,000 floor has been eliminated and the maximum that you can receive if you retire before you are eligible to start collecting full Social Security benefits (at age 65 to 67, depending on your year of birth) has been drastically diminished. If you call it quits at 55, you can now receive $35,500 to $40,600 at most, depending on the year of your birth. Benefits accrued prior to 1987 are not affected by the new limits, nor are employees of tax-exempt organizations.

Liberalized Vesting

Such bitter fruit of the reform act has obscured the only decidedly juicy plum. Corporate pension plans must now fully vest employees after five years of service or after seven years by vesting them with 20% of their benefits after three years, plus 20% in each of the next four years. The rules take effect for most plans in 1989, but years that you have logged with your employer by then count.

Lump Sums

Before tax reform, people at any age could roll over a lump-sum distribution from a retirement plan into an IRA within 60 days or take the money and calculate income tax on it using 10-year forward averaging, which allows you to pay tax as if you had received the cash over 10 years instead of all at once.

The new tax law preserves the rollover option but replaces ten-year averaging with five-year averaging. In addition, you can now use the averaging provision to calculate tax on only one lump sum and only after you reach age 59½. The increase in taxes under the new method is substantial. For example, the tax on a $300,000 lump sum taken in 1988 would be $76,613 under five-year averaging versus $66,330 using ten-year averaging.

There is one exception to the new rule: if you reached age 50 by January 1, 1986, you can choose either five-year averaging under the new tax rates or ten-year averaging under the 1986 rates to determine the tax on a lump sum, whether or not you have reached age 59½. Ten-year averaging will result in less tax than five-year averaging if the taxable lump sum does not exceed $473,739.

Large Nest Eggs

Watch out if all of your retirement benefits from your pension, company-sponsored savings plans, tax-sheltered annuities, and even your IRAs add up to a sum that Congress considers too princely. A 15% penalty now applies to taxable distributions from such plans in excess of $112,500 (adjusted for inflation) or $150,000 a year, whichever is greater. For lump-sum benefits, the tax kicks in on amounts over $562,500 (adjusted for inflation in the future) or $750,000, whichever is greater. In any event, if you must pay a 15% penalty and a 10% early-withdrawal tax on the same distribution, the amount of the 15% penalty is reduced by the amount of the 10% tax.

This section of the tax act features a grandfathering provision, but deciding whether to take it requires the sagacity of a soothsayer, or at least the advice of a tax adviser. If benefits you have accrued by August 1, 1986, are worth more than $562,500, all of those benefits can escape the 15% tax regardless of when they are distributed to you. You must, however, indicate your desire to take advantage of this provision on your 1987 or 1988 tax return, no matter when you intend to retire.

Money Tip

The tax reform law also affects the value of fringe benefits your company may offer. Under prior law, you could offset taxable perquisites such as financial planning or tax advice provided by your employer by deducting them as miscellaneous expenses. Now that you can write off only unreimbursed business and miscellaneous expenses that exceed 2% of your adjusted gross income, you may want to turn down perks that end up costing more than they are worth to you.

Money Basics

401(k). A salary reduction plan that allows an employee to contribute up to $7,000 of his salary annually before taxes. The earnings are tax-deferred until withdrawn.

403(b). An annuity available only to employees of some tax-exempt organizations. It works much like a 401(k), but has a $9,500-a-year cap.

Keogh. A retirement plan for employees of unincorporated businesses and persons who are self-employed full- or part-time. As in IRAs, earnings grow tax-deferred, and in some cases contributions are tax-deductible.

A Mixed Bag for Small-Business Owners

The loss of write-offs may increase taxes by 20%, but tax-deferred pension plans will still shine.

For the nation's 15 million small-business owners and self-employed individuals, the new tax law is like a glitzy piece of costume jewelry: at first glance it sparkles, but when you take a closer look, it loses most of its luster. The reductions in corporate tax rates are highly touted, but the benefit of those lower rates is more than offset in many cases by the elimination of deductions and other tax benefits.

For example, one of the biggest boons to small businesses—the 10% investment tax credit for such purchases as office furniture, automobiles, and other equipment—was axed by the new law. Business owners will also find their depreciation deductions scaled back for certain capital equipment, and self-employed individuals who work at home will now face tougher rules for taking home-office deductions. The bottom line: taxes will rise 15% to 20% for small businesses. Some businesses will be hurt more than others. Capital-intensive companies that used tax credits and depreciation to whittle down their taxes will find their tab is much higher. But service companies that could not take advantage of such credits and deductions and paid top rates anyway will suffer less under the new law, and some may even fare better.

The Good News: Lower Rates

Tax reform's biggest plus for businesses and self-employed individuals is lower corporate and personal income tax rates. Beginning July 1987, the top corporate tax rate dropped from 46% to 34%. This rate applies only to companies that earn more than $75,000 per year. For companies with smaller net incomes, lower, graduated rates apply—15% for the first $50,000 in earnings, and 25% for earnings between $50,000 and $75,000. This 26% cut in the top rate is not quite as attractive as it seems, however. The reason: a 5% surcharge is levied on companies with taxable incomes between $100,000 and $335,000. Your company's earnings that fall within that range are taxed at an effective 39% rate.

If you have set up your business as a partnership or sole proprietorship, you will be taxed at personal tax rates, which fell to 33% in 1988. Because the top personal rate is now lower than the top corporate rate, the owners of a small business structured as a regular corporation should consider changing it to an S corporation. This would allow income to flow through to the owners much as it does in a partnership.

Switching to an S corp can also avoid double taxation on gains when a company is sold. Under the new law, if you sell your company, both it and the individual pay tax on the gain. When an S corporation is sold, however, the gain is usually taxed only at the individual level.

But S corps have some drawbacks: medical insurance premiums for the shareholders are not deductible, the corporation can have no more than 35 shareholders, and an S corp must use a calendar year for tax purposes.

New Rules for Pension Plans

Among the most sweeping changes in the new law are those affecting company retirement plans. For most employees, the vesting period drops from ten to five years, though in some cases vesting may occur gradually over seven years. Pensions must also cover a larger percentage of employees after 1988, and employers can no longer use Social Security payments as a way to avoid making contributions for lower-paid workers.

Consider a SEP. There are also strict new rules for deferred-salary plans such as 401(k)s. The result is that many companies will have to rewrite their benefit plans. In view of the increasing complexity of corporate retirement plans, some tax accountants suggest that small-business owners consider switching to a SEP, or Simplified Employee Pension plan, which is as easy to establish and maintain as an IRA. The employer merely sets up a SEP account for each employee and then contributes up to 15% of the employee's salary to the account, to a maximum of $30,000 a year.

The new law has sweetened SEPs. In addition to the employer's contribution, employees themselves may put away as much as $7,000 of their earnings in the SEP. Taxes on their contributions are deferred, but the employer's and employee's contributions combined may not exceed $30,000. To take advantage of this new benefit, a company cannot have more than 25 employees and at least half must elect to contribute to the SEP.

Keep the Keoghs. These plans, the most popular retirement savings vehicles for unincorporated businesses, have survived virtually intact. By setting up a money-purchase Keogh account—one of two types—you can salt away and deduct up to 20% of your net business income to an annual maximum of $30,000. Once you decide what percentage of income you wish to put away under this type of plan, however, you must contribute that percentage every year for yourself and your employees. A profit-sharing Keogh—the other type—is more flexible. You can set aside up to 13.043% of your net business income—but no more than $30,000 a year—and you may change that percentage or decide not to contribute at all in a given year.

As with an IRA, this money compounds tax-free until it is withdrawn, usually upon retirement. Earlier withdrawals are subject to a 10% penalty. Unlike IRAs, Keoghs can be funded after April 15—as late as October 15, provided you file for the appropriate extensions. You cannot take a deduction for the 1987 tax year, however, unless you established your Keogh account by December 31, 1987. While Keoghs are not as complicated as corporate retirement plans, the annual reporting requirements can be burdensome. A SEP involves the least paperwork of all.

The Bad News: Fewer Deductions

Most of the new law's provisions partially or completely eliminate deductions or credits and, as a result, will boost business taxes. Among the targets with the greatest impact are the following.

Investment tax credit. The 10% credit has been so resolutely eliminated that not even equipment bought in 1986 before the new law was signed qualifies. This is one of the most significant losses for small businesses. Losing a tax credit, which cuts your tax bill dollar for dollar no matter what your marginal rate, hurts businesses in lower tax brackets more than the loss of a deduction, whose value is higher in upper brackets. One provision of the new law may help soften the blow: the amount of capital equipment you can directly write off rather than depreciate over time has been doubled from $5,000 to $10,000.

Depreciation. Two opposing forces are at work in the new depreciation rules. The depreciable lives of some assets have been increased—a move that lowers deductions—while at the same time the rate at which you can depreciate capital equipment has been increased by a third. This means larger deductions for some assets, smaller ones for others.

The biggest loser under the new depreciation rules is commercial real estate purchased after 1986. It must be depreciated over 31½ instead of 19 years. You will also get lower deductions on cars and light trucks you buy for your business, since they must be deducted over five instead of three years. You will get higher write-offs on computers, however, since they retain their five-year depreciable life and get the added bonus of accelerated depreciation. A provision in the new law lets you choose either the old or new rules to depreciate equipment placed in service between July

31 and the end of 1986. By using the new rules for a $20,000 computer system, for example, you can increase your deduction by a third—$4,000 instead of the $3,000 available under the old law.

Home-office deduction. Previously, you could deduct a proportional share of such expenses as mortgage interest, real estate taxes, depreciation, utilities, and maintenance as long as the total deduction did not exceed the gross income from your business. Now home-office deductions are limited to your business's net income alone. Thus if your business grosses $20,000 this year, all other expenses total $16,000 and your home-office expense is $8,000, you can deduct only $4,000. Under the new law, however, whatever home-office deduction you cannot use can be carried forward indefinitely. This is a plus for start-up companies that might not be able to use all their deductions in their first years of operations.

Yet another aspect of the new law—its overwhelming complexity—hurts almost all small businesses. Only 80% of business meals and entertainment expenses, for example, are deductible. While this modest reduction will certainly hurt small businesses, tax accountants say the bigger blow will be developing a system to account accurately for such expenses. The net result: small businesses will spend more time and money on record keeping and less on improving sales and earnings.

Money Basics

Employee Stock-Ownership Plan (ESOP). A program that allows employees to buy stock in their company, sometimes with matching contributions by the employer.

Simplified Employee Pension plan (SEP). A pension that consists of both an employee's and his employer's contributions. A SEP is similar to an IRA. The employee's contributions and earnings are tax-deferred.

Moonlighters: Running Up Deductions

Tax-sheltering rewards remain in force for part-time entrepreneurs.

Operating your own sideline business has long been a wise tax strategy—a way to boost your income and at the same time shelter it by taking advantage of tax deductions unavailable to salaried workers. While tax reform has eroded some of these deductions and may make others more difficult to take, moonlighting may pay off more than ever.

One major plus about being self-employed— whether full or part time—is that you can make substantial, tax-deductible contributions toward your retirement, even if you no longer qualify for a tax-deductible IRA under the new law. As long as your sideline business turns a profit, you can set up a Keogh account and stash away and deduct as much as 20% of your net business earnings to a maximum of $30,000 a year. Keoghs can involve considerable paperwork, however, so you might instead want to consider a SEP, or Simplified Employee Pension plan. A SEP is essentially the same as an IRA. The difference is that your tax-deductible contributions can be larger—15% of your net business income up to a maximum of $30,000. (For more on Keoghs and SEPs, see pages 55-56).

Starting a sideline business can also help you salvage deductions you might otherwise miss out on under the new law. The larger standard deduction and the tougher restrictions on miscellaneous deductions will make it harder to take personal deductions for unreimbursed expenses you incur for your employer. But moonlighting may provide a way to deduct these items as business expenses. If in your regular job, for example, you incur nonreimbursed expenses for professional dues, technical publications, business travel, and local transportation, you can now deduct them only to the extent that they exceed 2% of your adjusted gross income. If you are also self-employed part time, however, you may be able to take the full deduction on Schedule C, the form filed by sole proprietors.

Of course, as a self-employed individual you can also write off against business income other normal business expenses, such as depreciation on personal computers, automobiles, and other equipment. And if you operate your sideline business out of your home, you may be able to take a home-office deduction covering a proportionate share of such expenses as depreciation, utilities, real estate taxes, and mortgage interest.

Tax reform has put one new restriction on this popular deduction: your home-office write-off cannot exceed the net income from your business. In short, you cannot use this deduction to create a loss to offset other income. Unused home-office deductions may be carried forward to future years.

The IRS has always frowned on people who claim these deductions when their so-called business is actually a hobby, and the new law has adopted a still harder line. Now, unless you post a profit in three out of five years, instead of the old law's standard of two out of five, the IRS may decide your business is a hobby and limit your deductions to the amount of income the activity generates.

But you can flunk the hobby-loss test and still legitimately claim you operate a business as long as you can show that you are profit-motivated and are running your enterprise in a businesslike manner. Setting up a separate checking account and telephone line, getting the appropriate licenses to operate your business, and maintaining accurate records of income and expenses should prevent you from running afoul of the hobby-loss rule.

The Simple Science of Keeping Records

It's easy, it's wise, and it can save you $500 or so a year.

Along about March, taxpayers across the land begin an irritating paper chase that doubtless sets many to wondering whether there is not some system for keeping—and easily retrieving—all the documentation needed for tax returns. That concern is more critical than you may realize. The Internal Revenue Service can now compare your return with data sent to the agency by your employer, bank, brokerage house, and anyone else who pays you interest, dividends, and other kinds of income. The reporting and comparing is all done silently and efficiently by computer, and discrepancies can land your file on an IRS auditor's desk.

One other reason for keeping good tax records: it can save you tax preparation fees. When a tax specialist is preparing your returns at $100 an hour or more, a missing check or financial statement can keep the meter running unnecessarily long. And by regularly making note of any expenditure or receipt with tax implications, you are sure not to overlook the little sums that add up over the year. An accurate record-keeping system can conservatively save a middle-income taxpayer $400 to $500 annually.

Record keeping need not be tedious and time consuming. Since many miscellaneous deductions such as investment advisory fees, tax preparation costs, and union dues can be deducted only when they exceed 2% of adjusted gross income, you may have fewer records to keep. For example, there is absolutely no need to keep sales tax records anymore, since that deduction has been eliminated.

All you need by way of equipment to keep excellent tax records are three basic items: file folders for financial statements and receipts, a small notebook to record business-related travel and entertainment expenses, and your checkbook register. The actual work, if pursued regularly, is far easier than working with such complicated aids as $50 datebooks.

The file folders. Most tax documentation goes into file folders or the pockets of an accordian file. You should begin receiving documents early in the year: as of January 31, employers should have mailed out W-2 forms and brokers, their 1099 forms; mortgage companies will have sent 1098 forms to homeowners, detailing mortgage interest payments. If you have a car loan you repay with a book of coupons, the total yearly interest may appear on the last coupon of the year. (Otherwise you should ask your finance company for the information.) Do not forget that under the new tax law, it is still possible to deduct 65% of your consumer interest payments in 1987 (40% in 1988, 20% in 1989, and 10% in 1990). File checks with your bank statement.

Each securities transaction record and year-end mutual fund statement should be filed in its own compartment and kept until the investment is sold. Save all documents relating to your IRA. You must be able to show when the contribution was made, the amount, and the date and source of any rollover contribution. If you are ever audited, the IRS is going to want to know where your IRA money came from. As the years go by, it will become very difficult to keep track of your IRA if you do not keep careful records now.

It is also important to hold on to your K-1s, the annual statements you receive, usually in late March or early April, documenting income and losses in a limited partnership. If your shelter has amassed passive losses in the past year, the amount you are not permitted to use to offset current income may be carried forward until the end of the partnership, reducing your tax on any gain. But to arrive at the final figure, your accountant must have all the K-1s for the life of the partnership.

You should cherish and preserve all receipts for capital improvements to your home. You will need them to reduce any taxable capital gain when you sell it. Also, for home-equity loans taken out since August 1986, deductible interest is limited to the amount of the original cost plus capital improvements.

The business travel log. For the self-employed and for moonlighters, a log is essential. A log should clearly list details of incidental travel and entertainment expenses—what you spend, where, when, and for what business purpose. Such expenses are now only 80% deductible, and the IRS, which has been tough on taxpayers who claim them, will surely get tougher. The best response is to write down everything. For out-of-pocket business expenses less than $25—taxis, tolls, tips, and parking garage fees, for instance—a simple listing in your log will do. For expenses above $25, you have to save

all receipts.

If you drive a car for business, your log should show where you started and ended your trip, the number of miles traveled, the purpose of related business meetings and when they occurred. Keep receipts to substantiate all these deductions.

Your check register. This is one paper source that makes your record keeping easier. Besides being a straightforward chronological listing of deductible expenditures, your check register is a directory for the most important documents you can have if deductions are questioned: canceled checks. If your bank or money-market fund does not return canceled checks, you can refer to your register when you ask for copies of the checks you need. And even if checks are returned to you, it is a good idea to write the number of each check on the back of the corresponding bill or receipt you keep in your file folder so you can find the check in case of an audit.

Here are some further tips.
● Always keep original documentation. While copies of receipts, bills, bank statements, and canceled checks are usually acceptable, the real thing will always be preferred.
● Organize your papers regularly. Going through a year's worth at one sitting will only raise your blood pressure. Bringing your files up to date once a month should take most taxpayers half an hour or so. At the same sitting, make sure your pocket log is current. And in your checkbook register, put a mark next to tax-deductible entries. Total every category of deduction in one column of a 13-column sheet of accountant's paper (one column per month plus year-end totals). This master ledger will greatly simplify tax preparation next year. All you have to do then is make sure the 1099s, K-1s, and other forms you are due to receive come in on time.
● Save all tax documentation for at least six years in a fireproof file. (Use a safe-deposit box for hard-to-replace items needed for longer than that, such as K-1s, deeds, and records for property improvement.) But remember that if the IRS suspects you of fraud, it can audit you as far back as it desires.

Your Investments

Whatever your current investment stance is—bull, bear, or chicken—this is not the time to be a Pudd'nhead Wilson, the Mark Twain character who declared: "Put all your eggs in the one basket and—WATCH THAT BASKET." Indeed, the advice that Twain conveyed through his hero may help explain why Samuel Clemens was not a very successful investor.

You, however, should get healthier returns with less risk if you put your investment eggs in several baskets and—watch *those* baskets. Then, as your personal circumstances change or as expectations for different financial assets improve or worsen, you can transfer part of your wealth from one basket to another in hopes of finding the combination that is right for you and right for the times. Your quest need not be limited to markets in the United States; "Going Global" explains how foreign stocks and bonds can help offset the risk of holdings dominated by securities that respond solely to the stateside economy.

Commence your search for a well-balanced portfolio by concentrating on two sets of variables. Those in the first group are external and include the outlooks for interest rates, inflation, economic growth, and the dollar's value abroad. The other factors are personal: your age, your family and job situations, and your tolerance of risk. Retirees relying on investments to meet their living expenses obviously should lean toward safety—certificates of deposit, money-market funds, short-term U.S. Treasury securities—and study "Investing for Income." But preservation of capital could be just as important for a young couple struggling to get established financially.

If your time horizon is five years or more, you can afford to aim for the greater returns available from diversified holdings of stocks, bonds, precious metals, and the mutual funds that specialize, respectively, in these assets. That is because the market moves in cycles, usually going through a complete bull and bear market cycle within four to six years. If you can hold on to your investments for that long, you can generally be sure of outlasting periodic market downturns.

If you do not have the time or inclination to take an active role in overseeing your investments, you probably should concentrate on mutual funds, which offer professional management and broad diversification at a low cost. This chapter covers most types of funds, with tips on how to select the ones that best match your financial goals with your stomach for risk. You may even want to consider "Hiring Your Own Market Timer," which evaluates the performance of money managers who, for a fee, use mutual funds to move your money into the investments whose prospects seem brightest at the moment.

Investing for Income

Amid seesawing interest rates, there are still safe ways to boost your portfolio's yield.

The tax reforms that began taking effect last year were supposed to usher in a golden age for income investors. Reason: as the maximum tax rate on dividends and interest dropped from 50% in 1986 to 33% in 1988, investors would be allowed to keep a much greater portion of the income they earned. Moreover, the outlook for fixed-income investments seemed bright as 1987 began. Since May 1984, yields on 30-year Treasury bonds had dropped from 13.9% to 7.4% last March, rewarding bondholders with sizable capital gains as well as high, inflation-dwarfing income. Many economists predicted that interest rates would continue to decline and that inflation would remain under control.

Investors were understandably shocked when this glowing vision dissolved before their eyes as interest rates unexpectedly shot up in

March and April. Suddenly, inflation appeared to be resurging and bond prices plunged. By early May, newly invested bond owners and shareholders in fixed-income mutual funds had lost as much as 10% of their principal.

Chastened by that debacle, conservative investors face two dilemmas: first, should you sell bonds and bond mutual funds and take your losses, or hold on? Second, when you make new purchases, should you accept the lower yields available on safer, short-term investments such as money-market funds or reach for riskier, higher yields on longer-term investments? Further confusion has arisen because financial institutions continue to crank out innovative fixed-income investments that sometimes make misleading claims or fail to disclose certain pitfalls. For instance, bond funds report their yields in various ways and do not make clear how much principal you could lose as interest rates rise.

Devising a Defensive Strategy

To invest safely today, you need a strategy for constructing a fixed-income portfolio that will be partially insulated from the risk of rising rates. That is why many investment advisers recommend that you split your money between short-term and long-term investments when the direction of interest rates is uncertain. For example, you could put half your money in money-market funds or short-term bonds (maturities of four years or less) and half in long-term issues, thus substantially reducing your principal losses if rates rise.

An alternative is to purchase bonds with serial maturities—that is, issues that come due at equally spaced intervals. Say that you have $20,000 to invest. You could buy four lots of five $1,000 bonds maturing in two, four, six, and eight years. If interest rates rise, you will benefit by getting back some of your capital to reinvest at higher rates every two years.

The minimum recommended investment for fixed-income issues ranges from a modest $2,500 to as much as $25,000. (See the table on pages 64-65.) You will need at least $20,000 to assemble even a simple diversified portfolio. You can buy most fixed-income investments through your broker, who can also explain the more arcane aspects of fixed-income investing, such as how to avoid an early call on a bond and how to tell the difference between current yield and yield to maturity. For investors with $10,000 or less, however, mutual funds are the wisest choice. With the usual minimum investment of $1,000, you get a professionally managed, diversified portfolio. Funds sold by brokers, though, usually charge commissions, known as loads, that can run as high as 8.5%.

Going for Yield—and Safety

To assemble a list of safe income-producing investments that offer above-average returns,

Money surveyed 35 financial planners and stock and bond analysts. Here are the 10 types of securities (ranked from the lowest yield to the highest) you should consider for your income portfolio.

Electric utility stocks. Shares of such companies have long been a favorite of income investors because they pay higher, safer dividends than any other stock group. Most utilities trade on the New York Stock Exchange for $15 to $40 a share. The downward spiral of interest rates and oil prices over much of this decade has helped to lift the group's profits and market prices to record highs. But since the beginning of 1987, the stocks have lagged behind the market, while average yields have risen from 6.5% to 7.7% by late last year. Electric companies that offer double-digit yields may look attractive, but high payouts usually are a sign of major risks such as those associated with the completion and licensing of a troubled nuclear generating facility. As a result, many analysts suggest that conservative investors buy only shares of electric companies that do not need to build new plants. Such utilities will not have to borrow much and therefore can use excess cash to raise dividends.

Convertibles. These bonds and preferred stocks can be exchanged at the owner's option for a specified number of common shares, which are almost always those of the issuing company. By combining a yield close to that of a bond and the appreciation potential of a stock, convertibles are safer than low-dividend stocks, though their capital gains are usually smaller. The average yield on convertible bonds was lately around 9.5%.

When evaluating a convertible, ask your broker how much the conversion premium is. This is the amount by which the convertible's price exceeds the value of the underlying stock for which it could be exchanged. Convertibles with premiums above 60% are most sensitive to changing interest rates; their price swings closely resemble those of conventional bonds. A premium below 30% means that the security will principally move with the stock market.

Thus higher premium issues are the safer bet for income investors willing to hold a convertible for a long time, notes Jack Levande, manager of E.F. Hutton's Convertible Securities mutual fund.

Master limited partnerships. An MLP is a security that represents part ownership of a pool of income-producing assets; it is traded on a stock exchange or over the counter. Often the assets, such as oil in the ground, are being used up or depleted; therefore, holders of MLP units are actually receiving a return of some of their original principal as well as true income. MLP yields recently ranged from 10% to 15%. From 30% to 70% of these distributions may be considered tax-free returns of capital, depending on the rate at which assets are being depleted. David Bradshaw, a partnership analyst at Rauscher Pierce Refsnes in

Where to Get Safe, High Yields

There are a number of reliable investments that are more attractive than money funds and Treasury bonds. The first two columns below show the range and tax status of yields on sound issues of each type. Subsequent columns indicate capital-gains potential in a healthy economy with slowly declining interest rates, the risk that a payment of interest or principal will be missed, and the ease of selling in a declining market. Finally, the table lists the minimum recommended investment, the availability of income-oriented mutual funds in each of the areas, and the typical total cost to buy and sell the securities themselves.

Investment	Yield range	Tax status	Capital-gains potential	Default risk	Liquidity	Minimum investment	Mutual funds
Utility stocks	6% to 9%	Taxable	High	Low	High	$1,000	Yes
Convertible bonds	6% to 10%	Taxable	High	Low	Medium	2,500	Yes
Master limited partnerships	6% to 13%	30% to 70% tax sheltered	Medium	Low	High	1,000	No
Municipal bonds	7% to 9%	Exempt from federal tax	Medium	Low	Medium	5,000	Yes
High-yield stocks	7% to 12%	Taxable	High	Medium	High	2,500	Yes
Real estate investment trusts	7% to 12%	10% to 30% tax sheltered	High	Low	High	1,000	No
Real estate limited partnerships	7% to 13%	20% to 100% tax sheltered	High	Medium	Low	5,000	No
Mortgage-backed securities	9% to 11%	Taxable	Low	None	Medium	25,000	Yes
Junk bonds	10% to 12%	Taxable	Medium	Medium	Medium	5,000	Yes
Oil-and-gas limited partnerships	10% to 18%	30% to 100% tax sheltered	High	Medium	Low	5,000	No
Money-market funds	5% to 6%	Taxable	None	None	High	100	Yes
Treasury bonds	8% to 9%	Exempt from state and local taxes	Medium	None	High	1,000	Yes

Dallas, recommends oil and gas producers with reserves large enough to last as long as 15 years at present rates of extraction.

Municipal bonds. Historically, the interest on debt obligations issued by state and local governments and certain related institutions has been exempt from federal taxes. Income from these bonds has usually also been exempt from state and local taxes for individuals who reside in the same state as the issuer. For someone in the top tax bracket, a municipal paying 8% would yield as much after 1987 taxes as a taxable bond paying 13%.

Tax reform, however, has splintered the market, creating several classes of municipal bonds. Traditional general-obligation issues, which are backed by the taxing power of a state or local government, remain fully tax-exempt. Revenue bonds, whose interest and principal is paid with revenues from a specific project, such as a toll highway, are also fully tax-exempt if the project is considered to have a public purpose.

Causing the most confusion in today's market are the new types of bonds created *in response to* tax reform. For example, some bonds that finance a so-called private purpose—such as facilities for local companies—pay taxable interest. And even those private-purpose bonds whose interest is exempt from regular federal taxes are subject to the alternative minimum tax. Such issues, known as AMT bonds, yield about half a percentage point more than other munis. If your accountant is certain that you will not come under the alternative minimum tax, buying AMT bonds is an easy way to boost your income. Most muni analysts recommend high-quality issues—those rated AA or better by Standard & Poor's or Moody's Investors Service.

High-yield stocks. Recently the average dividend of stocks in the Standard & Poor's 500-stock index was only 3%. Yet diligent dividend seekers can find dozens of NYSE stocks—aside from electric utilities—that yield at least 7%. The higher the payout, though, the greater the risk that the company may be forced to reduce its dividend. William Lippman, manager of L.F. Rothschild's Rising Dividends mutual fund, points out that Texaco's 10% yield looked great—until it dropped to 0% when the company filed for bankruptcy last April. Lippman thinks investors will get the greatest total return—income plus capital appreciation—from stocks yielding 3% to 5% that are likely to have dividend increases of 8% or more a year. Among his favorites are insurance companies and regional banks.

Fees and commissions	Comments
2%	Avoid those currently involved in major new construction, especially nuclear plants.
2%	Expect lower yields than regular bonds but greater capital-gains potential.
2%	Income depends on the fluctuating price and life span of the underlying assets.
3% to 4%	Interest on home-state bonds is usually totally tax-free to state residents.
2%	Double-check the company's financial strength to be sure the dividend is secure.
2%	Mortgage REITs have higher yields; equity REITs have more appreciation potential.
15% to 20%	The best partnerships are those that buy properties that have little mortgage debt.
2%	They have higher yields than Treasuries but uncertain timing for principal repayments.
3% to 4%	Extra-high yields may indicate poor creditworthiness of the issuing company.
15% to 20%	Income includes a return of capital because irreplaceable reserves are being used up.
0%	Money funds offer the lowest yields but almost total safety.
0.5%	Treasuries are safe from default but not from losses resulting from rising interest rates.

Real estate investment trusts. A REIT is essentially a high-yielding mutual fund that buys real estate or makes mortgage loans. About a hundred different REITs trade on the stock exchanges or over the counter, generally ranging in price from $10 to $30. In addition to recent 7% to 12% yields, the shares also pass through some minor tax benefits and can appreciate in price as their properties increase in value.

There are three types of REITs: equity REITs own office buildings, apartment complexes, shopping centers, and industrial warehouses. They earn income through rent and depreciate their properties; some 10% to 30% of their dividends are tax sheltered. Mortgage REITs make mortgage loans, the same way a savings and loan does. Hybrid REITs are a combination; they make mortgage loans and also own a share of the underlying property.

Real estate limited partnerships. As a limited partner, you can own a share in a pool of properties or mortgages without being liable for more than your initial investment. Like REITs, real estate partnerships buy income-producing properties or make mortgage loans and pass the income and tax benefits to the limited partners. Unlike REITs, though, RELPs are difficult to sell in a hurry. Get into a real estate partnership only if you plan to hold the investment for seven to ten years.

Partnerships formerly served primarily as tax shelters, but the days of three-to-one write-offs are long gone. Now most of these partnerships are devoted to providing high current income. They lately have yielded 7% to 13% and can be bought through any broker, generally in minimum denominations of $5,000. Deals do still generate some tax benefits, however, which come from the depreciation of the properties they own. As a result, anywhere from 20% to 100% of your income may be tax sheltered.

Mortgage-backed securities. These issues represent shares in a large pool of mortgages that have been insured against default by a federally backed agency—such as the Government National Mortgage Association—and packaged by a brokerage firm. Such securities, known as Ginnie Maes, Fannie Maes, or Freddie Macs, are available from any broker, generally in minimum denominations of $25,000.

Mortgage-backed issues recently yielded between 11% and 12.6%, compared with a yield of 9% to 10% for a Treasury bond of the same maturity. Their only major drawback is that a mortgage-backed security returns part of your principal with each monthly payment. When interest rates fall, many people refinance their mortgages, causing mortgage-backed securities to repay principal even faster—and you have to reinvest at lower rates. An innovation called a collateralized mortgage obligation (CMO) or a real estate mortgage investment conduit (REMIC) offers an effective solution to the problem of early repayment of principal. CMOs and REMICs are usually offered in a series of maturities ranging from two to twenty years, and all prepayments of principal are applied to the security with the shortest life until it is fully repaid. A two-year REMIC recently paid about 9.2%, while a ten-year issue yielded around 10.7%.

If you find Ginnie Maes and REMICs too complicated or the minimum investment too high, you can participate through at least 20 mutual funds that lately yielded around 10%. Two of the most experienced managers are Franklin and Vanguard.

Junk bonds. They include debt obligations of troubled companies and bonds issued to finance takeovers and other corporate reorganizations. As such, these so-called junk bonds are inherently risky but pay as much as six percentage points more than Treasury securities with comparable maturities. Junk bonds can be bought through a broker; they generally have a face value of $1,000 and trade in minimum lots of five.

Some analysts warn that the default rate of these bonds, now a nominal 1% or less a year, could soar in a recession. Other bond market watchers say there are gems in the junkyard if you know where to look. If you do not have the $25,000 needed to buy a portfolio, you can still get payouts of as much as 12.4% through a self-styled high-yield corporate bond fund.

Oil and gas partnerships. As a limited partner, you can participate in a program of oil exploration or the development of existing oilfields without being liable for more than your initial investment. Partnership units are available through any broker, usually in minimum denominations of $5,000. Yields for such programs recently have ranged from 10% to 14%.

Income deals, which finance the development and production of proven oil and gas reserves, are far less speculative than new exploratory programs. Since the reserves are slowly being used up, 30% to 100% of the income you receive is tax sheltered by the depletion allowance. Because they are hard to sell, limited partnerships are best suited to investors who are willing to hold them for seven to ten years.

The Right and Wrong Ways to Buy Gold

Instead of panning for fast profits, most people should buy gold as insurance against rising inflation.

If all the gold that has been taken from the earth in all of recorded history could be molded into one cube, it would measure only 18 yards to a side—small enough to fit in a modest suburban backyard with room left over for a patio. The scarcity of this metal is what makes it precious, but few commodities are as unstable in value. Witness the price of gold during the first half of 1987. It shot up 19% from January 1 to May 20, going from $403 to $480 a troy ounce, sank to $437 in the next four weeks, then rose again to $450. In late 1987, bullion commanded between $450 and $470. Where it will head next, nobody knows.

The price of gold may be unpredictable, but the reason for its volatility is obvious: fear of rising inflation. Gold serves as a storehouse of value when the purchasing power of money is in steep decline. Investors swap their cash for it at such times, driving the price skyward. This is particularly so just before abrupt surges in the consumer price index—most notably in 1980, when gold more than doubled as the CPI was heading toward a record 12.2% annual rise.

So that you will own some inflation insurance when living costs take off, most analysts and professional money managers recommend putting at least 5% and at most 10% of your invested assets in gold. And even though gold investments yield little or no income, people nearing retirement should lean toward the higher figure, particularly if much of their savings is in fixed-income securities such as bonds and thus greatly exposed to the risk of lost purchasing power.

The challenge is to know where and when to buy gold and in what form. Should you buy it from your banker or broker or from a retail coin dealer? Should you invest with someone who sells it over the phone—a thieves' market these days? Should you invest now or wait for a drop in price? Should you buy gold bars, gold coins recently issued by the U.S. Treasury and several foreign governments, rare coins with extra value as collectibles, the shares of gold-mining companies, or the mutual funds that specialize in those shares? And if you choose the metal itself, should you take it home with you or let the seller arrange to have it stored for you?

Investors who try to time their gold buying in anticipation of inflation are risking trouble; not even the experts can agree on where gold is headed. If, for example, you heed the views of veteran gold watcher Albert Friedberg, head of the Toronto commodities firm Friedberg Mercantile Group, you would buy gold now. Friedberg has predicted that the price will surpass its record high of $875 before mid-1989. But if your gold guru is William Siedenburg, top-rated metals analyst at the brokerage firm of Smith Barney, you would squelch the urge to buy for now. Siedenburg has forecast that the price will sink and not rise above $420 until at least mid-1988.

Faced with such conflicting predictions, small investors should reduce their risk by buying gold systematically over a fairly long period. You can do that through installment purchase plans offered by banks and brokers. They permit you to buy a set dollar amount of gold at regular intervals, investing as little as $50 every month or quarter. That way you acquire more bullion when the price is low than when it is high.

Whichever way you buy gold, deal only with a seller you know and trust. Mark Twain described a gold mine as a hole in the ground with a liar standing next to it. Today's liars do not stand; they sit at telephones in establishments called bucket shops or boiler rooms, many of them in California and Florida. State regulatory officials estimate that these operations, using pressure-tested sales recipes, fraudulently extract $500 million a year from investors. The California Department of Corporations gets 50 to 100 complaints a week from boiler-room victims who have lost all the money they put in.

Also pass up invitations to dabble in gold futures or options—a legitimate arena where even trained mercenaries perish. These high-risk markets make it possible to speculate on large amounts of gold for a fraction of its price. But they expose you to the loss of all your money and, with futures, more than you put up. Consider instead the offerings described below and in the box on page 71.

Gold Bars and Coins

You can buy bullion in bars of 24-karat gold and in 22-to-24-karat coins minted by governments. Bars are available in sizes of one gram and up, but there is an advantage to buying bars of 10 ounces or one kilogram. They generally carry a lower premium for manufacturing costs than that charged for smaller bars,

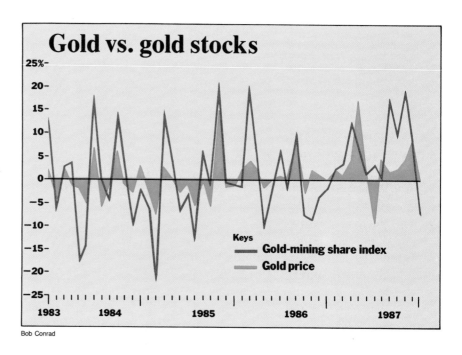

Gold-mining shares, measured here by the Toronto Stock Exchange gold index, usually exaggerate price swings in bullion. But the relationship changed briefly in 1985 and 1986, when investors fled South African mines.

Bob Conrad

usually $5 for a one-ounce wafer.

Unless you want to turn your house into a miniature Fort Knox, you can buy gold bars without having to take them home. Dealers will arrange storage for you in special bank depositories at annual fees of about 1% of the gold's value. If a dealer is arranging storage for you, be sure the depository is a major bank. In the past, charlatans have stashed away gold-painted bars—or nothing at all. So be wary of a company that volunteers to store the metal for you in its own vault as part of its sales pitch. Regulators suggest calling the depository—before you send money—to verify that your dealer has an account there and that customers' assets are kept segregated from those of the firm. That way, the dealer's creditors will not have a claim on your gold in case the firm goes bankrupt. Also verify with the dealer's insurance company that your gold in storage is covered for theft and fire damage.

Coins are more convenient than bars if you want to take possession of your gold; they are easy to sell and fit in a safe-deposit box. Although banks do not insure the contents of their vaults, you can cover your coins for a fee of $1.50 to $2.75 a year per $100 worth with a rider on your homeowners or tenants policy.

Coins such as the Canadian Maple Leaf and the American Eagle are favored by many investors for their easy marketability throughout the world—an attribute highly valued by people who fear that someday they may have to flee war or civil violence. As with smaller bars, you have to pay a premium to cover the costs of making coins. Brokers' commissions run between 2% and 8% of the transaction versus up to 15% on the smallest bars.

Gold coins of numismatic value are another alternative. Collectors price such coins according to their rarity, condition, and artistic value, and the prices are apt to be far higher than the worth of a coin's gold content. As with collectibles of all kinds, it takes special knowledge and a fascination with the objects if you hope to become a successful investor in numismatic coins. Furthermore, coin collections are less liquid than bullion. Coin prices reported in catalogues may be hard to duplicate unless you have plenty of time to wait for a dealer to find

you a buyer.

The least expensive way to invest in gold bullion is through certificate programs offered by many banks and brokerage firms and by Deak International, a precious-metals dealer with offices in 28 cities. The certificates, which you can usually buy for the price of an ounce of gold, give you title to a portion of a large amount of the metal that has been bought, stored, and insured at bulk rates. In some programs you can request delivery of your gold at any time; in others you cannot. In either case, you can liquidate your position through your dealer whenever you choose.

Dos and Don'ts for Bullion

Do select a dealer carefully. Stick with firms that can document that they have been trading in gold for at least five years; a dealer would have to have been in business that long to prove he can weather significant bear and bull markets. A legitimate dealer will always buy back the gold he has sold you. This saves you the cost of having gold bars assayed to prove their metal content—a requirement any other dealer would be likely to demand before buying your gold. Questions to ask the dealer: Who audits the firm, and is the audit conducted at least once a year? (Then call the auditor and verify that the dealer is a client.) Does the dealer belong to the local Better Business Bureau? (Check that out with the BBB in his city.) The Industry Council for Tangible Assets, the largest precious-metals trade association, responds to investor complaints about dealers and blacklists firms that do not live up to its code of ethics.

Do shop for the best price. With dealer markups ranging from 2% to 15%, you may save plenty. If you are in one of 45 states that slap a sales tax on gold, the dealer can save you money by having your gold stored in a state with no tax.

Do not fall for deals that involve buying gold with bank loans. Telephone salespeople may pitch you aggressively to put down, say, $3,000 on a $10,000 purchase of bullion and borrow the rest from a bank, which will keep the gold as collateral. The hype is that if gold rises a mere 15%, giving you a $1,500 profit on your $3,000, your gain is 50%. Maybe so, but even if the deal is legitimate, that rosy result does not take account of dealer commissions of 4% or more, storage or transaction fees as high as 2.5%, or interest at 8.5% and up. And if the value of your gold drops to $7,000, the bank will demand additional collateral.

Stocks and Mutual Funds

The only way to get income from gold holdings is to buy shares in gold-mining companies that pay dividends. When the price of gold goes up, dividends generally rise as well; when gold falls, so does your payout. Most publicly traded mining companies are in North America, Australia, and South Africa. Many Canadian companies are listed on U.S. stock exchanges, while shares of Australian and South African mines are available in the form of American Depositary Receipts, also traded on U.S. exchanges and representing mining shares held in U.S. banks.

South African mines used to be popular investments because they pay out most of their earnings in dividends, whereas North American companies pay 1% or less and plow the rest of their earnings back into production. But racial unrest in South Africa poses sizable risks to investors. The mines depend on the labor of poorly paid black workers, and repeated work stoppages would make them unprofitable.

A risk shared by gold-mine investors everywhere is the exaggerated ups and downs of mining shares, illustrated on page 68. Here is why: mining costs are fairly well fixed, so changes in the bullion price go straight to a company's bottom line, boosting or slashing profits exponentially. Mutual funds specializing in gold-mine companies at least allow you to diversify within the industry. Among the best performers in the 12 months to October 1, 1987, were Keystone Precious Metals, which was up 102%, and Vanguard Special Portfolio—Gold, up 92%.

Dos and Don'ts for Stocks

Do stick with mining companies that have at least $300 million worth of shares in public hands. The stock will then trade actively enough to make it easy to unload if the price of gold turns down sharply. You can get publicly held share values from your broker.

Do choose a mutual fund to help diversify your gold holdings. Especially in gold mining, opportunities change so quickly that you need portfolio managers with a global view who can make timely investment decisions.

Do not dabble in penny mining stocks. Exploration companies, which raise working capital by issuing shares that cost less than a dollar, are cheaper than producing companies. But 90% of them do not pan out, notes James Blanchard, president of the precious-metals firm James U. Blanchard in New Orleans.

Money Sources

Before buying gold from a dealer, you can find out about his reputation by calling the Industry Council for Tangible Assets (202-783-3500).

The Midas Market

Which type of gold investment is best for you? To help you answer that question according to your motives for owning the metal, this rundown of the options sorts out the differences in terms of suitability, cost, and risk.

Gold Bars

For whom: conservative investors prepared to hold large amounts of the metal for years; people who want insurance against political upheavals
Where to buy: large banks, coin dealers, stockbrokers
Smallest investment: tiny bars weighing one gram (0.032 of an ounce); more typically, one ounce, ten ounces, and one kilogram (32.15 ounces)
Price behavior: the same as the spot, or cash, price of gold on commodity markets
Advantages: low markup on large bars (2% to 3%); portability
Disadvantages: cost of storage (usually in a bank vault) and insurance (about $50 a year); cost of selling—dealers may require an assay at $25 or more a bar

Bullion Coins

For whom: conservative investors who wish to own small amounts of gold
Where to buy: most banks, stockbrokers, coin dealers
Smallest investment: 0.1-ounce coin; more typically one ounce
Price behavior: the same as the spot price of gold on commodity markets
Advantages: ease of buying and selling; portability
Disadvantages: higher markup than on bars; cost of storage and insurance (about $7 a year for each coin)

Collectible Coins

For whom: collectors
Where to buy: bullion and coin dealers, auctions, numismatic shows
Smallest investment: quarter-ounce $10 (face value) American gold piece minted between 1867 and 1933; cost: about $165
Price behavior: usually rises and falls less than the spot price of gold
Advantage: value may hold up better than for bars and bullion coins
Disadvantages: poorly defined market value and difficulty of finding buyers willing to pay top price; cost of storage and insurance

Gold Certificates

For whom: conservative investors, particularly those interested in buying small amounts at regular intervals
Where to buy: brokers, large banks, and one dealer, Deak International
Smallest investment: $250 in systematic buying programs that let you subsequently invest as little as $100 a month
Price behavior: the same as the spot price of gold on commodity markets
Advantage: low dealer markup (3% to 3.5%)
Disadvantage: annual storage fee (usually 1%)

Mutual Funds and Mining Shares

For whom: aggressive investors
Where to buy: stockbrokers, financial planners, by mail from no-load and low-load funds
Smallest investment: the price of one share of an individual company; usually $250 in a mutual fund
Price behavior: more volatile than the spot price of gold
Advantages: maximum gains when the gold price rises; dividend income; no storage costs; diversification and professional management in funds; ease of buying and selling
Disadvantages: maximum losses when gold prices fall; high political risk of South African mines; risk of loss if a mine becomes unprofitable

Mutual Funds for the Next Decade

Here are the pros' choices.

Faced with the maddening multiplicity of mutual funds—there are over 2,000 now—how do you choose the one that is right for you? To help you narrow the choices to a manageable number, *Money* surveyed the nation's top mutual fund portfolio managers and asked them where they would invest their money. The question put to this elite panel was straightforward but not simple: Which five stock or bond funds—in order of preference—would you choose personally over the next five to ten years? Participants were asked to exclude funds that they managed as well as those run by the company for which they worked. The pros' picks are listed opposite.

Clearly, foul-weather stability was prized by the managers polled, and seven of the twenty-three nominees fared better than the S&P 500 during its most recent pronounced dip prior to October 1, 1987. That falloff, according to Lipper Analytical Services, took place between June 23, 1983, and July 26, 1984, when the S&P 500 dropped roughly 6%. (Corresponding figures for the market plunge that began last October were not available when this book went to press.)

If there is any cause for disappointment in the survey results, it is that three of the top twenty-three—Windsor, Sequoia, and Loomis-Sayles Capital Development—were closed to new investors as of late 1987. But funds do not necessarily close forever. Mutual Shares and Pennsylvania Mutual were locked up earlier last summer before reopening in mid-July. Unfortunately, John Neff says Vanguard has no intention of accepting new investors in Windsor soon.

One other heartening fact is that although the top managers' salaries (some in seven figures) come out of fees collected by their firms, 20 of the funds charged a lower annual expense ratio than the 1.1% stock fund average. Then too, of the 23 funds on the list, 16 have no front-end loads, and none levy back-end loads.

Whichever fund you consider purchasing from our roster of stars, remember that the managers *Money* polled made their picks largely on the reputations of the people at the helm. It is therefore important, except perhaps in the case of the largely computer-driven Twentieth Century funds, to stay alert for staff changes or deterioration in performance. *Money*'s monthly "Fund Watch" column will keep you abreast of management turnover, but you should monitor your holdings regularly. If your fund's performance lags behind that of others in its category for a year or more, consider taking some of your business elsewhere.

And since the superstar managers we polled leaned so strongly toward funds that hold up well in down markets, you probably should also. Aggressive funds that stay locked into stocks—like Twentieth Century's entrants or Fidelity Magellan—should probably be considered only by truly long-term investors. Such funds are costly in an extended bear market, the most recent of which occurred nearly 15 years ago. The S&P 500 plunged 37.3% between January 1, 1973, and January 1, 1975, but precious few fund managers now even remember those days. On our list, however, are some of the best who do.

The Pros' Mutual Fund Picks

Fund name Manager, age (years managing fund)	Type	Comments
Vanguard Windsor* John B. Neff, 56 (23)	G&I	Fully 18% of the portfolio was recently in auto stocks. Unusual incentive fee structure means that if Windsor beats market, manager Neff prospers.
Mutual Shares Corp. Michael F. Price, 36 (13)	G&I	Bottom-fishing fund seeks to invest up to 50% of its assets in prospective mergers, consolidations, liquidations, and reorganizations.
Nicholas Fund Albert O. Nicholas, 56 (18)	Gro	Dearth of bargains, says manager, explains recent 30% cash position. Fund's price/earnings ratio was over 16 in fall 1987, nearly a 12-year high.
Acorn Fund Ralph Wanger, 53 (17)	SCG	Manager Wanger known for big bets on small U.S. companies. But as of July 1, 1987, 18.7% of portfolio was invested in Europe, Far East, Canada, and Israel.
Sequoia Fund* William J. Ruane, 62 (17)	Gro	Portfolio only 55% in stocks as of early fall, 1987; balance in Treasuries.
Pennsylvania Mutual Charles M. Royce, 47 (14)	SCG	Royce Value, smaller sister fund also run by manager Royce, has similar objectives and record but requires only $2,000 minimum.
Evergreen Fund Stephen A. Lieber, 62 (16)	Gro	Sizable stake in disappointing bank stocks explains mediocre one-year gain, according to fund's managers. Firm's Total Return Fund also suffered.
Fidelity Magellan Peter Lynch, 43 (10)	Gro	Many managers surveyed felt that fund's huge size jeopardizes future performance. Assets have tripled since November 1985.
Twentieth Century Select (Committee management)	Gro	Most conservative of Twentieth Century's growth funds. Buys only companies paying dividends. Stays 100% in stocks at all times.
Vanguard PrimeCap Howard B. Schow, 60 (3)	Gro	Schow is buy-and-hold man. Annual portfolio turnover for past two years has averaged 14% (typical fund's is 94% annually), IRA minimum is $500.
Loomis-Sayles Mutual G. Kenneth Heebner, 47 (11)	Bal	Balanced portfolio emphasizes stocks or bonds, depending on manager's investment outlook. In August 1987, 80% of holdings were in stocks.
Templeton Growth John M. Templeton, 74 (33)	Glo	Fund has loaded up on U.S. shares in past three to four years. Manager Templeton has bested S&P 500 in 20 of 32 calendar years at helm.
New England Growth G. Kenneth Heebner, 47 (11)	Gro	Manager Heebner makes big wagers on fast-growing firms. Fund sold through New England Life, but no policy purchase needed (except for faint of heart).
Gabelli Asset Mario J. Gabelli, 45 (1)	Gro	Gabelli is celebrated investor, pension manager. High expenses should drop as assets—smallest on list—increase. Minimum investment for IRA is $2,000.
Selected American Shares Donald A. Yacktman, 46 (4)	G&I	Buys large, overlooked laggards such as Fireman's Fund and Clorox, then waits. Manager Yacktman's strategy, said one peer, "lets you sleep nights."
AMEV Growth Stephen M. Poling, 55 (4)	Max	Minneapolis fund looks mostly for stocks of medium-size firms with prospects of strong earnings growth. Co-manager is Don Longlet, 42.
Weingarten Equity Harry Hutzler, 64 (18)	Max	Hutzler buys stocks with strong earnings momentum. Prospectus allows 100% cash position. Level in mid-1987 averaged a bullishly lean 3%.
Twentieth Century Growth (Committee management)	Max	Fund founder James Stowers, 63, is low-profile lead manager. Buys stocks similar to those of sibling Select, but not all pay dividends.
Loomis-Sayles Cap. Dev.* G. Kenneth Heebner, 47 (11)	Gro	Like New England Growth, which Heebner also runs, Loomis invests heavily in a few companies. Very high portfolio turnover rate (206% in 1986).
Neuberger & Berman Manhattan Irwin Lainoff, 56 (8)	Max	Holds value superbly in down markets, considering aggressive nature. In August, largest concentration of assets (15%) was in technology issues.
T. Rowe Price International Stock Martin G. Wade, 44 (7)	Intl	Fund's London-based advisory firm, Jardine Fleming, was praised by peers. Manager Wade is moving assets out of Japan and into Hong Kong, Britain.
Fidelity Equity-Income Bruce Johnstone, 46 (15)	EqI	Several rivals described Equity-Income as fund for all seasons. Busy manager Johnstone oversees 11 Fidelity funds in income/growth group.
Lord Abbett Affiliated John M. McCarthy, 60 (15)	G&I	Manager hardly ever loses money, noted several pollees. Fund has lowest expense ratio on list but assesses full 7.25% load on reinvested dividends.

Types: Bal Balanced; **EqI** Equity income; **G&I** Growth and income; **Glo** Global; **Gro** Growth; **Intl** International; **Max** Maximum capital gains; **SCG** Small-company growth ***Currently closed to new investors.**

How to Hold a Bond Fund's Feet to the Fire

By getting answers to a few simple questions, you can earn grade-A profits.

Corporate, government, and municipal bonds represent a rich and diverse mother lode for investors, but to buy individual bonds, you would need to plan on dividing at least $25,000 among five issues. For most small investors, the only practical way to tap into this vein is through mutual funds. You can pool as little as $500 with money from thousands of other small investors in a multimillion-dollar fund and gain all the clout you need to profit from the institution-dominated bond market.

Of course, a bond fund cannot insulate you from the market's uncertainties the way bank certificates of deposit can. The fund's yield and share value will fluctuate with those of the bonds in its portfolio. Shooting for the highest possible return thus means accepting a greater risk of losing principal.

Consequently, choosing a bond fund requires attention to detail. In addition to current yield, which is the annual rate at which a fund pays income, you must weigh such factors as a fund's capital gains and losses in recent years, the costs of investing in it, and, above all, the riskiness of its holdings. You can get most of this information from a fund's prospectus and annual report or by phoning the fund's customer service department. Other information can be culled from comparative listings of fund performances such as those in the back of this book. The factors you should consider include the following, in descending order of importance.

Current yield. Since this is the rate at which a fund produces income, it is the measure most investors look at first. When comparing yields, however, remember that funds do not calculate their yields uniformly—different funds measure income over different periods, and some include income other than interest and dividends, such as premiums from writing options. At the urging of the Securities and Exchange Commission, funds are likely to adopt a standard method soon, using only interest and dividends earned over the previous month. Meanwhile, you can compare funds by consulting the alphabetical listing in the back of this book, where yields are calculated on a uniform basis.

Past performance. By comparing a fund's total return over various periods with the returns of funds with similar investment objectives, you can get an idea of how the fund's managers perform in different kinds of markets. The one-year total return figures in the rankings beginning on page 198 will tell you how a bond fund did in the strongly bullish climate that prevailed until mid-October of 1987. Ten-year return figures record the fund's consistency over a period of both up and down markets. Also check the total return for calendar year 1981 to gauge how the fund weathered that bearish time. Total return figures may be published in a fund's prospectus; if not, call the fund and ask for them.

Maturity. Long-term bonds almost always yield more than their short-term cousins because they are riskier—they fluctuate more in price when interest rates change. For example, twenty-year Treasury bonds recently yielded close to 10%, compared with nearly 9% for three-year notes. If rates were to rise by one percentage point, however, the value of recently issued twenty-year Treasury bonds would fall about 9%, while three-year notes would drop only 2.5%. So if you think interest rates are going to rise, favor funds that keep maturities short; if you foresee falling rates, buy long-term bond funds. Each fund generally keeps its holding's maturities within a range specified in the prospectus. To find out a fund's current average maturity, you must call the fund.

If you are uncertain about interest-rate trends, many bond analysts recommend sticking with funds that hold bonds with short and intermediate maturities—that is, under 10 years. You will sacrifice a percentage point or so in yield, but in return, you get the comforting security of price stability. If you prefer, you can delegate the job of managing your maturities by investing in a fund that can shorten or lengthen its portfolio at will. A few such funds, including T. Rowe Price New Income and Strong Income, have almost no restrictions on maturity.

Quality. The more credit risk a fund takes, the higher its yield—but the less secure its share price. Funds can easily boost their yields by buying risky junk bonds, or those rated less than investment grade by Standard & Poor's or Moody's. But if that strategy does not work out, the resulting drop in the value of your principal can more than offset the fund's higher yield. For example, the Venture Income Plus Fund produced a 12-month yield through October 1986 of 15.5%—3.5 percentage points more than the average for other high-yield funds—by investing in the troubled energy and steel industries. Defaults in those industries cost the fund 8.9% in principal, however, giving shareholders a total return over the period of only 5.4%. Similar funds returned a total of 18% on average.

Expenses. Every fund incurs some costs in operating, administering, and marketing the fund. All of these expenses diminish your returns. The most onerous expense is a sales charge, or load, which can take as much as 8.5% off the top of your investment in a fund or up to 6% of money you withdraw from it. Front-end loads are deducted every time you purchase shares, thereby reducing the amount of money you have working for you. Back-end loads gradually decline to zero over four to six years. Load funds are chiefly sold by brokers and financial planners, so if you are confident of your own ability to choose a fund, pick a no-load. No-loads perform, on average, just as well as load funds.

All funds, load or no-load, charge fees for administering the fund and managing the investment portfolio. For bond funds the average ratio of expenses to total assets is about 0.9%. These expenses directly reduce your yield. As a result, if you are choosing among otherwise equally promising funds, pick the one with the lowest expense ratio.

Size. Bigness confers distinct advantages on a bond fund. For example, $100 million or more in assets lets a fund diversify widely, and the economies of scale generally mean that larger funds have smaller expense ratios. As a rule, also look for a bond fund with a minimum of 40 different issues in its portfolio, and with no more than 10% from the same industry.

Call or prepayment risk. If a fund's stated yield seems excessively high compared with yields of similar funds, chances are that many of the bonds in its portfolio are priced at sharp premiums to face value. The risk to you is that its bonds may be redeemed by issuers, and the fund will have to reinvest the proceeds in lower-yielding issues. In addition, if the call price—the price at which the bond can be redeemed by the issuer—is lower than the bond's price when you bought into the fund, you lose capital.

As a rule, you should be suspicious of funds with yields more than two percentage points above prevailing rates. In other words, if a yield seems too good to be true, it probably is.

Sizing Up Single-State Munis

These municipal bond funds can greatly enhance your tax-saving pleasure. But they are not for everybody.

For many high-bracket investors in high-tax states, tax-exempt single-state municipal bond funds are the nearest investment left to a day at the beach. Indeed, they assume added attractiveness now because tax reform, while lowering federal rates, generally means that state and local levies will constitute a greater portion of your total tax. And these funds generate more than income—lately between 7.5% and 8.3% on average—that is exempt from federal, state and, in some cases, local taxes as well. They can also produce substantial, if taxable, capital gains in the event that interest rates decline.

But single-state funds' per share values, like those of all bond funds, can also drop abruptly, as they did in many cases in the spring and fall of 1987. And choosing among single-state funds is not a simple matter of comparing yields or total returns—interest income plus capital appreciation. The shopping is far more complicated than that, and single-staters do not make sense for many investors.

If you are in the 28% federal tax bracket or lower in 1988 (that is, with taxable incomes of up to $43,150 for individuals and $71,900 for couples filing jointly), the after-tax yields produced by single-state funds generally will not be large enough to make them worth your while. Alas, even if you clear the 28% hurdle, your state may throw up yet another obstacle by taxing your fund income even if it is generated by in-state bonds. Illinois, Iowa, and Wisconsin do. In such an instance, a higher-yielding corporate or U.S. government bond

fund may be your best choice. In the District of Columbia, New Mexico, and Utah, muni bond income is tax-exempt, whether it is generated in or out of state. So there is no added benefit from limiting your tax-free fund choice to a single-stater. Thus your better bet is a conventional, or national, muni bond fund that diversifies its investments among many states. Such funds were recently yielding 8.3% to 9% on average.

Alaska, Florida, Nevada, South Dakota, Texas, Washington, and Wyoming levy no state income tax, which eliminates investors' incentives for owning single-state funds. But residents of about three dozen states could benefit from single-state muni bond funds. Of course, that is assuming a single-state fund is offered. Although nearly 200 such funds were available in mid-1987, they covered only 25 states, the District of Columbia, and Puerto Rico. High-tax states with large populations such as California, Massachusetts, Michigan, Minnesota, New York, and Ohio have the most choices. The following states have at least one single-state fund: Arizona, Colorado, Connecticut, Florida, Georgia, Hawaii, Indiana, Kentucky, Louisiana, Maryland, Missouri, North Carolina, Oregon, Pennsylvania, Rhode Island, South Carolina, Texas, Virginia, and West Virginia. For residents of these states (and others where the funds will eventually come), here is a primer.

Who needs them. If your state has such a fund, you first should determine whether the

Mutual Funds 77

yields currently offered by your state's entries beat the after-tax yields for you on funds in which the income is either wholly or partially taxable. One caveat: if you are among the 1% or so of taxpayers who are subject to the alternative minimum tax, you will need to do additional research. Specifically, you must find out if the single-state fund in which you are interested invests in recently issued private-placement muni bonds, most of which produce income that is subject to the AMT. If it does, the fund's after-tax yield for you could be only 96% or so of what it would be if the income was truly totally tax-exempt. That 4% margin could make a difference in a close comparison of yields.

How to shop. A bond fund cannot stand on yield alone; you must consider a host of other variables. Prime among them is total return, which is the only measure that tells you whether your fund is making money for you.

When interest rates rise, the value of single-state funds can be particularly hard hit, as was the case in the 12 months to October 1, 1987, when single-state bond funds posted losses ranging from 1% to 7.4%. The main reason is that the funds' managers trade the bonds of only one state and thus deal within a comparatively restricted universe of buyers and sellers (not to mention issues). Last April, for instance, Ohio funds gave back 7.2% on average, California entries 7.1%, and New York shares 7%, compared with 6% for the average national muni bond fund. The typical national tax-exempt fund holds 115 issues or so. Some single-state funds own fewer than 30. You can check a fund's annual report to see how many issues it holds. A greater number generally means that a fund manager will have more flexibility in bond trading, and clever swaps can curb losses when the bond market gets grizzly.

You can attain greater protection of capital by investing in one of two alternatives: single-state muni bond unit trusts or single-state funds with shorter maturities. Unit trusts, which are sold by such prominent packagers as Lebenthal, Nuveen, and Van Kampen Merritt, are best for long-term investors who are willing to lock into a bond portfolio for five to thirty years. The packagers assemble a portfolio of at least 12 bonds and sell shares—called units—for as little as $1,000. Since the bonds are held to maturity, you are guaranteed the return of your principal (barring a catastrophe for the portfolio) if you do not sell out before the trust matures. In the meantime, you collect yields that are currently comparable to those on single-state funds. Trusts commonly charge 4.9% in front-end loads.

Single-state funds that keep their average bond maturities under 12 years or so cushion capital in another way. Because their bonds involve shorter commitments, they fall less than longer-term funds when interest rates rise. Unfortunately, few such limited-term single-state funds exist. Among them are Park Avenue New York Tax Exempt-Intermediate, Limited-Term Municipal-California, and Benham California Tax Free-Intermediate.

An increasingly appealing alternative in jittery times is a single-state municipal money-market fund. More than 40 such funds were available recently, most of them for investors in populous states such as New York and California. Because the funds invest in short-term municipal paper generally of 120-day maturity or less, your share price will remain steady. Single-state municipal money-market funds lately yielded only 4% to 5%, but they could net highly taxed investors more than national tax-exempt or taxable money-markets.

The quality question. In evaluating a single-state fund, as with any bond fund, keep in mind the quality of its holdings. The higher the quality, the lower the yield—and the lower the likelihood that the fund's portfolio will be damaged by default. Also, higher-quality funds characteristically fall less during a prolonged rise in interest rates. Most single-state funds put at least 80% of their portfolios in investment-grade issues—those rated between BBB and AAA by Standard & Poor's and Moody's, the major credit-rating services. Funds with lesser-quality standards can expose you to interest-rate and credit risks you might prefer not to bear. Note too the types of bonds a single-state fund invests in. A fund that spreads itself among so-called revenue bonds that finance hospital, utility, housing, and education projects will be more balanced and stable than a fund that is heavily concentrated in just one type of enterprise.

To ease the minds of especially cautious investors, fund groups such as Dreyfus, Franklin, and Vanguard offer insured single-state funds. The insurance protects against default on interest payments and insures timely repayment of the bond's principal. But insurance does not shield investors from fluctuations in the value of fund shares. Moreover, if your fund is amply diversified, the cost of the insurance in terms of a lower yield is probably more than the impact any one failure in the portfolio could have. The risk of a rash of defaults is almost infinitesimal.

The crux is that while single-state funds may represent the nearest thing to a tax-free payday for fund investors, the task of picking them is, well, taxing.

The Return of the Money Fund

Investors fleeing risk are rediscovering the advantages of these secure refuges.

Since 1981-82, the heyday of money-market funds, the average yields of these funds have dropped from 15% to around 5.5% more or less in sync with the corresponding downturn in interest rates. As a result, money-market funds' total assets declined 20% in 1983, dipping to a low of $163 billion. But today money funds are enjoying another round of popularity because they offer solid security of principal in a post-crash period when many other investments look increasingly risky. As early as spring 1987, for example, long-term interest rates shot from 7.5% to 8.5% in a mere six weeks. During that time, stocks pulled back 8%, and the bond market plummeted; some debt issues lost as much as 12%. Seeking refuge, investors quickly shifted $5 billion from stock and bond funds into money funds in April alone.

In essence, money funds are simply mutual funds that buy short-term—and thus virtually riskless—debt issues with maturities as brief as 24 hours. The holdings of taxable funds can include U.S. Treasury bills, bank certificates of deposit, and corporate debt obligations known as commercial paper; tax-exempt money funds invest in short-term paper issued by municipalities. You can find funds that offer higher returns than the current average by consulting "Investor Scorecard" in monthly issues of *Money* magazine.

Since protection from market fluctuations, rather than yield, is the paramount reason for investing in a money fund, you should evaluate the character of a fund's current holdings. The three most important factors to look at are the average maturity of the securities in a fund's portfolio, their quality, and the size of the fund's annual management fees.

Maturity. As a rule, the risk of principal loss—slight as it may be—rises as a fund's average maturity grows longer. Under federal law, a money fund that claims it will hold its net asset value (the price at which you buy or sell shares) constant at $1 a share must limit the average maturity of its portfolio to 120 days or less. The most conservative investors should buy funds with average maturities of 90 days or less, advises Glen King Parker, publisher of

Income and Safety, a monthly newsletter that rates the safety of money-market and other fixed-income funds. Since 1972, two funds have suffered losses large enough to push their net asset values below $1 a share because they lengthened maturities too far; in one case, some investors lost 6% of principal.

Investors willing to take a bit more risk may want to consider funds with longer average maturities because of their higher yield. One such fund is Neuberger & Berman Money Market Plus, which recently yielded about 7%. Because of the fund's longer average maturity, its net asset value varies, though usually by less than one percentage point. By the same logic, you may want to consider short-term bond funds, which offer slightly greater risks but even higher yields—around 7.5% on average.

Quality. Issues in a money fund's portfolio can range from supersafe U.S. Treasuries to riskier commercial paper issued by companies with mediocre credit ratings. For example, the safety ratings calculated by the *Income and Safety* newsletter range from AAA+ to BB, depending on both the quality and the average maturity of a fund's holdings.

In general, lower-quality issues pay slightly higher yields. Nonprime commercial paper, for example, typically yields 0.2 percentage point more than top-rated issues. Thus, to accept a 100-day average maturity and a second-rate portfolio is foolish if you get a yield only 0.1 percentage point or so higher than that of a high-quality fund with a 40-day average maturity. A yield advantage of 0.4 percentage point, though, might make the lower-quality fund a reasonable choice.

Fees. All funds take a yearly charge, known as the expense ratio, against investors' assets for managing the portfolio. Such fees range from a low of 0.48% for Vanguard Money Market Prime to a high of 0.8% for Cardinal Government. Since higher fees do not really buy better management, you should favor funds with below-average expenses because this cost is subtracted from a fund's dividends.

Finally, before you settle on a money fund that pays taxable dividends, check to see whether a tax-exempt fund would offer you a better yield after taxes are taken into account. Single people earning more than $17,850 and couples with combined incomes of more than $29,750 who file joint returns will be in the 28% or the 33% tax bracket in 1988. For such investors, a tax-exempt fund with a yield of 4.8% or more in 1988 will offer the equivalent of a taxable yield of more than 6.6%.

To stay current on both tax-exempt and taxable money funds, a useful shopping tool is Donoghue's weekly *Money Fund Report*, which lists yield, portfolio composition, and average maturities for 411 money-market funds. Armed with the information in its columns, you should be able to choose the fund that gives you the best combination of safety and yield.

Money Sources

To subscribe to *Income and Safety* newsletter, write to 3471 N. Federal Hwy., Fort Lauderdale, FL 33306. Cost: $49 a year.

To subscribe to Donoghue's *Money Fund Report*, write Box 540, Holliston, MA 01746. Cost: $595 a year, $5 a copy.

Money Tip

Time your fund buys to avoid unnecessary taxes. Buy shares after a fund's annual capital-gains payout, which is often in January. If you get in just before a fund makes its distribution, the gains will be included in the price of the shares. In effect, you will get back part of your investment and will be taxed on gains you did not earn. After the payout, the fund's share price will drop, allowing you to avoid owing the extra taxes and to buy more shares as well. Before investing in a fund, call to find out when it will distribute capital gains.

Think Twice before Buying the House Brand

Investors pay high fees for these slow-paced funds.

If your broker tried to sell you a mutual fund that assessed steep annual fees and expenses, penalized you heavily for withdrawing your money or charged a front-end load, and more often than not stood to produce an average or below-average return on your investment, would you jump at it? Or jump out of the way? Despite the obvious answer, thousands of investors have settled for such comparatively unrewarding investments over the past few years by following their brokers' advice and sinking billions into major brokerage firms' house-brand mutual funds.

To see whether the funds operated by the largest national brokerage houses live up to their marketing hype, *Money* examined performance figures supplied by Lipper Analytical Services for the one-, three-, and five-year periods to May 1, 1987. Specifically, we looked at the four fund categories—government bond, mortgage-backed securities, growth, and growth and income—that were pushed most heavily by brokers in recent years. The conclusion: far from the "rock-solid, market-wise" performance touted in one firm's television ads, we found widespread mediocrity.

Hot Sales, Cold Performance

Most of the brokers' name-brand funds fell near or below the average total return for the four fund categories. Of the 40 funds studied, only five ranked in the top 20% of their category and a mere three beat the 102.9% total return of the Standard & Poor's 500-stock index over the three-year period. Only Merrill Lynch Basic Value, a growth and income fund that was up 216.5% for the five years to May, beat the S&P over that 60-month period. And all this *before* you deduct any sales fees. Here is a closer look at these categories.

U.S. government bonds. Three of six major brokerage house government bond funds beat the average 3.7% one-year return for all such funds. The largest, Hutton Investment Series Government Securities, with some $6.6 billion in assets, posted the worst record of all—a 1.9% total return. For the privilege of buying this fund, investors pay a 12b-1 fee of just under 1%. That 12b-1 charge allows Hutton to siphon off nearly 1% of the fund's average net assets each year for marketing and promotion, jacking up the expense ratio and thereby significantly eroding the investor's return. If a dissatisfied investor tries to bail out, however, he or she could be in for a nasty jolt: the fund imposes a 5% deferred sales charge if you cash in your shares within a year. The charge declines gradually until the seventh year, when you can redeem your shares without penalty. Despite these burdens, Hutton's legions of brokers had no trouble pushing this dud. In 1986, net sales totaled $2.5 billion.

Mortgage-backed securities. Among these popular income funds, six of nine brokerage house brands fell short of the average 4.8% one-year return for the 28-fund category. If you take sales commissions into account, Merrill Lynch's Federal Securities Trust, which charges a 6.25% load for purchases under $25,000, hit investors the hardest. If you had put $20,000 into this fund on May 1, 1986, and paid the broker his $1,250 commission, at the end of April a year later the fund's middling 4.7% gain would have left you with an investment worth $19,631—$369 less than you started with.

Growth stocks. The big houses did not fare much better in this broad stock fund category. Six of the eleven funds with three-year performance histories ranked in the bottom half of similar funds for the three-year period. And of the eight that had been around for five years, no more than four bested the 161.8% gain of the average growth fund. Noteworthy in this group is Merrill Lynch's best-selling stock fund for 1986—the $925 million Merrill Lynch Fund for Tomorrow, which seeks to invest in goods and services popular with baby boomers. Fund for Tomorrow gained 80% for the three years through April 1987, placing it in the middle among brokerage house funds with three-year records, but 76th among the 118 growth funds tracked by Lipper.

A Few That Delivered

Now for some good news. In the growth-and-income category, six of eight brokerage firm funds topped the average fund. Most notable were Merrill Lynch Capital, Merrill Lynch Basic Value, Drexel Burnham Fund, Smith Barney Income & Growth, and Dean Witter Dividend Growth.

And in the international and global fund groups the brokerage houses have some undisputed aces. For example, Merrill Lynch Pacific, up 868% over 10 years, has handily outperformed other international funds over the same period. Still, in the four fund categories that have recently been attracting the most money from investors, brokerage house funds are definitely also-rans.

Why Brokerages Fall Short

Given their vast capital, manpower, and research resources, why do the major brokerage houses do so poorly? One possible reason is that brokerage firms are relative newcomers to mutual funds, most having entered the business only in the past seven years or so. Thus they have not had time to cultivate their own superstar managers to rival Fidelity Magellan's Peter Lynch or Vanguard Windsor's John B. Neff. There is also speculation by mutual fund experts that, with a team of brokers to pitch their funds in person or by phone, brokerage houses need not place as high a premium as no-load fund companies on investment results to sell their products.

Brokerage house spokesmen insist that their portfolio managers often have 10 years or more of investing experience. The brokers also deny they are under less pressure to produce superior performance. Norman Harvey, senior vice president of Merrill Lynch Asset Management, insists that Merrill Lynch's funds have to be continuously competitive because the firm's brokers have the option to sell someone else's funds.

Brokers do sell funds other than those managed by their employers and, theoretically at least, a broker's recommendations are based on the client's overall financial goals and performance objectives. But if you walk into a broker's office, you stand a far better chance of being sold the house's brand of fund than one from any other single family, such as Putnam, Colonial, or Pilgrim.

The reasons are financial. When a brokerage house sells an outside fund, it collects only a portion, normally 55% to 70%, of the brokers' sales commission. But if the house sells its own fund, it not only may collect a sales commission but also a continuing annual management fee of 0.4% to 0.5% of average net assets. In 1986 brokerage houses pocketed an estimated $2.8 billion in investment advisory fees, much of it from their mutual funds.

When brokers sell their own company's funds, they also get to milk the 12b-1 cash cow. E.F. Hutton, for example, took in $46.5 million in 12b-1 fees in a single year from just two funds in its Hutton Investment Series—Government and Growth. The individual brokers benefit from this income stream too, because 0.25% of the fee is usually kicked back to them and included in calculating their commissions. In addition, brokers pocket a greater percentage of the commissions generated by house funds. For instance, the average Dean Witter broker gets 41% of the commissions he generates on Dean Witter funds but only 36% on outside funds.

Does this mean you should avoid your broker's house-brand funds? Not necessarily. But before you take a broker's recommendation, ask him to back up his pick with past perfor-mance figures. If his house fund has lagged behind the average fund in the past, do not buy unless the broker offers a sound reason why it will do better in the future.

As for government bond and mortgage-backed securities funds—the ones brokers have lately been flogging the most—there is little reason to invest in any brokerage house's fund. That is because there is generally a much smaller variation in total return among bond funds than among stock funds. Instead of paying a sales charge for your broker's advice, you will do just as well choosing a no-load government bond or mortgage-backed securities fund on your own.

When to Sell Your Funds

The toughest decision you face as a mutual fund investor is when to sell. Here are some objective sell signals to watch for.

Your fund limps badly. Every fund has a down quarter sometime, but if your fund's performance ranks in the bottom fifth of funds of its type over a 12- to 18-month period, consider selling.

Your investment objectives change. You may want more conservative holdings, for instance, as you head toward retirement. In that case, you could supplant your growth stock fund with a less risky portfolio that aims for total return.

The portfolio manager quits. You might elect to sell if you discover, perhaps in news reports, that the person behind your fund's admirable record has moved on to another fund.

Your stock fund gets too hot. Be wary when you buy a sizzling performer that continues to singe other funds of its type for several months or more. Reason: a sustained superheated per-formance relative to other funds with similar objectives suggests that your fund is either not of the type it purports to be or is taking exceptionally high risks with your money. Consider taking some gains early in such a fund if, for example, a small-company growth fund rises 50% faster than its peers over nine months or so. The steeper and more seductive the climb, the harder the fall.

Your stock fund gets too big for your tastes. Similarly, consider selling if your fund's torrid performance attracts a flood of new money that more than doubles its total assets. Fund managers who must contend with such hot cash have to invest it wisely and fast or performance will lag and the flighty money will pull out, possibly forcing your manager to sell stocks at an in-opportune time. Once a fund's assets swell to more than $200 million, the manager can no longer rely on a select group of carefully re-searched stocks to power the portfolio. By contrast, bigger is usually better in bond funds, since the more bonds a fund holds, the slimmer are its chances of being hurt should some of its bond issuers default.

Hiring Your Own Market Timer

A Money *study shows that clients can come out ahead.*

Most mutual funds, whether invested in stocks or bonds, tend to rise or fall in value more or less in concert with the general markets. As a consequence, you can improve your return significantly if you can deftly switch into a fixed-value money-market fund when stocks or bonds start slipping, then move back to more volatile funds when the bull returns.

Most fund investors, however, have neither the time nor the inclination to pursue such a strategy successfully. If you are among them, you may want to consider hiring one of the 50 or so money managers who specialize in timing the market with mutual funds. These investment pros usually pick your funds or help you do it. You need not be rich to sign on; the firms sometimes will accept as little as $2,000 in an Individual Retirement Account. Entry levels for regular accounts range from $2,500 to $100,000.

How Timers Work

As market timers, the managers' goal is to move your money into stocks when the market begins rising and then protect gains by switching to the safe haven of money-market funds as stocks start to head down. They are usually better at getting you out than at getting you in on time. Although few fund switching firms have been managing money this way long enough to have documented their prowess, several who participated in a *Money* study of their clients' results succeeded admirably in taking gains near market tops.

The fees that timers charge run high—2%

or more of your assets, which is about twice the typical mutual fund management fee. Some companies add to your costs by using load funds with initial sales charges of 4% to 8.5%. To shed light on whether mutual fund-switching market timers are worth their prices, *Money* sampled the actual results—after expenses—of 18 clients at nine firms that had records of clients going back five years or more and agreed to provide copies of the records for the study. Of 30 firms that were identified as eligible to participate, 21 either could not produce records for enough clients or declined to participate. The period studied, from July 31, 1981, through September 30, 1986, is just a bit longer than five years so that it could begin with the collapse in stock prices that occurred from August to September 1981. Since the prime goal of a timer should be to protect you against big losses, *Money* evaluated how well the firms in the study did at preserving investors' capital in that selling spree, in which the Lipper growth-fund index of 30 such funds dropped 18.2%. The period covered also took into account the 15% correction, as measured by the Lipper index, between January and May 1984. (To compare the five-year performance of the firms, see the table on pages 84-85.

Although a few of the investors did abysmally, 12 of the 18 got better results than they would have achieved if they had left their money sitting for the same period in an average growth fund, as represented by the 30 funds in the Lipper growth fund index. The composite result of the timers' clients was an average compound annual return of 15.2%, compared with 13.6% for the Lipper index. The comparison, however, omitted taxes, which would be higher for a successful timer's clients because frequent fund switches create additional taxable gains.

The two clients who did best, both under the management of J.D. Reynolds Company in the Cincinnati suburb of Terrace Park, Ohio, had compound annual returns of more than 20%. Reynolds and the other firms that showed up well in this survey chose stock funds that performed strongly while their clients' money was in them. Even so, clients whose accounts were successfully timed did far better than they would have if they had merely left their money in the same funds through the ups and downs of those five years.

This study bolsters the opinion of analysts that market timers do best not at matching the peak gains of bull markets but at protecting your assets when prices start to tumble. After all, if you stay in the market all the time, you can get the full gain when prices rise. If you are out, you will seldom get back in ahead of the next bullish move—and neither will a professional.

The timing firms whose results were analyzed vary considerably in size and methods. Their assets under management ranged from a low of $11 million at Portfolio Management Services in Mission Viejo, California, to a high of $500 million at R. Meeder & Associates in Dublin, Ohio. Some use load funds, some use only no-loads, and some use both. A few will apply their timing to almost any fund a prospective client already owns, but many limit you to a list of funds they have selected. In all cases, the client keeps the mutual fund account in his own name and can add or withdraw money at will. He simply gives written authorization for the timing service to switch among stock and money funds at the manager's discretion.

When market-timing money managers move millions of dollars at a time in or out of funds, as they often do, they force mutual fund managers to buy or sell large blocks of stock at inopportune moments. Hence, fund organizations view timers as disruptive. Some large no-load organizations, including T. Rowe Price

Putting Timers to the Test

Working from actual client records covering a bit more than five years, *Money's* consultant, Stephen Shellans of MoniResearch Corporation in Portland, Oregon, calculated the performances achieved by

Investment manager		Value of a $100,000 investment after the 62 months to October 1986
J.D. Reynolds Co. 706 Indian Hill Rd. Terrace Park, OH 45174	Client 1	$276,612
	Client 2	259,315
Portfolio Management Services 27001 E. La Paz Rd., Suite 148 Mission Viejo, CA 92691	Client 1	258,211
	Client 2	200,092
R.M. Leary & Co. 3300 E. First Ave., Suite 380 Denver, CO 80206	Client 1	256,043
	Client 2	224,044
Lincoln Investment Planning Benson East, Suite 1000 Jenkintown, PA 19046	Client 1	238,991
	Client 2	233,173
Portfolio Timing Inc. 402 Rainier Bank Bldg. 11th & Broadway Tacoma, WA 98402	Client 1	233,708
	Client 2	204,363
R. Meeder & Associates 6000 Memorial Dr. Dublin, OH 43017	Client 1	232,281
	Client 2	204,328
Average result for all clients		207,830
Comparative result in an average mutual fund without timing		193,489
William Mason & Co. 22801 Ventura Blvd. Woodland Hills, CA 91364	Client 1	189,641
	Client 2	185,747
Shoal P. Berer Associates 717 Grant St. Pittsburgh, PA 15230	Client 1	156,540
	Client 2	152,652
Managed Advisory Services P.O. Box 79100 Pittsburgh, PA 15216	Client 1	146,717
	Client 2	141,530

* Moved out of stock funds before the market peaked; the result shown includes earnings on cash at the Treasury bill rate.

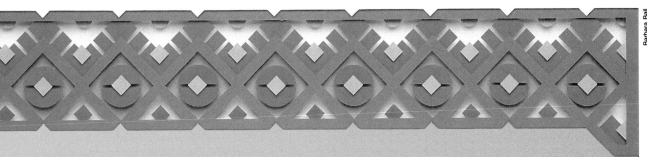

Barbara Ball

the nine managers in this table, all of whom time the stock market using mutual funds. To make the results comparable, Shellans assumed that each client had $100,000 in his account at the start of the study and did not add or withdraw any money for the next 62 months. Then Shellans followed exactly the moves of the manager, switching whenever he did between the same stock funds and money-market funds.

Compound annual return	Return on the funds without timing	% of capital preserved by selling before two big market declines		Average number of switches per year	Minimum investment	Highest annual fee
		18.2% drop from August to September 1981	15.5% drop from January to May 1984			
21.8%	9.0%	96.4%	95.1%	3.6	$25,000	2.0%
20.2	10.8					
20.1	18.4	96.4	89.1	3.2	None	1.5
14.4	11.0					
19.9	19.9	96.9	90.8	5.8	100,000	2.0
16.9	19.9					
18.4	12.3	105.2*	96.8	2.4	10,000	2.3
17.8	12.3					
17.9	12.5	97.1	97.2	5.2	35,000	3.0
14.8	12.5					
17.7	13.6†	105.1*	92.5	4.8	2,500 (in the firm's own mutual fund)	0.7
14.8	13.6†					
15.2						
13.6‡		81.8	84.5%			
13.2	7.9	96.9	94.1	4.8	10,000	2.0 plus $65
12.7	10.8					
9.1	18.4	101.8*	87.2	3.6	10,000	2.0
8.5	14.9					
7.7	20.8	101.5*	91.3	6.0	10,000	2.0
7.0	6.7					

† Compared with the Lipper growth fund index because the account was invested in many funds at the same time.   ‡ Based on the Lipper index.

Associates and the Vanguard Group, now limit to six and four, respectively, the number of switches you or your manager can make a year. Several timers who used no-load funds in the past say they have moved exclusively to load funds because these organizations are less likely to impose such restrictions. An even more powerful motivation for using load funds, however, is that many timing services get their referrals from stockbrokers, who earn more generous commissions from load funds than from stock trades. The sponsors of load funds reciprocate by tolerating frequent switches.

What to Watch

The results of the *Money* survey of timers, combined with the advice of specialists in mutual fund investing, suggest some points to consider in choosing a fund-switching money manager.

Weigh the tax consequences. Unless your money is in an IRA, a teachers' retirement fund, or some other tax-deferred account, any switch out of a stock fund that has risen will involve capital gains—to be taxed at a maximum of 33% beginning in 1988.

Be wary of frequent switching. Top-ranked timer J.D. Reynolds averaged fewer than four moves a year, which is about average for the firms studied. But some timers hop in and out of stocks more often. There is no evidence that more frequent switching adds anything but extra taxes.

Be skeptical of timers' performance claims. Ask whether the firm achieved its record entirely with money under management or partly with imaginary assets projected backward to a time before the firm was managing accounts. Ask if the timer can provide outside verification of his results by an independent advisory service. Switch-fund timers do not usually have their results audited, but Stephen Shellans of MoniResearch Corporation, who designed *Money's* study and did the statistical

work, ranks them six times a year on the accuracy of their timing signals in his *MoniResearch Newsletter*.

Choose no-load funds whenever possible. Though some firms using load funds fared relatively well in the study, the higher the fees that are deducted from an account, the higher return the timer must achieve to overcome those fees.

Do not expect miracles. Be satisfied if a firm can demonstrate that—after expenses—it has at least edged out average mutual fund performance. According to Robert James of *Timer Digest*, an advisory newsletter in Fort Lauderdale, what you need is for the combination of timing performance and mutual fund selection to be three or four percentage points better than average annually. In the long term, that compounded return will make a big difference to your profits.

Money Sources

Timer Digest (333 Sunset Dr., Fort Lauderdale, FL 33301; every three weeks, $175 a year) ranks the performances of published timing services.

MoniResearch Newsletter (P.O. Box 19146, Portland, OR 97219; $90 a year) ranks fund-switching timers six times a year.

Money Tip

If you will owe the alternative minimum tax (AMT), invest for income. You may owe this toughened wealth tax, especially if you claim tax-shelter losses. Under the AMT, however, any taxable interest and dividends will be nicked at a 21% rate. Thus for AMT payers, income-producing assets get a tax edge that they otherwise would not have.

Going Global

Financial boundaries are falling, opportunities growing.

Stand back, the old line goes, and gain perspective. So to gain global perspective—the prime requisite for a global investor—one must stand way back, far enough to see the world as a whole. From that height, the currents of the world economy, its borrowings and booms, the ceaseless tussle of supply and demand, appear like weather patterns swirling across the face of the globe.

There on the jade-green cheek of the China Sea, a broad stream of cash, billions of dollars, sweeps offshore from Japan and stretches swaglike across Asia and Europe to the eastern shore of America. This is the $3 billion or more that Japan invests in the United States each month. Not only does this cash flow help bankroll our prodigious federal deficit, the yen-stream also has a potent effect upon our interest rates: to attract bond buyers, the Federal Reserve Bank must set its rates alluringly high. But only part of the Japanese cash flow goes up the Potomac. A large tributary splits off and heads toward lower Manhattan, where it is absorbed into the stock and corporate bond markets with booming results.

Indeed, from a global perspective, many questions can be answered. Where, for instance, does Japan come by its abundance of cash? It is easy to see. The oceans are peppered with vessels carrying Japanese cars and electronics equipment to markets all over the globe, and from each of these markets a telltale ribbon of cash flow winds back to Tokyo.

Other patterns emerge. Notice the strong braiding of money currents between the European countries. London, in particular, teems with activity. Most of Latin America is overcast by debt. While theory suggests that the flow of money out of a country should be roughly balanced by the influx, large blocks flow into the Latin capitals from U.S. financial institutions, but we see only spurts and dribbles outward bound.

One observation, however, is unmistakable. The intertwining global financial patterns are gaining intricacy and breadth as jumbo jets and computers shrink time and distance. Boundaries are tumbling; the distinction between what is foreign and what is domestic grows blurry. Not since colonial times have how much we earn, what we can buy, and how fast our savings grow been so determined by forces outside the U.S. economy.

Even the Communist bloc is feeling tremors of global capitalism. In March 1987 the Soviet Union announced its first bankruptcy. A Leningrad construction trust—the nearest thing to a private company—was shut down because of persistent financial losses. Then Raisa Gorbachev, the Soviet leader's wife, was accused of using an American Express Gold Card. Last year China opened its fifth bond market, where citizens can invest their savings in industrial collectives. And American investors, in every form ranging from Exxon to egg-roll entrepreneurs, are hoping that the hard-line Asian colossus will continue to soften up to the blandishments of the profit motive.

It should be no surprise that American investors have been joyously singing *We Are the World*. In recent years most sallies into foreign stocks and bonds have been profitable ones because financial markets everywhere have boomed as global inflation has waned. In 1986, for example, the Standard & Poor's 500-stock index enjoyed a 14.6% boost in share value, while other markets, notably those in Italy, Korea, and Spain, rang up increases of 50% or better, measured in local currencies.

What should you know before you take the plunge overseas? First, be alert to the technical differences among the world's markets. Norway, for example, withholds a 25% tax on all dividends. In Switzerland, foreigners can buy stocks only at a premium above their cost to Swiss citizens. You often can circumvent such pitfalls of international investing by buying a foreign stock that trades in the United States as an American Depositary Receipt (ADR). These certificates, which trade on exchanges or over the counter, represent ownership of foreign shares held by a custodial U.S. bank. But newly issued ADRs can pose a problem: foreign investors often get wind of the fact that a local stock is going to be packaged as an ADR and bid up the price in advance. Small investors usually do better by investing through a mutual fund that specializes in overseas securities.

Traditionally, international investments have been viewed as a way to diversify a portfolio by imbuing it with what is called uncorrelated risk. The idea is to spread your money around geographically so it will not get mauled at the same moment by the same economic bad news. Look at the world as a collection of separate but interrelated economic units. Push one down here, and over there another pops up. Or so the theory goes.

But diversification through distance is becoming a less effective gambit. What has always been a world dotted with localized economies is increasingly becoming a single economic entity which, soufflelike, could rise or collapse at a stroke. Karin Lissakers, a professor at the School of International Affairs at Columbia University, worries that the electronic interlocking of stock exchanges and multinational investment firms makes today's world financial markets a daisy chain of transactions that is only as strong as its weakest link. A small failure in, say, Singapore could have disastrous repercussions.

François de St. Phalle, a director at Shearson

Lehman Brothers, has a more sanguine outlook. He believes globalization, far from being a threat, is an economic boon. He cites several debt-conversion programs masterminded by Shearson that could only have been devised and executed by a multinational institution of its size and influence. Under these programs, U.S. banks in effect forgive the notes of debt-burdened nations in exchange for equity shares in local industries, thus forestalling default.

Any transaction across national boundaries faces the risk of currency fluctuations. Say you use U.S. dollars to buy a share of stock on the Paris stock exchange when the dollar is valued at 10 francs. If the dollar value subsequently changes to five francs, when you cash in your shares and convert back to dollars, any profit you have made will be doubled, any losses cut in half. If, however, the dollar moves the other way and is worth 20 francs by the time you sell, you will then halve your profits or double your losses.

Two basic factors affect a currency's value—one natural, the other artificial. First comes the worth placed upon it by the rest of the world. People will place the highest value on currencies of nations blessed with political stability, military strength, and sound financial institutions. The second factor is the artificial manipulation of a currency's value by a nation's central bank. A strong currency makes imports cheap and thus quells inflation. So to boost their currency, a country's central bankers will buy it in the world market using the bank's stores of the specific foreign currencies they want to depreciate against their own. Of the two factors, the latter is the weaker force.

The question confronting American investors is whether the U.S. dollar, which has taken a tumble in recent years, will land on its feet or its nose. The bloody-nose scenario, according to Stephen Marris, senior fellow at the Institute for International Economics in Washington, D.C., would occur if our foreign creditors decide to eschew dollar debt. (The value in yen of all those Treasury bonds bought by the Japanese goes down with each drop of the dollar.) To finance the U.S. deficit, the federal government would then have to shoulder its way into the financial markets and scoop up investment capital by issuing more bonds at increasingly higher rates. Next stop: recession.

Even if recession is years away and you never buy a share of foreign stock, currency fluctuations are bound to jerk you around a bit. With the dollar's fall, Americans can expect to pay more for imported goods. On the other hand, our exports may pick up some sheen, thereby increasing corporate profits, creating jobs, and enhancing the nation's overall economy.

The Best Ways to Buy Foreign Stocks

Mutual funds are the simplest course, but if you insist, you can pick your own issues.

They talk different languages overseas—especially when it comes to investing. How fluent you must become depends on your objectives, pocketbook, and investment style. There are three approaches.

1) You can buy stocks abroad by opening overseas accounts or by dealing through a U.S. brokerage. The investment business plays by different rules over there, however. In some countries, it can take longer to execute a trade than to win a chess championship.

2) A simpler and less costly way to invest in some of the biggest companies is through American Depositary Receipts, or ADRs, which are a kind of warehouse receipt for shares stored in bank vaults. You buy ADRs through stockbrokers, but they represent less than 4% of all the stocks the world has to offer.

3) Or you can do what most Americans do to run with the global bulls and bears: buy mutual funds that invest entirely or partially outside this country. A minimum investment of $250 to $2,500 will buy you a smorgasbord of countries and their stocks—as well as professional management of your investments.

Mutual Funds

Mutual funds that buy foreign securities exclusively—known generically as international funds—were among the most spectacular performers in the 12 months to October 1987. They gained on average 46% versus 39% for the S&P 500 index. Much of this international good fortune came from the declining dollar. When a foreign currency strengthens against the dollar, it boosts the dollar value of your investments—and your profits.

But shareholders in these funds probably will not see the same magnitude of profits once the dollar stabilizes in value, and they could suffer losses if the dollar rebounds strongly against other currencies. Still, foreign holdings can balance the risk of a portfolio dominated by stocks that respond solely to the U.S. economy. Here then is an atlas of overseas investment routes.

Global funds. If you want to spread cash among foreign and domestic stocks, a global fund can do that for you. Globals can shift their assets between foreign and domestic markets largely as they see fit. As a group, they returned 37% over the 12 months to October 1, 1987.

Most globals lately have preferred to invest

The Lure of Investing Overseas

Since 1985, a falling dollar has boosted the returns American investors earned from most foreign stock markets. The German market, for example, rose only 5% in 1986. But the dollar's 22% drop against the deutsche mark gave U.S. investors a 33% return. Japanese stocks also soared in dollar terms, while British shares received a smaller bonus.

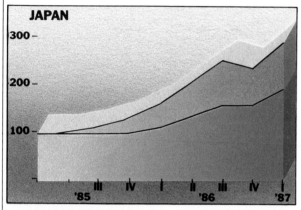

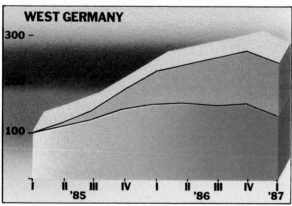

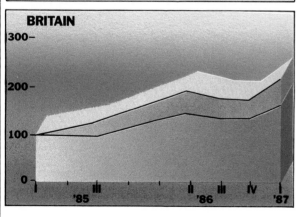

Stock market index   **Bonus for U.S. investors**

Bob Conrad

on this side of the sphere. For example, Wallace Wormley, manager of Prudential-Bache Global, considers U.S. stocks relatively attractive compared with companies in some high-flying foreign markets. And he plans to invest even more heavily stateside when he sees little more scope for the dollar's decline.

Each global fund has its own investment goals. You can choose a fund like Prudential-Bache, which aims for growth and income, or a more aggressive fund such as Putnam International, up 40% in the 12 months to October 1, 1987. Globals also may operate under various restrictions, as described in their prospectuses. For instance, Pru-Bache can put no more than two-thirds of its holdings in any one country, including the United States.

International funds. These are basically growth funds that invest almost exclusively in foreign stocks, though they may follow different approaches. For example, Fidelity Overseas searches for bargains among stocks of foreign companies that the manager believes are undervalued relative to the firms' assets. By contrast, T. Rowe Price International focuses on such fundamentals as earnings growth, interest rates, and currency trends. Since 1985, the falling dollar has made it deceptively easy for funds investing abroad to make money. One good way to evaluate an international fund is to gauge how well it did in years when it did not have that kind of help.

Single-country funds. If you know enough about overseas markets and currency trends, you may want to take on extra investment responsibilities by choosing funds that invest all their assets in one corner of the world. Say you think Japan's yen will rise against the dollar, while other Asian currencies will not. You can bet on your belief by buying a fund that invests only in Japan, such as Japan Fund and GT Japan Growth. (Japan Fund, originally a closed-end fund, converted to an open-end one last year. The $8.3 million GT Japan Growth, founded in 1985, is too small to be included in this book's fund listings.)

Almost all single-country portfolios are closed-end funds, which have a fixed number of shares that trade on stock exchanges or over the counter. Closed-end fund shares, in contrast to the more familiar open-end mutual fund shares, trade at whatever price the market sets—often at a large discount from or premium over the value of the stocks and other assets behind each share.

A typical closed-end fund goes public at a premium, then drops to a discount within six months, after the initial demand for it subsides. Therefore, Thomas J. Herzfeld, publisher of the *Investor's Guide to Closed-End Funds*, cautions against buying such funds when they are newly issued. The bigger the discount, the more shares you get for your dollars. Current discounts or premiums appear in the *New York Times* and some other dailies on Saturday, in the *Wall Street Journal* on Monday in a table titled "Publicly Traded Funds," and in *Barron's*.

Herzfeld says a good time to buy a fund is when its discount is five percentage points greater than its average discount over the previous six months. For example, First Australia Fund ranged between a 20% premium and a 24% discount in 1986. In the six months to October 1, 1987, it averaged a 12.4% discount. So the fund would appear to be attractive at a 17.4% discount.

Before you buy a single-country closed-end fund, ask your broker to get you a prospectus and check it for annual expenses, which range from 0.7% to 3% of your net asset value. Also look up the tax status of dividends. Foreign countries impose varying percentages of withholding tax on dividend income. The amount withheld will show up on the 1099 form that the fund sends you early in the year. You can claim a credit or a refund for foreign taxes by filing Form 1116 as part of your income tax return.

American Depositary Receipts

The quarrel with mutual funds, both foreign and domestic, is that they do not give you the thrill of stock picking. As a fund investor, you can never make a killing by spotting the next Sony. For that kind of opportunity, you must go it alone.

You can buy the stocks of many major Canadian, Israeli, and Philippine companies directly on U.S. exchanges, and more than 600 other foreign issues trade on U.S. stock markets as American Depositary Receipts. ADRs provide a fairly easy and inexpensive way to construct a portfolio. They are receipts issued by U.S. banks for one or more shares of a foreign company or, because some foreign shares cost several thousand dollars per share, a fraction of one share. Although you can find smaller growth companies this way, most ADRs are issues of the large established companies.

You can profit—or lose—almost as much with ADRs from changes in currency values as you can on foreign exchanges. To get the liveliest currency play, though, avoid the ADRs of multinational firms with large U.S. exports that are sensitive to our economy. Such firms tend to be heavily represented in the ADR universe.

Brokerage commissions are the same as on U.S. stocks. When you place a buy or sell order, the trade is settled in this country, so you experience none of the delays inherent in settling with a distant and perhaps less efficient foreign stock exchange. Dividends come in U.S. dollars, and the issuing bank sends you documentation for claiming credits on taxes withheld by other countries.

Not all issuers of ADRs, however, tell you as much about the company as you can find out about U.S. stocks. The most informative are about 120 ADRs that trade on the New York or American stock exchange or are registered with the National Association of Securities Dealers Automated Quotations (NASDAQ) system to trade over the counter. Almost all of these ADRs are listed in newspaper stock tables and must comply with strict SEC reporting requirements according to generally accepted accounting principles.

More than 500 other ADRs are not listed in the newspapers, and many are traded so infrequently that a spurt of buying or selling can quickly bump up—or knock down—prices. Before you buy an unlisted ADR, make sure you will not have trouble unloading your shares when sellers far outnumber buyers and the price falls. Ask your broker how many market makers, or dealers, stand ready to buy or sell the ADR for their own accounts. Find out from your broker how many market makers are behind the ADR. If there are eight or ten, there is a sufficiently active market in this country.

Foreign Exchanges

For the ultimate in worldly investing, you can buy foreign stocks directly. But it takes a sizable portfolio to diversify adequately—by many estimates, $50,000 is the minimum—and a special kind of broker to trade abroad.

To find the right broker, stick with major national firms that have international trading know-how. George Mulvey, vice president of national sales and marketing at Shearson Lehman Brothers, suggests you visit the local offices of several major brokerages. Bring along a list of stocks you are interested in and ask specifically how the firm can help you with them. If you meet a broker who can add to your list, all the better.

The brokerage firm you choose should have a trading office in each country in which you want to trade. Otherwise, the firm will have to hire a broker-dealer to execute your trades, and you will pay double commissions. Even the largest firms are unlikely to maintain offices in every country with a stock exchange. Merrill Lynch, for example, has offices in London and Tokyo but not in Madrid. In any case, be prepared to pay dearly for trading abroad. You must also put up with agonizing delays. When trading stocks in Italy, to cite an extreme example, some Americans have been known to be kept waiting six months for confirmation that their order was executed. Further, fees for converting dividends into dollars can take big bites out of your income.

Finally, a cheery word for you globetrotting big spenders attuned to foreign markets. If you have at least $100,000 to invest, want maximum control of your portfolio, and are not easily discouraged by long-distance annoyances, then you might be a candidate for your own overseas accounts at banks or brokerages in several countries. You can rest easy knowing that your broker is on the spot at the other end of an international telephone line to take care of all your needs. Your phone bills may be hefty, but at least you will not have to pay double commissions.

Money Basics

ADR. American Depositary Receipt; a document showing that you own one or more shares, or a fraction of a share, in a block of foreign stock held by a U.S. bank. ADRs trade on U.S. stock exchanges or over the counter.

Bourse. The French word (from purse) for stock exchange. The Paris exchange and several other markets in France, Switzerland, and Belgium are called bourses.

Closed-end fund. An investment company resembling a mutual fund except that it issues a fixed number of shares that trade on a stock exchange, usually at a premium or discount to net asset value.

Denationalization. The transfer of ownership of a company from government to private control, usually by a public stock offering.

SDRs. Special drawing rights; credits issued by the International Monetary Fund to its 151 member countries in amounts proportional to each nation's gross national product. A country can buy or sell SDRs on the open market when it wants to stabilize the value of its currency in the foreign exchange market.

Supranationals. Special agencies formed by groups of countries to support their economies and trade relationships and sometimes to finance economic development with supranational bond issues. Examples: the International Monetary Fund, World Bank, and Asian Development Bank.

Foreign Bonds: Portfolios of Call

For a shot at double-digit yields, try one of the new foreign fixed-income funds.

How does an annualized 25% yield on 30-day New Zealand bank bills grab you? Or a 14.3% yield on a three-year Australian government bond? Those are extreme examples of the robust—but risky—returns available from foreign bonds and money-market securities last year. But you do not really need Crocodile Dundee to protect you when you seek such high yields overseas. It is an underpublicized fact that American investors could have done better owning bonds of countries other than the United States in all but two of the past twelve years.

High yields are not the only siren beckoning you to bonds issued by other countries. Swift changes in currency values and interest rates can lift your total return if the changes go in the right direction—or submerge you if they do not. During the first three months of 1987, for example, the British pound climbed 8.2% against the dollar and interest rates slid lower in the United Kingdom. As a result, a 10-year British government bond returned a total of 20% to an American bondholder. That is dramatically better than the 0.2% return he would have received from a similar U.S. Treasury issue.

Two major problems confront you when you venture abroad, however: painfully high transaction costs and the global headache of trying to guess correctly which countries' bonds to buy at which times. Indeed, you may have trouble getting a brokerage or bank to handle your transactions at all unless you can flash a bankroll of at least $50,000 to invest.

Navigating Restless Currencies

What most people need is a professional money manager at reasonable cost. Enter the foreign bond mutual funds—and entering they are in rapidly growing numbers, from only one six years ago to more than a dozen today. But do not throw in your lot with these foreign bond professionals unless you understand the risks involved. Foremost are currency shifts.

To illustrate, suppose you buy a one-year British government note with a face value of £10,000 and a 10% interest rate. Ignoring commissions, if the exchange rate is $1.50 to the pound, the note will cost you $15,000. After a year, you will get back your £10,000 plus £1,000 interest. But suppose the pound's value has declined to $1.20. Then your £11,000 will be worth only $13,200, which is 12% less than you invested. On the other hand, if the pound has increased 20% against the dollar, your £11,000 will convert to $19,800, a 32% return.

In April 1987, for example, yields around the world ranged from the 25% on New Zealand money-market securities to 3.5% on Japanese short-term notes, with three-month U.S. Treasury bills near the low end at 5.5%. The reasons for the disparities show how the markets work. New Zealand's short-term rates were so high mainly because of the government's campaign to cut 12% inflation with a tight monetary policy. As Americans learned in 1981, a choked-off money supply usually leads to a recession, which in turn squashes interest rates. The prospect of those events in New Zealand has caused long-term bonds to yield less than short-term notes.

Economic pessimism and high inflation also prevail in Australia, where rates are averaging four percentage points lower than in New Zealand. But they are still high relative to rates in other countries. If inflation subsides, however, New Zealand and Australian bond yields will come down. Then bond prices, which always move in the opposite direction from interest rates, will climb.

Japan, by contrast, is contending with low inflation rates of 2% to 3%. Thus the 4.5% yields on its 10-year government bonds last April were more attractive to Japanese investors in real—or inflation-adjusted—terms than were New Zealand's comparable issues yielding 16.3%. Although the Japanese economy appears to be slowing down, most analysts agree that its trade surplus will keep the yen stronger than most other currencies.

In West Germany—another country with low inflation, a stout trade surplus, and a rising currency against the U.S. dollar—yields on 10-year government bonds were only 5.8%. Comparable U.S. Treasury bonds were paying 7.5%. But if the yen or the deutsche mark keeps rising against the dollar, American owners of Japanese or West German bonds could fare better than they would with their money in Treasuries.

Booking Passage with a Fund

A swiftly growing universe of mutual funds can get you into the international action. Last year several fund sponsors and brokerage houses, including Fidelity, E.F. Hutton, Kleinwort Benson, and Paine Webber, opened foreign bond funds or unit trusts, with more to follow. Only three open-end funds have been around long enough to compile any sort of record. By far the oldest is Massachusetts Financial International Trust Bond Portfolio. Since its founding in 1981, Massachusetts Financial has had an average annual total return of around 18%; over the 12 months to October 1, 1987, it returned an elegant 30%. Most

of those returns came from capital gains, however; the fund yields only about 6%. To minimize risk in pursuit of gains, fund manager Leslie Nanberg buys only government-backed issues. His largest holding lately has been 10-year West German bonds. Nanberg expects a double dose of appreciation: from falling interest rates in a slowing German economy and a further ascent of the deutsche mark against the dollar.

For a cautious fling in the New Zealand money market, you can try the new T. Rowe Price International Bond Fund. Since its debut in September 1986, it has provided an annualized total return of 13.5%.

Two new closed-end funds—the kind that trade on stock exchanges—can put you in foreign money markets or bonds. Global Yield Fund (traded on the New York Stock Exchange) owns foreign and U.S. money-market securities and lately yielded about 11.5%. First Australia Prime Income Fund (American Stock Exchange), with a recent 6.7% yield, invests in Australian, New Zealand, and U.S. debt instruments.

Charting Your Own Course

For individual investors who want to grapple with worldwide variables and can afford high transaction costs, two alternatives available through U.S. brokers may make sense. One is debt issued by American corporations in foreign currencies. Such securities offer you the advantage of receiving your interest—and eventually your principal—in dollars instead of the currency in which the bond is denominated. That means you do not have to pay your bank or broker to convert foreign checks you receive from overseas issuers. Jeffrey Diehl, a foreign bond expert with First Boston, a major investment banker, explains that from the standpoint of interest-rate and currency considerations, these bonds and foreign securities are virtually the same game. It is simply more practical to buy bonds that U.S. companies issue in foreign currencies, since American banks accept deposits only in dollars.

The other bonds with special appeal are

those denominated in European currency units, or ECUs. The ECU is essentially a mixture of European currencies weighted according to the predominance of each currency in trade and designed to simplify transactions within the European Common Market. Thus with ECU bonds, you can diversify in an assortment of currencies without having to pay for a bundle of bonds from different countries. Bonds issued in ECUs by companies around the world yield on average about 1.5% more than West German issues. For example, Federal Home Loan Bank's 10-year ECU bonds yielded 9.2% in late 1987 versus 7.6% for West German bonds and 10% for U.S. Treasuries of the same term.

Money Basics

ECU. European currency unit; an amalgam of Western European currencies developed by member nations of the European Common Market to simplify transactions among them. Some American and foreign corporations have issued bonds that are denominated in ECUs.

Eurobond. A bond issued by the government or a corporation in one country and denominated in its currency but sold outside that country. Companies all over the world float Eurobonds to tap additional sources of capital.

Great Investment Advice That Is Free

Information that could otherwise cost thousands of dollars a year is free for the asking if you know where to look.

● Start with your local public library, where you should find *The Value Line Investment Survey*, *Standard & Poor's*, and the annual *Wiesenberger Investment Companies Services*.

● Next, contact brokerage firms. Merrill Lynch, for example, gives away a 30-page booklet, *How to Read a Financial Report*, as well as a free brochure, *Short-Term Fixed-Income Investments*, which discusses Treasury bills, money-market securities, and commercial paper. E.F. Hutton offers *Corporate Bonds*, which explains bond market terminology and types of bonds.

● If you can do some advanced analysis on your own, send for free reports of economic data from the 12 Federal Reserve Banks. For a copy of *Dallas Fed Economic Review*, write to the Public Affairs Dept., Station K, Dallas, TX 75222. To get the St. Louis Fed's *Monetary Trends* and *U.S. Financial Data*, write to its Public Information Office, P.O. Box 442, St. Louis, MO 63166.

● Sometimes, the best advice you can get is how to avoid bad advice. The National Futures Association (800-621-3570, 800-572-9400 in Illinois) publishes a 20-page pamphlet titled *Investment Swindles—How They Work and How to Avoid Them*.

● For a broad market overview that can help you shape your portfolio strategy, read the most recent annual report of Berkshire Hathaway, a diversified holding company, and a compilation of chairman Warren Buffett's letters to shareholders from 1979-85. Buffett is widely regarded as one of the best investors in the world. These publications are available from Berkshire Hathaway, 1440 Kiewit Plaza, Omaha, NE 68131.

● Some of the best sources of ideas for investors in undervalued or emerging growth stocks are the annual and quarterly reports of top-performing mutual funds. Such information will necessarily be dated, so you should not treat it as a buy recommendation. Instead, compile a list of promising stocks that deserve further research. Among the funds whose managers' decisions merit such attention are: Growth Stock Outlook Trust, 4405 East-West Hwy., Bethesda, MD 20814; the Gabelli Asset Fund, P.O. Box 1634, Grand Central Station, New York, NY 10163; the Acorn Fund, 2 N. LaSalle St., Ste. 500, Chicago, IL 60602; Z-Seven Fund, 90 Broad St., New York, NY 10004; Over-the-Counter Securities Fund, Ste. 325, 510 Pennsylvania Ave., P.O. Box 1537, Fort Washington, PA 19034.

© 1987, Bob Gomel

Personal Finance

Ever since the first jolt of virulent inflation in the 1970s, consumers' common wisdom has been to spend and enjoy, and then borrow and enjoy, and then borrow some more. As a result, the average American family spends around 20% of what it earns to pay off consumer debt alone, not counting mortgages. Add mortgage costs and the fact that real household income has declined in the past decade, and it is no surprise that the Gallup poll reports 63% of families are worried that they might owe more than they can afford to repay.

This transformation from borrowing spree to debt squeeze, which is explained in "House of Credit Cards," has profound implications for your family's future prosperity. Consider this: If you use your next $1,000 to pay down your credit-card balances, you probably will save about 18% a year before taxes—or three times as much as you would earn by putting the same amount in a money-market fund. The borrowing bonanza is over, called on account of three broad economic changes that consumers can no longer ignore:

• Tax reform. The law enacted in 1986 makes it far less worth your while to borrow. The interest deduction on consumer loans is being phased out and will be gone by 1991. And the new tax rates, under which no one this year will pay more than a 33% marginal tax, make the few interest deductions left even less valuable.

• The retreat of inflation. It made sense to borrow when prices were rising sharply, because anything bought on credit would be paid for with dollars that were cheaper than at the time of the purchase. But since the double-digit inflation rates of the late 1970s and early 1980s, inflation has plunged as low as 1% per annum in 1986 before rebounding to a recent annualized pace of around 5%.

• The inevitability of a recession. Whether it comes this year or in the next five, it will be particularly hard on those who drink deepest from the debt trough. Even a fairly brief recession will trigger defaults at all levels—national, international, and personal.

For these reasons it is time to take a close look at your indebtedness. If your family is already overextended, you must change some spending habits in order to regain control of your loans. "Getting on Top of Your Debt" outlines steps you can take, from the least painful—a little belt-tightening—to the most drastic—declaring bankruptcy. Few of us, however, can live debt-free, nor do we have to. You just need to learn the best ways to use credit ("How to Borrow Like a Pro"), to impress creditors ("How Lenders Size You Up"), and to tailor your loans to specific needs ("A Savvy Borrower's Shopping Guide"). What is important is that you plan new moves, and that you start right now.

House of Credit Cards

Now is the time to rethink—and perhaps reduce—your debt exposure.

Consumption is the motor that drives all modern industrial economies, and in the United States, consumer spending is a turbo-charged V-8 engine. When Americans are buying avidly, as they have been since 1982, business booms. The expansion perpetuates itself as wages rise and new jobs are created, giving consumers more money to spend. Now, though, economists warn that the buying binge may be near an end. If they are right, the economic recovery will sputter out too, exposing you and your family's financial well-being to the vicissitudes of more stringent times ahead.

The heart of the problem is debt. While the growth in consumer spending has remained fairly strong since the economic recovery began, growth in personal income has been slowing since 1984. The difference between what consumers have to spend and what they actually do spend has been made up by borrowing. As a result, installment debt—balances on credit cards, auto loans, and other such nonmortgage borrowing—has soared to an all-time high of $592 billion.

This seemingly limitless willingness to borrow is most evident in the way Americans rely on credit cards. Almost all creditworthy adults have at least one card, and the typical cardholder has seven. The average balance per person is about $1,450, and millions of Americans have outstanding debt of $2,500 or more. For many families, debt levels are already too high. Defaults on credit cards have grown more common. By some estimates, more than 20 million households are now overextended on installment debt.

The mounting pile of IOUs is, in part, a

holdover from the double-digit inflation of the late 1970s and early 1980s. Then it made sense to borrow indiscriminately because anything bought one day cost more the next. But by the end of 1986 inflation had declined to 1.1%, and the consensus among economists is that prices will rise a modest 4% per annum over the rest of the decade.

Economists disagree about how dangerous these debt levels are for the economy as a whole and how long consumers will keep borrowing to finance exuberant spending. But one thing is clear: at some point during the next year or two, consumers will reach the limit of how much debt they are willing to carry. They will then retrench, buying less on credit. The chart below shows how closely the economy—measured by an economic index known as the coincident indicators—parallels fluctuations in the levels of debt. Since 1982, debt has risen from 12% to 16.8% of annual personal income. When the increase in borrowing stops, economic growth will almost certainly come to a halt as well.

Optimists point to several factors that could sustain consumer borrowing for a while longer. For one, the tremendous increases in the value of such assets as stocks, bonds, and

real estate since 1982 have made consumers richer and better able to take on debt. Further, the decline in interest rates on auto financing and certain other types of loans has made some borrowing less expensive.

Moreover, credit-card issuers may soon roll back their rates. While long-term interest rates have fallen from 13% in mid-1984 to 8.5% recently, rates on credit cards have scarcely budged. Most run from 18% to 20%. Recently, though, political pressure has been building to force card issuers to cut their rates—or at least to disclose all borrowing costs fully. A few banks around the country now offer cards with rates of less than 12%.

Nonetheless, while those factors may delay the downturn in consumer borrowing, one compelling new development suggests a crunch within the next year or so: tax reform. Under the new tax law, the deduction for non-mortgage interest is being phased out, with most of the benefit lost in 1987 and 1988. Thus even with lower rates, many taxpayers will face a whopping increase in the after-tax cost of borrowing.

Consider the case of a family that has been in the top 50% tax bracket and has been able to deduct $1,000 of annual interest on credit

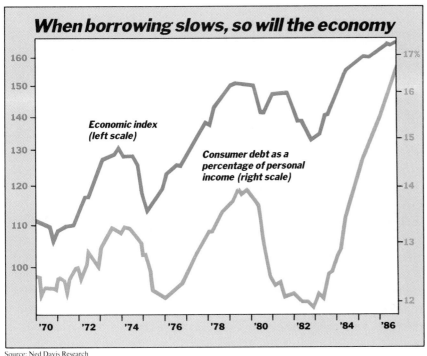

Source: Ned Davis Research

card balances and other nonmortgage debt such as auto loans. In 1986, this family's after-tax borrowing cost was $500. In 1987, though, the top tax rate fell to 38.5%, and only 65% of the interest was deductible. The family's real cost of borrowing works out to $750, a 50% increase over the 1986 cost. And in 1988, only 40% of the interest will be deductible; with a top marginal tax rate of 33%, the after-tax cost will rise to $868.

No one really knows how consumers are going to react to these staggering increases in the real cost of borrowing. Many economists believe that consumers have adjusted psychologically to the higher interest costs of future purchases but that the sharp rise in the after-tax cost of past purchases will take debtors by surprise. If consumers start to pay down their outstanding credit balances as well as shy away from new debt, consumer spending could suddenly plummet and the economy could slip into a serious recession.

Over the long term, however, the buildup in consumer debt does not pose as severe a threat. With a slowdown in spending, enough debt would be paid off to bring consumer borrowing and spending back into balance within a year or two. And there are ways you can protect yourself from temporary shocks that may develop in the short run. Your first step is to confront—and take control of—your indebtedness.

Getting on Top of Your Debt

What to do now so you will never find yourself in hock again.

Losing control of your debts is easier than regaining it. Getting back on top means changing spending and borrowing habits built up over years. In many cases it also means adjusting to a standard of living that is lower, at least temporarily, than you were accustomed to. While there is no simple way to undo the effect of years of overborrowing, the following guidelines can help you get back on track.

The first and most difficult step is to admit that you are in trouble and stop using credit. (See the quiz opposite.) If willpower alone cannot stop your borrowing, try plastic surgery: cut up your cards, cancel your credit lines, and close your overdraft accounts.

Those steps will prevent you from digging yourself in deeper. Next you need a plan for getting yourself out of the hole. Cathy Pietruszewski, director of Consumer Credit Counsel-ors of San Francisco, suggests breaking down the task into short-term goals. Figure out what it will take to repay some smaller bills in six months, and get rid of those first. Liquidating those debts will give you the momentum to tackle the next target. To raise cash for those goals, consider whether there is some unused earning power in your household—a spouse who can go back to work, perhaps, or moonlighting opportunities for you.

Track Your Cash Flow

For most families, however, coming up with extra cash every month usually means cutting back, maybe drastically, on current expenditures. To find the least painful way, you will first need to find out where your money is going now. Begin by recording your expenditures for one month. Chronicling the fate of every cent spent may not be your idea of high finance, but the results may surprise you. Most people think of their expenses as a few major fixed costs and then a lot of other things too minor to count. But when they total those miscellaneous expenses, they are shocked at how much money dribbles away on things such as entertainment, clothes, and restaurant meals.

To control impulse spending, credit counselors suggest that you give yourself the third degree before making any discretionary purchase. Do I really need this or just want it? Will anything terrible happen if I do not buy it? Why did I not need it three weeks ago? Will a less expensive item do as well?

Also give some thought to reducing expenses you might ordinarily consider fixed. For example, you can reduce utility bills by turning down the heat, cut long-distance telephone tolls by writing instead, and trim insurance premiums by raising the deductibles on car and homeowners policies. But make sure your new budget leaves an allowance for inevitable but infrequent costs such as annual insurance premiums and car and home maintenance. Once you have set goals to come up with the cash you need, put them in writing to keep yourself honest.

Talk to Your Creditors

If you need to buy time from your creditors to get your repayment plan on its feet, call your creditors immediately. Explain why you are having difficulty and emphasize that in spite of everything you want to pay your debts. Produce your new austerity budget as evidence of your sincerity. If your efforts do not elicit sympathy—and do not count on it—they should at least engage the self-interest of the lenders. The last thing they want is to write off a loan; many might be willing to make concessions, such as accepting interest-only payment for a few months, to help you get back on schedule.

A debt-consolidation loan, under which you borrow enough money from one source to pay

Are You Out of Gas in the Fast Lane?

To isolate subtle traits of potential overspenders, Money *asked 15 psychologists, credit-card counselors, and financial planners to draw up this test.*

1. You spend money on the expectation that your income will increase in the future. TRUE ☐ FALSE ☐

2. You take cash advances on one credit card to pay off bills on another. TRUE ☐ FALSE ☐

3. You spend more than 20% of your income on credit-card bills. TRUE ☐ FALSE ☐

4. You often fail to keep an accurate record of your purchases. TRUE ☐ FALSE ☐

5. You have applied for more than five credit cards in the past 12 months. TRUE ☐ FALSE ☐

6. You regularly pay for groceries with a credit card. TRUE ☐ FALSE ☐

7. You often hide your credit-card purchases from your family. TRUE ☐ FALSE ☐

8. Owning several credit cards makes you feel richer. TRUE ☐ FALSE ☐

9. You pay off your monthly credit bills but let others slide, such as doctors' bills and utility bills. TRUE ☐ FALSE ☐

10. When you eat out with friends, you like to collect cash from them and then charge the tab on your credit card. TRUE ☐ FALSE ☐

11. You almost always make only the minimum required payments rather than paying off your entire credit-card bill. TRUE ☐ FALSE ☐

12. You have trouble imagining your life without credit. TRUE ☐ FALSE ☐

Now score your response. How many times did you answer True?

1-4 True. You can probably keep going. You do not splurge uncontrollably.

5-8 True. Slow down, you have entered the caution zone. It is time to draw up a budget, pay off your bills, and re-evaluate your spending habits.

9-12 True. You have to stop. You might be wise to consult a credit counselor or financial planner to seek help in changing your spending habits.

off all your other outstanding loans, is another possibility. For the strategy to work, you must be serious about living on cash until the loan is paid off. Otherwise, you could simply dig yourself in deeper. That is why credit counselors advise caution in consolidating debts with home-equity loans, which are secured by borrowers' houses. If your willpower erodes, you could lose your house.

If you cannot win concessions from your creditors, and dare not consolidate, there is still help: one of the nonprofit counseling services that belong to the National Foundation for Consumer Credit. Counselors will help you draw up a budget and negotiate with your creditors for you. Because they usually have close ties with local lenders, the nonprofit counselors can often arrange more lenient repayment terms than you can on your own. If the lenders accept the repayment schedule, you pay a single monthly check to the service, which then apportions the money among your creditors. Nonprofit credit counselors are free or charge only a nominal fee.

If there are no nonprofit credit counselors in your area, you may decide to turn to a commercial credit counselor. At best, they do for you what a nonprofit counselor does—except they charge fees of as much as 15% of your debt. At worst, they take your money and ignore your problem, a practice so common that some states require practitioners to get licenses and others ban commercial counselors outright. Ask for references and check the counselor's reputation with your local Better Business Bureau.

When All Else Fails

If you have tried everything up to this point and nothing worked, your last resort is bankruptcy. Your credit record will be poisoned for 10 years, making it difficult or impossible to get another loan in that time. You could also end up losing your house and property. Moreover, it may not solve all problems: student loans, overdue taxes, alimony, child support, and loans you obtained fraudulently—for example, by lying about your income—cannot be discharged by declaring bankruptcy.

There are two kinds of personal bankruptcy, Chapter 7 and Chapter 13. If you have a lot of equity in your house, you will probably lean toward Chapter 13, which allows you to keep your property while you repay your debts. But you cannot qualify for Chapter 13 unless you make enough money to meet those payments.

In petitioning for Chapter 13, you submit a budget and detailed repayment plan, and if the court affirms the plan, your creditors are bound to discharge your debts once you complete the scheduled payments. Depending on your financial situation, you may not have to pay off the full amounts that you owe. You make your payments directly to a trustee appointed by the court. The trustee then parcels the money among your creditors. Unlike Chapter 7, Chapter 13 allows you to discharge student loans and fraudulent loans, but it will not let you off the hook for taxes, alimony, or child support.

If you are unemployed or simply in too deep to fund an acceptable repayment plan, you may have no choice but to file the more drastic Chapter 7. The court then cancels all your debts and hands your estate over to a trustee to be liquidated and split among your creditors. You can keep some of your assets. The exact amount varies from state to state, but you usually would be allowed to keep $7,500 of equity in your house ($15,000 for married couples), $1,200 of equity in a car, $4,000 in household goods, and about $500 worth of jewelry. If the equity in your home, for example, exceeds the protected amount, the trustee will sell the property and then return to you an amount equal to your full protected equity.

Money Sources

For a free directory of nonprofit credit counseling services, write the National Foundation for Consumer Credit at 8701 Georgia Ave., Silver Spring, MD 20910.

What the Killjoys Can Do to You

In Pennsylvania, creditors can take your house but not your Bible.

Although the days of debtors prisons are long past, an incensed creditor can make your life miserable if you default, or fail to make timely payments, on a loan. Under both federal and state law he may take any collateral securing the debt, collect part of your salary, or seize the funds in your bank account. A creditor may even reclaim your car by sending a repo man to jump-start it and drive it away.

In most instances, generalizations are difficult. Here, however, is an outline of your rights—and your creditor's recourse—for the three main classes of loans.

Unsecured loans. You are in default on a loan if you do not meet the specific terms of the loan agreement—even if that means you missed only one payment by one day. But it is unlikely a creditor will take immediate action on an unpaid credit-card balance or other unsecured loans for which you have not put up collateral. You will be charged a late penalty plus additional interest if that is spelled out in your loan agreement. Some agreements include a grace period to give you up to about 30 days from the payment deadline before interest or penalty charges begin to accrue. In all, a credit-card company might wait 60 to 90 days before canceling your card; if it does, you would still owe the balance as well as any interest and late charges.

There is no rule about how patient a creditor will be. Usually within two weeks of a missed payment the creditor will mail a friendly reminder, and then follow up with other letters or phone calls. Finally, if the creditor decides you are dodging him, he is likely to turn to a collection agency. And if you still do not respond, the creditor or collection agency will probably sue in civil court, though that is not likely unless you owe more than $200. (Only the Internal Revenue Service can seize property without taking you to court.)

Once in court, the creditor must win two judgments: one finding you in default and another permitting him to collect by seizing your property or garnisheeing your wages—an unpleasant procedure in which up to 25% of your net earnings after taxes per paycheck is sent to the creditor.

The creditor must attempt to satisfy the debt with money from your bank accounts, stocks, and other personal property before it can take your real estate. Many states have laws exempting household and personal possessions. In Pennsylvania, Bibles, clothes, schoolbooks, and $300 worth of items that you specify are exempt. Under the old homesteading laws in Texas, creditors may not touch a home and land of up to 200 acres in addition to clothes, furnishings, and $15,000 of personal property for each single adult. The IRS, however, can ignore this provision.

Another wrinkle worth noting is that if you live in Pennsylvania, South Carolina, or Texas, your salary cannot be garnisheed. And in Florida, all salary earned by those who head households is safe, even though their houses are not.

On a brighter note, you are protected by the Federal Debt Collection Practices Act passed in

1977. It prevents creditors from harassing you with threats of physical violence, abusive phone calls, any calls at all after 9 p.m., or direct calls to your employer. Nor can they pester you by posing as a government official.

Secured loans. When the creditor requires you to pledge the item you are buying, such as a car, the creditor gets a lien on it. If you miss a payment, he is entitled to take it. Also, the lien prevents you from selling the item without notifying the lender.

If you cannot meet your payments, you should notify the creditor to negotiate a new repayment plan. Or you may want the right to sell the item yourself; you will probably get a higher price than the creditor might. You should avoid repossession; besides losing your car, you will be hit with legal fees plus towing and storage costs.

State laws on notification vary. In Massachusetts, for example, the creditor must send you a certified letter when you are 21 days late. You must pay in full in 21 more days to avoid repossession.

A creditor will initially try to repossess an item peacefully without a court action under what is euphemistically called self-help. A repo man, who is paid either by salary or by fee for each item repossessed, can take your car from the front of your house or even from your driveway without a court ruling. He cannot, however, break into your locked garage. If the creditor goes to court and wins, then a sheriff can enter your home and take whatever is specified in the judgment. After the item is repossessed, the creditor must place a notice in a local newspaper for an extended period stating that he intends to sell your collateral. You could reclaim the item by paying off your debt and the creditor's costs up to the time of sale.

Even after an item put up as collateral is repossessed, you are not off the hook. For example, if a bank sells your car for less than what you owe, it can seek a deficiency judgment to collect the outstanding amount along with legal fees and other repossession costs. But if there is not a large sum of money involved, it is unlikely a creditor will seek a deficiency judgment.

Foreclosure. Financing the purchase of your home is another example of secured debt; a mortgage represents the lender's interest on your property. If you fail to pay, in this case, the consequences can be disastrous because the creditor can seize the collateral: your home. Thus the threat of foreclosure should never be taken lightly by anyone.

Some banks call or write to you 30 days after the due date while others call you first and follow up with a warning letter. If you still do not pay, the creditor will send you a certified or registered letter specifying its intent to foreclose unless you respond by a certain date, usually within 30 days. If you do not, the bank can advertise the forthcoming sale of your home. The notice must appear in a local newspaper for several weeks. During that period, you can pay the overdue balance, interest penalties, and other expenses to cancel the sale.

In about half the states, you may be able to reclaim your home even after a foreclosure sale. The longest redemption period is in Tennessee, where, unless you waived your right in the mortgage contract, you have two years after the sale to pay off the entire amount and move back into your house.

Money Basics

Collateral. Property or assets pledged by a borrower to a lender until the loan is repaid. If the borrower fails to repay the loan, the lender can seize the property and sell it.

Default. Failure of a borrower to pay interest and principal as they come due.

Garnishment. A court order requiring an employer to withhold a specified amount from an employee's wages in order to satisfy a debt.

Lien. A creditor's claim against real or personal property to satisfy a debt. A mortgage, for example, is a lien against a house.

How to Borrow Like a Pro

*The key is to learn how to manage debt deftly
instead of letting it manhandle you.*

Few Americans can live like Americans without some debt. The house, the car, and the college education are necessities that most of us must pay for on the installment plan. Until now we have tended to go in hock ad hoc. But with inflation leashed and interest payments no longer tax deductible, there is a new American way of debt. It calls for deploying more of our borrowing power to make money even as we spend it.

Smart credit management can send you soaring like Franklin Ohlin, a Merrill Lynch financial consultant in Colorado Springs. Ohlin is using a glider to test-pilot the firm's home-equity credit line, called Equity Access. In May 1986 he borrowed $10,000 against his $175,000 house to buy a single-seat Schweitzer 1-36 sailplane. He is learning to fly it on the Rocky Mountains' world-famous thermals, which can loft gliders to 18,000 feet.

At first glance, borrowing against your house to finance an adventurous hobby such as Ohlin's does not look too shrewd. But he is a member of Colorado Springs' Black Forest Soaring Society, and he immediately leased his plane to the society. Fellow members get to use it at 40% off the normal rate. He expects his plane to pay for itself in five years and then throw off income.

Treat Credit Like an Investment

As Ohlin will tell you, knowledgeable management of your borrowing power demands the same attention to detail as handling your investments does. You have to monitor your rate of return, the tax status of your loan, and, above all, what is happening to inflation and interest rates. And you must be able to get out if interest rates take a sharp upturn. The difference is this: professional investors have built a body of lore and a set of accepted maneuvers that are based on experience and research, while credit management as a discipline has not progressed beyond Home Economics I and II. So far nobody has defined the term credit management precisely. It can mean something as simple as knowing where to borrow at low rates when you have to. It can also mean making profitable moves such as paying off old debts with cheaper new money or using other people's money to your own gain. Either way, it is a smart new approach to debt that is worth learning.

Borrowing against one's house with a home-equity loan is the nation's handiest new credit tool and its most vast financial resource. These house-secured credit lines have all the attributes of revolving charge accounts, plus the flexibility of letting you repay the debt at your own pace. Some $1.2 trillion of borrowable equity resides in American homes. And the 1986 Tax Reform Act provides solid rationales for using it—particularly for home improvements, educational purposes, and long-term investments. While deductions on all other forms of consumer credit will be phased out by 1991, home-equity interest remains partly and in many cases fully deductible. Unless you know how to handle credit, though, the home equity dispensation could lead to excesses reminiscent of the tax-driven real estate deals that Congress hoped it had laid to rest with recent tax reforms.

Borrow with a Plan

What you need—what every prudent person needs—is a low-cost credit reserve with deep pockets and a medium-term (say five-year) plan for its possible use. Homeowners whose property has multiplied in value can raise a large amount by refinancing their mortgages, but in doing so they take on a 15- to 30-year obligation. Mortgage refinancing makes excellent sense when your first loan is still young and two or more percentage points higher than current interest rates.

More flexible borrowing power at variable rates is available from various sources, including home-equity credit lines and unsecured lines of credit from a bank. Each has strengths, weaknesses, and special uses. Here are the general purposes.

Refinancing. First see whether you can profit by restructuring your present debts. If you apply for a home-equity credit line, prospective lenders probably will insist that you use part of it to pay off any second mortgage on your house. They want to clear that off the books so that they are not third, fourth, or fifth in line for their money in case you default.

The typical household has additional cleaning up to do. Take this scenario supplied by William T. Kirkpatrick, manager of the Ready Equity Department at Citizens & Southern National Bank in Atlanta. A family owes $20,000 on a car loan, home improvements, an unsecured vacation loan, and Sears, Penney, and MasterCard accounts. Interest on these debts averages 15%, with tax deductibility waning on all but the home improvement loan. (If you itemize in the 1987 tax year, 65% of your consumer interest is deductible; the following year 40%; then 20%, 10%, and out.)

Loan payments for this hypothetical household total $762 a month, or $9,144 a year. Since there is plenty of equity in the family home, Kirkpatrick arranges a tax-deductible Ready Equity line of $25,000, of which $20,000 is drawn down to settle the other debts. Assuming a 9.5% interest rate, monthly payments of 2% of the balance start out costing $400, freeing up $362 a month and $4,300 a year. If the family takes Kirkpatrick's advice, it will use at least some of that saving to accelerate repayment of the home-equity loan and will earmark the rest for investments in their family's health and welfare, such as orthodontics and college.

Conserving capital. By commanding credit when you need it, you can escape having to sell assets with growth potential to raise cash in a hurry. A $350,000-a-year chief executive officer in the Washington, D.C., area was hit in 1986 by a six-figure personal tax bill and found himself with a $40,000 cash deficit. Neither he nor his wife believed in personal borrowing, but their alternative was to sell some of the stock he owns in his fast-growing company. Joan Bickel, their financial planner, showed them that if the stock appreciated at its present rate, in five years it could make them richer by half a million dollars or more.

The planner's solution was a $100,000 unsecured line of credit at an adjustable rate of one percentage point above the prime rate—the interest banks charge their best corporate customers. The planner's clients kept their stock, paid their taxes, spent $20,000 on other needs, and quickly began reducing their loan. They do not have any plans for the remaining $40,000 of borrowing power at their disposal. On the other hand, it does not cost them anything.

Another way credit lines can help you make better use of your assets is to serve as a substitute for an emergency fund. Instead of tying up three months' salary in a money-market fund—as many financial planners recommend—open a home-equity line and do not hesitate to lock up your emergency money in a short- to medium-term bank certificate of deposit or a U.S. Treasury bond, where it will be safe but earn a higher return.

Investment leverage. If most of your wealth is tied up in your house, you may want to consider a gentle form of leverage to diversify this investment, counsels Mark Tucker, a tax lawyer whose Decision Support Group in Alamo, California, provides training materials on investment management and other aspects of financial planning as a fringe benefit for corporate employees. Tucker states the basic rule of leverage in one sentence: the after-tax rate of return on a leveraged investment must exceed the after-tax cost of borrowing.

One strategy for diversifying the money in your house is to take out a home-equity line and draw from it an equal sum each month or quarter to invest in mutual funds. Especially when house and stock prices are appreciating steadily, this strategy, called dollar-cost averaging, prevents you from investing all your money at the market's top. Meanwhile, your home's value will increase as much as it would have without the loan. (Not all advisers agree with this strategy. See page 115.)

Investing in a business. Using your house as collateral for a loan to start a business is more perilous than investing in mutual funds. If a bank will not back your venture on its merits, perhaps you need to think again about whether it has merits. Even when a bank says yes to a small-business loan, however, the rate probably will top what you would pay for a home-equity line.

Betty Ross, a Washington, D.C., travel writer, took a chance on a home-equity business loan and seems to be winning. Ross, who did a stint as press secretary to inflation czar Alfred E. Kahn in the Carter White House, says that she was brought up to pay cash for everything and hates borrowing money. She was writing a guide book, though, and wanted to be its publisher.

Overcoming her credit aversion, Ross took out a $30,000 equity line in December 1985 on her mortgage-free house in the District, which she has owned since 1955. The bank, American Security, charged her $398 up front and a variable rate that began at 11% and later fell to 8.5%. The money she drew down, $25,000 at its peak, covered the fees of her editor, in-

dexer, designer, engraver, printer, and other specialists. She began making $298 monthly payments out of her freelance income.

Ross's Americana Press published her handsome paperback, *A Museum Guide to Washington, D.C.*, in June 1986. By marketing it herself to museum shops as well as through regional and national distributors, she has sold 9,000 copies, and last February paid off the balance of her loan. Now in its second printing, the guide will earn her $10,000 in 1987, she estimates. Does she intend to finance a third press run with home equity? You bet.

A caveat. Be aware that, as flexible and useful as they are, home-equity loans do have drawbacks. Loan rates are adjustable and seldom capped, so if interest rates rise, your payments could swell beyond the limits of your budget. And if your loan ends in a huge balloon payment and you cannot pay it off or refinance at that point, you could lose your house.

Money Basics

Equity. The market value of your property, minus the mortgage and other liens against it.

Home-equity loan. A line of credit secured by your house. The credit line can equal up to 80% of the current appraised value of your house, minus your mortgage balance. Interest rates are variable and not capped, but interest is due only on the portion of the credit line in use. You must also pay an origination fee of 1% to 2% of the credit line.

Leverage. A means of enhancing the value of or return from an investment without increasing the amount of the investment.

Refinancing. Restructuring a loan to take advantage of lower interest rates and to secure lower payments.

How Lenders Size You Up

A yea or nay on a loan depends on scoring the right points.

Applying for credit used to mean cajoling, pleading, or begging a lender to give you a loan. Ignominious groveling is still part of the lending process, except today it is the creditors who are on their knees. Five years ago banks generally approved just 30% to 50% of those who applied for credit cards. Today approval rates are running to 60%, and banks that push their plastic through pre-approved mass mailings sometimes approach 80% acceptance rates.

The lenders' shift from arrogance to accommodation is not grounded in altruism. When they are paying 6% for money and lending it at 18%, they will approve more accounts. One reason they can boost their approval rate so dramatically is the advent of a new social science: credit scoring. Arcane mathematical models are used to scan your loan application plus reports about your credit history. If you are applying for a credit or charge card or just about any type of personal loan, chances are the creditor will use a point-scoring system to size you up and make a decision about whether to accept or reject you.

Credit scoring is usually a two-step process. First, you are awarded points on your application form depending upon your answers to questions about your occupation, income, and the length of time you have held your present job. The higher you score, the better credit risk you are in the lender's eyes. Although upwards of twenty questions may appear on the form, usually only eight to twelve are scored. Other questions asking for your telephone number or names and addresses of relatives merely provide information for the creditor's records.

The weight given to each scoring question depends on the particular creditor's experience and judgment. If homeowners in his area proved to be good credit risks, while renters tended to skip town, high points would go to the homeowner. A typical system would require that you get at least 200 points out of a possible 300 for approval. The correct answer to a heavily weighted question might win you as many as 50 points, while another question might carry only 10 points. Federal law prohibits creditors from discriminating on the basis of sex, race, or age. Still, you can be scored on the basis of age, but if you are 62 or older you must get at least as many points for your age as any person under 62.

After reviewing your life's history on the application, the lender goes to the second scoring step: buying your credit bureau report. This is where you can win—or lose—50% or more of the points you need for approval. A credit report that shows you frequently let payments slip for 60 days or so can knock you out of contention. Before applying for a credit card or loan, you should get a copy of your report and look for any errors. Clearing up mistakes or, in the case of a disputed bill, putting your side of the argument onto the report, can improve your chances. (For more on credit bureaus, see page 112.)

Lenders are notoriously tight-lipped about which of the items weighed are considered most significant. Sears, one of the largest non-bank consumer lenders in the country with some 60 million cardholders, has 700 different credit scoring models, almost one for each of its stores. Scoring systems are usually updated every three years so they reflect the lender's most recent experience with borrowers. Thus lenders in a booming city that has attracted affluent professionals from other parts of the country may deem such standard measures as how long you have had your job or the same home as a poor predictor of creditworthiness.

Still, some items generally tend to score higher than others. Knowing which those are can help you get approved or, in the event you are rejected, help you prepare an appeal to the lender. The following factors usually carry the most extra weight.

Number of creditors. Simply having credit with other lenders can win you 30 or more points in many systems. Bank credit cards—such as MasterCard and Visa—and travel-and-entertainment cards such as American Express score highest. Major department store cards are also good scorers. You can actually lose points for having loans with finance companies, since they are associated with bad credit risks. Yet a good payment record on such loans wins back at least as many points as you might lose.

Traditionally, the more creditors you have, the more creditworthy you are. But as the pile of personal debt teeters at dangerous heights, a new trend is emerging. Some banks will reject you outright if you already have three or more credit cards. Others may subtract points if you have more than five cards.

On the other hand, having no credit references reduces your chances. To win approval without a credit history, you will have to score high in all other areas of the application. To begin building a credit history, start by applying for department store credit cards, which are generally easier to get. By showing that you make your monthly payments on time, you will accumulate points that will help persuade other creditors to extend you credit.

Credit payment history. A sterling bill-paying habit can earn you 25% or more of the points you need. That is usually more than any other single item. Most credit bureau reports list loans, credit cards, and charge accounts and note whether you are paying them on time or if you are ever 30, 60, 90, or 120 days delinquent. Delinquencies with a MasterCard or Visa will generally detract from your score more than late payments to a department store. Since bank credit cards have far more uses than a store card, lenders have found that borrowers try to keep these current even when undergoing financial difficulties. Thus lenders view delinquencies in these cards as cause for alarm. One credit card that is 30 days delinquent will not rob you of all your points in this category, but delinquencies of 60 days or more—regardless of what kind of account—may scuttle your chances for approval.

Suits, judgments, and bankruptcies. If you have declared bankruptcy, a lender has taken you to court to force repayment of a debt, or a tax lien has been filed against you, that information will usually show up in your credit report. Even fully paid suits, judgments, and liens remain on your record for seven years; a bankruptcy stays on for ten. Such derogatory items—"serious derogs" in creditors' jargon—are often not scored per se, but they can cause an immediate rejection. Lenders do ignore some derogs, such as small medical bills, because they usually indicate a dispute over how much is owed. Others, such as personal bankruptcy, are almost insurmountable.

If you have what you believe are unwarranted negative entries on your credit reports, you can add an explanatory statement to your report. You may also argue your case to the lender.

Length of time at your job and residence. Lenders prize stability. Their payment records show that people who settle down tend to pay their debts better than those on the move. Thus under many scoring systems a person who has lived at the same address for three years may get twice as many points as someone who moved in the past year. In parts of the country noted for mobile populations—Washington, D.C., for example, where administrations come and go—moves may be of little or no consequence.

Similarly, you earn more points the longer

you stay at one job. While leaving for a better-paying job should make you a better credit risk, most point-scoring systems do not take this into account. If the points you lose in this category mean the difference between approval and rejection, pointing out that you have an employment contract and are in the process of purchasing a home may persuade a lender to review your case.

Income. A higher income will get you more points. This does not mean, however, that someone earning $40,000 gets twice as many points as someone earning $20,000. In a typical scoring system, a monthly income of $1,500 might win you 10 points, while earnings of $2,500 a month might merit 12 points. Generally, lenders stop awarding additional points if you earn more than $35,000. Make sure you list all sources of income, such as alimony, child support, and interest income (all of which lenders must recognize as income).

Your debt-to-income ratio—a convenient measure of your ability to handle debt—usually is not factored into credit scoring systems. Lenders rely heavily on this ratio, however, in the less clinical decision-making process used for larger loans such as home mortgages and home-equity lines. A decade ago, lenders were loath to lend to you if the monthly payments for all your debt—mortgage, auto, credit-card, and other loans—exceeded 35% of your monthly income before taxes. Now many lenders are willing to go to 40% and even 50% in the case of home-equity lines made to borrowers with incomes of $50,000 or more.

Wary of the growing burden of consumer debt, some lenders are beginning to develop credit scoring systems that will factor in debt-to-income ratios for mortgages and home-equity lines. The score you get under these systems may also vary according to the amount of equity you have in your home. For example, if your house is worth $100,000 and the total debt secured by your house—including both mortgage and home-equity line—was $60,000, you would probably score higher than a similar homeowner who has racked up $80,000 in debt against his house.

Occupation. Most scoring systems place applicants into one of eight job categories: professional, managerial, blue-collar supervisor, clerical, sales, self-employed, skilled trade, and unskilled worker. Executives and professionals usually rate the most points, around thirty, while unskilled laborers may get only five. In some cases, the type of employer is also considered. Thus a checkout clerk for a thriving supermarket chain might get more points than a higher-paid assembly-line worker at an auto manufacturer with a history of layoffs.

Age. Generally, the older you are the more points you rack up. But it is possible for an 18-year-old, in some cases, to get more points than a 30-year-old. Young borrowers who live at home with their parents often have more disposable income to devote toward debt payment than a 30-year-old burdened with a monthly mortgage and car payment.

Checking or savings account. Lenders have found that people with checking accounts tend to manage their finances better than those who only have savings accounts. As a result, checking accounts may get up to twice as many points. Having both will get you the maximum number of points.

Homeowner versus renter. Owning your own home could give you as much as 15% of the points you need. Creditors are convinced that homeowners are less likely to default. The importance of this characteristic varies around the country, however. In areas with a high concentration of retirees who rent, home ownership may not mean much. The importance of this factor also varies by the kind of credit. Scores of home improvement applications would ignore this item for a simple reason: everyone applying is a homeowner.

All lenders must play by certain rules. The federal Equal Credit Opportunity Act stipulates that you must be notified, in writing, within 30 days after you have completed an application, if you have been rejected. If a creditor turns you down, he must give you specific reasons or tell you of your right to request a written explanation. A lender who rejects you through a point-scoring system does not have to reveal your actual score, but he must specify the categories that dragged you down. If an unfavorable credit report did it, the lender must name the credit bureau.

You need not despair if a lender rejects you. A failing score at one bank could be a passing grade across the street. And while they do not widely advertise it, many creditors are willing to listen to a rational appeal and sometimes override the scoring system. In fact, many lenders find that people who get irate and call are usually people whose creditworthiness is fairly good. Sometimes structuring the loan differently or lowering the amount of credit allows an approval.

How Much Debt Can You Handle?

▶ Experts say the secret to a healthy home balance sheet is to keep your monthly consumer debt payments down to around 10% to 15% of your total monthly net income. The absolute maximum: 20%. This includes payments due on credit cards and personal, school, and car loans—but not first mortgages, home-equity loans, or rent. Those obligations can account for as much as an additional 35% of your total monthly expenditures. Your own safe personal debt ceiling, however, depends largely upon who you are:

▶ If you are earning $20,000 a year or less, debt counselors say your net income may leave only enough for essentials. Avoid borrowing at all.

▶ If you are single, middle-aged, and net $40,000 a year, you can probably afford 20% in debt. But knock that back to 15% if your income is based upon commissions instead of a regular salary.

▶ If you and your working spouse take home $50,000, you can probably carry 20%. If you have children, make it 15%.

▶ If you are retired on a fixed income, stay within a 10% limit.

To find your personal debt ratio, calculate your monthly income in net terms by subtracting all taxes, Social Security, and IRA contributions. Then use this worksheet to tally up your monthly payments and determine exactly where you stand.

List Loans and Charge Accounts	Average Monthly Payments
$	$
$	$
$	$
$	$
$	$
$	$
$	$
$	$
$	$
$	$
$	$
$	$

1. Total your monthly consumer debt payments. $_____

2. Enter your monthly net income. $_____

3. To calculate the most you can afford each month, divide your monthly net income by 5 for a 20% limit, 6.7 for 15%, or 10 for 10%. $_____

To find whether your payments are within your means, subtract line 1 from line 3. That sum is your safety margin. If line 1 is larger than line 3, however, you should start reducing your debt immediately. $_____

Watching the Credit Watchers

As far as lenders are concerned, your credit report is the best nonfiction reading this side of the bestsellers list. Such reports—usually compiled by data-base companies as a service for creditors—can account for half the reason you are either accepted or rejected for a loan. Though comprehensive, these computerized records can contain mistakes. And one negative mark, correct or incorrect, can cause lenders to reject you for up to seven years. Fewer than one percent of the consumers who have read their report find they need to take advantage of federal consumer laws to correct errors. Still, unless you request a copy, you probably will not learn whether you are one of the unlucky applicants stuck with an error until after you have been rejected for a loan or credit card.

Credit reporting agencies. There are five national agencies. TRW, based in Orange, California, and Trans Union, based in Chicago, are the largest. These two agencies maintain files on more than 135 million consumers. Most lenders prefer to have reports from two credit bureaus. Ask your banker for the names of the agencies he uses. To get a copy of your file, check your phone book for local offices. But you will have to write the agencies yourself; federal law prohibits your banker from disclosing your record to anyone, even you.

Because credit reporting agencies rely on information supplied by stores and banks, only those that regularly report information to them will appear on your report. You may be surprised by what is not on your report. Student loans in good standing are often unreported. And while an increasing number of mortgage lenders are beginning to report to credit agencies, your house payment history is not likely to be there. Even American Express does not supply payment information. Yet a payment that is even one day late to Visa or MasterCard can stay on your record seven years.

Your credit report. Once you get your report, making sense of it is the next task. You will see your past and current credit-card accounts and fixed loans with notations that characterize them as positive or negative. On the back of your report you will find a key to the codes and abbreviations. You will also find reference to a 1971 federal law that prescribes the necessary steps to correct any wrong information. The law requires that agencies maintain reasonable procedures to assure accuracy. If they do not, you can sue them for punitive damages.

Settling disputes. If you disagree with the report data, start by writing a letter to the credit reporting agency, disputing the information. The burden will then be on the agency and creditor to prove that the information is correct. You can expect an answer in 30 days. Incorrect information must be removed from your record.

But some disagreements are not so simple. If, for example, you refused to pay a department store charge because you decided the merchandise was shoddy, you are allowed to add a 100-word justification to your report. If an irregular payment was caused by a serious illness or divorce, an explanatory note may help smooth future problems before they begin. Most credit agencies maintain a staff that will help you draft a statement.

What creditors fear most. Any compelling reason you have for not paying the dispute should be in your records. What lenders fear most is the implication that you did not pay your bills simply because you did not feel like it. Before adding the statement, consider getting in contact with the creditor who reported the negative information to see whether there is some way to reconcile the matter. If you succeed, your creditor can have the negative remark completely removed from your record.

A Savvy Borrower's Shopping Guide

How you can get the best deals for five common needs, from buying a car to financing college.

How do you know which is the best place to go for a loan and which one to choose once you get there? Given the wide range of offerings, the charge to borrowers these days is to learn about lenders and what they have to offer. By doing a thorough credit check of your own, you are more likely to borrow on your own terms.

Your purpose for borrowing, the amount you need, your ability to repay, and your creditworthiness will dictate from whom you can borrow and the type of loan you get. Say you need a loan to help pay for your daughter's college tuition. You apply for a Guaranteed Student Loan, but your family income is too high to qualify. The banker suggests a home-equity loan. Unlike other college borrowing, all the interest is tax deductible. Great, you say. The terms: a variable rate pegged at three percentage points over prime and closing costs amounting to 1.25% of the loan. Not so great. By scouting around, you can do much better.

All loans fall into one of two broad categories, secured or unsecured. Secured loans use an item, commonly your home or car, as collateral, which protects the lender's interests. Aside from first mortgages, they include home-equity lines of credit, automobile loans, and borrowing against your portfolio of securities held in a margin account by your broker. Unsecured debt includes personal loans, lines of credit, and credit cards, and tends to carry higher interest rates. Here is a guide to help you pick the right loan for your purposes.

Home Renovation

No matter who your lender is, the most popular loan these days is a home-equity line of credit. Reason: unlike interest on debt that does not use your home or second home as collateral, interest on home-backed debt is almost always fully deductible up to the price you paid plus improvements. And with your house securing the line of credit, the interest rates on these medium- to long-term (seven to twenty years) variable-rate loans are among the lowest around; rates are usually one to two percentage points over the prime rate, lately around 9.25%. Also, you pay interest only on the amount you actually draw down.

But there are potential problems. Fall behind on your payments and you could lose your house. If inflation and interest rates revive, you could find yourself facing far heavier payments than you ever imagined. Few lenders have caps on how high the variable interest rates can go. Payments on a seven-year, $40,000 loan at 9.5% are $654 a month; at 14% they would be $750. If the prime returned to its 1981 high of 18.8% and you were paying prime plus 2%, you would need to lay out $908 a month.

You can get more predictable payments, but at higher rates, with a second mortgage or a secured home improvement loan. Second mortgages differ from home-equity lines of credit in that you usually borrow a fixed amount at a fixed rate for a fixed term. In late 1987, interest charges were about 11% to 14%; the typical term is 10 to 15 years. With home improvement loans you must submit a contractor's estimate and plans and then prove to the lender that the improvements were done. The lender puts a so-called junior lien on your home; he can claim his money if you default and the house is sold, but he cannot foreclose. The rates are somewhat higher than second-mortgage rates (around 13%) and the terms are much shorter (three to five years). Your payments would be $455 a month on a $20,000, five-year loan at 13%.

Banks, savings and loans, and credit unions are the most frequent sources of home-backed loans, but finance companies such as the Loan Depot and Beneficial Finance have become serious competitors. Finance companies are more liberal—lending up to 85% of the value of your home less the mortgage balance, compared with 80% for other creditors—and often lend to applicants with so-so borrowing histories. The price: interest rates that are one to five percentage points higher than banks, depending on your creditworthiness.

There are other ways to get the cash to fix up your house. Most company retirement or pension plans let employees borrow up to $50,000 of the vested balance in their accounts for home renovation. Interest rates are competitive, usually one percentage point over the prime rate, and you can repay the money over five years through salary deductions. Or, if you have cash-value life insurance, you can borrow against the accumulated value at rates set forth in the contract. Loans on older policies go for as little as 5% or 6%, while recently issued variable-rate policies are around 8% now. You do not have to pay back what you borrow, but if you die with a loan outstanding, the debt is subtracted from the policy's face value before the proceeds are paid out. The major drawback of borrowing from your pension or life insurance is that such loans are treated as consumer debt by the IRS, so interest is not fully deductible.

College

Because the IRS is phasing out the deductibility of interest on college loans, a home-equity line is the most convenient way to borrow money for college and still deduct the interest.

If you have little or no equity in a house or prefer not to risk borrowing it, try the college itself. Many institutions have become low-interest lenders to help supplement the limited programs offered by the government. The Consortium on Financing Higher Education, a group representing 30 of the country's top colleges—including Amherst, Harvard, and the University of Chicago—organized a loan program called SHARE in March 1986. Parents of students at any of the Consortium schools can borrow $15,000 a year for four years and take up to fifteen years to repay. The interest rate is variable, but it is never higher than prime plus two percentage points. There are no income requirements.

You might also consider a government loan—if you can qualify. Guaranteed Student Loans (GSLs), available through most banks, are more difficult to get under the new rules that became effective last January. GSLs are now restricted to families who can demonstrate need, based on such criteria as income and size of family. The interest rate on 10-year GSLs is 8% for the first four years and 10% thereafter. Students can borrow up to $2,625 a year for the first two years and $4,000 a year for the second two years of undergraduate study and $7,500 annually for graduate and professional courses. The Supplemental Loan program, open to all income levels, picks up where GSLs leave off. Undergraduates can borrow $4,000 a year at a variable rate, based on the one-year Treasury bill rate—lately about 7.5%—plus 3.75 percentage points. The maximum: 12%.

Parents can also tap life insurance policies or retirement or pension plans, the same as for home renovation. The government stipulates, however, that borrowing from retirement or pension plans for any purpose other than to buy or improve a primary residence must be repaid within five years. If you borrow $20,000 at 8.5%, your monthly payments would be $410 a month over five years, compared with $209 a month on a 15-year, 9% home-equity loan.

Automobiles

Many banks and credit unions have countered the car companies' low-interest financing offers with attractive loans of their own. The average bank rate for a conventional car loan is about 11%, down from 12.7% in 1986. Some banks are offering long-term loans with no down payments. At most banks, however, you can get a better rate on shorter-term loans.

Manufacturers' incentives have ranged from American Motors' 0% financing to General Motors' choice of 2.9% financing or a $1,500 rebate. But you may not get the exact model—much less the colors and options—you have your heart set on. In fact, popular models that sell on their own are often not offered. If you have a choice, take a rebate and borrow elsewhere. George Rose, a lawyer in the consumer affairs department of Montgomery County, Maryland, calculates that if you finance $10,000 at 2.9% for two years, you would pay $10,304.88, or $891.32 more than if you took the $1,500 rebate and financed $8,500 at 10% for two years with your friendly banker.

Many banks are touting low-interest, long-term home-equity lines for car purchases. But they may not be bargains when you consider that upfront costs on a $10,000 home-equity loan may run from $400 to more than $1,000.

Vacations

The easiest way to pay for a vacation is to whip out your Visa, MasterCard, or American Express and say: "Charge it, please." But cards are also the most expensive way to get away. The interest rate for the average revolving credit account is a whopping 18.2%. If you are shopping for a card to use for vacations or any other purposes, you should also consider the annual fee and the grace period—the gap between when you charge something to the time interest starts to accrue.

If you can plan ahead, you may want to apply for an unsecured personal loan to help pay for your vacation. The average rate: 15.5%. Terms are one to five years.

Do not even think about using the equity in your home to pay for a fleeting few weeks of R&R. Andrew McA. Hunter, a vice president of Germantown Savings Bank near Philadelphia, was so distressed about misuse of the bank's home-equity program that the bank took out a full-page ad in the *Philadelphia Inquirer* that read: "Although you have always wanted to go on safari, ask yourself whether your home is worth a few snapshots of wild giraffes."

Investment

Borrowing to invest is risky business. But if you are going to do it, ask your broker to lend you the money using your securities as collateral. Interest paid on such margin accounts is deductible up to the extent of your net investment income—from interest, dividends, and capital gains—for the year. Interest that cannot be deducted one year because of the cap can be carried forward and deducted in future years when there is enough investment income to offset it, such as when you sell the investment at a gain. Interest on loans against tax-exempt bonds is not deductible.

Another plus: interest rates are relatively low, usually .5% to 2% over the call rate, which is what brokers pay for the money (recently around 8.8%). Investors can margin up to half their stockholdings and an even greater percentage of fixed-income securities. You can also use margin for noninvestment purposes via a cash-management plan, but the interest is not fully deductible.

Proceed cautiously if you are thinking of using a home-equity loan for investing. Ask yourself: Is the deal worth risking your house? Unless you are anticipating an exceptionally large return, the answer is probably no. Even if you are putting the money into an ultrasafe investment such as Treasury bills, financial planner Charles Hughes of Bay Shore, New York, figures your net after-tax return needs to be 115% more than the net cost of the loan for the deal to make economic sense. If you are in the 30% bracket and the net cost of a 9% home-equity loan is 6.3%, you would need to earn at least 7.25% on your investments.

Family Matters

One of the most vexing issues confronting today's families is the decision about how much life insurance they really need and how to find the most cost-effective means of obtaining that coverage. These are vital questions for anyone with dependents, yet all too many of us come up with the wrong answers. On average, according to one unbiased study, married men need about twice as much insurance as they have, and married women require about three times as much. Adequately insured or not, Americans have a tendency to overpay for their protection. More than half of all parents with insurance on their own lives also buy policies for their children—almost always unnecessarily.

Compounding the complexities of your family's coverage is the fact that life insurance is no longer a straightforward contract that provides your dependents with financial protection against your untimely death. Inspired by the crackdown on the most abusive tax shelters and enflamed by tax reform, insurance companies are cranking out new types of policies that, in some cases, have so many investment-related options that you need a stockbroker's license to sell them. The result is an array of enticing, all-purpose instruments encompassing a death benefit, a high-yield or growth investment, and a source of instant cash.

These new policies, which are detailed in "Should Your Life Insurance Double as an Investment?" and "Your Life as a Tax Shelter," give you tax-deferred gains and tax-free access to your policy's earnings. You can save or invest for a purpose such as a college fund for your children and, at the same time, create a handsome instant estate in case you die before they enroll. But if you do not look hard at the numbers behind your salesman's spiel—examples of which are scrutinized in "Wicked New Spins on Old Sales Pitches"—you could get smacked with sales charges heavy enough to slow the growth of your insurance fund to a ponderous crawl.

Insurance agents can walk you through tables and formulas designed to help you determine your family's coverage requirements. But you can do your own calculations using the worksheet "Figuring Out How Much Life Insurance You Need." In addition to tallying your family's living expenses, you will have to estimate the total cost of your children's college education. That sum recently averaged about $24,000 per graduate for public schools and $42,000 for private ones, and is sure to rise significantly over time. Do not assume that your survivors can invest the entire proceeds of your insurance and live off the income. Few people can afford that much insurance. Realistic planning, based on the gradual use of the principal, will allow you to provide for your family without depleting your resources.

Should Your Life Insurance Double as an Investment?

Even stockbrokers are pitching new policies.

Not since federal revenuers torched the three-for-one write-off promised by some tax-sheltering limited partnerships has any type of security been marketed as zestfully as life insurance is now. Some of the new policies so closely resemble an account for trading stocks and bonds that you need a broker's license to sell them.

Insurance that doubles as an investment comes under such generic names as whole life, variable life, universal life, flexible-premium variable life, and single-premium life. The policy most heavily promoted by brokers is single premium, but in all forms the new insurance got a tremendous lift in 1987 from the twin forces of a rousing stock market and a confusing tax code. Now that most other shelters have either been eliminated or sharply re-stricted, the insurance lobby's successful campaign in 1986 to preserve the tax breaks on insurance policies has made investing in them one of the few ways left to protect your stock market gains from immediate taxation.

But do not let the bells and whistles distract you from the risks of mixing family protection with the vagaries of the stock and bond markets. Despite the investment wrapping in which policies are now advertised, you should not forget that making certain your survivors will not suffer financially after your death still remains the most compelling reason to buy life insurance.

Buying it unhitched from investments is still one of your options. You can get pure protection in a term policy, which pays off if you die but not if you live. Because you are buying only protection against death, term insurance generally costs far less than any policy that builds cash value. Nevertheless, term policies have been losing sales in recent years to plans that offer tax-sheltered savings.

Single-premium variable life thus far has been sold primarily by stockbrokers, not insurance agents. But brokers, being more familiar with the investment aspect than with the insurance side of the deal, may be ill-equipped to advise you whether the policy will adequately fill your family's insurance needs. Worse, they may not warn you that the policy loans being ballyhooed as a benefit will come out of your survivors' pockets if you die with a big balance due. In either case, a broker as insurance salesman could aggravate the most common life insurance problem facing families: insufficient coverage.

The big push on investment-oriented insurance comes at a time when U.S. households would benefit most from professional guidance in buying policies primarily, if not exclusively, for survivor benefits. As the number of two-income and female-headed households grows, women are increasingly buying separate coverage. In 1975 men purchased twice as many life insurance policies as women. By 1985 the ratio had narrowed to 1.6 to 1. But the most pertinent demographic force in life insurance is the baby boomlet. The populous generation born between 1946 and 1964 has entered its prime child-rearing years, when insurance is most important. This generation now accounts for about half of all life insurance purchases, a percentage that will inevitably rise over the next decade.

It adds up to this: planning your insurance program, never a simple task, has become even more daunting. You must look at your policy as a document that requires periodic review, much as you would monitor your Individual Retirement Account, to make sure you are always getting the most for your money.

Your Life as a Tax Shelter

Cash-value life insurance policies will cut your IRS bill if you are patient and can pay for the privilege.

Tax reform has made your own life one of the better shelters around. If you are underinsured, a policy that doubles as an investment can be a splendid way to provide for your dependents, save for some future expense, and get tax benefits along the way. But now, even if you own enough insurance to protect your family in case you die, you may be tempted to buy a cash-value policy. And perhaps you should, if you are sitting on a pile of cash. In that case the only type of additional coverage you should consider buying is single-premium whole life or single-premium variable life for their roomy shelters.

The cash value in a policy is a growing pool of money that belongs to you. It is there because the premiums you pay in this type of contract are higher than necessary to cover the risk of your death. Whereas term insurance premiums cover only a death benefit, cash-value insurance is priced higher so that each year there is an increasing surplus. That extra capital is then invested by the insurer according to the type of policy or your own wishes.

In a financial crisis you can retrieve your cash value and give up the policy. But you can also borrow from it at low interest. And although the tax deduction on interest is phasing out, if you do borrow, you are not required to repay the loan. (If you die, however, the balance due comes out of the death benefit.) Some policies even let you withdraw part of your cash value interest-free.

The tax breaks from this type of insurance are hardly new. Ever since the modern income tax began in 1913, cash-value forms of insurance have been tax favored because Congress has always viewed insurance as a way citizens can provide for one another without drawing on public funds. Policyholders were granted three inviting loopholes:
● The earnings on your cash value grow tax deferred.
● You can borrow earnings from your policy tax-free.
● If you do not cash in your insurance, your beneficiary will get the policy's proceeds free of federal income taxes when you die.

These tax advantages do not come cheap, however. As a rule, a cash-value policy will give you a decent investment return only after you have held it for at least 10 years. It takes that long for your investment income to exceed the commissions and fees deducted by the insurer. Further, your investment choices are limited. At most, you can choose from only a few mutual-fund-like bond and stock portfolios for the savings portion of your premium. More typically, the insurance company makes all the decisions for you.

It is also tough to tap a cash-value policy in the early years. Although you can borrow from a policy or cash it in, you cannot generally take out as much money as you have put in until you have owned the policy for a considerable period. The major exceptions, single-premium policies, do offer a large amount of immediate cash value but are likely to levy a surrender charge if you cancel them in the first five to ten years.

What is more, the borrowing privilege is a tax break that could backfire. The tax-free status of policy loans, especially those on single-premium life, is so large a loophole that a deficit-dogged Congress might be forced to close it. Even if this tax deal continues, you risk a nasty consequence by borrowing heavily without repaying the loans. If drained of most of its cash value, your policy could lapse—that is, be canceled. Then the Internal Revenue Service will sock you with a mammoth tax bill on the unpaid loans on the ground that they are investment income.

As long as you understand its limitations, however, cash-value insurance can serve you well as a tax-favored vehicle. The next question is which type to buy, and that depends on what you want from your policy. Use the following profiles of the cash-value alternatives—whole life, universal life, and variable life—to help you determine which types are most appropriate for you.

Whole Life

This classic policy still makes sense for those who can afford the premium, need the discipline of enforced savings, and will not need to cash in the policy for at least 15 years.

Death benefit: a fixed amount that you choose when buying the policy.

Premium: a fixed amount paid monthly, quarterly, or annually.

Investment choices: none.

Rate of return on cash value: not disclosed. A guaranteed cash value accumulates, growing each year to a new level stated in the original contract.

Access to cash value: policy loans generally at fixed-interest rates of 6% to 8% or variable rates, lately around 8.5%.

In sum, whole life removes many of the uncertainties of an insurance contract, but the guarantees inflate the premium. The annual outlay for a 35-year-old man needing $200,000 of insurance might be $2,500 for whole life versus $275 for the same amount of term. The price of term insurance increases yearly, however, while whole life's never changes.

Letting the insurer decide how to invest your premiums safely can be comforting. But expect to wait about 15 years before your cash value, including any dividends, revs up to full throttle. The insurer never delineates how much of your premium goes to pay for insurance or what rate of return your cash value is earning. Your premiums are invested conservatively in long-term government and corporate bonds, mortgages, and blue-chip stocks.

One drawback of whole life is the sales charge. Your friendly agent usually pockets between 50% and 100% of the first year's premium. With so much of your initial investment drained away, many policies have a negative return for a year or two. On the other hand, most whole life contracts pay yearly dividends, which in effect lower your cost. These so-called participating policies charge higher premiums, but their dividends (which can be taken in cash, premium reductions, or additional paid-up insurance) make them cheaper in the long run than nonparticipating policies.

One way to shop for whole life is to check out the consistency of an insurer's annual payouts. If an agent will not divulge his company's dividend history, think twice before signing up with him. For a listing of whole life policies and their dividend records, get the December 1987 issue of *Best's Review* magazine, found in most large libraries. The most useful figures appear in the column headed interest-adjusted surrender cost index, which compares policy performances over the past 20 years. Highest marks went to Northwestern Mutual Life, Union Mutual Life, and Central Life of Iowa.

Single-Premium Whole Life

If you need little or no insurance but could use a tax shelter, take a hard look at single-premium whole life.

Death benefit: a fixed amount that you choose when buying the policy.

Premium: one lump-sum payment of $5,000 to $1 million.

Investment choices: none.

Rate of return on cash value: 4% generally guaranteed, above that variable. The rate usually changes every one to three years and lately has been about 8% before commissions, fees, and the cost of insurance are taken out.

Access to cash value: policy loans generally at 2% to 4% net interest on your original investment and free of charge on your own earnings. Interest is not tax deductible.

Under most circumstances it is foolish to pay for insurance in a lump sum up front. If you die shortly thereafter, much of what your beneficiaries get will be your own money. But the appeal of single-premium whole life is its enormous potential as a tax shelter. In catering to the demand, the 100 or so companies now selling single-premium whole life contracts try to keep the guaranteed death benefit to the legal minimum. For example, a 60-year-old who pays a $10,000 single premium might get a mere $30,000 of insurance.

Clearly, you should not invest in single-premium life for the short term. Cashing in early costs you part of your premium—usually 9% of it the first year and one percentage point less each year after that. And since it takes some years to accumulate earnings that you can borrow, you also dilute one of your key advantages: the right to tap those earnings as tax-free loans at no net interest cost.

Also, if you borrow from a single-premium policy routinely, you could owe income taxes. Borrowing annually for, say, college tuition could prompt the IRS to assert that you are withdrawing taxable earnings. To thwart such a ruling, borrow a slightly different amount each year and make at least token repayments.

If you expect to take advantage of the loan privilege, buy only a policy that guarantees a zero net interest rate on your earnings and a maximum rate of 2% or less on your original premium. Avoid any policy whose surrender charges—the service fees levied for exercising loan privileges or cancelling the policy—extend longer than seven years. Some of the best single-premium policies, according to analysts, are sold by Equitable of New York, Fidelity Bankers Life, and Life of Virginia.

Universal Life

If you want cash-value insurance with a spacious tax shelter but cannot put in a whole lot of money up front, this is probably the policy you should consider first.

Death benefit: variable. You choose a fixed amount when buying the policy and you can raise or lower it annually.

Premium: a fixed or variable amount paid monthly, quarterly, or annually. You can increase or reduce it from time to time and even skip a year occasionally if you are in a bind.

Investment choices: none.

Rate of return on cash value: 4% generally guaranteed, above that variable. Rates change from day to day and recently have ranged from 6% to 11% before commissions, fees, and the cost of insurance are taken out.

Access to cash value: partial withdrawals at a $25 fee; policy loans generally at 6% to 8%.

Universal life offers you more bang for your premium bucks. You often pay about a third less than for a whole life policy with the same death benefit. Universal also provides more flexibility than whole life, allowing you to vary your premiums, coverage, and investments. Furthermore, the insurer informs you of the current rate of return on your cash value, before expenses, and how much of your premium is paying for company costs. But if you fail to pay enough in premiums to cover mortality charges, the insurer will take what is needed by dipping into your cash value.

Some universal life policies do allow the option of paying exactly the same premiums every year. Insurers say that such a commitment on your part helps them boost the yield on your cash value because they know in advance the amount of their investable capital. Decline the offer nonetheless. Giving up a little yield is a fair price to pay to retain the flexibility that is this policy's main appeal.

Some of the best buys in universal life are no-load policies, which cost you no agents' commissions, and policies with comparatively low loads of 1% to 10%. Recommended low-loads include those sold by American Life of New York, Bankers Life of Nebraska, and Lincoln Benefit Life; a no-load sold through the mail by USAA Life is available to the military and their dependents. No-load insurance means you and your dependents will never be able to talk to an agent face to face with questions about the policy. Some purchasers, of course, see this as a plus.

Variable Life

If you need protection and are willing to take investment risks with your insurance in hopes of a potentially larger cash value and death benefit, this could be the answer.

Death benefit: an amount that you choose when buying the policy. It can increase if your investments do well.

Premium: a fixed amount paid monthly, quarterly, or annually.

Investment choices: stock, bond, and money-market portfolios. You can switch among them by writing to the insurer.

Rate of return on cash value: none guaranteed. The rate fluctuates with investment performance.

Access to cash value: policy loans generally at 6% to 8%.

This type of insurance lets you invest your premiums in portfolios resembling mutual funds. If they do well, you can accumulate a substantial sum. If your investments bomb, your cash value will be less than in whole life. Your beneficiary will still get the original death benefit, but as Indiana University insurance professor Joseph Belth points out, if you invest in a variable life policy, your beneficiary's best hope is that you will "die on an uptick."

Variable life investment portfolios bear such a striking resemblance to mutual funds that a few have begun to appear in the Lipper Analytical Services monthly ranking of fund performance, available in most brokerage offices. One stellar performer, the New England's Zenith Capital Growth Fund, topped the Lipper list in 1986 with a total return of 95%. But some of that appreciation was swallowed in fees larger than those of even the most expensive load funds.

When a 40-year-old man makes $1,000 annual premium payments to buy Zenith, about 35% goes to pay commissions and other expenses in the first year. The load then eases a bit, to 18% in years two through four and 15% after that. (Of course, unlike a mutual fund, insurance protection is included.) Thus, after fees are subtracted, Zenith's results are less sensational. James Hunt, a director of the National Insurance Consumer Organization

(NICO), figures that if Zenith earns an average annual rate of 12% before expenses are deducted, its actual return to policyholders will be 6% annually in 10 years and 8.7% in 20 years. You can get a similar analysis of any cash-value policy from NICO for $25.

Assess a variable life policy's investment portfolios as you would a mutual fund, by looking at the long-term past performances shown in the prospectus. Unfortunately, you are at some disadvantage here because variable life is so new. At most companies, three years is considered a long track record. It is too early to tell how a prolonged down market will test the managers' investment footwork.

A bond portfolio is available but is not advisable for variable life policyholders. If you cancel the policy after interest rates rise, you could lose part of your principal. Whole life and universal life also invest in bonds but guarantee your principal.

Lipper so far ranks only two stock and two bond variable life portfolios with three-year records, all from Monarch/Merrill Lynch. From 1984 through 1986, the Capital Stock fund was up 69% and Growth Stock fund was up 60%. The Standard & Poor's 500-stock index rose 66% during that period.

Single-Premium Variable Life

This is the policy for the patient high roller in search of a tax-sheltered investment with a bit of insurance protection thrown in.

Death benefit: an amount that you choose when buying the policy. It can increase if your investments do well.

Premium: one lump-sum payment of $5,000 to $1 million.

Investment choices: stock, bond, and money-market portfolios. You can switch among them by writing to the insurer.

Rate of return on cash value: none guaranteed. The rate fluctuates with your investment performance.

Access to cash value: policy loans generally free of charge on earnings and 2% to 4% on your single premium. Interest is not tax deductible.

Single-premium variable life is sometimes likened to a gigantic Individual Retirement Account. The analogy is valid in more ways than one. Because much of your premium will normally get gobbled up by expenses over 10 years, this is definitely an investment for the long haul. Unless you are really strapped, do not borrow much from your cash value while it is invested in a stock portfolio. In a hot market, you would deprive yourself of big gains on the borrowed money; the most the insurer will credit to you is a return equal to your loan interest.

Some single-premium variable life policies worth considering, according to insurance analysts, are those sold by Guardian Life, Monarch Life, and Provident Mutual Life.

Flexible-Premium Variable Life

If you need family protection and desire both payment and investment flexibility, this type of policy (also called universal life II) is the ticket.

Death benefit: an amount that you choose when buying the policy. It can increase if your investments do well.

Premium: a fixed or variable amount paid monthly, quarterly, or annually. You can increase or reduce it from time to time and even skip a year occasionally.

Investment choices: stock, bond, and money-market portfolios. You can switch among them by writing to the insurer.

Rate of return on cash value: not guaranteed. The rate fluctuates with your investment performance.

Access to cash value: policy loans generally at 6% to 8%.

After universal variable life has been around a few more years, it could prove to be an excellent cash-value policy. First sold in 1985, it blends the best features of regular universal life and variable life: flexibility of payments, coverage, and investment choice. But the insurance is so new and the investment record of its portfolios so short that no policy can possibly stand out yet purely as an investment. The only identifiable universal life stock portfolio as yet followed by Lipper for a full year is Equitable Hudson River Common Stock, which in 1986 underperformed the S&P 17.3% to 18.7%.

A final word of advice. In picking any type of cash-value policy, limit yourself to financially strong insurers. A solid company is one that has had an A+ rating for 10 years from Best's, the independent rating service whose annual yearbook, *Best's Insurance Reports*, is on many libraries' reference shelves. For $2, you can get the issue of the newsletter *Insurance Forum* that lists the 113 companies meeting this test. You can widen your sights, however, without taking much extra risk by also looking at insurers rated A by Best's.

Money Sources

Members of the military services can buy insurance through USAA Brokerage Services, P.O. Box 33277, San Antonio, TX 78265. Or call 800-531-8000.

For analyses of cash-value policies, write to National Insurance Consumer Organization, 121 N. Payne Street, Alexandria, VA 22314.

For a copy of *Insurance Forum*, send $2 to P.O. Box 245, Ellettsville, IN 47429.

It Is Still Life Insurance, After All

What most families require is ample protection at low cost.

While tax advantages and investment opportunities add glitter to life insurance, most people still buy it for one simple reason—to protect the financial well-being of their dependents. Children come first. With the number of births in the United States increasing since 1983, an ever-rising number of American families face ballooning insurance needs on limited budgets.

Two-career couples also have to revamp their thinking. In the days when most families relied on one income, only the husband needed to be covered. Now more than half of all mothers with children under age 18 are working for pay. When both parents are breadwinners, both should be insured.

The primary goal of the life insurance buyer sounds elementary: securing all the protection you require at the lowest possible cost. But your choices have never been more complicated. To cut through that confusion and pin-

point your family's solution, begin with a survey of your finances using the worksheet on pages 126-27. Then, having determined the amount of necessary coverage, you can pick the type of policy that suits your pocketbook. Building savings tax-free is for most just a frill. Term insurance, a contract with no investment value, often provides the bare-bones coverage you need without prohibitive costs.

A well-designed insurance plan like the one in the worksheet will allow your family to live comfortably if you die before your children have left the nest. But it will not make them better off than they are now. Do not commit the error of trying to soothe emotional losses with a luxury-level death benefit. Rather than pouring money into an extravagant policy, aim for coverage that will maintain your current standard of living. Invest any surplus funds with the aim of enhancing a long life, a far more likely scenario than an early grave. The first step in judging how much insurance you need is to hold a frank discussion with your family. The agenda should include such hypothetical issues as whether a surviving parent would work or stay home with the children and for how long; how expensive a college, if any, your insurance should provide for; and whether you want to buy extra coverage to pay off the mortgage.

How Much Do You Need?

It is an axiom of insurance planning that your policies should be large enough to cover your family's economic needs if you were to die tomorrow. So you should evaluate your coverage every two years to keep it up to date—and take an extra look whenever there is a dramatic change in your situation. Getting a big raise or having another baby, for example, can boost your insurance needs significantly.

In addition to providing for long-term income, your life insurance can smooth out more immediate financial snags. The payoff from insurance does not go through probate, which can tie up an estate for at least four months. The beneficiary of your policy has only to send it, along with a death certificate, to the insurer's claims department. Within a month a check will arrive for the face value of the policy—in time to ease your family through a cash pinch.

If you do not have financial dependents, you probably do not need life insurance for its own sake. But if you have a substantial interest in a closely held company, consider whether the business would suffer financially without you. An insurance policy would allow colleagues to buy your share from your heirs without draining the business of cash.

Life insurance agents may use a series of calculations at least as thorough as those in our worksheet, but agents are not necessarily disinterested parties. Many agents suggest you follow simple formulas—a common one is that your death benefit should equal five times your gross income. But such rules of thumb mean little because they do not take into ac-

count the unique circumstances and concerns of your family.

Some agents and financial planners advise buying enough insurance so that your family can invest the death benefit and live off the income from it. That is too grandiose a plan for most purses. Instead, the worksheet assumes that your family will invest most of the insurance proceeds and gradually spend both income and capital. Do not overlook the fact that your spouse and dependent children would probably be eligible for Social Security after your death. So-called survivor benefits can cut your insurance needs substantially. Glance down the columns in Table A of the worksheet. A person with three young children who dies at age 45 with a salary over $40,000 and full Social Security coverage can count on more than $18,000 a year in benefits going to his or her family for several years.

Coverage at your office may also reduce the insurance you need to buy on your own. But do not fall into complacency just because your employer provides a generous insurance package. A company benefit of $40,000 in group life insurance, along with $10,000 in policies that you purchase on your own may sound adequate—until you realize that your situation calls for $250,000.

Which Kind Is Best?

That amount of coverage is sure to be expensive if you buy the whole life and universal life policies that most salespeople plug. At age 30, for example, a man who is healthy and does not smoke would generally pay around $2,650 a year for whole life from a solid, efficient company. The premium for a woman under the same conditions is about $2,500. Your agent may not volunteer that the same protection is available for only a fraction of the cost. A yearly renewable term insurance policy with a $250,000 death benefit costs about $435 for the man and $405 for the woman. Though the term premium ratchets up every year, as your children mature your insurance obligations drop. In 20 to 25 years, you may not need any coverage for their sake.

Figuring Out How Much Life Insurance You Need

This exercise aims to nail down how much insurance you need while your children are growing up. It does not include the much larger sums required to finance a surviving spouse's later life or retirement. The presumption these days is that he or she could take care of that. But families with lifelong dependents—a handicapped child, for example—should ask a financial planner for help in their calculations.

Most of the lines on the worksheet explain themselves. Here is some coaching for those that do not:

Line 1. In two-paycheck households, lump together both after-tax incomes. Payroll deductions for retirement funds and health insurance count as take-home pay; life insurance deductions do not.

Line 2. People usually spend a third of their income on themselves. You may want to figure more or less than that.

Line 6. In totaling your present assets, do not forget Individual Retirement Accounts, company savings plans, and survivor's benefits from your pension fund.

Lines 7 and 8. Consider here whether your spouse, if she or he is now working, would wish to stay home with the children for a year or two if you die. Then subtract that year or two from the number on line 4. If your spouse would choose not to work for several years, do not count on any take-home pay. Enter 0 on line 7.

Line 10. Social Security survivor benefits can become a major source of income. Table A, at right, indicates the annual amounts currently paid to a non-working spouse and children and the maximum available per family. Benefits decline swiftly for a working spouse earning more than $6,000 a year. Children will continue collecting until they graduate from high school or turn 19,

1. Current total family take-home pay $_____
2. One-third of your own take-home pay $_____
3. Annual family expenses without you (line 1 minus line 2) $_____
4. Number of years until your youngest child finishes high school x_____
5. Total family expenses (line 3 times line 4) $_____
6. Savings and investments $_____
7. Spouse's annual take-home pay $_____
8. Number of years of that income x_____
9. Total spouse contribution (line 7 times line 8) $_____
10. Total Social Security benefits $_____
11. Total assets and income (add lines 6, 9, and 10) $_____
12. Total income deficit (line 5 minus line 11) $_____
13. Average annual income deficit (line 12 divided by line 4) $_____
14. Lump sum that, if invested, would provide the amount on line 13 for the number of years on line 4 (factor from Table B times $1,000) $_____
15. College costs per child $_____
16. Number of college-bound children x_____
17. Total college costs (line 15 times line 16) $_____
18. Funeral and estate costs $_____
19. Lump sum for a mortgage or emergency fund (optional) $_____
20. Total lump sum needed at death (add lines 14, 17, 18, and 19) $_____
21. Present life insurance coverage $_____
22. Total insurance needed (line 20 minus line 21) (if negative, you have more than you need) $_____

Table A: Social Security benefits. Here are estimates of annual survivor payments for your spouse and children.

WORKER'S PRESENT AGE		WORKER'S 1986 INCOME		
		$20,000	$30,000	OVER $40,000
25	Benefit per survivor	$6,312	$7,764	$9,060
	Maximum family benefit	14,940	18,132	21,132
35	Benefit per survivor	6,228	7,716	8,724
	Maximum family benefit	14,795	18,000	20,352
45	Benefit per survivor	6,216	7,488	7,944
	Maximum family benefit	14,772	17,484	18,528
55	Benefit per survivor	6,216	7,224	7,572
	Maximum family benefit	14,760	16,872	17,544
65	Benefit per survivor	5,868	6,804	7,092
	Maximum family benefit	13,908	15,888	16,560

Source: Social Security Administration

Table B: Lump-sum factors. Here are the amounts needed to replace income (multiply by $1,000).

DOLLAR AMOUNT (FROM LINE 13)	NUMBER OF YEARS (FROM LINE 4)								
	5	7	9	11	13	15	16	17	18
$5,000	24	33	41	49	57	65	72	79	85
10,000	48	65	82	98	114	129	143	157	170
15,000	71	98	123	147	170	193	214	235	255
20,000	95	130	164	196	227	257	286	313	340
25,000	118	163	205	245	284	321	357	391	425
30,000	142	195	245	294	340	385	428	469	510
35,000	166	227	286	343	397	449	500	548	594
40,000	189	260	327	391	454	513	571	626	679
45,000	213	292	368	440	510	578	642	704	764
50,000	236	325	408	489	567	642	713	782	849
55,000	260	357	449	538	624	706	785	860	934
60,000	283	390	490	587	680	770	856	938	1,019
65,000	307	422	531	636	737	834	927	1,016	1,104
70,000	331	454	571	685	794	898	999	1,095	1,188
75,000	354	487	612	734	850	962	1,070	1,173	1,273

whichever comes first. A spouse's benefits expire after the youngest child reaches age 16. Estimate your total benefits by counting the years of maximum and lesser benefits at your income level in the table. Multiply the benefits by the number of years you would collect them and add the results. (For further help, call your local Social Security office or write to the Social Security Administration, Office of Public Inquiries, Baltimore, MD 21235.)

Line 14. The average annual income deficit resulting from your death (line 13) overstates what your family would need unless you adjust the amount for investment income. Much of the lump sum you are calculating could earn interest or dividends for several years before the whole amount is spent. The number shown in Table B, at left, most nearly corresponding to your annual deficit and the years your family would need income (line 4) is a factor that, when multiplied by $1,000, approximates the lump sum needed. It is based on the conservative assumption that after taxes and inflation the fund would earn a 2% return.

Line 15. Enter an amount here if you want your insurance to finance the college education of your child or children. Four years at a private college, including room and board, now costs an average of $40,100, and public colleges average $22,416. For children at least five years away from college, those amounts should be adjusted now for inflation. Assuming 5% annual increases, raise them to $52,000 and $28,600—and in five years review them against actual costs.

Line 18. Funeral and estate costs, including the settlement of debts, generally amount to one year's take-home pay.

Line 19. If you wish, you can provide money that your family could use to pay off the mortgage or keep for emergencies.

Line 21. Take into account any coverage you already have from your employer as well as your own policies.

As the life cycle rolls on, retirement ends most remaining financial responsibilities. Your own income stops, leaving you to enjoy the fruits of your labors: Social Security, perhaps a company pension, and a lifetime of savings and investments. While you and your spouse may be a fiscal unit, he or she will presumably inherit most of your assets, leaving little need for insurance. The only reason to pay for coverage in that case is to give your estate some liquidity or to leave money to a charity. Otherwise, if you are so inclined, you can get yourself one of those bumper stickers that says: "We're spending our children's inheritance."

Besides, at retirement age any insurance will be expensive. Term insurance premiums skyrocket when you pass 65. A $250,000 policy that cost $435 at age 30 may well run $10,000 at age 70. Nevertheless, you can build a safeguard into your term coverage when you first buy it by choosing a policy that lets you convert some part of it to whole life at least until age 60 without having to pass a new physical. Almost all annual renewable term policies are convertible, and so are most group insurance plans when you leave your job or retire. If you still need coverage in your retirement, say for liquidity, you can convert perhaps $25,000 of your term to whole life and drop the rest.

Many insurance agents will try to discourage you from buying term because such a policy pays comparatively low commissions. Given the same face amount, the agents can make five to ten times as much selling whole life or universal than they can selling term. An agent or financial planner may tell you that term premiums are wasted because you have nothing left after paying premiums for many years. But the money you save on term premiums is hardly wasted because you can spend it on something else or invest it.

Cash-value policies may make sense for those who can afford them. Just do not skimp on the death protection because you are hungry for tax-deferred savings. You should first explore other tax-free savings accounts such as a 401(k) at your job and an Individual Retirement Account (even if you can no longer deduct your contribution) before you plunk down the money for a cash-value policy.

Shop for the Best Deal

Now that you have nailed down how much and what kind of insurance you need, it is time to go comparison shopping. You can save hundreds or thousands of dollars over the years by insuring with a low-cost company, but first make sure it is financially secure. A bargain policy is no bargain if the company behind it is shaky. So avoid any insurer with a rating of less than A from A.M. Best & Company.

Your final cut will be made on the basis of cost, a task that sounds simpler than is the case. You must grapple with a host of variables: how much the premiums rise in a term policy; how fast the cash value will grow in whole life; what, if any, dividends the company will pay; and how much of your premium will be consumed by commissions and expenses. Given the endless permutations, you cannot just compare premiums or be swayed by agents' price illustrations. Most companies write a dozen or more basic policies and several riders, or optional clauses, that may be added to nearly all the basic policies.

To help you comparison shop, the National Association of Insurance Commissioners has adopted two cost indexes. Prudential, for example, was recently offering a $100,000 annual renewable term policy for a 35-year-old nonsmoking man with a 10-year net payment cost index of 2.31. A comparable policy from USAA, a well-regarded company that markets to the military and their dependents by mail, came in at 1.55, making it much the cheaper policy.

The shortcoming of the indexes is that they tell you which of two policies is cheaper, but they do not help you determine whether both are overpriced. To help you judge whether a policy is providing the insurance you need at a competitive price, the National Insurance Consumer Organization recommends getting premiums and cost indexes for a policy of the size you need and for a person your age from USAA. You can then use that figure as a benchmark for comparison.

It is much trickier to assess the true cost of a cash-value policy because it has more variables than term. These include the rate at which the cash value increases and the flow of any dividends, which are annual refunds of excess premiums. (Dividends are a much greater cost factor in whole life than in term.) NICO will estimate for you the rate of return on a whole life policy by comparing it to an annual renewable term policy that provides the same death benefit. You have to furnish a printout that your agent can provide, illustrating the costs of the policy year by year. NICO's fee for an estimate is $25 for one policy and $20 for each additional policy that you send in the same envelope.

Discounts for so-called preferred risks can save you a bundle on premiums. Nonsmokers frequently pay 10% to 15% less than smokers, according to the American Council on Life Insurance. If you are physically fit and a non-smoker from a family free of chronic diseases, ask about discounts that run 15% to 20%. Women have longer life expectancies than men and therefore pay premiums that are typically 5% to 10% lower.

Finally, your agent may suggest a variety of riders that will boost your costs for little value. A guaranteed insurability rider lets you buy more coverage at specified times of your life without a physical. But most such riders cancel

the guarantee if you skip one increase. An accidental death benefit rider doubles your coverage if you are killed in an accident. But accidental deaths do not increase your insurance needs, and the gamble rarely pays off. Only 3% of all deaths occur in accidents.

Money Sources

To get a list of the maximum rates that the National Insurance Consumer Organization recommends for annual renewable term policies, write for the booklet *Taking the Bite Out of Insurance*, 121 N. Payne Street, Alexandria, VA 22314. The cost is $8.25.

One way to make price checking easier is to pay someone to do it for you. A firm called Insurance Information Inc. (800-472-5800) will send you the names, prices, and A.M. Best ratings of the five cheapest term policies it can find for a person of your age, sex, place of residence, and smoking habits. Be sure to specify the size of the policy you want. The fee is $50.

Wicked New Spins on Old Sales Pitches

Be prepared to face some sharp new twists.

Life insurance agents, financial planners, and stockbrokers are all pushing the presumed extra tax benefits of their life insurance policies now. Since their pitches may sound persuasive, here is a scouting report to help you handle their fresh deliveries (in italics), as well as the trickiest twirls of yore.

The Tax Reform Fastball

You should buy life insurance because of the new code—regardless of whether your taxes rise or fall.

In the trade magazine *Life Insurance Selling*, a vice president of Liberty Life in Greenville, South Carolina, advised agents: "If the prospect will owe more taxes, then he needs to save taxes. If the prospect will owe less taxes, then he must use the money to work toward financial security goals and other needs." His solution is the same for both cases: buy more life insurance. The response to that contorted view is simple: increase your coverage only if you need more.

The Free-Insurance Slider

This policy is a great investment, and we throw in the insurance for free.

Fat chance. You may not see an explicit charge for insurance when you buy a single-premium whole life policy. But to cover that protection—as well as a profit margin—about 2% of the yield is deducted from the earnings paid on your cash value account.

The Interest-Rate Floater

You can earn double-digit interest on your tax-sheltered cash value.

Policies on which an agent can quote a rate of return usually guarantee that rate for one year at most and often for a mere month. Today's enticing interest rate could soon be switched to a lower one. Some insurers also quote artificially inflated gross rates, not telling you that sales charges and expenses will come out of your interest. Before comparing proposals, eliminate companies now promising interest rates higher than recent market rates on Treasury and quality corporate bonds. An insurer can sustain such a figure only by taking bigger investment risks than the competition or by playing accounting games.

The Tax-Free Knuckler

You can borrow against your single-premium policy's cash value at 7% interest, and my company will credit your policy with the same 7%. Your net cost is zero, and the income you receive will be free of federal taxes.

This pitch catches a lot of customers looking. What agents may neglect to add is that if you unwittingly borrow the bulk of the cash value, your policy may lapse. Then you will owe income tax on the difference between what you paid over the years and what you borrowed. Some insurance companies warn policyholders about their borrowings, but others do not. So you cannot depend on being warned that you are too deep in debt. Furthermore, Congress may soon eliminate or restrict this tax break.

The Municipal Bond Change-Up

Sell your tax-exempt municipal bonds and use the proceeds to buy single-premium whole life.

An article in *Broker World* arms agents with the argument that insurance is superior to municipal bonds because a single-premium policy lets you automatically reinvest earnings while a muni bond's coupons must be redeployed elsewhere. Apparently the insurance industry has never heard of municipal bond mutual funds, which also allow you to reinvest dividends automatically.

The Term Sinker

Buying term is like renting your house, while buying whole life is like owning it.

Many salesmen have for years scorned term insurance because it does not offer the cash-value savings feature of whole life (and because it pays a smaller commission). Author Andrew Tobias provided the perfect riposte in his book about the insurance business, *The Invisible Bankers*: "But when homes are overpriced and good rental units are available at cheap rates (with guaranteed renewable leases), it makes sense to rent."

The No-Risk Fork Ball

If what you want is peace of mind, I can assure you that our policies are risk-free.

The federal government does not insure or guarantee life policies as it does bank accounts. There are guaranty funds in 38 states, which pay claims and continue coverage when an insurer is declared insolvent. The other 12 states, including California, New Jersey, and Ohio, have no such backup funds. If your insurer goes belly up, you or your beneficiaries might not receive all your contracted benefits. For safety's sake, buy life insurance only from companies rated A or A+ for the past 10 to 15 years by A.M. Best & Company, an independent rating firm.

Taking the Pulse of Your Health Plan

Everyone needs a stopgap strategy to safeguard against rising medical costs and interruptions in coverage.

Most people's health insurance is tied to their job. But what if your company goes under or restructures, laying you off, among thousands of other employees? What if your family breaks up? What if you decide to go into business for yourself or retire early? And what will your children do when they outgrow your group coverage? Such events increase the numbers of Americans—35 million in 1985 versus 30 million three years earlier—who have no health insurance.

A sudden loss of coverage or drop in protection becomes an immediate threat to your family's financial well-being. A coronary bypass costs $25,000, a kidney transplant upwards of $75,000, including drug therapy. Thus the most important checkup you can have may be a self-examination of your insurance to make sure that you and your family have reliable coverage and to formulate a contingency plan in case you get separated from your present policy.

Replacing first-rate group coverage (as defined in the box on page 135) with an equally good individual policy can be difficult. In an attempt to make money in the market, leading insurers such as Prudential have reduced the benefits on their individual policies. New York Life, Lincoln National, and other big companies have gone a drastic step further by no longer writing individual plans at all. Aetna, Equitable, and Prudential have withdrawn from the market for individual coverage in the District of Columbia because they cannot require applicants there to take a test for the AIDS virus. California has also enacted legislation to ban testing, and at least half a dozen other states are considering such bans. So insurers may withdraw from those states as well. Insurers are also threatening to pull out of Massachusetts, South Carolina, and other states that have rejected premium increases. To put further pressure on state regulators, some companies are switching from plans that cannot be canceled to collectively renewable policies, which can be terminated by dropping all customers in any state where the policy is losing money.

Your coverage is best measured against what is offered in a comprehensive company group plan. Group members can generally choose between the traditional fee-for-service insurance and the fast-multiplying prepaid health maintenance organizations (HMOs). Under a typical fee-for-service plan you go to your own doctors, pay them, and file insurance claims. Your coverage usually divides into two parts: a basic plan that pays 100% of your hospital expenses and a major-medical plan that covers a high percentage of most other costs in and out of the hospital. You are responsible for paying the first $100 or so of costs under the major-medical plan—known as the deductible—and a portion on the rest, usually 20%. Your costs stop, as a rule, if they reach about $1,000 in any one year.

An HMO can be a single-clinic facility for everything but in-patient care, which is provided by a local hospital. More and more HMOs, however, are networks of private physicians practicing at their own offices. In either form, the HMO's prepaid yearly membership fee entitles you to nearly all the doctoring, hospitalization, and surgery you may need.

Those who must pay their own way will have to scour the market to match such group benefits in an individual policy. Nevertheless, shopping for as comprehensive a policy as possible is by no means futile. First, keep in mind five facts about health insurance.

• Your premiums will rise as you age and become more susceptible to major illness.

• How much you pay will depend on where you live. New Yorkers with Park Avenue zip codes, for example, are likely to pay twice as much for health care—and thus for insurance—as are residents of, say, Minneapolis.

• Women usually pay more than men. This has nothing to do with maternity, which in most states is an optional extra. Childbearing aside, women as a group see doctors more often than men do.

• A policy that is guaranteed renewable is well worth the 50% to 100% extra cost.

• Big deductibles offer big savings. Consider a policy with a deductible of at least $250 a year, which will be about 20% cheaper than one with a $100 deductible.

Beyond those rules, adjust your insurance shopping to the predicament you face: inadequate coverage on your job, interrupted coverage, or a desire to supplement Medicare.

If Coverage Is Inadequate

Whether you are self-employed or get little or no insurance from your employer, first look into association plans. The best of them come close to matching topnotch company plans. Association group insurance may be sponsored by your professional society, college alumni as-

sociation, labor union, or some other membership organization. Such plans are often 10% to 50% less expensive than individual policies—the difference shrinks as you age. Group plans are also easier to get into.

New York Life, Aetna, and a few other large companies are making group insurance accessible to more individuals by marketing them through easy-to-join consumer groups. Aetna, for example, has an agreement with the Alliance for Better Health, an independent organization that helps members control health-care costs. You can join the Alliance for $12 a year and immediately become eligible for AetnaCare Extra, a policy that covers all expenses in and out of the hospital. The insurer picks up 80% of your medical costs above a deductible that you can set at any of seven levels, from $100 to $10,000. Your share of total medical bills cannot exceed $1,000 a year as an individual or $3,000 for a family of four, but there is no limit on total benefits that you may receive over a lifetime.

There is a two-year waiting period before AetnaCare Extra covers illnesses you contracted before signing up. The policy is guaranteed renewable only in certain areas—Maryland, for one. For a plan with a $250 deductible, a man or woman in Baltimore, at age 23, would pay $717 a year. A couple that age with two children would pay $1,822. Add $725 for maternity benefits.

Another possibility is joining a health maintenance organization. About half of the nation's 750 HMOs, some operating as many as 45 clinics, accept individual applicants. The average annual cost is $900 for an individual and $2,472 for a family. While that up-front cost may be higher than the premium on a fee-for-service policy, your out-of-pocket expenses during the year will be next to nothing. All HMOs are not equal, however. Measure the benefits of plans in your area against the yardstick on page 135. Other options to consider include the following:

Small group policies. Many insurance companies will consider writing small group policies for business owners with at least one employee. Prudential actually has a "group" policy for one—a plan for a proprietor or professional who works alone. A single, 30-year-old man doing business in St. Louis, for example, would pay $578 a year for a Prudential plan that covers 80% of his expenses after a $500 deductible and limits his out-of-pocket costs to $1,000 a year. A plan for a family of four would run $2,251.

Individual major medical. Buy a comprehensive or major-medical plan that pays the cost of expensive hospital and medical care. Shop at independent insurance agents who represent several companies so you have a choice of policies. Local chapters of the National Association of Life Underwriters will supply names of reputable agents.

One of the best major-medical plans for individuals is offered by American Republic of Des Moines. After a $250 deductible, the policy covers 100% of your annual medical expenses, with a maximum of $1 million per illness. Cost in the Boston area: about $712 a year for a 35-year-old male nonsmoker and $1,086 for a female nonsmoker, including maternity benefits. Add $72 to $120 if you smoke. A family plan averages $1,480. The policy is guaranteed renewable.

If you are covered by a group but inadequately so—say you have a $25,000 lifetime limit—you can buy what is known as a piggyback policy, a major-medical plan with a $25,000 deductible that will pick up where your group plan leaves off. Mutual of Omaha writes a piggyback policy that costs $742 a year for a family of four in suburban Chicago.

If Coverage Is Interrupted

You might fall into this category if you are laid off, recently divorced or widowed, or you have reached the age of ineligibility for your parents' group plan (usually 23). The options:

Group continuation. Under the Consolidated Omnibus Budget Reconciliation Act of 1985 (COBRA), the divorced spouse, widow, or widower of an employee, or an employee who quits or has been laid off through no fault of

his own, has a right to remain temporarily in the company's group plan. The coverage, which is paid for by the insured person, continues for 18 months if you leave your job and for 36 months for your family if you die or get divorced. This rule applies only to companies with 20 or more employees. Your premium: 2% more than the group rate, which averages $1,800 per employee nationwide.

If your benefits under COBRA run out before you get into a new group, you can convert the company plan to a much less adequate individual policy. The advantage of staying with the same insurer is that you remain covered for an illness you already have. Conversion policies have severe limitations, however: their maximum benefit may be as low as $25,000 a year, they generally exclude mental disorders, and the price is high for what you get. So if you are in good health, you would be well-advised to shop for a better deal such as an association plan or an HMO.

Stopgap individual plans. If a job offer is imminent, you can purchase a temporary major-medical policy. Most large health insurers offer short-term policies. Prudential, for example, has one spanning three or six months that provides unlimited reimbursements for the cost of treating any new illness or injury. A sample premium for a 35-year-old man in St. Louis: $183 for a three-month policy with a $200 deductible.

When Medicare Is Not Enough

Medicare, the Social Security program for people 65 and over, pays for only 60% of the average person's health care. Legislation that would vastly improve Medicare's protection— while more than doubling the premiums—has passed the House of Representatives and commands strong Senate backing. But the measure was still pending as of late 1987.

The current Medicare hospital plan, called Part A, covers continuous or intermittent hospitalizations for "benefit periods" of 90 days. During the first 60 days of each benefit period, Medicare pays all but $520 of the total cost.

During the remaining 30 days, it pays the costs above $130 a day. New 90-day benefit periods can begin after you have been out of the hospital for 60 days. Between benefit periods, you can fall back on a lifetime "reserve" of 60 days for which Medicare pays only your costs above $260 a day. Doctor bills, whether incurred in or out of the hospital, come under Medicare's optional Part B program, the cost of which, $214.80 a year, comes out of your monthly Social Security checks. The government dictates how much it will pay doctors for office visits, treatments, surgery, and all other procedures. Unless your doctor agrees to accept this amount, you must pay him the difference. But many "medigap" policies are available to pick up the slack.

Group coverage. Three-quarters of all workers over 65, whether active or retired, receive lifelong health-care benefits from their employers that fill most of the Medicare gaps. If your company does not extend your plan into retirement, perhaps your group plan can be converted to an individual medigap policy.

Individual medigap. Retirees with no company coverage face a bazaar of policies that are at best confusing and at worst useless. A policy worth its premium should cover most of the deductibles and your share of the costs under Medicare, as well as the important costs that Medicare does not cover. Be sure the policy you are considering is called "Medicare supplementary insurance," a name that insurers can use only for policies that meet or exceed federal minimum standards of coverage. As part of its $5-a-year membership fee, the American Association of Retired Persons offers three solid Prudential plans. One, called Medicare Supplement Plus, costs $311 a person annually and pays for most of what Medicare does not, including extended stays in a hospital or a "skilled nursing home" (one staffed with doctors and registered nurses), and foreign hospital and medical care. The supplement does not pay for custodial nursing homes, which are for patients who mainly need help with dressing, eating, and personal hygiene.

HMOs. Medicare recipients can trade their government benefits for HMO membership. Medicare pays all but, at most, $600 a year of the HMO fee. Another advantage of joining an HMO: you escape the onerous paperwork involved in filing Medicare claims.

Long-term care. A number of insurance plans are emerging to help cushion the devastating, previously uninsurable costs of care for patients with stroke, Alzheimer's disease, and other chronic disabilities. With the cost of a skilled nursing home averaging $23,725 a year, about two-thirds of all patients who start out paying their own bills are impoverished within a year.

A dozen companies, including Aetna, CNA, and Fireman's Fund, offer policies that pay as much as $120 a day toward the cost of a skilled or custodial-care nursing home. You buy these plans through independent agents. An Aetna policy that pays $100 a day for up to four years of nursing-home care and $50 a day for two years of home care would cost a 55-year-old policyholder $420 to $550 a year and a 65-year-old $770 to $1,240.

The Untouchables

What if you need insurance for a current illness but have no company plan to convert? Are AIDS victims and other high-risk patients, such as those with cancer or liver disease, doomed to die in total poverty? The options certainly are few: in a recent survey of health insurance companies, 91% said they consider an AIDS-infected applicant "uninsurable at any price."

Not so. Nearly half of all Blue Cross/Blue Shield organizations offer plans to anyone, including victims of AIDS, during open-enrollment periods. The coverage and cost vary by locality. In New York City, patients pay no deductible as long as they go to one of the plan's participating board-certified physicians. Hospitalization is limited to 120 days, and the premium is $1,980 a year for an individual and $3,089 for a family. Open enrollment usually lasts for one month a year. To get details, call the local Blue Cross.

For the totally uninsurable, 11 states have organized high-risk health insurance pools: Connecticut, Florida, Idaho, Illinois, Iowa, Montana, Nebraska, New Mexico, Rhode Island, Tennessee, and Wisconsin. In Iowa, for example, you need only be rejected by one insurer to qualify for the pool, in which all companies that sell health policies in the state are required to participate. The policy has a $500 deductible and a $250,000 maximum lifetime benefit. The cost for a 35-year-old man is about $978 annually. A 45-year-old woman pays $1,534. For a family policy, add $485 per child.

Money Sources

Alliance for Better Health is a consumer group whose members are eligible for AetnaCare Extra. Write to Alliance for Better Health, 295 Plus Park Blvd., Nashville, TN 37202.

For help finding a reputable agent who can offer you a choice of individual major medical policies, write the National Association of Life Underwriters, 1922 F St. N.W., Washington, DC 20006.

The American Association of Retired Persons offers supplemental insurance to retirees. Write to 1909 K St. N.W., Washington, DC 20049.

Compare Your Plan with These

Group Major Medical
Annual deductible for one person: **$100**; for a family: **$200**
Your share of costs above the deductible: **20%**
Your maximum cost per year: **$1,000**
Hospital and surgical coverage per year: **unlimited**
Lifetime maximum coverage: **unlimited**
No second opinion required for full surgical coverage
Home health-care coverage: **200 visits**
Psychiatric care in the hospital: **365-day lifetime limit**
Psychotherapy in the doctor's office: **50% of fee**
Employee's average annual contribution for one person: **$156**; for a family: **$492**

Group HMO
Federally qualified
Percentage of board-certified doctors: **60%**
Your share of fees of specialists not available at HMO: **zero**
No second opinion required for coverage of surgery
Cost of coverage when you need treatment out of town: **zero**
Your contribution to prescription drugs: **$2 per prescription**
Waiting time for nonemergency appointments: **one to two weeks**
Waiting time for emergency treatment: **none**
Employee's average annual contribution for one person: **$90**; for a family: **$569**

Medicare Supplement
Pays 100% of the $520 Medicare hospital deductible
Pays patient's share of Medicare-covered doctor and hospital bills
Hospital coverage after Medicare runs out: **365 days**
Private-duty nursing care in the hospital: **up to $30 a shift**
Nursing home (skilled facility): **$65 a day from day 21 to 100; $130 a day from day 101 to 365**
Reimbursement for prescription drugs
Foreign hospital and medical care: **80% after a $50 deductible**
Average annual cost for one person: **$725**

Your Home

Within only a generation or so, a lifetime of buying and selling homes has become the cornerstone of American affluence. Indeed, for most middle-income people, this process is now the primary way of building family wealth. You begin the housing cycle deep in debt and end up, if all goes well, with a tidy retirement treasure that in many cases is absolutely *tax-free!* You may encounter some steep hills and nasty potholes along the enriching route from your first home to your final golden one. But this chapter should help you stay the course.

Say you bought a starter house five years ago for $54,100 with a mortgage of $43,300. Assuming annual appreciation of 5%, you might sell the house today for $69,100. (The family you sell to might begin its own grand tour with a $55,300 mortgage, $3,800 in savings, and a $10,000 gift from their parents.) After paying off your loan you would pocket roughly $25,800 in cash. You could use $20,300 of this for the 20% down payment on your $101,500 trade-up house and pour the remaining $5,500 into savings—unless you need it to cover the cost of a real estate broker, who usually collects 6% of the sale price. Mortgage closing costs can run to another 6%.

As your income and family grow, you may itch for more room and comfort. You could trade up again or, more likely, remodel after five years with a $22,400 home-equity loan. When you sell, you may get back as much as 70% of the cost of a room addition and 50% of the money spent on landscaping. Together, $20,000 for a new room and $2,400 for landscaping boost the value of the trade-up by $15,200. That plus 5% annual appreciation gives the remodeled house a market price of $144,700.

Once your children have left the nest, the time may come when you want to look for the right house for your retirement years. Often this means trading down to a smaller home loaded with creature comforts. The remodeled house would be worth $235,700 after 10 more years of 5% appreciation. By then you will have paid off $14,000 of your mortgage, leaving $67,200 of the principal to go. If you sell the house for $235,700, you are left with $146,100 after paying off the mortgage and home-equity loan. Use $20,300 for the 20% down payment on a $101,500 retirement house, and you can stash most of the $125,800 profit tax-free—if you qualify for the one-time $125,000 capital-gains exclusion available to house sellers age 55 or older.

Where does that leave you? Free to loll in the pool, dote on your grandchildren, and contemplate the rewards of successfully pyramiding the assets you have lived in.

Starter Home: Your First Step Is the Biggest

Changing mortgage rates and tax write-offs make first-time buying even more bewildering.

Spring's seasonal house-buying binge turned more feverish than usual last April following a sudden spike in mortgage rates from 9% to 11%. Panicked buyers hurried to close their deals before rates headed higher, and homeowners who had bought before the dawn of double-digit mortgages scrambled to trade up to their dream house. Yet for those now poised to buy, sell, or trade, the advice of experts is simply SLOW DOWN. Most economists do not expect rates to move more than half a percentage point up or down before spring of 1988. If a 10.5% mortgage rate has you seething, keep in mind that two years ago the same rate seemed so low that it triggered a home-buying frenzy.

This perspective is particularly important for first-time buyers, who generally lack the income and assets of those who are trading up, remodeling, or trading down to retirement. If you are among these neophytes, you will have to plan your every move with care. You will likely have to scrape to come up with your down payment, then budget hard to meet your monthly payments. And one stiff interest-rate breeze could wipe you out just as you are getting ready to buy. For instance, monthly payments on a $120,000, 30-year 10% mortgage may fit your budget—but a rate increase of only 1% increases monthly payments by about $100, enough to make homes unaffordable for some cash-strapped first-time buyers. In fact, higher rates are for some a signal to go on renting and postpone ownership.

Buying your first house need not be overwhelmingly difficult. Here is what you need to know to get through the process.

The Price

To determine roughly how much house you can afford, begin by applying the same rules used by banks to size up prospective borrowers. That way you can, in effect, prequalify yourself for a loan and reduce the risk of being denied a mortgage or falling for a house way beyond your means. Here are three rules of thumb worth noting.

● The price of a house should not exceed approximately twice your family's gross annual income.

● Your monthly mortgage payment, property taxes, and homeowners insurance should not exceed 28% of your family's gross monthly income, or about 35% for a Federal Housing Authority or Veteran's Administration mortgage. (Many banks, savings and loans, and mortgage companies make FHA and VA mortgages. But the maximum FHA loan is $90,000. Only veterans and sometimes their surviving spouses can apply for VA loans.)

● Your debt payments on all loans of 10 months or longer, including your mortgage, should not exceed 36% of your gross income, or about 50% for an FHA or VA loan.

For example, a couple with gross income of $60,000 and a monthly debt load of $500 or less might look for a $120,000 house with total monthly housing payments of about $1,300. The couple could most likely qualify for a 30-year fixed-rate loan, assuming that mortgage rates stay below 12%.

Next consider how far you are willing to commute to work. Generally, the farther a house is from a city, the less it costs. For many first-timers this factor could be the one above all that makes ownership affordable.

Once you have selected a few desirable towns or neighborhoods, read the weekend newspaper's real estate ads for prices of local homes in your range. This is when you should start looking for a seasoned real estate agent who has worked full time in your target areas for at least three years. Ideally, the agent will be one recommended by someone you know. The agent will figure out exactly how large a mortgage you can afford, explain financing terms, grade the local school system, answer questions about the character of particular neighborhoods, and guide you in making reasonable purchase offers.

But do not forget that most real estate agents are double agents. They are hired by both buyer and seller but paid by the seller. So both the seller and the agent profit by getting you to pay top dollar for the house.

Before looking at any houses, find out if it is customary in your area to hire a lawyer. If it is, get one to help you draw up a purchase contract. Expect to pay the lawyer roughly $300.

As you start the actual quest, plan to look at no fewer than 10 to 15 houses in your price range. Do not miss out on ones advertised for sale by owners, which your agent cannot show you. If a low price is paramount, do not neglect condominiums. Understand, however, that a condo will require you to pay a monthly maintenance fee for upkeep of common areas such as parks or swimming pools. On the other hand, do not feel obligated to buy the priciest house a lender will allow. Give yourself a cushion of $2,000 to $5,000 for unexpected fix-up expenses.

In your hunt for the perfect house, you need to carry the gear appropriate to the task. Bring a Polaroid camera for instant snapshots that will help you recall appearances. Take along a note pad to jot down impressions and data. For example, ask sellers how much their utilities cost. The expense can equal half your monthly mortgage payments, particularly in hot and cold climates, according to Kenneth Austin, chairman of HouseMaster of America, a home inspection franchise.

The Opening Bid

Your ability to negotiate a better price on a house often depends on when and where you are shopping. Sellers are generally most willing to cut prices from October through March, when the number of buyers dwindles. You also will have the most bargaining clout in a buyer's market where prices are flat, such as in most of Texas today.

If your housing market is not tilted toward buyers or sellers, offer a seller an initial bid 10% below the house's fair market value. Estimate the fair market value by looking at your agent's book of recent sales prices for comparable houses. And expect to haggle through at least two rounds of bids and counterbids. You can negotiate from strength by asking your agent for details about the owner's experience selling the house so far. Find out how long the house has been on the market—more than three months usually suggests the house is overpriced.

You can, of course, win on price and lose in the small print. Accordingly, never sign a sales contract without contingency clauses nullifying it if a home inspection turns up major structural damage or defects or you fail to get financing within, say, 60 days at your specified mortgage terms. Your agent or lawyer can write in such clauses.

The Financing

You can comparison shop among banks, savings and loans, and mortgage companies. Not only do terms vary, but rates, which once moved at a stately pace, rise and fall faster than you can say Fannie Mae. One reason is that Fannie Mae (the government-chartered Federal National Mortgage Association) and its brother Freddie Mac (Federal Home Loan Mortgage Corporation) now pool and sell to investors 45% of their mortgages, versus only 19% in 1981. Investors compare rates on these mortgage-backed securities with those of conventional bonds, so when bond rates fluctuate wildly, mortgages do too.

Because mortgage rates do not move in precise lockstep, however, there are chances to make huge savings. Ask your real estate agent or a lender whether any companies publish weekly mortgage comparisons for your area. If you find such a service, call for the current issue (typical cost: $10 to $20). It is likely to show local mortgage rates differing by as many

as two percentage points, says Victor Peeke, publisher of the Peeke Report, a mortgage data service based in Gaithersburg, Maryland.

But prepare for a nasty surprise if you need a mortgage exceeding $153,100. Lenders call such loans jumbos and usually charge a rate about half a percentage point higher than on smaller loans. That is because Fannie Mae and Freddie Mac are prohibited by law from buying mortgages larger than $153,100. The figure, set by the Federal Home Loan Bank Board, is adjusted annually and pegged to national house prices.

Determine the type of mortgage you prefer before you shop. You might opt for a 15-year loan if you can afford the 8% to 20% higher payments than on a 30-year mortgage. For example, a 15-year, $80,000 mortgage cost about $835 a month in mid-1987, versus $700 for a 30-year loan. Your rate will be 0.25% to 0.5% less than on a 30-year mortgage, and you will cut your total interest payments roughly in half. The less interest you pay, the less you can deduct from your taxes, of course, though lower tax rates have diminished the value of the write-off.

Adjustable-rate mortgages, or ARMs, are enticing with mid-1987 rates of 6% to 10.5%, compared with 9.5% to 11% on fixed-rate loans. Lenders can usually twist a borrower's ARM rate—painfully, if rates are headed up—either annually or every three years. Shun ARMs whose rates can rise by more than two points a year or six points over the life of the loan. Dennis Campbell, a senior vice president of Fannie Mae, recommends three-year ARMs for buyers who expect to move within seven years and thus will see their rates rise only twice, if at all. One fetching type of ARM, now widespread, even lets you convert the loan to a fixed-rate mortgage in two or three years. The conversion fee is usually less than lenders charge to refinance a conventional mortgage taken out when rates were higher.

Points, one type of loan-origination fee, are a lurking danger to any loan shopper. Each point equals 1% of your mortgage. Lenders typically charge one to three points on mortgages. Many lenders have raised points lately rather than increasing mortgage rates because buyers often compare only rates. Points can hurt—a lot. Here is how: four points on a $150,000 loan cost an eye-popping $4,500. As a rule, if you plan to move within five years, look for a loan with no more than two points. The points you pay are tax deductible in the year you buy the house.

Always figure the total cost—basic rate plus points—of a mortgage by computing the effective annual interest rate. Multiply the mortgage rate by the number of years you plan to live in the house. Add the points charged and divide the total by the number of years you will own the house. For example, take a 10% mortgage with three points on a house you plan to live in for five years: 10% times five equals 50 plus three equals 53 divided by five equals an effective rate of 10.6%.

Once you choose a lender and complete a mortgage application, do not dawdle over your unfinished loan business. Otherwise, you could miss your closing date and lose the house. Immediately arrange for a home inspection and, if necessary, a termite inspection, and shop for homeowners insurance. Be sure your employer sends the lender verification of your earnings.

The Down Payment

If you are like many first-time buyers with steady incomes, making the mortgage payments will be a breeze compared with amassing the cash for the down payment, points, and other settlement costs. Lenders prefer a down payment of at least 20% of the purchase price, though many accept as little as 5%.

Try if possible to put 20% down even if it is not required. A smaller down payment will cost you by increasing your mortgage amount and thus the interest you will owe. Most lenders also require that a borrower putting down less than 20% buy private mortgage insurance, or PMI, generally available through the lender. (Federal mortgage insurance is included on VA and FHA loans.) You pay PMI until your home equity equals 20% of the fair market value, usually in seven to nine years. But this can happen faster if you can prove

your house has appreciated quickly.

The tinier your down payment, the more pricey the PMI. Put down 10% and you will pay the equivalent of 0.5% of the amount of the mortgage at closing ($400 or so) and then roughly $20 a month. Put down 5% and you will have to pay 1.25% ($1,000 or so) and about $30 a month.

A minimal down payment will also boost the cost of any points you must pay the lender. For example, two points on a $150,000 house with a 20% down payment would cost you $2,400. They would cost $2,850 with a 5% down payment.

If you can draw your down payment entirely from your savings, you will increase the chance that your mortgage application will sail through with the greatest of ease. Failing that, add to your savings by asking your parents or any charitable relatives for a gift with a letter for the lender noting that the money need not be repaid. If that gambit fails, try to borrow from relatives and pool their cash with your savings. Increasingly, lenders say, first-time buyers get help from their parents, though there are no reliable statistics on this phenomenon. Lenders sometimes jokingly call this aid G.I. financing, not "government issued" but "good in-laws." But be careful. If you borrow for the down payment, your repayments could put you over the lender's debt limits and disqualify you for the mortgage.

If you have exhausted your savings and asked your family for help and still need more cash, look for inexpensive ways to borrow. Some sources are life insurance policies, company savings plans, and credit unions.

Other down payment sources, in strategic order: Withdraw tax-free your pre-1987 contributions to an after-tax company savings plan. Next, tap your 1987 after-tax savings plan contributions—some of this cash will be taxable, and you will also owe a 10% tax penalty. Then, dip into your Individual Retirement Account, paying taxes and the 10% penalty. Finally, if you are in a 401(k) savings plan and your company will let you pull out your contributions to buy a house, do so. Count on paying taxes and the 10% penalty on this money too.

The Settlement Costs

Do not deplete all your savings for the down payment and any mortgage insurance. Other settlement costs could amount to several thousand dollars or 3% to 6% of your purchase price. One common surprise for first-time buyers is that lenders often require borrowers to write escrow checks for a year's worth of property taxes and homeowners insurance.

The nationwide real estate brokerage firm ERA recently polled 400 brokers and came up with this list of median settlement costs, which excludes the cost of hiring a lawyer:

Escrowed property taxes	$1,000
Loan-origination fees	760
Title search	400
Homeowners insurance	340
Appraisal fee	188
Home inspection	150
Survey fee	125
Termite inspection	45
Credit check	37
Deed recording fee	20
Total	$3,165

After you get the seller's house keys at the closing, your first go-round in the housing life cycle begins in earnest. From here on out, chugging along on that cycle becomes much easier. You will enter the later stages with experience and, if all goes well, lots more cash from your buildup of home equity. Finding the right house is lovelier the second time around.

Money Tip

Keep records of all improvements on your house. When you sell, you reduce any taxable profits by adding the amount spent on improvements to your original purchase price. Bona fide improvements include such things as putting in a new kitchen, refurbishing a basement, and building a tennis court or gazebo. But repairs, painting, and ordinary maintenance do not qualify as improvements.

Money Basics

Adjustable-rate mortgage. A loan whose interest rate can be raised or lowered by the lender, usually either annually or every three years.

Condominium. A house or apartment that requires you to pay a mortgage and a monthly maintenance fee for upkeep of areas shared with other condo owners.

Escrow. The custody of money or contracts by a neutral third party until specified conditions are met.

FHA mortgage. A loan of $90,000 or less that is insured by the Federal Housing Administration. The down payment is lower than with a conventional mortgage.

Jumbo mortgage. A loan exceeding $153,100. Jumbo mortgage rates are often half a point higher than those of smaller loans.

Loan application fee. A lender's charge ranging from $75 to $300, that you must pay when you apply for a mortgage.

Private mortgage insurance (PMI). An insurance policy lenders generally require for a borrower making a down payment of less than 20% of the purchase price. PMI is paid monthly, usually for seven to nine years.

Settlement costs. Expenses paid by a home buyer to take possession of a house. They generally amount to 3% to 6% of a house's purchase price.

Title search. The process of proving that the seller can transfer the title free and clear of liens and other encumbrances.

VA mortgage. A loan guaranteed by the Veterans Administration for U.S. veterans or, sometimes, their surviving spouses. The down payment is lower than that required for a conventional mortgage.

When Renting Is Right

For many Americans, the decision to buy a home is more emotional than economic. If you are in a quandary about whether to go on renting, these questions may help you sort it out.

Do you have enough money saved? While your monthly payments on a mortgage may be no more after taxes—and perhaps even less—than rent, the initial costs of home ownership are considerable. For a $100,000 house, you will need a minimum of $28,000: $20,000 for the down payment, $6,000 for closing costs, and a $2,000 cushion for contingencies.

Are you the roving kind? Richard Peach, a senior economist with the Mortgage Bankers Association of America, says that with hefty borrowing and closing costs on both ends of the deal, it does not make sense to buy if, say, you

stand a good chance of being relocated by your employer in a couple of years. You need to live in a house for at least five years to make buying the good investment it can be.

Do you live in a region where renting makes sense? In cities such as Baton Rouge, Houston, and Tulsa, where there is a housing glut and values have been flat or falling, renting ends up being a bargain while buying becomes a risk.

Are you a born renter? Some Americans cannot imagine dealing with clogged drains, malfunctioning heating systems, or dandelion-dotted lawns—things that, for better or worse, a landlord is responsible for. Some renters also savor the delicious freedom of being able to pick up and move without the complications of liquidating a property.

The Trade-Up: An Indulgence That Pays

Buy the best location, materials, and amenities you can afford. You will come out ahead, now and when you sell.

There are two important comings of age in America, according to George Sternlieb, director of the Rutgers University Center for Urban Policy Research. One is the transition from renter to owner. The other is trading up to a better house. A quick look at recent home sales shows that this second rite of passage—trading in the old homestead for a larger, more expensive and luxurious one—has sparked much of today's real estate boom.

Consider:
● Of the 4.3 million houses sold in 1986—the highest level this decade—roughly two-thirds went to repeat buyers, most of whom used the equity in their old house to step up to a bigger and better home. This marks a major shift from the housing boom of the 1970s, when first-timers accounted for almost half the homes sold in the United States.
● Price appreciation, which showed signs of

disappearing in the early 1980s, is now standing tall. The median price of a house nationwide rose to $80,300 in 1986—a smart 6% gain compared with a sluggish 2% in 1982. But many areas easily outperformed the national average. Of the 52 metropolitan areas surveyed by the National Association of Realtors, almost half beat the average in 1986. Among the winners: Providence, up 37%; Hartford, up 30%; and the New York City metropolitan area, up 20%.

● New houses are getting bigger, another sure sign of strength in the move-up market. Lately, a third of new houses built measured 2,000 square feet or larger, up from a quarter of all new houses five years or so ago. To lure homeowners into new houses, builders are stocking them with more and more options: fireplaces, whirlpool tubs, two-story Palladian-inspired windows, and designer kitchens. These and other amenities provide the distinctive look that today's houses must have to win over high-income, luxury-seeking, and status-conscious buyers.

Going for the Dream House

If you are still sitting in the cramped condo or starter house you bought five years ago, you need not fret that you have missed your big chance to cash in on this craze. The trade-up market is where the action will be until the mid-1990s, according to Michael Carliner, an economist for the National Association of Home Builders (NAHB). As a result, trade-up houses will increase in value more than will starter houses over the next five to ten years. Thus if you own a starter house, now is the time to move up.

A combination of financial and demographic factors has spurred this move-up mania. The biggest boost has come from maturing baby boomers. Of the 76 million people born between 1946 and 1964, the NAHB estimates that about 40% have already bought their first house. Statistics indicate that it is likely to be a two-bedroom condominium or townhouse measuring less than 1,500 square feet. But now that these buyers have started families and crave more space and creature comforts, they are anxious to parlay the equity in their starter home into a down payment on the archetypal American dream: a single-family detached house with four bedrooms, two baths, a family room, and a big yard—with or without a white picket fence.

But they are not the only ones who are trading up. People in their fifties are spending their discretionary income on bigger houses too. These buyers, often trading up for the third or fourth time, are looking for status, not space.

Falling interest rates have contributed to the trade-up craze. Since 1982 mortgage rates dropped from around 15% to as low as 9.25%. This 40% slide meant buyers could afford a much more expensive house for the same monthly payment. For example, a couple earning $50,000 a year and living in a $125,000 house with a $75,000 mortgage could only afford to trade up to a $142,000 house when rates were at 15%—hardly worth the cost and inconvenience of a move. But with rates at 9.25%, the same couple could afford a $192,000 house.

The irrepressible itch to move up has gained impetus from tax reform. For most people, the deduction for mortgage interest, points, and real estate taxes is the last remaining shelter under the new tax law. Of course, the lower marginal rates introduced by tax reform have reduced the value of those deductions. But the tax benefit most important to people trading up has been left intact: you can sell your existing house for a huge profit and, as long as you buy another house of at least equal value two years before or after the sale, you can defer the tax on your gain.

You can use this deferral only once every two years unless the Internal Revenue Service considers your move work-related. Otherwise, you can continue to roll over such gains indefinitely until you eventually sell for a lower-priced house or move into an apartment. And even then, most sellers 55 or over can shelter $125,000 of the gain from taxes. (While you do not pay tax on gains when you trade up to a more expensive house, you still must report them to the IRS on Form 2119.)

Timing Your Move

The biggest challenge for homeowners who want to trade up is timing: you want the sale of your present house to coincide as closely as possible with the purchase of the house you are buying. You thus avoid the predicament of owning two houses at once and having to make double mortgage payments. The strategy you use to accomplish this juggling act will vary depending on how quickly houses are selling in your market. In areas where houses are appreciating and turning over quickly, you can take the aggressive approach of buying your trade-up first and then putting your present house on the market.

To make the most of this approach, you ideally should buy in January, before prices begin their traditional spring climb, and try to hold off closing until May or June. Then list your present house in March or April and try for a June close. This way you buy your house at winter's prices and get the full benefit of appreciation on the selling side. Even in a fast-moving market, however, you run the risk that you will wind up buying your new house before you can sell the old. So you should adopt this aggressive approach only if your budget can handle dual mortgage payments for at least a couple of months.

Take a far more conservative stance if you live in a depressed housing market. Realtors recommend that you do not buy a new house until you have your other one sold. In Houston, for example, a house can easily sit on the market four to six months before it is sold; some have languished as long as two years. Should you find a house you feel you cannot pass up, ask the seller to accept a contract that makes the deal contingent on the sale of your present house. If you cannot sell your house within a specified period—usually 60 to 90 days—the contract expires. If you do offer a contingency sales contract, be prepared for the seller to ask for a contingency release. Under this arrangement, the seller accepts the contingency contract but reserves the right to continue showing the house. If the seller receives a bona fide offer on the house, you usually have up to 72 hours to buy the house at your original offer or release him from the contract.

If you wind up buying your new house before unloading the old, you will probably have to turn to a bridge, or swing, loan for the down payment. This type of loan allows you to borrow against the equity in your old house until you are able to sell it. Lenders charge one to two percentage points more than the prime rate for such financing. You usually make interest payments only until the entire principal balance comes due, usually within 30 to 120 days. Often, a real estate agent can help you arrange this financing through a local commercial bank or savings institution.

Buying with an Eye to Resale

When trading up, strive to select a house that meets your family's needs but at the same time has the best appreciation potential. Start not by looking for a house but by scouting out a prime location. The best neighborhoods always enjoy the highest appreciation. Real estate agents can tell you which neighborhoods carry the most prestige, but you should also look for other characteristics such as a highly rated school system and proximity to shopping, employment, parks, and other recreation facilities.

Once you have chosen a neighborhood, you can launch your search for a house. You first must decide whether to buy an existing house or a new one. While that decision largely boils down to whether you prefer the charm and character of an older house or the modern conveniences of a new one, keep in mind that new houses are more energy-efficient, require less maintenance than older homes, and usually appreciate 5% to 20% more than older houses.

For the best resale value, stick to large houses with 2,000 square feet or more and at least three bedrooms and two baths. Move-up buyers also show a distinct preference for the privacy of detached homes. As important as the amount of space is the interior design—how the space is divided up. Here are the areas home buyers consider most important in a trade-up house.

Master-bedroom suite. This is the room that really sells a house to a move-up buyer. The master bedroom should have a den or alcove leading off it with enough space for a desk, library, or exercise equipment. It should also have its own bathroom, preferably large enough for a whirlpool tub, separate shower, and dual lavatory basins.

Foyer. More prevalent in new houses than older ones, a spacious entry foyer carries as much snob appeal as design appeal. Since interior space is so expensive, a splurge in an area that is not even being lived in suggests wealth. It is one of the most sought-after elements in today's new houses.

Formal dining room. Since smaller starter houses generally lack a separate dining room, it is one of the first things home buyers look for when trading up. In new houses, the trend is to give it added privacy by closing it off from the rest of the house with French doors. This room should be large enough to seat at least 10 people comfortably.

Kitchen. Even though many of today's working couples spend little time there, the kitchen still serves as a showcase of luxury, convenience, and conspicuous consumption. The country kitchen look is popular today, with a quarry-tile floor, high-ceilinged eating area, and exposed rustic beams. Add a full complement of top-of-the-line appliances and solid wood—oak or cherry—cabinetry, and you have the perfect kitchen.

Just because a house does not contain each of these features does not mean you should reject it. But you should pay particular attention to the quality of design and construction. Marble-tile baths, cedar-shake roofs, oak floors, French doors—these and other touches separate the moving-upper from the starting-outer.

Ultimately, you will probably sell your trade-up house. When you do, remember that the buyer will give it the same careful going-over you did. Move-up buyers are the most discriminating and demanding ones out there. After all, they do not *have* to move.

Money Basics

Bridge loan. Also known as a swing loan, this type of financing tides you over if you must purchase your new house before you sell the old one. A bridge loan lets you borrow against the equity in your present house so you can use the money as a down payment to finance the new one. Interest rates usually run one to two percentage points over prime.

Contingency clause. A clause in the sales contract stipulating that if you are unable to sell your present house within a specified period of time—usually 60 to 90 days—the deal to purchase the new house is off.

Contingency release. A seller who agrees to a contingency arrangement may add a contingency release clause. This allows the seller to accept your offer but keep his house on the market. If the seller receives another offer on the house, you usually have 72 hours to purchase the house at the price in your sales contract. Otherwise, the seller is free to accept the other deal.

Capital-gains deferral. A provision of the tax code that allows you to sell your present house at a profit and defer paying tax on that gain as long as you buy another house of equal or greater value within two years before or after the sale. You may roll over such gains until you sell for a lower-priced house or sell and then stop buying entirely. Even then, most sellers at age 55 can shelter $125,000 in gains.

The Make-Over: When It Pays to Remodel

Renovating can be the most cost-effective—and least traumatic—route to your dream house.

To move or to improve? That is the question facing owners who have grown dissatisfied with the house they currently call home. Whether the problem is cramped living quarters, antiquated amenities, or exorbitant fuel bills, Americans are increasingly opting to remodel their way into more comfortable homes.

Last year homeowners were expected to spend a record $65 billion on professionally installed renovation projects, up from $33 billion five years earlier, plus another $20 billion or so on do-it-yourself remodeling jobs. The projects range from such simple maintenance work as reroofing, re-siding, and replacing old windows and doors to more elaborate jobs, such as building additional rooms or overhauling kitchens and bathrooms.

Economics is the main impetus. With prices of new single-family homes averaging $111,800 in 1986 and rising 9% a year, many people simply cannot afford the house they really want. Meanwhile, financing improvements to a dwelling you already own has never been easier because of the widespread availability of low-interest-rate home-equity lines of credit.

Still, for many homeowners the decision to upgrade is more than dollars and cents. In many cases, remodeling is the best way to create exactly the kind of dwelling you want where you want it. Just how far you will want to go with your remodeling efforts depends partly on how long you plan to live in your home. The longer you intend to stay put—and thus enjoy the improvements that you make—the less you need to worry about the dollar value that future buyers will place on your alterations.

You should also take into account the value of your remodeled home compared with that of other homes in the area. In general, the highest return on improvements comes from bringing your place up to par with others in the neighborhood. Furthermore, especially if you are already in the same price range as nearby homes, you will want to stick with improvements that are likely to increase the value of your property, such as the creation of additional living space, modernization of bathroom and kitchen facilities, improvements in energy efficiency, and the installation of amenities—patios and shrubbery, for example—that will enhance the house's appearance and comfort. But no matter what specific improvements you choose to make, try to keep the cost of the entire renovation project to no more than 20% of the average value of homes in your neighborhood if you want to avoid losing money when it comes time to sell the old homestead.

Here are the most common types of renovations, listed roughly in order of the size of the project, from the biggest to the smallest.

Expanding. The reason for moving most commonly cited by prospective sellers is insufficient space. It is also one of the housing problems that remodeling can best resolve. You can create an extra bedroom, family room, or home office for a relatively modest outlay by converting an attic or basement currently used for storage into livable space. Because these areas already have floors, ceilings, walls, and rudimentary wiring, the cost of conversion is usually far lower than the cost of building a new room from scratch.

Take, for example, the results of a recent survey by *Practical Homeowner* magazine. It found that a typical 16-foot-by-36-foot two-room attic conversion, which might require the installation of new wiring and windows, costs around $9,500, but would return about 104% of your outlay if you sell your home within a year. A basement conversion is cheaper—a 24-foot-by-20-foot room runs about $6,600. But because prospective buyers put less value on subterranean living space than they do on aboveground rooms, you will get a lower return, about 97% on average.

You can also remodel your way into larger living quarters by building an addition to your home. But room additions do not come cheap. According to the *Practical Homeowner* survey, building an addition onto a standard three-bedroom suburban ranch house could run from $23,000 for a basic 20-foot-by-24-foot room to upwards of $27,000 for a 15-foot-by-25-foot addition that includes such finishing touches as skylights and sliding-glass patio doors. Moreover, if the additional space makes your home considerably larger or more luxurious than the houses that surround it, the extra rooms may be viewed as an overimprovement, meaning that you may be unlikely to recoup your costs.

Modernizing. If your main gripe with your home is its old-fashioned facilities—say, rusty plumbing or a Stone-age kitchen—remodeling may be a better bet than going through the hassle and expense of moving. Indeed, kitchen and bath renovations done with an eye toward modernization are the most common major home improvement projects being commissioned today, according to James Tolliver, executive director of the National Association of the Remodeling Industry.

Figure on spending from $4,600 to $8,800 for a minor renovation of the kitchen and from $7,800 to $27,000 for a major overhaul, which includes installation of all new appliances, cabinets, and countertops. There are ways to cut the costs to more manageable sums, however. Refinishing cabinets rather than replacing them, for example, can reduce the expense of a kitchen renovation by roughly 20%. You can also cut costs by removing parts of the old kitchen yourself; demolition labor can account for about a third of the labor charges you will incur. You are likely to recover anywhere from 70% to 90% of the expense of redoing your kitchen.

A bathroom make-over costs between $4,200 and $10,400 these days and provides around a 75% return on your investment. Adding a full bath averages about $7,300 and ranks among the most cost-effective improvements you can make. You will probably recover all the money you spend on the project and then some.

Upgrading energy efficiency. A leaky, energy-guzzling house is another problem that remodeling can frequently fix, although you no longer get income tax credits on such work. You can cut your annual fuel bills at least in half by completing three fairly simple tasks: weatherstripping and caulking doors and windows; insulating the attic floor, basement walls, ducts and pipes; and upgrading your heating system. The total cost of these improvements would be roughly $3,000 to $4,000. As a general rule, you can expect to recover about two-thirds to three-quarters of the money you spend to upgrade your home's energy efficiency.

Adding amenities. If you hope to recoup most of your costs on resale, focus on those improvements that are prized most highly by prospective home buyers. Topping the list are fireplaces and decks. A fireplace, which costs roughly $3,000 to install, can return from 85% to 125% of the money you spend on it when you sell your home, according to remodeling surveys by *Practical Homeowner* and *Remodeling Contractor*. A deck, which costs about $15 a square foot to build, can return from 80% to

100% of its cost in added market value.

You can probably expect to recover about three-quarters of the cost of adding skylights, another popular feature, but only about half of the price you pay for landscaping. The worst renovation you can make from a cost-recovery standpoint is the installation of a swimming pool, which many prospective home buyers regard as a danger to small children and an unnecessary encroachment of backyard space. The likely return: only 30% to 45%.

When you do decide that it is time to move on, consider putting some money into yet another kind of remodeling job: the interior facelift, as it is called in remodelers' parlance. In most markets, money spent on painting, papering, and general sprucing up of the inside of your home will bring a 100% recovery or better upon resale. Even if you do not find a buyer or you change your mind and decide to stay put, giving your house a facelift will probably add considerably to your enjoyment of your home—which, after all, is really the main purpose of remodeling.

The Trade-Down: Your Golden Home

Whether you plan to stay in your present house or move, you will have to plan your strategy carefully.

When you retire, your home will seem more important to you than ever before. Beyond the fact that probably nothing else you own will hold more value, both sentimental and monetary, you will probably spend an average of more than four-fifths of your time at home. Therefore, it is not surprising that an estimated 70% of retired Americans prefer to stay put rather than move to unfamiliar surroundings.

On the other hand, many retirees feel that the place where they lived during their working years is too big, too costly, too hard to keep up, or too far from warm weather. They are more than willing to trade in their house for one that better suits them.

Either way, you have options. If you stay where you are, you may want to consider converting some of your home equity into cash. If you opt to move, you will have other tough decisions. Should you buy or rent? Pay cash or take out a mortgage? Defer or exclude from taxes the capital gain you receive from the sale of your old home?

When you think of retiring, consider the following housing strategies.

Tapping equity. Conventional methods such as second mortgages, refinancing, and home-equity lines of credit are generally not available to anyone living on fixed incomes from pensions and investments. But other programs for converting home equity into cash are slowly coming available. One is a variation on a home-equity loan designed for the elderly and is called a reverse mortgage. Such an arrangement is offered by a few banks and savings and loan associations in 12 states, including California, New York, and Ohio. With a standard reverse mortgage, you receive a fixed monthly payment from the bank for seven to ten years. The amount will depend mainly on how much equity you have to borrow against. For example, an $80,000 reverse mortgage with a 10% interest rate will pay you $500 a month over eight years.

The catch is that at the end of the period—if you live that long—you must pay back what you borrowed plus interest. Most retired people who survive until the loan comes due would have to sell their property to repay the money. But a Senate bill passed last year would create a federally funded insurance program enabling borrowers who outlive a reverse mortgage's term to remain in their homes. If the provision becomes law—about a fifty-fifty possibility—such loans could soon become much more popular.

Meanwhile, an offshoot of the reverse mortgage developed by American Homestead, a mortgage banker in Mount Laurel, New Jersey, appears to be gaining favor among some homeowners 62 and older. More than a thousand of the loans have been made since they were first offered in 1983. Now available in five eastern states, including Connecticut and Maryland, the loan allows you to continue collecting payments until you either die or sell your home. In return for the indefinite term of the mortgage, you must give up a portion of the property's future appreciation. If you do not move before you die, the loan, accrued interest, and the bank's share of the appreciation will be repaid out of your estate upon the home's sale. Before taking out such a loan, discuss its merits and risks with an accountant or other financial adviser.

Arranging a sale-leaseback. Another way to bolster your finances is to sell your home, most likely to one of your children, and then pay rent to the buyer while you continue to live there. In a typical sale-leaseback, as these arrangements are called, the buyer gives you a 10% to 20% down payment. You usually finance the rest by providing the mortgage yourself. Income to you from the mortgage more than covers the rent you pay, leaving you with some extra money. The buyer, who benefits from any appreciation, also becomes obligated for property taxes, insurance, and maintenance expenses. Thus the buyer, now a landlord, gains the tax breaks produced by rental property, though these deductions have

become less attractive under tax reform.

The trick to arranging sale-leasebacks is finding prospective buyers—your children or relatives are among the best candidates—who are willing to rent out the property to you for life. Because sale-leasebacks are complex transactions, you will need to consult a real estate lawyer who has experience writing the required documents.

Renting out a room. If your house feels too big for you now that your children have moved out, renting part of your excess space could generate some valuable income. Creating an apartment in a split-level home or one with a walkout basement can be relatively inexpensive. With other types of properties, however, renovation costs may be prohibitive—and might not increase the value of your home. Before creating a so-called accessory apartment, check with your local zoning agency about the rules governing your neighborhood.

Moving out. Sometimes the only practical step is to move. Regardless of your reasons for abandoning the old homestead, it is crucial that you plan carefully. One of your primary concerns relates to the capital gains you receive upon the sale of your current home. Under the law, if either you or your spouse is age 55 or over, you may exclude from taxes a gain of up to $125,000 if you lived in the home for three of the preceding five years. But you may elect the exclusion only once.

Most taxpayers over 55 who sell their home and intend either to buy a less expensive place or to rent should take the exclusion. But if the cost of your new residence exceeds the sale price of your old one, then you are better off deferring the tax rather than electing the exclusion. All taxpayers, regardless of age, can postpone taxes on capital gains from a home sale if they buy a more expensive property within two years. If you realize a capital gain that exceeds $125,000, you can defer tax on the excess even if you reinvest the money in a less expensive home.

About 40% of elderly home buyers pay all cash for their new house. With mortgage rates in the double digits, paying cash makes sense if you can afford it. Retirees who do take out a mortgage should be sure to get one with a fixed interest rate rather than a variable-rate mortgage, whose payments could zoom unexpectedly. When shopping for a new place to live, also remember that no matter how energetic you may feel now, you will probably face health problems later on. So focus on such places as condominiums, townhouses, retirement communities, or rental properties, where the maintenance will be taken care of for you.

Money Sources

For a list of banks and other firms that offer reverse mortgages, send a stamped, self-addressed envelope to the National Center for Home Equity Conversion, 110 E. Main St., Madison, WI 53703.

Money Basics

Accessory apartment. An independent living area, including a kitchen and bathroom, usually created from excess space in a home. Renting the apartment can augment a retiree's income.

Capital-gains exclusion. A provision in tax law that allows homeowners age 55 or over to avoid paying taxes on a gain of as much as $125,000 from the sale of a home. You can take the exclusion only once.

Reverse mortgage. A loan against the equity in your home that pays you a fixed sum monthly until the loan's term expires, you sell your home, or you die.

Sale-leaseback. An arrangement in which you sell your home but continue to live in it while you pay rent to the buyer.

Your Future

Appropriate or not, comparisons of last October's stock market collapse with the 1929 crash that presaged the Depression have served to remind us all of how quickly one's family wealth can wane. Today the economic tectonics that threaten to undermine your financial foundations are less visible, but they are more varied. Besides the ever-present possibilities of drops in the stock and bond markets, adversity lurks in the form of higher taxes, rekindled inflation, and hard times for your company that might reduce your pension or even cause you to lose it.

By adroitly shielding yourself from such money menaces, you can put together and preserve a significantly bigger retirement bundle and have the earthly pleasure of knowing you will be able to pass all or most of it on to your chosen heirs. Begin your asset-amassing program by making the most of your house, company benefits, and investments, as described in "Building Family Wealth." In addition, the worksheet "Figuring Your Future Fortune" will help you come up with a working estimate of your net worth at retirement. The results could also show that you will have a roomy enough estate to warrant careful attention now.

The biggest obstacle to your financial security is complacency, particularly since the major threats to your prosperity seem somewhat subdued. Income tax rates have been slashed, inflation has run out of steam, and pension funds have grown fat since the bull market's start in 1982. But there is always the danger that you will get blindsided when the economy or your family's circumstances change. And they will change, if for no other reason than your own mortality.

Unsettling as it is, estate planning is one defense no family should be without. Most people probably would rather ignore the whole painful subject. But you cannot take it with you, and the legal mess you could leave behind if you do nothing could haunt your survivors. It is not particularly costly or difficult to ensure that this will not happen if you heed the advice set forth in "A Short Course in Estate Planning" and "Planning a Hassle-Free Legacy."

You can use a simple will to make sure that you pass assets to your desired heirs. A more complex estate plan that involves trusts and gifts to dependents is in order if at least one of the following situations applies to you: you have minor children; you want to protect your survivors from the delay, expense, and public disclosure of probate, the process by which a will is proved valid in court; or your estate is large enough to be taxed—the federal tax code exempts $600,000 for individuals or twice that amount for a couple.

Building Family Wealth

Your strategies should center around your house, your company benefit plans, and some disciplined market moves.

Having money in the family. What an idle dream it seemed when you started out in your first apartment with a few wedding presents and a batch of furniture the Salvation Army would not take. Your rent seemed bigger than the national debt and, to make ends meet, you drove an Own-a-Wreck and survived on a diet of meatless meat loaf.

Now that you have progressed in life and career, it is easy to see how your standard of living has advanced. And if you are in your forties or fifties, you may be surprised to discover when you tot up your assets that you have accumulated a stunning sum. If you are younger, you may be equally amazed at your potential for doing so. Indeed, wealth—a term once reserved for the few—is beginning to touch the many. Internal Revenue Service surveys of estates reveal that the number of millionaires doubled between 1976 and 1982, the most recent year for which figures are available. Another 850,000 people had assets of at least $500,000, and half a million owned more than $250,000.

Most people on their way to such wealth consider themselves solidly middle-income folks who will work, save, and invest their way to upper assetdom. Yet with affluence comes responsibility: on the one hand the risk of mismanagement and loss, on the other the opportunity to enlarge your net worth and to pass some of it along to your heirs.

Start your asset-building program by making the most of what you have. Your house is probably the foundation of your family wealth because its value has boomed over the past decade or so. Yet it may diminish in relative importance in the future even though it keeps pace with inflation. Second, pay close attention to your employee-benefits plans—particularly those to which you contribute. They have gained greatly in value because they allow you to stack up tax-deferred savings. Last, examine your investments: there may be sensible ways to invest that you have never thought of. By coordinating these three elements, you can achieve both security and growth.

Your House

This remains the most valuable asset most families acquire. Indeed, in 1984, the Census Bureau estimated that a house represented about 41% of a typical family's worth. Housing economists, however, are not forecasting the same heady gains for houses that they enjoyed in the inflation-ridden late 1970s and early 1980s. Expect instead that the single-family house (median price today: $107,000) will track inflation over the long run. That means your home will more likely be a source of capital preservation rather than capital growth.

Owning an asset whose value keeps pace with inflation is just one of the reasons for pursuing the American dream of home ownership. For example, making regular payments on the mortgage is a method of disciplined saving that works well for those who would normally spend every dollar they earn. Owning a house also qualifies you for one of the few remaining tax shelters available to individuals: deductions for property taxes and mortgage interest. When you sell, you can defer taxes on the profits if you put them into a new house within two years. And at age 55, you can exclude $125,000 of your gain from taxation.

Your Benefits

The funds stored in your employee-benefits plans may well turn out to be the stars of your future personal finances. That is because these plans typically offer more opportunity for tax-free buildup and more choice of investments than you might otherwise have access to.

While every company has its own wrinkles, employee-benefits plans fall into two major categories: defined benefit and defined contribution. The first, which has been around for decades, is simply your pension plan. Defined benefit means that the company puts away money for you and decides what you get—based on a formula—when you retire.

Spurred by tax breaks for themselves as well as their employees, more and more companies have added defined-contribution plans. These allow employees to put aside a portion of their salaries in a fund to which the company also adds. There are two types of such plans: matching programs, in which a company contributes a specified percentage—usually 50%—of what you invest, and profit-sharing arrangements under which your employer adds a portion of profits to your savings. Additionally, you may be offered an Employee Stock-Ownership Plan (ESOP). Your employer will typically match up to 50% of the amount you invest in shares of company stock.

In both types of plans, defined-benefit and defined-contribution, funds accrete quietly and inexorably until they total surprisingly large sums. At the Bechtel Group last year, a $55,000-a-year design engineer who left after 21 years of service walked away with $314,000 from various plans. An ESOP would have added even more. The National Center for Employee Ownership in Oakland, California, found that employees who earned $35,000 a year at companies with ESOPs can generally leave their jobs after 20 years with proceeds from an ESOP of more than $200,000.

Defined-contribution plans offer far more opportunity for wealth building than do pension plans. If you leave your company, you can take all your contributions with you, and the company's contribution vests more quickly than in pension plans—usually after one to three years of employment. Furthermore, many companies let you contribute to these plans as part of 401(k) salary-reduction programs. That is the best arrangement of all because it puts you three giant steps forward. First, you can exclude your contribution—up to $7,000 in 1988—from your taxable income. Second, you get an immediate gain on your investment because your employer matches it. Finally, the earnings are not taxed until you begin withdrawing them at age 59½. If you change jobs before then, you can roll over the funds into an IRA that continues the tax-deferred buildup.

Perhaps even more important, defined-contribution plans usually give you more than one investment option. The choices may include your company's stock, diversified portfolios of stocks and bonds that operate much like mutual funds, and guaranteed investment contracts—loans to large insurance companies that promise a fixed rate of return slightly higher than bank certificates of deposit. With most plans you can choose between two different types of investments, usually a growth fund and an income fund. If you are close to retirement and are leery of taking risks with your money, you will probably want to choose an income fund or guaranteed investment contract that pays steady dividends. If you have just started your career, however, you may prefer to invest for growth in, say, stock funds. Although you may go for growth when the stock market is about to take a deep dive, such moves are at least partly offset by the company's matching contribution. The same holds true for your ESOP. Even if your employer's stock sags, the match will compensate for temporary drops in value.

When you retire, your company may offer you several payment options for your pension. The two most common choices are a monthly check or a lump sum, which is typically based on your length of service, final five years' pay, and life expectancy. Deciding which to take requires detailed computations. The wealth-building point that many Americans are learning to take with increasing seriousness: if you believe you can invest the lump sum profitably enough to equal the pension you would otherwise get, you can also leave behind a sizable legacy. An added incentive: the tax bite on lump sums taken at retirement can be moderate. Everybody who retires after age 59½ is eligible for five-year forward averaging, which lets you spread out the lump as though it were paid in equal installments over five years. While the entire tax bill must be paid the year

you receive the lump sum, averaging will significantly lower your bracket.

Your Investments

One factor you should take into account in designing your investment portfolio is the security of your income, notes Gerald Perritt, editor of the *Mutual Fund Letter*. That is because people's investment inclinations often mirror the way they earn their money. For example, a freelance writer, a musican, or a salesperson on commission might earn $35,000 one year, $60,000 the next, and $10,000 the third year. Yet these are the type of people, says Perritt, who tend to invest in chancy emerging growth stocks, risky venture-capital deals, and highly leveraged real estate projects. Such an individual might instead be better off hedging with safer vehicles—CDs, Treasury bills, or mutual funds with holdings in stocks that pay dividends and promise some growth. By contrast, a corporate employee with a secure job who earns $50,000 a year and has a generous, diversified portfolio in his employee-benefits plans is often inclined to invest his spare cash in a safe but stodgy mutual fund. In this case, advises Perritt, the person can obviously afford to look for a little more bang in his investments.

If your analysis of your income tells you that you should be investing some of your spare cash more aggressively, but you are the type of person who frets over every decision, you might adopt a strategy called dollar-cost averaging. With this technique, you merely pick a mutual fund that matches your investment goals and tolerance of risk and invest equal sums periodically. This way, you will be purchasing fewer of the fund's shares when securities prices are high and more when prices dip. To make dollar-cost averaging work, you have to have the discipline to keep writing those regular checks even when your investment plunges. No-load growth mutual funds are ideal vehicles for this approach.

Another wealth-building avenue is to invest in mutual funds inside tax-deferring envelopes such as rollover IRAs. (If you are covered by a company pension plan and earn more than $25,000—$40,000 for a couple—you can no longer fully deduct your contribution to a standard IRA.) Single-premium deferred annuities, sold by insurance companies, operate in a similar fashion. You buy an annuity—the lowest priced is $5,000—with after-tax dollars, but your gains accumulate tax-free. Some annuities promise a specified annual return; others may offer a choice among as many as 15 different funds and allow you to add small deposits monthly or quarterly so that you can dollar-cost average. You have to choose carefully, however, because many insurance companies extract hefty fees.

However impressive the fortune you ultimately create, you probably will have a harder time in the future ensuring that your family—and not the IRS or your state—is your prime beneficiary. Currently, estate taxes do not inhibit the passage of wealth in most families; the federal tax code exempts $600,000 for individuals ($1.2 million for a husband and wife). Above those limits, the IRS takes 40% to 55%. So if you and your spouse die at the same time and leave $1,200,001, the most the estate will owe in federal taxes is 40¢.

Those generous limits are being scrutinized by an increasingly stingy Congress, which is threatening to toughen death taxes. Raising the percentage that the IRS can claim, scaling back the exemption for individuals and couples, and taxing appreciated assets are all ways that Congress may choose to respond to the pressure to increase revenues and help reduce the budget deficit.

No matter how confiscatory estate taxes become, it is still better to have created a small family fortune than not. And who knows what it might grow to in another generation or two?

Protecting Your Hard-Won Wealth

A lifetime of savings and investments can be wiped out by a lawsuit. And if the judgment exceeds the value of your assets, the plaintiff can attach your wages for years to come.

You can protect yourself from financial ruin with an excess liability policy. Most major insurance companies charge between $100 and $200 a year, depending on where you live and how much property you are insuring, to put an umbrella of $1 million—the minimum coverage offered—over both your auto and homeowners liability coverage.

It could be a bargain. In 1985, the last year for which complete figures are available, there were 488 jury awards at or above the $1 million mark, according to Jury Verdict Research in Solon, Ohio, a firm that monitors damage awards nationwide. And although many large awards are reversed or reduced on appeal, the 1985 tally is still more than three times the number of seven-figure awards in 1980. Of course, even a settlement that falls shy of the million-dollar mark can easily breach the $100,000-to-$300,000 liability limit of a typical homeowners or car insurance policy.

In addition to more dollar coverage, an umbrella policy also protects you from a variety of transgressions not even mentioned in a standard auto or homeowners policy, including libel, slander, and defamation of character. Most umbrella policies also pay all legal costs. By contrast, standard auto and homeowners insurance policies do not cover legal expenses if the total cost of the case exceeds the amount of the coverage.

Almost every major insurance company sells umbrella policies. But in some states a few insurers, including State Farm and Allstate, write excess coverage only for clients who already have home and auto policies with the firm. Others have restrictions. For example, you may first have to purchase $500,000 in primary liability coverage; but that costs only about $20 a year more than a $300,000 policy.

Figuring Your Future Fortune

Filling out the worksheet at right will help you make a rough estimate of your assets at retirement.

Step 1. List in the first column the current value of your assets. Include only those you will not need until retirement. For example, exclude your checking account and emergency fund. Also leave out any assets earmarked for specific purposes such as your children's college expenses. (The worksheet assumes that you will pay off your mortgage and other liabilities before retirement.)

Record the balances of your company benefits, such as a 401(k) or stock-ownership account, separately because their growth rates will differ. (Here you can add the projected value of any lump-sum pension payments. Enter them directly in the "future value" column.)

Once you have evaluated what you own, pick a reasonable annual total return for each type of investment. Start by considering historical growth rates. The large-company stocks in the Standard & Poor's 500-stock index have returned 10.3% annually on average since 1926, according to Ibbotson Associates, a financial consulting firm in Chicago. The stocks of smaller companies have done better, with a 12.7% annual total return. Long-term government bond yields have averaged 4.3%, while high-grade corporates came in at 4.9% and municipals at 3.5%. Housing prices have grown an average of 8.1% a year. Since 1960, gold has risen 9.3% and silver 7.7% annually. For mutual funds, see pages 198-203 for compound annual returns for the past five years.

The past is no guarantee of future performance, of course, so follow your own instincts if you have well-reasoned expectations for growth. But be realistic. If you have a consistently superior record as an investor, you can safely estimate a little higher return than the historical averages. If you have trouble matching the averages or are new to investing, shoot a bit lower.

Next, for each type of asset, list in the second column the factor from

Step 1: What Do You Have Now?

Type of asset	Current value		Factor from Table 1		Future value
Residence	_____	x	_____	=	_____
Company plans	_____	x	_____	=	_____
	_____	x	_____	=	_____
Mutual funds	_____	x	_____	=	_____
	_____	x	_____	=	_____
Stocks	_____	x	_____	=	_____
Bonds	_____	x	_____	=	_____
Real estate	_____	x	_____	=	_____
Limited partnerships	_____	x	_____	=	_____
Life insurance cash value	_____	x	_____	=	_____
Money-market funds or accounts	_____	x	_____	=	_____
Collectibles	_____	x	_____	=	_____
Other	_____	x	_____	=	_____

TOTAL _____ **(A)**

Step 2: What Will You Add?

Type of asset	Annual dollar value you expect to add		Factor from Table 2		Future value
_____	_____	x	_____	=	_____
_____	_____	x	_____	=	_____
_____	_____	x	_____	=	_____

TOTAL _____ **(B)**

Step 3: How Wealthy Will You Be?

Future value of assets (add A and B)   _____

Grand total after accounting for annual taxes   _____

Source: Westbrook Financial Advisers

Table 1

Expected Yield	Years to Retirement					
	5	10	15	20	25	30
1%	1.05	1.10	1.16	1.22	1.28	1.35
2	1.10	1.22	1.35	1.49	1.64	1.81
3	1.16	1.34	1.56	1.81	2.09	2.43
4	1.22	1.48	1.80	2.19	2.67	3.24
5	1.28	1.63	2.08	2.65	3.39	4.32
6	1.34	1.79	2.40	3.21	4.29	5.74
7	1.40	1.97	2.76	3.87	5.43	7.61
8	1.47	2.16	3.17	4.66	6.85	10.06
9	1.54	2.37	3.64	5.60	8.62	13.27
10	1.61	2.59	4.18	6.73	10.83	17.45
11	1.69	2.84	4.78	8.06	13.59	22.89
12	1.76	3.11	5.47	9.65	17.00	29.96
13	1.84	3.39	6.25	11.52	21.23	39.12
14	1.93	3.71	7.14	13.74	26.46	50.95
15	2.01	4.05	8.14	16.37	32.92	66.21

Table 2

Expected Yield	Years to Retirement					
	5	10	15	20	25	30
1%	5.10	10.46	16.10	22.02	28.24	34.78
2	5.20	10.95	17.29	24.30	32.03	40.57
3	5.31	11.46	18.60	26.87	36.46	47.58
4	5.42	12.01	20.02	29.78	41.65	56.08
5	5.53	12.58	21.58	33.07	47.73	66.44
6	5.64	13.18	23.28	36.79	54.86	79.06
7	5.75	13.82	25.13	41.00	63.25	94.46
8	5.87	14.49	27.15	45.76	73.11	113.28
9	5.98	15.19	29.36	51.16	84.70	136.31
10	6.11	15.94	31.77	57.28	98.35	164.49
11	6.23	16.72	34.41	64.20	114.41	199.02
12	6.35	17.55	37.28	72.05	133.33	241.33
13	6.48	18.42	40.42	80.95	155.62	293.20
14	6.61	19.34	43.84	91.02	181.87	356.79
15	6.74	20.30	47.58	102.44	212.79	434.75

Table 1 that corresponds to the annual yield you expect and the number of years before you retire. Multiply the factor by the current value of the investment and enter the result in the "future value" column. That shows what your assets will be worth if they grow at the rates you project.

Step 2. Because you will undoubtedly add to your savings before retirement, estimate how much you expect to put away annually and how you might distribute the money among your investments. (For example, you might regularly stash $2,000 a year in your Individual Retirement Account, putting half of it in growth stocks and half in corporate bonds.) Then enter these figures under "annual dollar value you expect to add."

Next choose the yield you expect for each type of investment as you did in Step 1. Find the factor in Table 2 that corresponds to the yield and the number of years between now and your retirement. The factors in Table 2 assume that you invest the money at the end of the year. If you put it away earlier, you will receive a bigger payoff in the end.

Step 3. Most of your assets may be in tax-deferred or tax-exempt investments, such as a house, an IRA, or a 401(k). Any wealth that is taxed annually, such as mutual fund dividends, will not grow nearly as impressively. To get a ballpark figure of what will be left after yearly Internal Revenue Service invasions, multiply the fraction of your total (the sum of A and B) that is taxed annually by 100% minus your tax bracket (for example, multiply by 72% if you are in the 28% bracket).

Should you wish to account for inflation in the future value of your assets, multiply your grand total by 78% if retirement is roughly five years away, 61% for 10 years, 48% for 15 years, 38% for 20 years, 29% for 25 years, and 23% for 30 years. That will reflect the 5% average annual inflation rate that many analysts foresee.

How to Make Your Assets Grow

An Individual Retirement Account is still a great way to save—despite tax reform.

Although Individual Retirement Accounts have lost some of their allure as short-term, tax-sheltered savings vehicles, they can still be your ticket to a comfortable future. For most people, the impressive gains of long-term, tax-deferred compounding of earnings generated within the account are too good to pass up.

It is true that the new tax law's lower marginal rates raise the cost of contributing to your IRA. For example, if you were in the 42% bracket prior to tax reform, it cost you only $1,160 to put $2,000 into your IRA each year. Uncle Sam kicked in the remaining $840 in the form of tax savings. At the new 28% rate, which affects couples earning more than $29,750 and singles earning more than $17,850 after 1987, that same $2,000 contribution gets you 33% less—$560—in tax savings.

Figuring out whether you can still deduct your IRA contribution beginning with the 1987 tax year is easy. If neither you nor your spouse is covered by a company pension or profit-sharing plan, you can stash away and deduct up to $2,000 for yourself and an additional $250 for a nonworking spouse, regardless of your income. If you are single and covered by such a plan—even if you are not yet vested—you rate a full deduction only if your adjusted gross income is $25,000 or less. Your allowable deduction drops $10 for each $50 you earn above $25,000 until you hit $35,000, when the deduction phases out entirely. Married couples filing jointly, with either spouse covered by a company plan, get the full deduction only if their adjusted gross income is $40,000 or lower. Their deduction also disappears in $10 increments for each additional $50 in income up to $50,000, when the deduction vanishes.

Here are some ways to shape your IRA strategy in the wake of tax reform.

Getting under the Income Limits

Savvy investors may be able to salvage part of their IRA deduction even if they earn more than the $35,000 or $50,000 ceilings. One way is to participate in a 401(k) plan if your company has one. Under such a plan, you direct your employer to put away up to $7,000 of your salary toward retirement. Some employers kick in 25¢ to a dollar for each dollar you contribute. Since the amount you put away under this plan is not taxable income, it lowers your adjusted gross income.

Example 1: If you and your spouse earn $52,000—and therefore are not eligible for an IRA deduction—and you put $7,000 into a 401(k) plan, your adjusted gross income would drop to $45,000, qualifying you for a $1,000 IRA deduction. Contributions to a Keogh and Simplified Employee Pension may also help you reclaim part or all of your IRA deduction.

Tax reform will also force you to re-examine how you invest your IRA money. Previously, it made sense to concentrate on high-yielding investments for your retirement account and do your growth-oriented investing outside an IRA. Since withdrawals from IRAs are taxed at ordinary income rates, investing in growth stocks or investments that reaped capital gains effectively squandered a tax break by converting a long-term capital gain into ordinary income. But now that capital gains and regular income will be taxed at the same rate, load up your IRA with the investments you believe will give the highest return, regardless of whether income, capital appreciation, or a combination of the two generates that return.

If you are undecided how to divvy up your IRA funds between stocks and income-oriented investments, consider the new breed of mutual fund that will make the decision for you. Known as asset allocation funds, these funds strive to get the best return by dividing their assets among stocks, bonds, and money-market securities.

And do not overlook one newly qualified IRA investment—U.S. gold and silver coins. Like any other IRA investment, these coins must be purchased through—and held by—such official IRA custodians as a bank or a brokerage firm. In general, however, you should consider this investment only if you are looking to hedge 5% to 10% of your retirement portfolio against losses related to a resurgence of inflation.

Alternatives for Saving

Faced with the loss of most or all of your IRA deduction, why should you continue socking away $2,000 a year in an investment that you will not be able to get at—without incurring the 10% withdrawal penalty—until you are 59½? The answer is easy: your IRA, whether deductible or not, should outperform other tax-favored investments provided you have at least five years until you retire.

If, however, you want to have the option of raiding your IRA fund before retirement—for a down payment for a house, say—then you ought to think twice before investing in an IRA. The reason is that tax reform's lower rates make the initial contribution to a nondeductible IRA more expensive and, at the same time, dilute the benefits of tax-deferred compounding of earnings.

Prior to tax reform, it often paid to use your IRA as a sort of medium-term savings account that you could readily dip into before you retired. If you were in the top tax bracket and stuck $2,000 into an IRA account earning 9%, you could withdraw the money five and one-half years later, pay the tax and 10% penalty for early withdrawal, and still come out ahead of someone who put $2,000 into a taxable investment paying 9%. Assuming the same 9% return today, however, it would take a person in the 28% bracket six years to break even after tax and penalty with a deductible IRA, and almost eleven years with a nondeductible IRA. As a result, investors who might have to draw on their IRA early should consider such alternative tax-sheltered investments as municipal bond funds.

Example 2: If you put $2,000 into a deductible IRA earning 8% and pulled out all your money in 10 years, after paying tax and an early-withdrawal penalty you would have $19,400. But if you had invested $1,440 ($2,000 minus 28% tax) in a municipal bond fund paying 6%, in 10 years you would have $20,119—on which you would owe no federal tax or penalty. In fact, it would take roughly 14 years until a deductible IRA outpaced the bond fund and roughly 25 years until a nondeductible IRA beat the bond fund.

Given the IRA's reduced status as a short-term tax shelter under the new law, you can expect some pressure from the purveyors of competing shelters. Among the most shrill will be insurance companies and brokerage houses pushing variable annuities and such life insurance products as variable life. Both these alternatives have serious shortcomings. Annuities typically carry back-end loads of up to 7% that phase out after seven years. They also charge annual fees of 2%. Finally, if you withdraw your money from an annuity before you reach age 59½, you will pay the same 10% penalty as for an early withdrawal from an IRA.

Variable life insurance offers tax-free buildup of earnings and gives you access to your money without the 10% penalty, but sales commissions and other expenses often make such policies poor alternatives to an IRA.

Taxes and Withdrawals

If you do decide to make nondeductible contributions, steel yourself for some daunting bookkeeping chores. You will need to keep accurate tax records distinguishing between deductible versus nondeductible funds in your IRA accounts. Deductible contributions, plus all earnings in any of your IRA accounts, are taxed upon withdrawal. If you withdraw before age 59½, you will also pay a 10% penalty. Nondeductible contributions are not subject to income tax nor the 10% penalty for early withdrawals.

Obviously, if you are in need of quick cash, you would dip into nondeductible contributions first since neither tax nor penalty is assessed against them. Unfortunately, Congress has outlawed this strategy. To discourage people from using nondeductible IRAs as tax-free savings accounts, the tax law stipulates that each withdrawal contains the same proportion of taxable and nontaxable funds as all your IRAs combined.

Example 3: Say that your IRA has a total balance of $16,000, including two years' non-deductible contributions totaling $4,000, and you make an early withdrawal of $4,000. Since only 25% of your total IRA balance consists of nontaxable funds, you must pay tax and the 10% penalty on the taxable portion—$3,000, or 75% of the $4,000 withdrawal. At the 28% rate, you would owe tax of $840 and a 10% penalty of $300 on the taxable portion of the withdrawal. Deducting tax and penalty from the $4,000 withdrawal leaves you with $2,860.

Some taxpayers, however, might be able to use spousal IRAs to sidestep this rule's full impact. The IRS requires withdrawals to take into account only the balance of your own IRA, not your spouse's. So if you already have a substantial amount of money in your IRA and are eligible for, but have not yet begun, an IRA for your nonworking spouse, opening such an account and putting most of the $2,250 contribution into it could be a way of keeping access to nondeductible funds without incurring harsh penalties.

Example 4: If your IRA is worth $10,000 and you make nondeductible contributions of $2,000 each year for the next three years to your own account and $250 to the spousal account, the balance of your account would be $20,097, assuming the account earned 9%. If you withdrew $6,000—the amount of your nondeductible contributions—after paying a 28% tax of $1,178 and a 10% early-withdrawal penalty of $421, you would wind up with only $4,401. If you had stashed only $250 into your account and $2,000 into your spouse's, the balance in that account would total $7,146. Since the bulk of that amount consists of nontaxable funds—$6,000 in nondeductible contributions—pulling out $6,000 would result in a tax of only $270 and a $96 penalty. Pulling out the same $6,000 would leave a net of $5,634—$1,233 more than you would have left making the withdrawal from your own account.

Financial machinations aside, the best reason to continue funding an IRA is also the simplest. When it comes time to call it a career, even those of us who wind up with a comfortable pension and Social Security can probably do with some extra savings to fall back on. The IRA is still an ideal way of saving for retirement without dealing with a lot of complicated investments. If you are going to have a long, healthy retirement, you will enjoy it more if you do not run out of money.

> ## *Money* Tip
>
> If you are self-employed and married, hire your spouse. Then he or she will be eligible to invest up to $2,000 in an IRA. Just make sure the service performed is legitimate, employment records are maintained, and you pay the going rate for the work.

A Short Course in Estate Planning

A well-drawn estate plan can keep your wealth in the family long after you are gone.

Of all the possible threats to your family's wealth, from inflation to bear markets to natural disasters, only one is certain to occur: your death. So while estate planning may not be the most pleasant of topics, it is one defense you can be sure your family will need.

If you die without a will, in most states you partially disinherit your spouse and condemn your estate to an unnecessarily prolonged and expensive wait in probate. Similarly, if you fail to prepare for estate taxes, your legacy could be clipped by federal transfer taxes at rates as high as 55%. With proper planning, most estates could reach their intended heirs without losing a penny to federal taxes.

A good estate plan has two aims: to make sure your wealth reaches your intended heirs in the manner you choose, and to minimize your estate's erosion by federal and state taxes. To accomplish both, you must manipulate the forbidding tangle of ancient common-law traditions and modern tax regulations that govern estate transfers. Do not attempt it without the help of a practiced estate attorney; if you go it alone, you risk having the orderly transfer of your wealth disintegrate into an ugly court battle among your heirs. Even with a lawyer, though, you need to understand the process in order to pass on your wealth. The more you know about the fundamentals of estate planning—wills, trusts, joint ownership, lifetime gifts, the marital deduction, and the $600,000 exemption—the better you will understand what the obstacles are and what you must do to succeed.

Your Will

You need a will whether you are single or married, old or young, healthy or ill. This document not only instructs your survivors about how to distribute your property but also enables you to nominate a guardian to care for your children if they become orphaned. Another crucial function is to designate someone as your estate's executor, the person who will be responsible for taking inventory of all your property, paying your estate's creditors and taxes, and ultimately splitting your estate among your heirs.

If you die without a will—intestate, in legal jargon—the courts take control of your estate and, in effect, write a will for you in accordance with your state's intestacy laws. It is unlikely that the result will match your wishes. For example, in most states your mate does not automatically inherit all your property if you have children. New York's intestacy law would award your spouse $4,000 plus one-third of the balance of the estate. The rest would be evenly divided among your children, regardless of their ages or special needs.

In the absence of a will, the court must also appoint an administrator for your estate and a guardian for your children. Normally the courts prefer a relative as administrator, but if one is not available or willing to serve, your estate could end up in the hands of a professional administrator. This official generally takes 3% to 5% of your estate in fees a year, an arrangement that gives him little incentive to settle your estate quickly or to minimize your estate for tax purposes. The court would also select a relative as guardian if the children were orphaned, but there is no guarantee it would choose the one you prefer. And since the court's appointment does not carry the moral weight of your last wishes in your will, your children could become the object of a bitter custody battle.

Considering the anguish it prevents, a will is a bargain. If your estate is simple—less than $600,000 with no out-of-state real estate—you can expect to pay between $50 and $200 for a will. You could draft one even more cheaply on your own by using a do-it-yourself form. But the savings are hardly worth the risk that your homemade testament could founder on a technicality.

Probate

Whether you write a will or not, your worldly effects will generally be subject to the ponderous process known as probate. At this time your executor (or the court-appointed administrator) values your assets, pays off your creditors, files the estate's taxes, and finally awards what is left to your heirs. Probate occurs under the supervision of a local court known in various states as probate, surrogate, or orphan's court. In addition to approving your will—or writing one for you if you failed to—the probate court rules on the legitimacy of any creditors' claims against your estate and supervises the actions of your executor until your affairs are completely settled. If your minor children inherit any property directly, the court also oversees the guardian's use of that property until the children reach legal adulthood. All guardians—even the children's surviving parent—must keep records of their routine use of the children's inheritances and must petition the court for any unusual expenditures on the children's behalf. To spare your offspring this red tape, do not leave property directly to them. Instead, bequeath it to a trust established for their benefit and name their guardian as trustee.

Other than that, the major drawback to probate is that even with a fairly efficient court and executor, the process takes a minimum of four to eight months. If disgruntled relatives contest the will or if you owned property in another state, your heirs might have to wait years. Administrative and legal expenses during probate normally run between 5% and 10% of the estate, and naturally, the longer your estate lingers in probate, the more these costs grow.

Minimizing delays. A properly drafted will holds probate delays and expenses to a minimum. In most cases, you should give your executor broad powers to settle disputes or sell property as he or she sees fit without having to ask the court for permission. Your will should also avoid provisions likely to be invalidated by the probate court or to spark a challenge from disappointed heirs. For example, in most states you cannot leave your spouse less than the portion he or she would receive under intestacy laws. Disinheriting a child, on the other hand, is permissible everywhere but Louisiana. If total disinheritance is your aim, be sure to specify in your will that you know you are doing it. Otherwise, the child might claim to have been overlooked by mistake. Also be careful about bequests, no matter how well intentioned, that could be interpreted as favoritism or slights by disgruntled heirs. For example, do not cut off the daughter who married the millionaire without explaining that her struggling siblings need your legacy more than she does. Her hurt feelings could spur a contest over the will or at least cause a lasting rift in your family.

You can also avoid probate problems by keeping your will up to date. You need to have it reviewed whenever your circumstances change significantly—if, for example, you divorce or move to another state. In any event, have a lawyer look over your will every five years.

In addition, keep your affairs in order. Maintain an inventory of all your assets and make sure your executor knows where that inventory is. Your estate should have enough cash on hand to meet your cash bequests and to pay off your estate's creditors, including the state and federal tax collectors. If your wealth consists largely of illiquid assets such as real estate or stock in a family business, you can provide liquidity by purchasing additional life insurance. You might, for example, have your business purchase insurance on your life in an amount roughly equal to the value of your stock in the company. When you die, the firm could use the proceeds to buy back the shares from your estate. Otherwise, your executor might have to unload the stock at fire-sale prices to raise cash.

Avoiding probate. The surest way to avoid probate is to keep your property beyond the probate court's jurisdiction. In fact, a surprisingly large amount of your estate is likely to pass outside probate without any effort on your part. For example, the proceeds of a life insurance policy and the balances in your employee retirement plan, Individual Retirement Account, or Keogh account will pass directly to your beneficiaries. Any property you own jointly with rights of survivorship will pass automatically to the co-owner at your death. If you live in one of the eight community property states—Arizona, California, Idaho, Louisiana, Nevada, New Mexico, Texas, and Washington—half of any possessions that you acquired during your marriage (except gifts or inheritances) belongs to your spouse; the other half passes under your will.

If you live in one of the more numerous common-law states, holding some—but not all—assets jointly with your spouse is smart estate planning. By putting at least your home and checking account in joint title, you will ensure that your surviving spouse at least owns the roof over his or her head and can get some cash immediately after your death. Owning everything jointly with your spouse, however, is no substitute for a will. If the two of you were to perish at the same time, your children's inheritance would be left to the rough justice of your state's intestacy laws.

The most practical mechanism for skipping probate altogether is probably the so-called revocable living trust or *inter vivos* trust. A revocable living trust is one that you set up while you are alive, in which you have the power to change or revoke the terms of the trust. (A trust that you establish in your will, called a testamentary trust, does not keep you out of probate.) You may designate yourself as trustee of a revocable living trust; you may prefer to have a bank or trust company as co-trustee if you want to have your assets managed professionally. (For more information on the relative advantages of wills and revocable living trusts, see "Planning a Hassle-Free Legacy" on page 168.)

Taxes and Trusts

Keeping your estate out of probate, for all its advantages, does not protect your wealth against taxation. Probate concerns itself only with property that you own in your own name when you die. By contrast, the federal transfer tax, known as the Unified Estate and Gift Tax, potentially counts as fair game every piece of property that you transfer to someone else, regardless of whether you give it while you are alive or have it transferred on your death. Your taxable estate at your death includes not only the property you own in your own name but also half your jointly held property; the face value of any life insurance you own, regardless of the beneficiary; and any property you do not directly own but over which you have general power of appointment, that is, the right to take it yourself or give it away. (This includes all the principal held in a revocable living trust.) This all-encompassing tax base is accompanied by a particularly voracious bite: this year the maximum estate tax is 55% on taxable estates of more than $2.5 million.

Lowering the tax bill. Fortunately, the estate-tax law leaves enough escape routes so that you can avoid federal estate and gift taxes altogether, provided you plan ahead. To begin with, your estate can deduct all its administrative costs, the value of any debts you leave behind, and any bequests to charity. But the most valuable deduction by far is the so-called marital deduction, which lets you leave any amount of property to a spouse tax-free.

The trouble is, if you leave everything to your spouse, some of your wealth will end up in the tax man's hands when your spouse dies and your property passes to your children. To minimize the tax liability on that second estate, you can make use of a second crucial sheltering provision of the estate-tax law: a credit that allows you to give away during your life or leave at your death a total of $600,000 free of federal gift or estate taxes. Moreover, you can also give away as much as $10,000 per person per year—$20,000 if you are married—without using up any of the $600,000 exemption. As long as you give away less than those amounts, your executor will be able to apply the full $600,000 exemption against your estate taxes.

Together, the $600,000 exemption and the marital deduction enable parents to pass an estate of up to $1.2 million to their children without federal estate tax. For example, consider a husband who has assets of $1.2 million. In his will he bequeaths half the property to a testamentary trust called a bypass, or family, trust. He directs that the income from the trust go to his wife for the rest of her life and that the principal pass to their children at her death. The husband's estate owes no tax on this bequest, thanks to the $600,000 exemption. And, because the wife does not control the property in the trust, the tax code excludes it from her estate as well. The husband leaves the remaining $600,000 to his wife. This property escapes taxation at his death because of the marital deduction. Though the assets are now in the wife's estate, she can use her $600,000 exemption to bequeath them tax-free to the children.

Marital and QTIP trusts. Tax-skirting trusts allow some variation on this basic strategy. Suppose, for example, that the husband does not want to leave property directly to his wife, perhaps because she is infirm. He can instead put the money in a so-called marital trust with, say, an adult child as trustee and his wife as sole beneficiary with general power of appointment. The contents of the trust would be considered part of her taxable estate; so even though the husband has not left the property to her directly, his bequest still qualifies for the marital deduction.

Giving the wife general power of appointment allows her to leave the trust property to whomever she chooses—including a new husband. Thus the first husband has no guarantee under this arrangement that the property he leaves in the marital trust will ever reach his children. To allay that concern, he could leave the property in a qualified terminable interest property, or QTIP, trust. In this arrangement, the trust agreement, not the spouse, controls who gets the property at the spouse's death. Such a trust would still qualify for the marital deduction provided it meets two requirements: all the trust's income must go to the wife during her lifetime and be paid at least annually, and the principal must be considered part of her estate.

Charitable bequests. To avoid taxes on an estate larger than $1.2 million, you first need to reduce the estate by charitable bequests or, better yet, by giving away assets while you are alive. If you leave property to a charity in your will, you get a deduction against your estate taxes. But if you donate property to a charity while you are alive, you not only reduce your eventual estate but also get a deduction on your income taxes. You need not make all your gifts to charity, of course. You can also give property to your family. As long as you and your spouse keep the gifts below $20,000 annually per heir, you do not use up any of your $600,000 exemption.

The best assets to give away are those you expect to appreciate rapidly. Suppose you intend to bequeath your $300,000 portfolio of stocks, currently appreciating 15% a year, in trust to your grandchildren. If you give the stocks away now, you will still have roughly half of your $600,000 exemption to apply against your estate taxes. But if you keep the stocks and live another five years, your portfolio will have grown to more than $600,000. Leaving that amount to the grandchildren will absorb your estate's entire exemption.

You can get an asset out of your estate without making an outright gift by transferring ownership to what is known as an irrevocable living trust. In this arrangement, you give up any right to trust income and principal as well as the power to change the trust agreement. Because you have, in effect, renounced the benefits of owning the property, it is not considered part of your taxable estate. When you draw up the trust, however, you are free to give the income to any beneficiary and to specify who inherits the principal. Note, though, that property transfers to an irrevocable living trust are considered gifts to the trust. So you may owe gift taxes if you put in more than $10,000 a year.

Obviously, the realm of QTIP trusts and irrevocable living trusts is no place for a layman—or even a lawyer who is not skilled in estate planning. Ask your accountant or financial planner for names of estate attorneys. They deal with such lawyers regularly and ought to know which ones are best in your area. In fact, it makes sense to coordinate all your estate planning with your accountant and financial planner since they are the experts most intimately familiar with your finances.

In selecting your attorney, interview at least three, telling them as much about your estate as you can. While you may lack the expertise to judge the legal merits of their proposals, you can gauge how well they listen and judge how comfortable you feel discussing family and financial matters with them. Avoid lawyers who seem inclined to dictate an estate plan rather than to hear you out. A good attorney will tell you what you may do and the best way to do it. But it is for you to decide what you really want for your family after you are gone.

Money Basics

Administrator. A person, often a family member, appointed by a court to handle an estate in the absence of an executor.

Bypass trust. A trust that allows the surviving spouse of the grantor to receive income from the property during the spouse's lifetime, after which the property passes to the grantor's other heirs.

Conservator. A person named by a court to manage the property of someone judged mentally incompetent or physically incapacitated.

Executor. A person named in your will to manage your estate. He or she collects your assets, pays your debts and taxes, and distributes property as you have directed.

Guardian. A person chosen by you—or by a court if you die without a will—to care for your children if they are orphaned. Guardians can also manage the children's property.

Irrevocable living trust. A trust you establish during your lifetime from which you receive no income and in which you retain no power to change the terms. Upon your death, the contents of the trust usually pass to your heirs free of federal estate taxes.

Marital trust. A trust in which property passes tax-free to the surviving spouse upon the grantor's death.

Revocable living trust. A trust that you establish during your lifetime in which you can change or revoke the terms as you wish. You can act as trustee or name a co-trustee such as a bank. You may also name a successor trustee to take over if you die or become mentally incompetent or physically incapacitated. Property in the trust is considered part of your taxable estate but skips probate.

Testamentary trust. A trust that is created by your will to take effect upon your death.

Unified Estate and Gift Tax. The federal transfer tax applied to all property you give away during your lifetime or transfer to an heir upon your death.

Planning a Hassle-Free Legacy

While a will is a must, your heirs will remember you even more fondly if you also draft a living trust.

Who would actually want to die without a will? Your financial plan, no matter how carefully crafted, would be forgotten, your assets would be disposed of according to a rigid legal formula, and your estate might be diminished needlessly by taxes.

The problem with a will is that it must be proved valid in probate court. Your heirs may have to wait four months to two years for their inheritances, depending upon the efficiency of your executor and the local court. The procedure can drag on even longer if your survivors squabble over who gets what. If you own property in more than one state, your heirs may have to deal with two or more probate proceedings. Worse yet, 5% to 10% of your legacy will be lost to court costs and attorney's and executor's fees.

Though probate procedures and fees are less onerous in some states than others, you can spare your heirs those nightmares by establishing a living—sometimes called an *inter vivos*—trust. (A living trust should not be confused with a living will, a document in which you formally, and in some states legally, express your wish to forgo extraordinary medical treatment when you become terminally ill.) Property placed in a living trust bypasses probate, as does your share of assets that are jointly owned or have named beneficiaries, such as pension and profit-sharing plans, Individual Retirement Accounts and life insurance policies.

Even if you establish a living trust, you will still need a simple will. The chief reason is that you cannot use a trust to name a guardian for your minor children. In addition, your will should include a "pour-over" clause stipulating that any property that you forgot to place in your trust should go there after your death. These assets will be subject to probate, but the process should not be lengthy or expensive, assuming you shifted most of your property to your trust before your demise. That is because most states have simplified probate procedures for small estates that can take as little as a day or two to complete and may not even require the services of a lawyer. The definition of a small estate varies by state, with limits ranging from $500 in New Hampshire to $60,000 in California. To find out what the ceiling is in your state, ask an attorney who specializes in estate planning or call your local probate court. And the price of a living trust should not break the bank. For a modest and uncomplicated estate, a living trust and a will with a pour-over clause cost about $400 to $1,000. A simple will runs $50 to $200.

Living trusts may be either revocable or irrevocable. But revocable ones are preferable because of their greater flexibility. For instance, you can keep any or all income a revocable trust produces, change its provisions, or terminate it. Many people even act as their own trustees. As a result, trust income is taxed at your rate (and reported on your tax return if you or your spouse serves as trustee). In addition, property in a revocable living trust is included in your taxable estate.

If you create an irrevocable living trust, on

the other hand, you cannot control property in it. If you serve as trustee you can act only as an administrator; you cannot change the trust's provisions. Since you part with your assets forever when you place them in an irrevocable trust, they are not included in your taxable estate unless you receive income from the trust. But there are better ways to avoid or reduce estate tax that do not require you to relinquish control of your assets during your lifetime, as outlined in "A Short Course in Estate Planning."

After your death, a revocable living trust can remain intact for the benefit of your heirs, or it can terminate with assets distributed to those same survivors. Your wishes, which you set down in your trust document, are carried out by a successor trustee of your choice. A relative, friend, or one of your beneficiaries may agree to perform this service free; banks and trust companies generally charge a fee equal to 2% of the assets distributed. There are no fees associated with living trusts during your lifetime unless you hire an institution, attorney, or a professional money manager to act as your co-trustee.

Even those fees seem reasonable compared with the expense of probate. Traditionally, attorneys' fees have been based on the size of an estate or dictated by local custom. Only 13 states have set fee schedules, usually 1% to 11% of an estate's gross value. Generally, fees consume greater percentages of smaller estates. In California, for example, a lawyer handling a $100,000 estate would earn at least $3,150, or 3%; for probating a $3 million estate, he would earn $61,150, or 2%. The attorney could charge additional fees for selling assets, preparing an estate tax return, or defending the estate against claims by creditors or dissatisfied survivors. You can obtain a fee schedule from your county's probate court.

Unlike a will, a living trust can also shield your estate from creditors. With a will, your executor is required to notify your creditors of your demise by mail and newspaper advertisement so they can submit their claims against your estate. If you placed your assets in a living trust, however, no such publicity is necessary. But you cannot escape your creditors

during your lifetime by transferring your assets to a revocable living trust. (They would be safe in an irrevocable living trust that you do not benefit from, though.) Say you cause an automobile accident and are liable for damages that exceed your insurance coverage. In most states, assets in your revocable living trust could be attached to satisfy court judgments against you.

Privacy is another advantage of living trusts. Nosy neighbors cannot find out how you apportioned your assets. In fact, the terms of your trust may become public only if someone objects to your provisions or lack of provisions for him or her. That is unlikely, however, because it is more difficult to contest a living trust than a will. Instead of filing a challenge against your estate in probate court, an unhappy survivor must sue your successor trustee as well as your beneficiaries.

Another benefit is that you can serve as trustee while you are in good health, but your successor trustee can take over if your physician certifies that you are no longer mentally or physically capable of managing your money. This arrangement is less costly and time consuming than a court-appointed conservatorship. A conservator must make an annual accounting to the court and may have to get its approval to make major expenditures or investments. Your successor trustee, on the other hand, simply follows the wishes you have set down in your trust document.

Once you decide to set up a living trust, you must transfer title to all your assets to it. Your attorney should handle the paperwork required to shift your house and other real estate into your trust. He or she should also prepare a document called an assignment of personal property to transfer personal possessions to a living trust. Standard legalese covers appliances, furniture, and other household goods, but you should list valuable antiques, art, and jewelry separately.

It is ordinarily up to you to put the rest of your assets in your trust unless you want to pay for the time it takes for your lawyer to do this. To transfer bank accounts to your trust, for example, you must either have your banker retitle your existing accounts or you must open new ones.

The easiest way to transfer stocks, bonds, and other intangible investments is to have your broker open a new account in your trust's name and place your securities in it. If you intend to trade on margin or buy and sell options, say so in your trust document. You can transfer motor vehicles by applying for new titles at your state's motor vehicles bureau.

Special rules apply if you live or have lived in Wisconsin or a community property state (see page 165). In those states, all income earned and assets acquired during marriage, except for individual gifts and inheritances, are considered community property. Each spouse shares equally in this property, so half of it is included in each spouse's estate. There is no problem if spouses agree to transfer community property to a trust created for their mu-

tual benefit. But if you want to put community property in a trust that benefits only you, your partner must agree to give up his or her rights to the property.

Money Basics

Living will. A document in which you formally, and in some states legally, express your wish to forgo life-sustaining medical treatment if you become terminally ill.

Successor trustee. A person, bank, or trust company named by you to become trustee of your revocable living trust if you die or become mentally incompetent or physically incapacitated.

The New ABCs of Asset Shifting

There are still tax-saving ways to accumulate funds for your children sooner so they can benefit later.

One of the lovelier loopholes lost to tax reform was the easy shifting of assets from high-bracket parents to low-bracket children through gifts and trusts. The device was the most cost-effective way to fund a child's college education, launch him or her in a business, or provide the down payment on a first house.

But with the new tax law came a provision dubbed the kiddie tax. Now any interest, dividends, or other investment income over $1,000 earned by a child under 14 is taxed at his or her parents' rate—as much as 33% this year. In the year in which a child turns 14, he or she goes through an economic rite of passage, and such investment income above $500 is taxed at his or her own rate, which presumably will be lower than the parents'.

Grim as the changes are, they have not knocked the life out of asset shifting. You can continue to give a child up to $10,000 a year ($20,000 if giving with your spouse) without paying a gift tax. And most financial advisers believe there are sizable tax advantages to be reaped from doing so. Assuming a hefty return of 10%, a child under 14 could still have assets of $10,000 and not be taxed at his or her parents' rate. At age 14 or older, the child could have assets of $178,500 before being pushed above the 15% bracket.

Of the shifting techniques still available, the one for you depends on how old your child is, when you want your child to make use of the money, and how much money is involved. Here are the choices.

Custodial Accounts

The easiest way to give money to a child under 18 is to set up a custodial account under the Uniform Gifts to Minors Act (UGMA) or its newer sibling, the Uniform Transfer to Minors Act (UTMA). These accounts, which cost nothing to set up through a banker or broker, are administered by a custodian—preferably someone other than yourself. The reason: if the assets are in your control, they are considered part of the donor's estate and would be taxed as such if you die.

UGMAs and UTMAs are essentially the same, except for two key provisions. In an UGMA, parents are limited to gifts of cash or securities. Another drawback: in most of the 23 states that permit UGMAs, the assets automatically come under your child's control when he or she turns 18. If the child would rather have a BMW than a B.A., that is his or her choice. With UTMAs, which have been adopted over the past three years in 27 states* and the District of Columbia, distribution of the assets can be deferred until the child reaches age 21—or 25 in the case of California. Also, the law allows you to place a wider range of property in an UTMA, including real estate, royalties, patents, and paintings.

If you set up a custodial account, you should take your child's age into consideration when making gifts. Richard Coppage and Sidney Baxendale, accounting professors at the University of Louisville, have computed the ideal amounts and timing of parental gifts in custodial accounts. Say the parents of a newborn wanted the child's UGMA to total $100,000 by the time he or she turns 18. (That, incredibly, is how much four years at a top private college may cost by 2006.) Assuming a yield of 8% annually, Coppage has calculated that parents in the 28% bracket who time their gifts properly (see the box on page 173) would have $9,458 more for their child's education than parents who ignore timing.

Tailor an UGMA's investments to your child's age too. If he or she is well under 14, financial advisers suggest that you go for long-term growth by investing in growth-stock mutual funds. If your child will not reach 14 for

five years, you could give him or her supersafe Series EE U.S. savings bonds, which if held for a minimum of five years have a guaranteed yield of 6% (recent yield: 7.2%). They are only federally taxable and not until the bonds are cashed in—by which time the child will be taxed at his or her own rate. When the child reaches 14, parents should shift into more conservative fixed-rate instruments such as certificates of deposit or corporate bonds with maturities matched to the time of need.

Minors' Trusts

You need a lawyer to set up a minors' trust, also known as a 2503(c) trust (which will cost about $500), and you must file annual trust tax returns. For those reasons, a minors' trust usually makes sense only when substantial amounts of money are at stake, at least $50,000. At that point, the expense will be more than offset by the two advantages of minors' trusts over custodial accounts, taxes and control.

With regard to taxes, the first $5,000 earned by the trust, no matter what the child's age, is taxed at 15%; any amount above that is taxed at 28%.

Control of the income and principal is in the hands of the trustee (normally you) until the child reaches 21, as with an UTMA. But in a minors' trust your child has 30 to 60 days from the time he or she turns 21 to demand the assets from the trust; if the child fails to do so, the trust continues until whatever time you have specified.

Charitable Remainder Trusts

You might want to consider a charitable remainder annuity trust if you are about to realize a large capital gain—$20,000 or so—and you want to avoid paying a hefty tax. Say you bought stock for $10,000, and it is now worth $50,000. In setting up such a trust, stipulate that a beneficiary—usually a child—be paid a fixed amount from the trust's income, say $5,000 a year over four years beginning when he or she reaches 18. A nonprofit institution chosen by you has use of the assets in the trust during its four-year term and then owns them when the trust terminates. The advantages to you: you avoid paying capital-gains tax, you get a charitable deduction (worth $11,033 in this example if your bracket is 28%) over the life of the trust, and your child pays tax on the principal he or she receives at the 15% rate.

Splits and Grits

An elaborate yet effective asset-shifting device for wealthy families is a split-interest purchase, commonly known as a split. It is essentially an arrangement in which an adult—usually the parent, although it could be anyone--buys majority interest in an asset and the child buys the rest. The parent then gets the income from that asset for a specified number of years, after which the child receives the property tax-free. Not only is this a cheap way for your child to acquire assets at a fraction of their cost, but it is also a way for a parent or grandparent to eliminate or reduce death taxes. But to set up a split, a child must have money—given by someone other than the person setting up the split—to pay his share.

If your child has no cash to kick into a split, you can consider a grantor-retained income trust, or GRIT. The adults retain the income interest as they do in a split, but they put up the entire purchase amount. What will take true grit is paying the bill from a tax or estate lawyer for setting up either of these arrangements: a nondeductible $1,000 or so.

Money Basics

Charitable remainder annuity trust. A trust from which a beneficiary, often a child, receives a fixed annual payment. When the trust dissolves according to the grantor's wishes, a nonprofit charity chosen by the grantor gets the remaining assets. The grantor qualifies for charitable deductions and pays no capital-gains tax on the assets.

Grantor. A person who places money in a trust for the benefit of someone else.

Minors' trust. A trust set up for the benefit of a child but managed by a trustee who controls the income and principal until the child turns 21—sometimes longer if the child does not demand the assets within 30 to 60 days after turning 21. The first $5,000 in earnings is taxed at 15%; any amount above that is taxed at 28%.

Uniform Gifts to Minors Act. A law that provides for accounts in which cash and securities given to a child are held in his or her name but are administered by a custodian. The child gains control of the assets at age 18. Under the new tax law, income from an UGMA account over $1,000 is taxed at the parents' rate until the child is 14, when all earnings over the $500 standard deduction are taxed at the child's rate.

Uniform Transfer to Minors Act. A law that provides for accounts similar to UGMA accounts except that the child does not gain control of the assets until age 21 (25 in California). Real estate, royalties, patents, and paintings are allowed in the accounts, as well as cash and securities.

*The states that had adopted the Uniform Transfer to Minors Act as of September 1987 were Alabama, Arkansas, California, Colorado, Florida, Hawaii, Idaho, Illinois, Iowa, Kansas, Kentucky, Louisiana, Massachusetts, Minnesota, Missouri, Montana, Nevada, New Hampshire, New Jersey, North Carolina, North Dakota, Oklahoma, Oregon, Rhode Island, South Dakota, West Virginia, and Wyoming.

How to Time Your Gifts

Shifting income to your best tax advantage can be tricky now that children under 14 must pay taxes at the same rate as their parents on investment income over $1,000. When a child reaches 14, such income above $500—but less than $17,850—is taxed at 15%. Nevertheless, properly timed gifts of income-producing property can be an effective way to reduce taxes. Richard Coppage and Sidney Baxendale, both accounting professors at the University of Louisville, computed the amounts and timing of such gifts so that parents can give as little money as possible before the child reaches 14 and still accumulate enough savings for college.

Say you have a 10-year-old daughter and your tax rate is 28%. By the time she enters college in 1996, total costs for four years at a private school are expected to average $50,000. To build up that amount in a custodial account,

Coppage and Baxendale calculate that you should give her a gift of $12,500 right away, $1,558 on her 13th birthday, and $20,000 on her 14th birthday, when the income from the account will be taxed at 15%. (A parent can give a child up to $10,000 a year—$20,000 with a spouse—without paying a gift tax.) With the contributions compounding at 8% a year, the child will end up with $3,357 more in the account than if her parents had invested the money on their own and paid taxes on the income at their rate. (The table can be used to figure smaller amounts. For a 10-year-old and a target amount of $25,000, for instance, divide the appropriate numbers in half.)

Target amounts are estimates of the average cost of tuition, room, and board for a private college when the child is 18, assuming 5% annual increases.

Age of child	Target amount	Gifts						Tax savings
		At birth	Age 5	Age 10	Age 12	Age 13	Age 14	
Newborn	$100,000	$12,500	—	—	$3,453	$20,000	$20,000	$9,458
5-year-old	$70,000	—	$12,500	—	—	$10,119	$42,000	$5,924
10-year-old	$50,000	—	—	$12,500	—	$1,558	$20,000	$3,357

Trends That Will Shape Your Future

Prosperity always comes at a price, and the bill we pay for our unmatched standard of living is a nagging insecurity. The stock market plunge last October was a painful reminder of how fickle good fortune can be. Since 1972 the number of families defined as upper income—more than $60,000 a year in 1987 dollars—has more than doubled. A real estate boom and spectacular bull markets in stocks and bonds have propelled many into a lush early retirement and given them a new worry: estate planning.

Yet few Americans have settled comfortably into this unprecedented affluence. Even the striving, upwardly mobile achievers of the baby-boom generation see their prosperity as precarious. They are unsettled by the debt-laden economy, uncertain whether career success can coexist with a happy family, and unsure that they can maintain their cherished life style through retirement. This nervousness could be their salvation.

While the next 15 years will offer fresh chances to shore up today's affluence, opportunities will be less likely than ever simply to come your way. Managing your finances will become increasingly complicated and demanding. The simple forms of planning that may have served your parents well will no longer be enough to ensure economic security. If you doubt this judgment, consider *Money*'s nominations for the major trends in personal finance over the next decade or so.

We Will Save More—at Last!

The credit card has become the talisman of the consumer society: since 1972, the personal savings rate has fallen from 7.3% to 3.7% of after-tax income, as Americans have bought on credit what they once would have saved for. Over the next 10 years, though, consumers will restrain their passion for plastic. A low and stable inflation rate will make the effort to save more worthwhile, and the phaseout of most tax deductions for consumer interest will discourage borrowing.

Rising income will also help build up bank and brokerage accounts. Not only will there be many more households in the high-saving upper-income category but more as well among the traditionally thrifty middle-aged. The average household income of those 35 or older will climb 16% by 1995, according to A. Gary Shilling, president of an economic consulting firm in New York City. As a result, Shilling forecasts that the overall savings rate will reach 10.5%. Investors should note that stocks of retailers depending on free-spending consumers will suffer, while shares in industries that benefit from saving and investment—financial services and capital equipment, for example—will shine.

Children May Be Your Best Investment

At today's prices, two-income households will typically spend more than $100,000—on everything from day care to Reeboks—raising their first child to age 18. Yet baby boomers with children will fare better than those without. In fact, says Cheryl Russell, editor of *American Demographics* magazine: "The best long-term investment for a baby-boom couple will be to have children."

Baby boomers are likely to live as long as 20 years after they retire, exhausting their savings. Government benefits will not make up the difference. Despite the 1983 reforms, intended to shore up the system through 2025, Social Security will provide only about $13,000 a year in 1987 dollars for couples retiring after 2012. Careful retirement planning will be a top priority for the foresighted. Yet many will need both financial and practical help, especially after 80. Currently, half of those over 85 have some disabilities, and families typically provide 80% of their nursing care and personal services.

College Costs Will Get Easier to Handle

You would hardly know it from the numbers. By the year 2000, tuition, room, and board for four years will jump 140%—to $150,000 at top private colleges. Neither federal aid nor parental income will keep up with the increase. Rather, the enormously enhanced prospects of the students themselves will enable them to assume the burden. The scenario: jobs will grow more than 12% by the late 1990s, while the number of 16- to 24-year-olds in the work force drops by as much as

14%, opening new opportunities for applicants from respected colleges. Although economists forecast that unemployment will average 7% to 8% over the next 10 years, compared with 6% now, for young males with college degrees the rate will remain below 3%.

Close to full employment will translate into wage levels for recent college graduates that could be 40% higher than today's in 1987 dollars. It will be clear in advance that this flush new generation of workers will be able to carry significantly more debt, and increasingly students, not parents, will take on the bulk of college loans. Some education financing experts see repayment schedules stretching out over entire careers, if need be.

Company Benefits Will Include Parental Day Care

"Today's benefits packages were designed for the family of the 1950s," says Cheryl Russell. The biggest flaws: no flexibility and almost no day-care benefits. "At present, only 1% of employees in medium-size and large companies have child-care benefits available to them," she says, despite the fact that seven out of ten baby-boom women are in the work force. An additional need that will increasingly be felt by two-career couples: day care for elderly parents.

Responding to demand, companies will switch from old-fashioned rigid benefits packages to cafeteria-style plans, where employees can pick and choose among a number of options. The hitch: total benefits will not rise very fast. Nonetheless, two-earner couples will gain, swapping duplicated medical coverage for day-care benefits, additional vacation, legal services, or extra life insurance.

Health Care May Cost As Much As Food

What the average American must pay, out of pocket, for health care will triple over the next decade or so, as medical costs continue to surge and health-care benefits lag. Retirees will feel the worst pinch of all: health-care costs, which now consume 12% of their budgets on average, will surpass the 18% share of income that they spend on food. For starters, medical costs may outpace inflation by as much as 7% a year, principally because of expensive new technology, according to William B. Schwartz, a professor at the Tufts University School of Medicine. Medicare, which provides nearly half the $120 billion spent annually on health care for those over 65, will run out of money between 2000 and 2005. Other government programs, such as Medicaid, and many private insurers will also be strapped, partly because of the fearsome financial toll of AIDS. By the 1990s, AIDS could add $16 billion annually—and probably much more—to already bloated health-care costs.

Silver-lining note: some of the best investment opportunities will be in health-related stocks. Drugs and medical high-tech will be the leading growth-stock sectors of the 1990s. But investors should be wary of stocks whose profits could be hurt by public cost-control programs, such as the shares of hospital management companies.

Hot Housing Markets Will Finally Cool

As long as inflation stays at bay—and most economists think it will—home prices will rise slowly. Even where increases have outpaced inflation by more than 10% annually, such as New York City and Washington, inflation-adjusted returns will thin out to less than 4%. As a result, there will be no repeat of the spectacular profits homeowners reaped in the past decade, when an annual inflation rate as high as 15% drove house prices up 222%. Yet you should still own your own home, if only because it forces you to save. As long as you resist the temptation to take out a home-equity loan, your house will probably add 25% to your net worth when you retire.

There Will Be a Second Coming for Stocks and Bonds

In the aftermath of last October's market crash, prices of both stocks and bonds may tumble again this year. Bonds may also fall further because interest rates could rise another percentage point or so, says Steven Leuthold, chairman of the Leuthold Group in Minneapolis. After that, though, he sees interest rates dropping sharply and a new bull market for bonds.

Stock prices were so overvalued in 1987 that a sharp correction was inevitable, says Richard C. Young, president of Young Research & Publishing in Newport, Rhode Island. As he correctly predicted last September: "We're going to have that correction because the divergence between share prices and their real worth has become too extreme." Dividend yields, one measure of value on which Young relies, were at their lowest levels since 1929. After the correction runs its course, though, he expects stocks to advance strongly again. With inflation between 4% and 6%, "corporate profits could be marvelous," says Young.

Boom times for real estate investing, by contrast, are gone for the rest of the century. You are likely to fare poorly whether you buy commercial properties outright or invest through limited partnerships or real estate investment trusts. Reason: widespread overbuilding has set the stage for a bust.

Domestic Stocks Will Outperform Foreign Shares

American capital has been globetrotting. Since 1972, purchases and sales of foreign stocks by U.S. investors have grown twentyfold to more than $100 billion annually. And during the next 15 years, investing overseas will become even easier and more popular. But U.S. stocks are likely to offer better performance.

"Our stock market is screamingly cheap compared with other markets," says David

Bostian, president of Bostian Research Associates in New York City. In recent years foreign stocks have outperformed the U.S. market, largely because the falling dollar increases the value of foreign shares to U.S. investors. But such phenomenal gains are unlikely to recur, he says, because corporate profits in some countries will not live up to investors' expectations. And since the dollar will probably not fall more than another 10%, U.S. investors cannot count on big currency bonuses in the future.

Entrepreneurs Will Make Big Money Selling Time

Businesses that sell convenience will be winners. By the mid-1990s, more than half of all U.S. households will run on two paychecks. Among baby boomers, that figure rises to 70%. As a result, Americans will have more money than ever to spend and increasingly less time to spend it. "Time is becoming a marketable commodity," says Thomas Miller, who edits a publication for clients of the Roper Organization, the polling firm.

Companies that satisfy this temporal need will be growth marvels of the 1990s, and many will be ideal for entrepreneurs—low-cost, low-tech start-ups. Likely candidates include home-delivery dry cleaners and lawn-care specialists; innovative mail-order and cable-TV home-shopping businesses; convenience stores purveying fancy takeout foods; interior decorators with mobile display units; and pick-up-and-deliver car repair.

Mutual Funds Will Invest in Furniture

In the past decade or so, institutions have rolled out ever more arcane vehicles for investments. Among them: stock index options, Ginnie Maes, and junk bonds. That is nothing compared with what is envisioned for the future. "I would not be surprised to see new mutual funds that buy trays of diamonds, portfolios of art, and antique furniture," says John Markese, director of research for the American Association of Individual Investors in Chicago. Other exotica aborning might include junk securities backed by farm loans or by Third World debt and limited partnerships in restaurants and theaters.

Flaky as they may seem, some will be worth a closer look. Offbeat securities can give small investors opportunities once available only to institutions. And vehicles that are insured or use options and futures to limit losses may actually reduce risk. But be skeptical. Untested securities can have pitfalls.

Computers Will Make Stock Market Bargains Scarce

Computer literacy—100 million adults will know how to use computers by 1995—will raise the small investor to a level of competence that rivals that of professionals. "Computers will improve the individual's ability to get information and analyze stocks and bonds," says Dan DiBartolomeo, a specialist in investment technology at the Boston Computer Society, an association of computer users. Bargains will be rare, however: so many investors will be scouring the market that undervalued shares will quickly be discovered and snapped up.

As on-line computer data bases grow and the cost of using them drops, it will be even easier than it is today for small investors to call up news reports and financial statistics on almost any publicly traded company as soon as they are announced. Sophisticated software will enable small investors to screen stocks and evaluate them just as a professional securities analyst does. As an added bonus, more efficient trading by computer will translate into sharply lower commissions.

The Best Stockbrokers in 50 Cities

To compile this directory of topnotch brokers in 50 major metropolitan areas, *Money* sought recommendations from Yale Hirsch, editor of the investment newsletter *Smart Money* and the author of the *Directory of Exceptional Stockbrokers*; executives in the head offices of the brokerage firms themselves; and experienced investors, financial planners, and other knowledgeable sources in each city. *Money* correspondents then interviewed the candidates about their investment philosophies and methods of handling accounts. Last, the list was checked against Securities and Exchange Commission records to weed out brokers who had ever been fined, censured, or suspended for professional misconduct by the SEC, the National Association of Securities Dealers, major stock exchanges, or state regulators.

To be considered for this directory, brokers had to be willing to take on new accounts of $20,000 or less for investment in individual securities. This requirement cut out many well-known brokers who accept only accounts of $100,000 or more. It also eliminated brokers who will accept a $20,000 account only if all the money goes into mutual funds, which demand less attention than do stocks and bonds. While mutual funds may be a fine way to invest such a sum, you do not need a broker to buy them.

As it is almost impossible to verify how well a broker's stock recommendations have performed, *Money* looked for brokers whose experience suggests strong stock-picking skills. Favored were those with independent opinions who did at least some of their own research. Expertise not available elsewhere, such as familiarity with fast-growing local companies, also gained points for a broker, as did evidence that a broker gives exceptional service and is readily accessible. While he or she may have assistants who can handle queries about housekeeping matters, you should be able to reach your broker quickly for answers to important investment questions.

The list below offers a capsule description of the investment approach of each broker, including areas of specialization. You are likeliest to find happiness with a broker if you first think through carefully what kind of investor you are and then seek out a broker whose philosophy matches your own.

Albany, New York

Tony Malatino (E.F. Hutton, 41 State St., Albany 12207; 518-447-1305) Concentrates on blue-chip stocks and municipal bonds

John A. Phelan (First Albany Corp., 41 State St., Albany 12207; 518-447-8430) Attentive to small accounts; also makes sell recommendations

Albuquerque, New Mexico

Lanny Rominger (Dean Witter Reynolds, 6400 Uptown Blvd. N.E., Albuquerque 87110; 505-883-6262) Favors a conservative approach using high-yield stocks

Jim Shafer (Eppler Guerin & Turner, 1650 University Blvd. N.E., Albuquerque 87102; 505-842-0303) Follows blue-chip and growth stocks

Atlanta, Georgia

Beth Dale (Robinson-Humphrey, 3333 Peachtree Rd. N.E., Atlanta 30326; 404-266-6316) Specializes in stocks of local companies

William B. Jones (Paine Webber, 3340 Peachtree Rd. N.E., Atlanta 30326; 404-262-5812) Specializes in small accounts and investment clubs

William A.H. Rhodes (Merrill Lynch, 3500 Piedmont Rd. N.E., Atlanta 30305; 404-231-2425) Prefers blue-chip stocks for small accounts

Larry Taylor (Drexel Burnham Lambert, 3495 Piedmont Rd., Atlanta 30305; 404-266-5813) Emphasizes client understanding of investment risks; follows mostly blue chips

Baltimore, Maryland

Harry M. Ford, Jr. (Legg Mason Inc., 7 E. Redwood St., Baltimore 21202; 301-539-3400) Seeks stocks with low price/earnings ratios

Edwin Reynolds, Jr. (Baker Watts & Co., 100 Light St., Baltimore 21203; 301-685-2600) Does own research on local companies

George Strum (Legg Mason Inc., 1777 Reisterstown Rd., Baltimore 21208; 30l-486-8010) Concentrates on stocks for long term

Marie Van Deusen and Carole Oliver (Paine Webber, 100 S. Charles St., Baltimore 21201; 301-576-3278) Work as team; know bonds and blue-chip stocks

Birmingham, Alabama

Arthur E. Malone, Jr. (J.C. Bradford & Co., 505 N. 20th St., Birmingham 35203; 205-251-8000) Knowledgeable about small, regional companies

Bob McLain (Merrill Lynch, First National Sonat Bldg., Birmingham 35203; 205-326-9548) Follows large-company stocks and bonds

Boise, Idaho

Dick Petso (Piper Jaffray & Hopwood, 923 W. Idaho St., Boise 83702) Favors blue chips for long-term growth

Michael Thompson (E.F. Hutton, 945 Bannock St., Boise 83702; 208-344-5800) Follows mostly large-company stocks but also researches local firms

Boston, Massachusetts

Peter Annicelli (Paine Webber, 265 Franklin St., Boston 02110; 617-439-8352) Favors blue chips; also knows local high-technology stocks

Edward D. Cook, Jr. (Smith Barney Harris Upham, Exchange Place, Boston 02109; 617-570-9564) Follows a wide range of stocks, including computer companies; works with investment clubs

Gary D. Markoff (E.F. Hutton, Chestnut Hill Plaza, Chestnut Hill MA 02167; 617-739-8720) Follows a mixture of large- and small-company stocks; likes to use stop-loss orders

Joseph McGraw (Homans McGraw Trull Valeo & Co., 131 State St., Boston 02109; 617-973-0509) Mixes fundamental and technical analysis

David Messaline (Tucker Anthony & R.L. Day, 1 Beacon St., Boston 02108; 617-725-2032) Also a certified financial planner; specializes in bank and utility stocks; does some of own research

John Stockwell (Alex. Brown & Sons, 1 Boston Place, Boston 02108; 617-723-7300) Recommends a mixture of blue chips and small retail clothing stocks

Buffalo, New York

Dennis J. Galucki (Dean Witter, 610 Norstar Bldg., Buffalo 14202; 716-846-2640) Focuses on stocks of "socially responsible" companies, avoiding arms manufacturers and electric utilities with nuclear plants. Likes food, clothing, and health-care stocks

George T. Gregory (Kidder Peabody, 3737 Marine Midland Center, Buffalo 14203; 716-849-3853) Follows a combined growth-and-income approach

Peter O'Keefe (Trubee Collins & Co., 1 M&T Plaza, Buffalo 14203; 716-849-1481) Favors a buy-and-hold approach

Chicago, Illinois

Ross Baumgarten (Rodman & Renshaw, 120 S. LaSalle St., Chicago 60603; 312-977-7882) Seeks stocks selling at low P/E ratios

Roy K. Crispe (First of Michigan Corp., 135 S. LaSalle St., Chicago 60603; 312-263-7444) Follows a mix of large- and small-company stocks; makes sell recommendations

Mary D. Esser (Forest Securities, 475 River Bend Rd., Naperville, IL 60540; 312-983-2960) Knowledgeable about both growth and income investments

David J. Klein (Paine Webber, 707 Skokie Blvd., Northbrook, IL 60062; 312-564-7542) Makes sell recommendations

Shirley Litt (Bear Stearns, 3 First National Plaza, Chicago 60602; 312-580-4103) Favors a mixture of bonds and mostly blue-chip stocks

Connie Manchester (Mesirow Financial Corp., 135 S. LaSalle St., Chicago 60603; 312-443-5778) Looks for large-company, well-researched stocks just below the best-known, blue-chip level

Leon F. Strauss (Drexel Burnham Lambert, 1 S. Wacker Dr., Chicago 60606; 312-977-3061) Welcomes small accounts; follows mostly large, well-known companies

Cincinnati, Ohio

Paul Parker (Cowen & Co., 3 E. Fourth St., Cincinnati 45202; 513-579-8100) Follows a mix of bonds and large-company stocks

Hank Schmidt (Gradison Financial Services Inc., 580 Building, Cincinnati 45202; 513-579-5046) Favors primarily blue-chip stocks but also looks for small, fast-growing Ohio companies

Laurence J. Wulker (Paine Webber, 425 Walnut St., Cincinnati 45202; 513-369-4181) Also a certified financial planner; frequently recommends high-yield stocks; makes sell recommendations

Cleveland, Ohio

Sam Alberico (Merrill Lynch, 30100 Chagrin Blvd., Pepper Pike OH 44124; 216-292-8020) Specializes in undervalued small to medium-size U.S. companies; also follows foreign stocks

Bud Klein (Cowen & Co., 1375 E. Ninth St., Cleveland 44114; 216-623-7755) Favors stocks selling at a discount to their asset values; looks for special situations such as corporate restructurings

Ralph E. String (McDonald & Co. Securities, 2100 Society Bldg., Cleveland 44114; 216-443-2323) Specializes in income-producing investments; many of his clients are retirees

Columbia, South Carolina

John Allison (Smith Barney, First National Bank Bldg., Main Street at Washington, Columbia 29201; 803-771-8990) Favors mostly blue-chip stocks, convertible securities

Tom Kepley (Chapin Davis & Co., 1401 Main St., Columbia 29201; 803-765-9900) Prefers blue-chip stocks; makes sell recommendations

George T. McCutchen (Robinson-Humphrey, 1310 Lady St., Columbia 29201; 803-771-8818) Welcomes small accounts; recommendations mix blue chips with smaller fast-growing companies

Dallas/Fort Worth, Texas

Kenneth D. Ferguson (E.F. Hutton, 500 N. Ackard, Dallas 75201; 214-720-1200) Specializes in entertainment companies

Raymond E. Jennison (Canterbury Properties & Securities, 311 Interstate 30, Rockwall TX 75087; 214-722-8008) Does own research; suitable for high-risk investors

Miriam S. Kindred (E.F. Hutton, 5050 Quorum Dr., Dallas 75240; 214-934-4800) A service-oriented broker who is also a certified financial planner

William T. Melms (A.G. Edwards & Sons, 1701 River Run, Fort Worth 76107; 817-338-1401) A certified financial planner; adept at options trading

Alice Dye Rollins (Rauscher Pierce Refnes, 1600 RPR Tower, Dallas 75201; 214-978-0111) Does own research; good for investors seeking income

Denver, Colorado

Jerry Bruni (Smith Barney, 102 S. Tejon St., Colorado Springs CO 80903; 303-633-1793) Does own research; good for conservative investors

Terry Erbert (Drexel Burnham Lambert, 717 17th St., Denver 80202; 303-294-7725) Favors blue chips and out-of-favor stocks

Dan Harty (Paine Webber, 1600 Broadway, Denver 80202; 303-861-2400) Does own research; favors large-company stocks

Peter Mindock (Drexel Burnham Lambert, 717 17th St., Denver 80202; 303-293-7700) Prefers blue chips as well as over-the-counter stocks

Gregory P. Watson (Boettcher & Co., 1919 14th St., Boulder CO 80302; 303-441-0612) Does own research; favors blue-chip stocks

Des Moines, Iowa

Hobie Bannister (Piper Jaffray, 717 Mullberry St., Des Moines 50309; 515-244-9111) Follows both blue chips and stocks of regional companies

Douglas A. West (A.G. Edwards, 309 Court Ave., Des Moines 50309; 515-244-2255) Specializes in companies selling for less than break-up value; suitable for long-term investors

Detroit, Michigan

James Agee (Merrill Lynch, 200 Renaissance Center, Detroit 48243; 313-446-1264) Willing to help clients set objectives; favors growth stocks

Robert B. Clark (Paine Webber, 111 W. Third St., Rochester MI 48063; 313-652-3200) Generalist; good for conservative investors

Janice M. Gilmore (Kidder Peabody, 3290 W. Big Beaver, Troy MI 48084; 313-649-5700) Favors blue chips

James A. Lark (Fahnestock & Co., 23400 Michigan Ave., Dearborn MI 48126; 313-563-5060) Specializes in emerging growth and turnaround companies

Paul Messimer (Merrill Lynch, 400 Town Center Dr., Dearborn MI 48126; 313-336-4500) Favors large-company stocks

Alfred B. Moran (A.G. Edwards, 333 W. Fort St., Detroit 48226; 313-962-5525) Specializes in drug and utility stocks and Michigan municipal bonds; for income investors

Bob Stoetzer (First of Michigan Corp., 100 Renaissance Tower, Detroit 48243; 313-259-2600) Knowledgeable about income-producing securities such as utility stocks and municipal bonds

Greensboro, North Carolina

Brad Clasby (Paine Webber, 3608 W. Friendly Ave., Greensboro 27410; 919-299-9940) Knowledgeable about a wide range of investments including real estate limited partnerships and annuities as well as stocks

Jim Kirkpatrick (Merrill Lynch, Drawer F-1, Greensboro 27402; 919-373-1711) Favors stocks of large companies

Hartford, Connecticut

Jay E. Bigman (Advest, 280 Trumbull St., 1 Commercial Plaza, Hartford 06103; 203-241-2044) Does own research; favors small stocks

Terrance Herr (Smith Barney, 1 State St., Hartford 06103; 203-275-0744) Likes to use options as a hedging device

Honolulu, Hawaii

Richard Behnke (Abel-Behnke Corp., 1188 Bishop St., Honolulu 96813; 808-536-2341) Heads own firm; specializes in local stocks and turnaround situations

Peter Higuchi (Shearson Lehman Bros., 1585 Kapiolani Blvd., Honolulu 96814; 808-946-8377) Likes to use covered options

Robson Hind (Dean Witter, 1001 Bishop St., Honolulu 96813; 808-525-6946) Specializes in small stocks

Phil Norris (E.F. Hutton, 1001 Bishop St., Honolulu 96813; 808-521-2961) Knowledgeable about local stocks and emerging growth companies

Houston, Texas

Bert Clark (Paine Webber, 1200 Milam St., Houston 77002; 713-654-0250) Does own research

John Ford (Prudential-Bache Securities, 1331 Lamar St., Houston 77010; 713-951-4431) Tries to identify major market turns

Virginia Hodge (Paine Webber, 1200 Milam St., Houston 77002; 713-654-0200) Knowledgeable about the health-care field

Jerome Levy (Prudential-Bache, 1331 Lamar, Houston 77010; 713-654-4477) Specializes in options

Indianapolis, Indiana

John T. Kelsey (Thomson McKinnon, 5 E. Market St., Indianapolis 46204; 317-632-3501) Concentrates on chemical, oil, computer, and pharmaceutical industries

Scott Mullins (Edward D. Jones, 26 Public Square, Shelbyville IN 46176; 317-398-3143) Favors blue chips

William G. Schaefer (Dean Witter, 251 N. Illinois, Indianapolis 46204; 317-263-5570) Specializes in high-technology stocks

Jackson, Mississippi

Melanie Dowell (Prudential-Bache, 188 E. Capitol St., 1 Jackson Place, Jackson 39201; 601-948-4414) Favors blue chips; makes sell recommendations

Fran Hall Finch (Merrill Lynch, 111 E. Capitol St., Jackson 39201; 601-968-9505) Clients include many retirees

Kansas City, Missouri

Maureen Gamble (Drexel Burnham Lambert, 801 W. 47th St., Kansas City 64112; 816-561-4444) Favors blue chips

Joseph Kain (Joseph Kain & Associates, 10540 Barkley, Overland Park KS 66212; 913-642-3820) Does own research; makes sell recommendations

Margo Shepard (E.F. Hutton, 920 Baltimore St., Kansas City 64105; 816-283-7200) Evaluates client's needs thoroughly; good for conservative investors

Robert Williams (Piper Jaffray, 1100 Main St., Kansas City 64105; 816-421-1550) Specializes in low P/E stocks and companies with undervalued assets

Las Vegas, Nevada

Alan J. Duncan (Prudential-Bache, 20001 E. Flamingo Rd., Las Vegas 89119; 702-796-0135) Bear market veteran; specializes in the gambling industry

Randall I. Garcia (Paine Webber, 3800 Howard Hughes Pkwy., Las Vegas 89109; 702-731-1121) Does own research; favors blue-chip stocks

John P. Mojica (Merrill Lynch, 300 S. Fourth St., Las Vegas 89101; 702-383-6130) Specializes in options and municipal bonds; tries to identify major market turns

Little Rock, Arkansas

J. Ogden Mayhugh (Merrill Lynch, P.O. Box 1980, Little Rock 72203; 501-370-2027) Good advisor for conservative, long-term investors

Frank Satterfield (A.G. Edwards, 1501 N. University Ave., Little Rock 72207; 501-664-9135) Specializes in small stocks

Los Angeles, California

Elias Argyropoulos (Shearson Lehman, 15303 Ventura Blvd., Sherman Oaks CA 91403; 818-788-2800) Specializes in pharmaceutical and biotechnology companies

Andrew Basch (Dean Witter, 10900 Wilshire Blvd., Los Angeles 90024; 213-208-4541) Knowledgeable about savings and loan and biotechnology stocks

Richard A. Bock (Bear Stearns & Co., 1800 Century Park East, Los Angeles 90067; 213-201-7809) Does own research in biotechnology stocks

Patrick M. Burke (Paine Webber, 4675 MacArthur Court, Newport Beach CA 92660; 714-253-6324) Concentrates on high-yield stocks

Bill Carr (E.F. Hutton, 650 Town Center Dr., Costa Mesa CA 92626; 714-641-7715) Prefers buy-and-hold approach

Neil Kneitel (Oppenheimer & Co., 2029 Century Park East, Los Angeles 90067; 213-552-3880) Specializes in restructuring companies; also knowledgeable about bonds

Peter M. Malis (Prudential-Bache, 16501 Ventura Blvd., Encino CA 91436; 818-788-7460) Specializes in bonds and other income investments

Ti Nguyen (Kidder Peabody, 610 Newport Center Dr., Newport Beach CA 92660; 714-644-7040) Takes a contrarian approach to blue-chip stocks; also knowledgeable about the waste-management industry

Larry M. Phillips (Dean Witter Reynolds, 3501 Sepulveda Blvd., Torrance CA 90503; 213-214-5901) Looks for well-known but out-of-favor stocks

David J. Pollock (Oppenheimer & Co., 1 Century Plaza, Los Angeles 90067; 213-552-7581) Seeks stocks with undervalued assets

Victor E. Refkin (Shearson Lehman Bros., 9601 Wilshire Blvd., Beverly Hills CA 90210; 213-858-4100) Does own research; specializes in restaurant-industry stocks

Mark C. Roukas (Bateman Eichler Hill Richards, 700 S. Flower St., Los Angeles 90017; 213-683-3955) Specializes in income-oriented investments; does own research

Kristin Stockmar (Kidder Peabody, 333 S. Grand St., Los Angeles 90071; 213-485-1100) Knowledgeable about the pharmaceutical industry

Louisville, Kentucky

Howard Linker (J.C. Bradford, 315 S. Fourth Ave., Louisville 40202; 502-589-7660) Does own research; likes out-of-favor issues

Robert Liter (E.F. Hutton, First Trust Centre North, 200 S. 5th St., Louisville 40202; 502-561-4007) Prefers blue chips; tries to identify major market turns

Robert Matlock (Advest, 2400 Meidinger, Louisville 40202; 502-589-8302) Does own research

Miami, Florida

Mark E. Gold (Thomson McKinnon, 11601 Biscayne Blvd., North Miami 33181; 305-891-8000) Tries to identify major market turns

Gloria Llewellyn (Paine Webber, 2500 Ponce de Leon Blvd., Coral Gables FL 33134; 305-448-5444) Does own research; specializes in Florida bank stocks

Tony Rodriguez (Shearson Lehman, 777 Arthur Godfrey Rd., Miami Beach 33140; 305-674-5900) Specializes in medium-size out-of-favor companies

Carole Salmon (Smith Barney, 777 Brickell Ave., Miami Beach 33131; 305-379-1000) Tries to identify major market turns

Milwaukee, Wisconsin

Donald V. Anderson (Dean Witter, 250 Wisconsin Ave., Milwaukee 53202; 414-291-7624) Does some of own research; welcomes small accounts

James F. Herget (Blunt Ellis Loewi, Grafton State Bank Bldg., 101 Falls Rd., Grafton WI 53024; 414-375-4040) Favors low P/E stocks, buy-and-hold strategy

Thomas F. Schmid (Robert W. Baird & Co., 777 E. Wisconsin Ave., Milwaukee 53202; 414-765-3525) Specializes in small, regional stocks

Minneapolis/St. Paul, Minnesota

Gary Donath (Paine Webber, N. 100 First National Bank Bldg., St. Paul 55101; 612-291-7979) Does own research; specializes in regional stocks

Sharon Erickson (Prudential-Bache, 80 S. Eighth St., Minneapolis 55402; 612-340-4537) Does own research

Jack Feltl (R.J. Steichen, 1414 First Bank Place West, Minneapolis 55402; 612-341-6212) Does own research; concentrates on turnaround situations

Ross Paden (Merrill Lynch, 2700 IDS Tower, Minneapolis 55402; 612-349-7992) Favors blue chips

Douglas K. Savitt (Paine Webber, 320 Opus Center, 9900 Bren Rd. East, Minnetonka MN 55343; 612-936-4858) Specializes in emerging growth companies and convertible bonds

Bruce Wiessner (Dain Bosworth, 6600 France Ave. South, Edina MN 55435; 612-925-7046) Specializes in small stocks, including high-technology issues

Nashville, Tennessee

Larry Fuldauer (E.F. Hutton, 1 Commerce Place, Nashville 37219; 615-244-2500) Likes blue chips; also follows some secondary stocks

Fred T. McLaughlin (J.C. Bradford, 330 Commerce St., Nashville 37201; 615-748-9315) Prefers mainly blue chips but also follows some riskier over-the-counter issues

Mimi Wallace (J.C. Bradford, 330 Commerce St., Nashville 37201; 615-748-9391) Favors blue chips; likes to use stop-loss orders

New Orleans, Louisiana

C.B. Brewster III (Dean Witter, 639 Loyola Ave., New Orleans 70113; 504-587-9624) Follows over-the-counter stocks; familiar with oil and gas companies

Nolte C. DeRussy, Jr. (Thomson McKinnon, 1 Shell Square, New Orleans 70139; 504-581-4881) Does own research; follows emerging growth stocks

Stuart Singer (Howard Weil, 900 Energy Centre, 1100 Poydras St., New Orleans 70163; 504-582-2758) Follows low P/E stocks; welcomes small accounts

New York, New York

Jeff Armstrong (Dean Witter, S. 61 Paramus Rd., Paramus, NJ 07652; 201-712-4053) Concentrates on out-of-favor issues

Michael Baum (Woodmere Securities Inc., 1215 Station Plaza, Hewlett, NY 11557; 516-374-5050) Does own research; looks for turnaround stocks

John Claghorn (Tucker Anthony, 535 Madison Ave., New York 10022; 212-303-0557) Advocates a balanced portfolio mixing growth and income stocks

Richard Clark (Legg Mason, 63 Wall St., New York 10005; 212-428-4985) Likes stocks in companies with strong cash flow

Alan Denzer, Jr. (Drexel Burnham Lambert, 60 Broad St., New York 10004; 212-480-6598) Makes sell recommendations; tries to identify major market turns

Robert Gorman (Paine Webber, 1221 Ave. of the Americas, New York 10020; 212-730-5959) Favors a balanced approach, using municipal bond unit trusts, blue chips, and emerging growth stocks

Julie Habers (Shearson Lehman, 2 Broadway, New York 10004; 212-412-4781) Attentive to small accounts; prefers buy-and-hold strategy with blue chips

Robert Kraut (Shearson Lehman, 666 Fifth Ave., New York 10103; 212-373-6423) Also a certified financial planner; knowledgeable about a wide range of investments

Richard Matteo (Swartwood Hesse Inc., Heights Plaza, 777 Terrace Ave., Hasbrouck Heights, NJ 07604; 201-288-8500) Looks for smaller, lesser-known companies with good growth potential

Robert Petruski (Dean Witter, Mack Centre IV, S. 61 Paramus Rd., Paramus, NJ 07652; 201-712-4101) Tries to identify major market turns; knowledgeable about high-yield stocks

Charles Roden (Rosenkrantz Lyon & Ross, 6 E. 43rd St., New York 10017; 212-986-6700) Prefers out-of-favor stocks in well-known companies

Todd Semon (Philips Appel & Walden, 185 Bridge Plaza, Fort Lee, NJ 07024; 201-461-8041) Does own research; seeks low P/E stocks in companies with strong cash flows

Robert Shapiro (E.F. Hutton, 605 Third Ave., New York 10158; 212-878-3948) Thoroughly evaluates client's needs; seeks low P/E stocks

Myron Wein (Prudential-Bache, 100 Gold St., New York 10292; 212-791-3222) Favors lower-priced NYSE issues; good for long-term investors

Oklahoma City, Oklahoma

Barbara Crabtree (E.F. Hutton, 211 N. Robinson, Oklahoma City 73102; 405-232-9181) Likes stocks in medium-size to large companies

Bill Grooms (Dean Witter, 6305 Waterford Blvd., Suite 240, Oklahoma City 73118; 405-841-3981) Does own research; bear market veteran

Rosemary Allen (Thomson McKinnon, 777 First National Center, Oklahoma City 73102; 405-272-9711) Specializes in small accounts; good for conservative investors

Omaha, Nebraska

Dick Kelley (Dain Bosworth, 9290 W. Dodge Rd., Omaha 68114; 402-392-6100) Likes blue chips; also knows regional stocks

Marshall Lewis (Blunt Ellis Loewi, 1901 Farnam St., Omaha 68102; 402-344-0100) Does own research; seeks low P/E stocks and stocks in companies whose assets are undervalued

Robert Prendergast (Piper Jaffray, 910 N. 96 St., Omaha 68114; 402-397-1600) Knows regional stocks, has many retired clients

Philadelphia, Pennsylvania

Mitchell Dressler (Merrill Lynch, Foxcroft Square, Jenkintown PA 19046; 215-576-3176) Favors stocks in large companies; welcomes small accounts

Joel P. Feldman (Tucker Anthony, 1760 Market St., Philadelphia 19103; 215-972-8600) Contrarian who favors large companies

Kenneth A. Friedman (Fuhrman-Matt Securities, 1608 Walnut St., Philadelphia 19103; 215-875-4680) Prefers balanced approach using blue chips and some speculative issues

John H. Geary (Boenning & Scattergood Inc., 121 S. Broad St., Philadelphia 19107; 215-875-1660) Seeks out-of-favor high-yield stocks

Robert Goldberg (Janney Montgomery Scott, 5 Penn Center Plaza, Philadelphia 19103; 215-665-6255) Does own research; specializes in small, emerging companies

Alan H. Meyers (Prudential-Bache, 1515 Market St., Philadelphia 19102; 215-241-6793) Emphasizes diversification among fixed-income and equity holdings

Andrew Palashewsky (Janney Montgomery Scott, 530 Walnut St., Philadelphia 19106; 215-625-6800) Looks for high-quality stocks selling for less than $60

Arnold M. Peskin (Collings Legg Mason, 2310 Fidelity Bank Bldg., Philadelphia 19109; 215-735-1000) Also a C.P.A.; looks for out-of-favor stocks

Anthony W. Tedeschi (Drexel Burnham Lambert, 3 Mellon Bank Center, Philadelphia 19102; 215-561-8060) Specializes in tax-free bonds, high-yield securities; good for fixed-income investors

Phoenix, Arizona

Lewis Carns (Shearson Lehman, 15456 N. 99th Ave., Sun City AZ 85351; 602-933-0191) Frequently recommends a mix of stocks and tax-exempt bonds; makes sell recommendations

Peter Johnson (R.G. Dickinson & Co., 7373 N. Scottsdale Rd., Scottsdale AZ 85253; 602-483-3201) Does own research on small, fast-growing companies in biotechnology and pharmaceutical industries

Edward F. Muhlenfeld (Rauscher Pierce Refsnes, 6607 N. Scottsdale Rd., Scottsdale AZ 85253; 602-991-0803) Looks for undervalued stocks followed by only a few securities analysts

Vince Zamis (Private Ledger Financial Services, 14901 N. Scottsdale Rd., Scottsdale AZ 85254; 602-483-8408) Does own research; seeks stocks with undervalued assets

Pittsburgh, Pennsylvania

Tim Beck (Shearson Lehman, 1 PPG Place, Pittsburgh 15222; 412-392-5800) Emphasizes client service; favors blue chips

Nancy T. Brown (Legg Mason Masten, 2579 Washington Rd., Pittsburgh 15241; 412-833-0310) Bear market veteran; thoroughly evaluates client's needs; suitable for long-term investors

James J. Garcia (Merrill Lynch, 2 Gateway Center, Pittsburgh 15222; 412-566-6742) Prefers large-company stocks and blue chips; likes to use stop-loss orders

Thomas B. Rieck (Thomson McKinnon, 300 Sixth Ave., Pittsburgh 15222; 412-456-1746) Follows quality blue chips; suitable for long-term investors

Ruth C. Robinette (Legg Mason, 2 Oliver Plaza, Pittsburgh 15222; 412-261-7300) Likes out-of-favor blue chips

Richard J. Scarton (Legg Mason, 2 Oliver Plaza, Pittsburgh 15222; 412-261-7300) Favors established NYSE or OTC companies, but can accommodate aggressive investors

Nancy C. Snyder (Paine Webber, 3 Gateway Center, Pittsburgh 15222; 412-288-2715) Bear market veteran; suitable for conservative, long-term investors

Portland, Oregon

Moonja S. Hollosy (Dain Bosworth, 1 S.W. Columbia, Portland 97258; 503-295-5885) Does own research; follows regional stocks and blue chips

David Jarman (Piper Jaffray, 101 S.W. Main, Portland 97204; 503-224-9020) Does own research; follows regional stocks and emerging growth companies

Jim Liss (Birr Wilson, 180 S.W. Harrison, Portland 97201; 503-224-1800) Contrarian; concentrates on small and medium-size growth companies

William H. Scott (Dean Witter, 10300 S.W. Greenburg Rd., Portland 97223; 503-293-4252) Does own research; tries to identify major market turns

Providence, Rhode Island

Barbara Kenerson (Tucker Anthony, 1000 Fleet Center, 50 Kennedy Plaza, Providence 02903; 401-457-1914) Teaches investment seminars; seeks turnarounds, other special situations

Steven Pitassi (Janney Montgomery, 236 Westminster Mall, Providence 02903; 401-274-8600) Caters to small investors; favors small local companies

Judith D. Struck (Tucker Anthony, 1000 Fleet Center, 50 Kennedy Plaza, Providence 02903; 401-457-1925) Teaches investment seminars; seeks low P/E stocks

Richmond, Virginia

P. Robert Kremzir (Scott & Stringfellow, 901 Moorefield Park Dr., Richmond 23236; 804-323-1012) A former mechanical engineer, he looks for undervalued capital-equipment stocks; makes sell recommendations

William R. Via (Paine Webber, 901 E. Cary St., Richmond 23219; 804-644-4111) Specializes in utilities and other high-yield stocks; has many retired clients

St. Louis, Missouri

Robert C. Kenny (A.G. Edwards, 10401 Clayton Rd., St. Louis 63131; 314-991-7800) Advocates a balanced portfolio of bonds and well-known stocks

Tony Kirk (Drexel Burnham Lambert, 7701 Forsyth Blvd., St. Louis 63105; 314-889-4924) Often recommends a buy-and-hold strategy with bonds, including zero-coupon issues

Bernard Kohm (Stifel Nicolaus, 500 N. Broadway, St. Louis 63102; 314-342-2756) Looks for little-known or out-of-favor stocks selling at low P/E ratios

John R. Moulton (Shearson Lehman, 8000 Maryland Ave., St. Louis 63105; 314-725-3700) Emphasizes low-risk strategies using large, well-known stocks

Salt Lake City, Utah

Randy Carlson (Fitzgerald DeArman & Roberts, 5241 S. College Dr., Salt Lake City 84123; 801-263-1900) Specializes in rapidly-growing OTC stocks

Karen Tafuri (Prudential-Bache, 50 W. Broadway, Salt Lake City 84101; 801-534-0088) Concentrates on well-known stocks with strong earnings growth; also knows gold-mining and energy issues, real estate investment trusts

San Antonio, Texas

Kent J. Cooper (Rotan Mosle/Paine Webber, 425 Soledad St., 100 NBC West, San Antonio 78205; 512-220-3838) Favors a mixture of stocks and municipal bonds; knowledgeable about the oil industry

Ronald Keller (Rauscher Pierce Refsnes, 300 Convent, San Antonio 78205; 512-225-6611) Believes in stocks as long-term holdings but does set sell targets to cut losses

San Diego, California

Dennis A. Costarakis (Prudential-Bache, 701 Palomar Airport Rd., Carlsbad CA 92009; 619-931-6800) Knowledgeable about technology companies

Rhett Dodson (Kidder Peabody, 701 B St., San Diego 92101; 619-236-1165) Seeks financially strong, small, fast-growing companies

William Kopenhaver (Merrill Lynch, 16787 Bernardo Center Dr., San Diego 92128; 619-485-0950) Specializes in fixed-income securities, blue chips

San Francisco, California

John Arkoosh (E.F. Hutton, 580 California St., San Francisco 94104; 415-954-9381) Researches undiscovered stocks in companies with little or no debt

Kenneth Brown (Birr Wilson & Co., 353 Sacramento St., San Francisco 94104; 415-983-7758) Favors a mixture of stocks and tax-exempt municipal bonds

Joseph J. Craig (Sutro & Co., 201 California St., San Francisco 94111; 415-445-8548) Favors mostly blue-chip stocks and urges clients to hold for the long term

Butler Crittenden (Wedbush Securities, 160 Sansome St., San Francisco 94104; 415-986-3330) Does own research, specializing in medical stocks

Lawrence E. Goodfriend (Sutro & Co., 201 California St., San Francisco 94111; 415-445-8300) Generalist; makes sell recommendations

Lawrence Marcus (Drexel Burnham Lambert, 555 California St., San Francisco 94104; 415-627-3182) Specializes in high-risk, potentially big gainers among little-known stocks; will take only a portion of any client's portfolio

Rod Miller (Dean Witter, 101 California St., San Francisco 94111; 415-955-6000) Specializes in medium-size but little-known over-the-counter stocks

Cecily Monahan (Thomson McKinnon,1970 Broadway, Oakland CA 94612; 415-834-2390) A former nurse who specializes in medical-industry stocks; makes sell recommendations on declining issues

San Jose, California

Donald Davies (Prudential-Bache, 150 Almaden Blvd., San Jose 95115; 408-291-2007) Favors conservative approach, using blue-chip stocks and bonds rated BBB or better

Gayl Stevenson (Bateman Eichler, 99 Almaden Blvd., San Jose 95113; 408-298-2727) Seeks stocks with high yields

Betty Chambers Toguchi (Kidder Peabody, 730 Welch Rd., Palo Alto CA 94304; 415-853-3250) Favors blue chips and tax-free bonds

Seattle, Washington

Arne R. Domas (Piper Jaffray, 1700 IBM Bldg., Seattle 98101; 206-223-3841) Likes blue chips; also favors medium-size companies overlooked by analysts

Jack Hanover III (Dean Witter, 350 106th Ave. N.E., Bellevue WA 98004; 206-455-8062) Does own research; specializes in regional stocks and tax-free bonds

Mary Ann Heeren (Dain Bosworth, 999 Third Ave., Seattle 98104; 206-621-3230) Contrarian; does own research

Eric Olanie (Dain Bosworth, 999 Third Ave., Seattle 98104; 206-621-3234) Does own research; specializes in growth stocks

Peter Rettman (Kidder Peabody, 1001 Fourth Ave. Plaza, Seattle 98154; 206-628-8542) Does own research; specializes in small, local companies

Tampa, Florida

J. Thomas Hartung (Dean Witter, 2560 Enterprise Rd. East, Clearwater FL 33546; 813-797-1611) Favors blue chips

Jim Bockenek (Dean Witter, P.O. Box 22500, Tampa 33630; 813-873-5647) Favors low P/E blue chips with undervalued assets

Washington, D.C.

Renee Frederick (Ferris & Co., 7101 Wisconsin Ave., Bethesda, MD 20814; 301-986-7613) Specializes in turnaround stocks and private real estate limited partnerships

John F. Glenn (Legg Mason, 8251 Greensboro Dr., McLean VA 22102; 703-821-9100) Seeks long-term growth; welcomes small accounts

Martin M. Gray (Drexel Burnham Lambert, 1850 K St. N.W., Washington, DC 20006; 202-862-2870) Looks for top-quality bonds and stocks of out-of-favor companies

Horace V. Lurton (Johnston Lemon & Co., 7101 Wisconsin Ave., Bethesda, MD 20814; 202-842-5367) Specializes in stocks overlooked by analysts

Richard Malone (Dean Witter, 1 Bankers Square, Alexandria, VA 22314; 703-838-8611) Does own research; contrarian who seeks low P/E stocks

Michael C. Neviaser (Financial Service Group, 1953 Gallows Rd., Vienna, VA 22180; 703-790-0543) Favors small, fast-growing companies

John J. Parise, Sr. (Dean Witter, 2 Wisconsin Circle, Chevy Chase, MD 20815; 301-961-1808) Favors local growth stocks and companies that do business with the federal government

The Best Financial Planners

The men and women listed below are among the most qualified financial planners in the United States. All have demonstrated a mastery of budgeting, insurance, investing, taxes, retirement planning, trusts, and other estate planning techniques. They were nominated by prominent planners and then interviewed by *Money* reporters. Of necessity, the directory omits many qualified people because others received a greater number of recommendations from their peers. Also left out are a handful of front-runners who are not now taking new clients. No one is listed in Alaska, Montana, and Wyoming because we found too few practicing planners there to carry out our peer review.

A good time to seek the help of a financial planner is when your household income or your investable assets hit $50,000. In making your choice, try this process of elimination.

Limit your search primarily to those with a C.F.P. or Ch.F.C. designation. C.F.P. stands for certified financial planner; Ch.F.C., for chartered financial consultant. To earn either title, a planner has to pass a series of exams administered by a professional board or an accredited academic institution. A few planners who are identified on our list as enrolled agents have either worked for the Internal Revenue Service or passed a special IRS exam for tax preparers. Other initials that may be listed after a planner's name are C.F.A., for chartered financial analyst, a designation for investment professionals; C.L.U., for chartered life underwriter, indicating a highly trained life insurance agent; M.S.F.S., for master of science in financial services; R.F.P., for registered financial planner, someone who has passed state insurance and securities exams;

R.H.U., for registered health underwriter, a specialist in health insurance; and the more familiar M.B.A., C.P.A., and J.D. or LL.B. (law degrees).

Look for membership in the Registry of Financial Planning Practitioners. (This is noted by the word "Registry" in the listings.) The 735 men and women in this group, sponsored by the International Association for Financial Planning (IAFP), have at least three years' experience as planners and a C.F.P. or Ch.F.C. designation or a business or law degree. They have also passed an especially comprehensive examination. A free list of registry members is available from the IAFP (Suite 800, 2 Concourse Pkwy., Atlanta, GA 30328).

Ask planner candidates how they are compensated and what you will pay. Be careful of planners who say their plans are free, because they live on commissions earned on financial products bought by clients. Such planners could be tempted to sell you what you do not need. Instead, lean toward fee-only or fee-and-commission planners, who will tend to be more objective. An hourly rate of $100 is fairly typical of both groups; a flat fee for a written plan usually costs $500 to $1,000 if commissions add to the planner's compensation and as much as $5,000 if the fee is the only compensation.

Ask planners what their typical client's income is. When that figure is $150,000 or more, we note it for planners on our list. Do not automatically rule out such planners if your income is lower. Ask whether they welcome people with your income or assets. But if you are earning $50,000 and none of their clients make less than $150,000, look elsewhere.

Alabama

Jim Conrad, C.F.P., C.P.A. (Conrad Burnett & Co., 1 Independence Plaza, Birmingham 35209; 205-870-0311) **Compensation:** fee only. **Specialty:** retirement planning

Stewart Welch, C.F.P., Ch.F.C., C.L.U. (Welch Financial Advisors, 200 S. 28th St., Birmingham 35233; 205-323-7100) **Compensation:** fee + commission. **Specialties:** small-business owners and medical professionals

Peter Weston, C.F.P., Registry (Wesban Financial Consultants, 1 Chase Corporate Dr., Birmingham 35244; 205-987-9484) **Compensation:** fee only

Arizona

Neal Barnes, C.F.P. (Taurus Financial Corp., 110 E. Roosevelt St., Phoenix 85004; 602-257-8826) **Compensation:** fee + commission

David Hammond, C.F.P., Registry (Hammond & Nutt Associates, 1636 N. Swan Rd., Tucson 85712; 602-326-1786) **Compensation:** fee + commission

Philip Johnson, C.F.P., Registry (Financial Planning Resources, 1990 W. Camelback Rd., Phoenix 85015; 602-242-4000) **Compensation:** fee + commission. **Specialty:** retirement planning

Mark Moritz, C.F.P., Ch.F.C., C.L.U. (Engle O'Callaghan, 5050 N. 40th St., Phoenix 85018; 602-952-0700) **Compensation:** fee + commission. **Specialty:** small-business owners

Carl Seiter, C.F.P. (Financial Security Advisors, 3033 N. 44th St., Phoenix 85018; 602-371-8300) **Compensation:** fee + commission. **Specialty:** estate and retirement planning

Arkansas

Mary Ann Campbell, C.F.P. (Money Magic, 2923 Imperial Valley Dr., Little Rock 72212; 501-227-6644) **Compensation:** fee only

Barry Corkern, C.F.P., Registry, C.L.U. (Barry Corkern & Co., 1050 Tower Bldg., Little Rock 77201; 501-376-7171) **Compensation:** fee + commission. **Typical client income:** $150,000

William Kelly, C.F.P., Ch.F.C., C.L.U., LL.B. (First Financial Planners, 1100 N. University, Little Rock 72202; 501-663-1292) **Compensation:** fee + commission

James Thorpe, C.F.P., Ch.F.C. (Financial Management Inc., 10 Corporate Hill Dr., Little Rock 72205; 501-223-2222) **Compensation:** fee only

California

Arlene Atherton, C.F.P. (Atherton Advisory, 1333 Lawrence Expressway, Santa Clara 95051; 408-243-1558) **Compensation:** fee + commission. **Specialty:** computer executives. **Client income:** $150,000

Jack Blankinship, C.F.P., Registry (Blankinship & Associates, 2775 Via De La Valle, Del Mar 92014; 619-755-5166) **Compensation:** fee + commission

John Cahill, C.F.P., M.B.A. (Carroll/Cahill Associates, 250 Executive Park Dr., San Francisco 94134; 415-468-3880) **Compensation:** fee + commission

Graydon Calder, C.F.P., C.L.U. (Financial Planning Consultants, 7860 Mission Center Court, San Diego 92108; 619-291-7974) **Compensation:** fee + commission. **Specialty:** retirees

Andrew Castiglione, C.F.P., M.B.A. (Financial Planning Consultants, 7860 Mission Center Court, San Diego 92108; 619-291-7974) **Compensation:** fee + commission

Colin Coombs, C.F.P., C.L.U. (Petra Financial Group, 6351 Owensmouth Ave., Woodland Hills 91367; 818-346-8601) **Compensation:** fee + commission

Rich Costa, C.F.P. (Financial Plan Resource Group, 820 Bay Ave., Capitola 95010; 408-476-5954) **Compensation:** fee + commission

Elfrena Foord, C.F.P. (Foord Van Bruggen & Ebersole Investment Planning, 2255 Watt Ave., Sacramento 95825; 916-487-8700) **Compensation:** fee + commission

Philip Gainsborough, C.F.P. (Gainsborough Financial Consultants, 1901 Ave. of the Stars, Los Angeles 90067; 213-553-5405) **Compensation:** fee + commission

Lawrence Krause, C.F.P. (Lawrence A. Krause & Associates, 500 Washington St., San Francisco 94111; 415-362-1200) **Compensation:** fee + commission

Mark Pash, C.F.P., Registry, M.B.A. (Pash International, 4303 W. Verdugo Ave., Toluca Lake 91505; 818-842-9700) **Compensation:** fee only or fee + commission. **Specialty:** retirement planning

Gail Pendell, C.F.P., Registry (Gail Pendell & Associates, 5871 Oberlin Dr., San Diego 92121; 619-458-1165) **Compensation:** fee + commission

Ruth Rockey, C.F.P., Registry, M.B.A. (Ruth Rockey Financial Services, 2659 Townsgate Rd., Westlake Village 91361; 805-496-6400) **Compensation:** fee + commission

Julian Smith, C.F.P., Registry (Smith & Tucker; 128 E. Carillo St., Santa Barbara 93101; 805-963-6628) **Compensation:** fee + commission. **Specialty:** small-business owners. **Client income:** $100,000 to $200,000

Lewis Wallensky, C.F.P., Registry, R.H.U. (Lewis Wallensky Associates, 1901 Ave. of the Stars, Los Angeles 90067; 213-557-2007) **Compensation:** fee + commission

Colorado

Sally Button, C.F.P. (Button Financial, 1115 Grant St., Denver 80203; 303-861-5290) **Compensation:** fee + commission

Carolyn Hamil, C.F.P. (Wagner & Hamil, 410 17th St., Denver 80202; 303-892-6928) **Compensation:** fee only

Eileen Sharkey, C.F.P., Registry (E.M. Sharkey & Associates, 2755 S. Locust St., Denver 80222; 303-759-4262) **Compensation:** fee + commission

Andrea Sullivan, (Cigna Financial Services, 950 S. Cherry St., Denver 80222; 303-691-3000) **Compensation:** fee + commission

Connecticut

Marty Baron, C.F.P., Ch.F.C., C.L.U. (1 Civic Center Plaza, Hartford 06143; 203-240-6229) **Compensation:** fee + commission

Robert Dowd, (Security Financial Corp., 2074 Park St. Central, Hartford 06106; 203-236-6145) **Compensation:** fee only. **Specialty:** dentists

James Hofmann, C.F.P., C.P.A. (J/M Financial Advisors Inc., 360 Tunxis Hill Rd., Fairfield 06430; 203-334-7878) **Compensation:** fee only. **Client income:** $175,000

Robert Maloney, C.F.P. (R.E. Maloney Associates, 73 Redding Rd., Georgetown 06829; 203-544-9369) **Compensation:** fee only

Stanley Sadlack, C.F.P., Ch.F.C., C.L.U. (S.T. Sadlack & Co., 175 Main St., Hartford 06106; 203-728-5594) **Compensation:** fee + commission

Delaware

Alan Benson Brown, C.F.P. (Delmarva Ltd., 3828 Kennett Pike, Powder Mill Square, Wilmington 19807; 302-655-7400) **Compensation:** fee only. **Specialty:** retirement planning

District of Columbia

Alexandra Armstrong, C.F.P., Registry (Alexandra Armstrong Advisors, 1140 Connecticut Ave. N.W., Washington 20036; 202-887-8135) **Compensation:** fee + commission. **Specialties:** single women and professionals

Joanne Bickel, C.F.P. (American Security Bank, 1501 Pennsylvania Ave. N.W., Washington 20013; 202-624-3772) **Compensation:** fee only. **Client income:** $150,000

John Freeman Blake, Registry, J.D. (Silverstein & Mullens, 1776 K St. N.W., Washington 20006; 202-452-7978) **Compensation:** fee only

John Cammack, C.F.P., Registry, M.B.A. (Alexandra Armstrong Advisors, 1140 Connecticut Ave. N.W., Washington 20036; 202-887-8135) **Compensation:** fee + commission. **Specialties:** pensions, ethical investing

LeCount Davis, C.F.P., enrolled agent (Financial Services Network, 1511 K St. N.W., Washington 20005; 202-638-4894) **Compensation:** fee only. **Specialties:** tax planning and small-business owners

Dennis Gurtz, Registry, C.F.A., C.P.A., M.B.A. (Dennis M. Gurtz & Associates, 4910 Massachusetts Ave. N.W., Washington 20016; 202-364-3060) **Compensation:** fee + commission

Paul Yurachek Registry, C.P.A., former IRS agent, J.D. (Dennis M. Gurtz & Associates, 4910 Massachusetts Ave. N.W., Washington 20016; 202-364-3060) **Compensation:** fee + commission. **Specialties:** tax and estate planning

Florida

Stephen Conway, C.F.P. (Stephen Conway Financial Advisors, 1515 N. Federal Hwy., Boca Raton 33432; 305-428-2455) **Compensation:** fee + commission. **Specialty:** small-business owners

Jack Coulter, C.F.P., M.B.A. (First Financial Planners, 825 South U.S. 1, Jupiter 33477; 305-747-7200) **Compensation:** fee + commission

Harold Evensky, C.F.P., Registry (Evensky & Brown, 2701 Ponce de Leon, Coral Gables 33134; 305-448-8882) **Compensation:** fee + commission. **Specialty:** fixed-income portfolio management

Margaret Starner, C.F.P. (Raymond James & Associates, 136 Madeira, Coral Gables 33134; 305-442-4490) **Compensation:** fee + commission. **Specialty:** tax planning

Laura Waller, C.F.P. (Laura Waller Advisors, 201 E. Kennedy Blvd., Tampa 33602; 813-221-1956) **Compensation:** fee + commission

Georgia

Jack Harmon, C.F.P., Registry (Consolidated Planning Corp., 400 Colony Square, Atlanta 30361; 404-892-1995) **Compensation:** fee + commission. **Client income:** $150,000

David Homrich, C.F.P., C.P.A. (Acorn Financial Services, 3525 Piedmont Rd. N.E., Piedmont Center, Atlanta 30305; 404-266-3641) **Compensation:** fee only. **Specialty:** small-business owners. **Client income:** $200,000

Lewis Walker, C.F.P., Registry, M.B.A. (Walker Capital Management, 4340 Georgetown Square, Atlanta 30338; 404-452-7222) **Compensation:** fee + commission

Hawaii

Robert Chamberlain, C.F.P., Registry (Chamberlain & Associates, 737 Bishop St., Honolulu 96813; 808-536-1985) **Compensation:** fee + commission

Bryan Enos, C.F.P., Ch.F.C., Registry, C.L.U. (Bryan D. Enos & Associates, 1188 Bishop St., Honolulu 96813; 808-536-3502) **Compensation:** fee + commission. **Specialty:** small-business owners

Bill McRoberts, C.F.P., Ch.F.C., C.L.U. (McRoberts & Associates, 1188 Bishop St., Honolulu 96813; 808-538-0816) **Compensation:** fee + commission

Idaho

Stan Mock, (Financial Planning Services, 4720 Emerald, Boise 83706; 208-343-3993) **Compensation:** fee only or commission only

Illinois

Marilyn Capelli, C.F.P., Registry (Forest Financial Advisors, 475 River Bend Rd., Naperville 60540; 312-983-2950) **Compensation:** fee only

Mike Kabarec, C.F.P., Registry, C.P.A. (M.P. Kabarec & Associates, 800 E. Northwest Hwy., Palatine 60067; 312-934-7777) **Compensation:** fee only

Michael Leonetti, C.F.P., Registry (Leonetti & Associates, 1130 Lake Cook Rd., Buffalo Grove 60089; 312-520-0999) **Compensation:** fee only

Gary Mandell, C.F.P., Registry, M.B.A. (The Mandell Group, 222 S. Riverside Plaza, Chicago 60606; 312-454-8515) **Compensation:** fee + commission

Mike Ryan, C.F.P., Registry (Ryan Financial Advisors, 1000 Skokie Blvd., Wilmette 60091; 312-256-6700) **Compensation:** fee only. **Specialty:** retirement planning

Indiana

James Morrison, C.F.P., J.D. (Financial Perspective, 4755 Kingsway Dr., Indianapolis 46205; 317-251-0766) **Compensation:** fee only

Thomas Searcy, Ch.F.C., Registry, C.L.U., M.S.F.S. (Financial Priorities, 244 Waterfall Dr., Elkhart 46516; 219-293-7103) **Compensation:** fee + commission. **Specialty:** retirement planning

Chuck Yeager, C.F.P., Ch.F.C., Registry, M.S.F.S. (SYM Financial Corp., 2513 E. Center St., Warsaw 46580; 219-267-2300) **Compensation:** fee only. **Specialty:** estate planning

Iowa

J. Michael Cavitt, C.F.P. (Cavitt Financial Management, 323 Third Ave., Iowa City 52240; 319-338-9211) **Compensation:** fee only

Pat McGoldrick, Ch.F.C., C.L.U. (Johansen McGoldrick Financial Planners, 317 Sixth Ave., Des Moines 50309; 515-243-3212) **Compensation:** fee + commission

David Strege, C.F.P., Registry (Bryton Capital Management, 2900 Westtown Pkwy., West Des Moines 50265; 515-223-1600) **Compensation:** fee only

Joe Young, C.F.P., Registry, C.L.U., J.D. (918 Equitable Bldg., Des Moines 50309; 515-244-5141) **Compensation:** fee only

Kansas

Beth Bateman, C.F.P., Registry (Bateman & Associates, 240 N. Rock Rd., Wichita 67206; 316-684-1440) **Compensation:** fee + commission

J. Randall Hedlund, C.F.P. (Financial Management Consultants, 4500 College Blvd., Overland Park 66211; 913-491-4222) **Compensation:** fee only. **Client income:** $150,000

David King, C.F.P. (David M. King & Associates, 103 W. 13th St., Hays 67601; 913-625-7393) **Compensation:** fee + commission

Kevin Tucker, C.F.P. (Reeves & Co., 712 S. Kansas Ave., Topeka 66603; 913-233-9262) **Compensation:** fee + commission

Kentucky

Bob Cole, Ch.F.C., C.L.U. (Financial Architects, 1484 Starks Bldg., Louisville 40202; 502-589-1772) **Compensation:** fee only. **Specialties:** small-business owners and women

Alan Griffes, C.F.P., Registry, R.H.U. (First Financial Advisor Corp., 9200 Shelbyville Rd., Louisville 40222; 502-425-8011) **Compensation:** fee + commission. **Specialties:** business owners and retirement planning

Kimble Johnson, C.F.P., C.F.A., M.B.A. (Capital Planning Services, 1484 Starks Bldg., Louisville 40202; 502-589-5092) **Compensation:** fee only. **Specialty:** estate planning

Louisiana

L. William Peters, C.F.P., M.B.A. (Peters Financial Services, 7909 Wrenwood Blvd., Baton Rouge 70898; 504-923-2273) **Compensation:** fee + commission

Robert Reed, C.F.P., Registry (Robert J. Reed & Associates, 202 N. Jefferson, Covington 70433; 504-892-8337) **Compensation:** fee + commission

D. Randolph Waesche, C.F.P., Registry (Resource Management, 3300 W. Esplanade, Metairie 70002; 504-833-5378) **Compensation:** fee only. **Specialty:** business owners

Judith Zabalaoui, C.F.P., Registry, M.B.A. (Resource Management, 3300 W. Esplanade, Metairie 70002; 504-833-5378) **Compensation:** fee only. **Specialty:** business owners

Maine

Daniel Duff, C.F.P. (Daniel P. Duff & Associates, 49 Acme Rd., Brewer 04412; 207-989-6082) **Compensation:** fee + commission. **Specialty:** estate and retirement planning

Raynold Gauvin, C.F.P., R.F.P. (The Center for Financial Planning Services, Rice and N. Main Sts., Presque Isle 04769; 207-764-3191) **Compensation:** fee + commission. **Specialty:** small-business owners

Maryland

Robert Ginsburgh C.F.P., Ch.F.C., Registry, C.L.U., enrolled agent (Neville Associates, 5319 Oakland Rd., Chevy Chase 20815; 301-951-0557) **Compensation:** fee only

William Kissinger, Registry, C.P.A. (Kissinger Financial Services, 1919 York Rd., Timonium 21093; 301-252-3400) **Compensation:** fee + commission

Donald Lebowitz, C.F.P., Registry (Lebowitz & Associates, 711 W. 40th St., Baltimore 21211; 301-366-1180) **Compensation:** fee + commission

Richard Wagener, C.F.P., Registry, C.L.U. (Financial First Advisors, 9861 Broken Land Pkwy., Columbia 21046; 301-720-5757) **Compensation:** fee + commission

Wade Webster, Registry (Webster Financial Group-The PlanFirst Co., 6 N. Park Dr., Cockeysville 21030; 301-683-0600) **Compensation:** fee + commission

Massachusetts

Dick Boardman, Ch.F.C., C.L.U. (The Boardman Co., 5 Hooper St., Marblehead 01945; 617-631-0994) **Compensation:** fee + commission. **Specialty:** small-business owners

Jim Hughes, C.F.P., C.L.U., M.B.A. (Hughes Financial Management, 21 Pleasant St., Newburyport 01950; 617-462-9500) **Compensation:** fee + commission

Robert Martel, C.F.P., Ch.F.C., Registry, C.L.U. (Financial Planning & Management, 3 Militia Dr., Lexington 02173; 617-863-1230) **Compensation:** fee + commission. **Specialty:** estate planning

Nancy Penhune, C.F.P., Registry, M.B.A. (Penhune Financial Planning, 57 Causeway Rd., Vineyard Haven, Martha's Vineyard 02568; 617-693-0350) **Compensation:** fee + commission

Iris Taymore Schnitzer, C.F.P., C.L.U. (The Financial Forum, 50 Milk St., Boston 02109; 617-451-9242) **Compensation:** fee only

Richard Wojcik, C.F.P., Registry (New England Financial Planning Group, 10 Mall Rd., Burlington 01803; 617-273-4575) **Compensation:** fee + commission

Michigan

Dan Boyce, C.F.P., Registry (Daniel H. Boyce Financial Advisory Services, 877 S. Adams, Birmingham 48011; 313-642-4000) **Compensation:** fee + commission. **Specialty:** retirement planning

Robert Finnigan, C.F.P. (Roney & Co., 1 Griswold, Detroit 48226; 313-963-6700) **Compensation:** fee + commission

Dale McClelland C.F.P., Registry (Financial & Tax Planning, G-4080 Miller Rd., Flint 48507; 313-733-5140) **Compensation:** fee + commission. **Specialty:** retirement planning

Isabel Francis Smith, C.F.P., Registry (Integrated Financial Strategies, 30200 Telegraph Rd., Birmingham 48010; 313-645-6357) **Compensation:** fee + commission

Minnesota

Patrick Farley, C.F.P., C.L.U. (Comprehensive Financial Planning, 821 Raymond Ave., St. Paul 55114; 612-645-4699) **Compensation:** fee + commission

Paul Kenworthy, C.F.P., Registry, M.B.A. (Source Financial Group, 8300 Norman Center Dr., Minneapolis 55437; 612-893-9900) **Compensation:** fee + commission. **Specialty:** business owners

Ross Levin, C.F.P. (Creative Energy Resources, 501 Union Plaza, 333 N. Washington Ave., Minneapolis 55401; 612-332-2300) **Compensation:** fee + commission. **Specialty:** tax planning

C.R. Moen, C.F.P., Ch.F.C., Registry (Creative Financial Cos., 9801 Dupont Ave. South, Bloomington 55431; 612-884-9311) **Compensation:** fee or commission

Diana Risdon, C.F.P. (Private Ledger Financial Services, 202 W. Superior St., Duluth 55802; 218-727-1989) **Compensation:** fee + commission. **Specialties:** retirement and tax planning

Helen Stecklein, C.F.P., M.B.A. (Stecklein Financial Services, 1988 N. Wheeler St., St. Paul 55113; 612-644-8304) **Compensation:** fee + commission. **Specialty:** retirement planning

Keith Witter, C.P.A., J.D. (Americap Financial Planners, 100 First Ave., Rochester 55903; 507-281-4100) **Compensation:** fee + commission. **Specialties:** tax and estate planning

Mississippi

Tim Medley, C.F.P. (Medley & Co., 1640 Lelia Dr., Jackson 39216; 601-982-4123) **Compensation:** fee + commission

Lynn Phillips, (325 University Dr., Starkville 39759; 601-324-2889) **Compensation:** fee + commission. **Specialties:** women and small-business owners

Donald Ray, C.F.P., LL.B., R.F.P. (Financial Review Services, 120 N. Congress St., Jackson 39201; 601-353-2555) **Compensation:** fee + commission. **Specialties:** business owners and estate planning

Missouri

Stewart Koestin, Ch.F.C., Registry, C.L.U. (Koestin & Co., 8080 Ward Pkwy., Kansas City 64114; 816-926-0860) **Compensation:** fee only

Michael Searcy, C.F.P., Ch.F.C., Registry (Searcy Financial Services, 1 Ward Pkwy., Kansas City 64112; 816-931-8686) **Compensation:** fee + commission. **Client income:** $150,000

Wayne Starr, C.F.P., Ch.F.C., C.L.U., M.B.A. (Neill & Associates, Ninth and Main Sts., Kansas City 64199; 816-842-1935) **Compensation:** fee only

Jim Stevens, C.F.P., Ch.F.C., C.L.U., M.S.F.S., R.H.U. (Creative Planning Inc., 8880 Ward Pkwy., Kansas City 64114; 816-926-2626) **Compensation:** fee only

Nebraska

David Rice, C.F.P. (David S. Rice & Associates, 11414 W. Center Rd., Omaha 68144; 402-333-0777 **Compensation:** fee + commission

Nevada

F. Gard Jameson, C.F.P., C.P.A., M.B.A. (Laventhol & Horwath, 300 S. Fourth St., Las Vegas 89101; 702-384-1120) **Compensation:** fee only

New Hampshire

Paul Pignone, C.F.P., Ch.F.C., Registry, C.L.U. (Boston Financial Services, 8 Stiles Rd., Salem 03079; 603-893-6650) **Compensation:** fee + commission. **Specialties:** small-business owners and corporate executives

Timothy Riley, C.F.P., Registry (The Harbor Group, 52 Riverway Place, Bedford 03102; 603-668-1832) **Compensation:** fee + commission. **Specialty:** retirement planning

Elliot Snow, Ch.F.C., Registry, C.L.U. (Baldwin & Clarke, 116B S. River Rd., Bedford 03102; 603-668-4353) **Compensation:** fee + commission

New Jersey

David Bugen, C.F.P., Registry, M.B.A. (Individual Asset Planning, 66 Maple Ave., Morristown 07960; 201-539-2300) **Compensation:** fee + commission

Charles Lefkowitz, C.F.P., Registry (Financial Blueprints, 248 Columbia Turnpike, Florham Park 07932; 201-966-0930) **Compensation:** fee + commission. **Specialty:** corporate executives

George Leupold, Ch.F.C., Registry, C.L.U. (Leupold Financial Planning Associates, 1902 Fairfax Ave., Cherry Hill 08003; 609-424-2233) **Compensation:** fee + commission

Robert Oberst, C.F.P., Registry, R.H.U. (Robert J. Oberst Sr. & Associates, 218 Broad St., Red Bank 07701; 201-842-2300) **Compensation:** fee + commission

Ron Subber, C.F.P., Ch.F.C., C.L.U. (Economic Concepts, Hwy. 31 South, Lebanon 08833; 201-735-4000) **Compensation:** fee + commission

New Mexico

Stephen Ciepiela, C.F.P. (Charles Stephen Financial Group, 2400 Louisiana Blvd. N.E., Albuquerque 87110; 505-884-0451) **Compensation:** fee + commission. **Specialty:** small-business owners

Bradley Greer, C.F.P., C.P.A. (First National Bank of Albuquerque, P.O. Box 1305, Albuquerque 87103; 505-765-4470) **Compensation:** fee only

Lindell Mitchell, C.F.P., Ch.F.C., Registry, C.L.U. (Mitchell & Associates, 5907 Alice N.E., Albuquerque 87110; 505-266-8795) **Compensation:** fee + commission. **Specialty:** mutual fund market timing

New York

Lewis Altfest, Registry, C.F.A., C.P.A., M.B.A. (L.J. Altfest & Co., 140 William St., New York City 10038; 212-406-0850) **Compensation:** fee only

Terrence Downing, C.F.P., C.P.A. (Downing & Young Associates, 5725 Main St., Williamsville 14221; 716-632-8234) **Compensation:** fee + commission

Steven Enright, C.F.P. (Seidman Financial Services, 15 Columbus Circle, New York City 10023; 212-245-1080) **Compensation:** fee only. **Specialties:** medical professionals and corporate executives

Charles Hughes, C.F.P. (C.G. Hughes Co., 260 Montauk Hwy., Bay Shore 11706; 516-665-7881) **Compensation:** fee + commission

Dennis Kelly, C.F.P. (Janney Montgomery Scott, 26 Broadway, New York City 10004; 212-510-0650) **Compensation:** fee + commission

Kenneth Leichman, C.F.P., Registry (First Albany Corp., 41 State St., Albany 12207; 518-447-8575) **Compensation:** fee + commission

Claire Longden, C.F.P., Registry (Butcher & Singer, 65 Broadway, New York City 10006; 212-422-1111) **Compensation:** fee + commission. **Client income:** $175,000

Andrew Rich, C.F.P. (AMR Planning Services, 146 Manetto Hill Rd., Plainview 11803; 516-433-0828) **Compension:** fee + commission. **Specialty:** tax planning

Alan Vogt, C.F.P., Registry, C.L.U., J.D. (Paramount Planning, 1325 Millersport Hwy., Amherst 14221; 716-634-6113) **Compensation:** fee + commission. **Specialty:** retirement planning

North Carolina

Larry Carroll, C.F.P., Registry, C.P.A., M.B.A. (Carroll Financial Planning Associates, 5950 Fairview Rd., Charlotte 28210; 704-553-8006) **Compensation:** fee + commission

Gerald Townsend, C.F.P., Registry, C.P.A. (Townsend Financial Group, 5120 Bur Oak Circle, Raleigh 27612; 919-782-9689) **Compensation:** fee + commission

North Dakota

Jerry Dockter, C.F.P. (Jerry Dockter & Associates, 418 E. Broadway, Bismarck 58501; 701-258-3053) **Compensation:** fee + commission

David Vanderscoff, C.F.P., Ch.F.C. (Vanderscoff Financial Planning, 217 W. Rosser Ave., Bismarck 58501; 701-255-6417) **Compensation:** fee + commission. **Client income:** $150,000

Ohio

Edwin Morrow, C.F.P., Ch.F.C., Registry, C.L.U. (Confidential Planning Services, 2507 N. Verity Pkwy., Middletown 45042; 513-424-1656) **Compensation:** fee + commission. **Specialties:** corporate executives and small-business owners. **Client income:** $250,000+

Stephen Polk, (Polk Financial Services, 2164 Riverside Dr., Columbus 43221; 614-488-6597) **Compensation:** fee + commission. **Specialty:** small-business owners. **Client income:** $150,000

Larry Waller, C.F.P., Ch.F.C., Registry, C.L.U. (Waller Financial Planning Group, 921 Chatham Lane, Columbus 43221; 614-457-7026) **Compensation:** fee + commission. **Specialty:** retirement planning

Oklahoma

Alan Ross, C.F.P., J.D. (Ross & Associates, 7666 E. 61st St., Tulsa 74133; 918-250-7803) **Compensation:** fee + commission

Oregon

Kim Colin, C.F.P. (Diversified Financial Planning, 8196 S.W. Hall, Beaverton 97005; 503-641-5198) **Compensation:** fee + commission. **Specialty:** dual-income families

Dale Hadley, C.F.P., Registry (Interwest Financial Advisors, 121 S.W. Salmon, Portland 97204; 503-227-3988) **Compensation:** fee + commission. **Specialty:** retirement planning

Robert Keys, C.F.P., Registry (Interwest Financial Advisors, 121 S.W. Salmon, Portland 97204; 503-227-3988) **Compensation:** fee + commission. **Specialty:** retirement planning

Al Jeanfreau, C.F.P. (Al Jeanfreau Associates, 200 S.W. Market, Portland 97201; 503-224-5766) **Compensation:** fee + commission

Pennsylvania

Joann Bay, C.F.P., Registry (J.R. Bay Associates, 5022 Sylvia Rd., Drexel Hill 19026; 215-853-2222) **Compensation:** fee only

Roy Diliberto, C.F.P., Ch.F.C., Registry, C.L.U. (RTD Financial Advisors, 1500 Walnut St., Philadelphia 19102; 215-893-4000) **Compensation:** fee + commission

Roger Gibson, C.F.P., Registry, C.F.A., M.B.A. (Allegheny Financial Group, 3000 McKnight East Dr., Pittsburgh 15237; 412-367-3880) **Compensation:** fee + commission

Jan Gotshall, C.F.P., Registry (GM Financial Planners, 15 N. Devon Blvd., Devon 19333; 215-688-4034) **Compensation:** fee + commission. **Specialties:** women and retirees

Daniel Hey, C.F.P., Registry, enrolled agent (417 Longwood Dr., Exton 19341; 215-363-7306) **Compensation:** fee + commission. **Specialties:** tax and estate planning

James Hohman, C.F.P., Registry (Allegheny Financial Group, 3000 McKnight East Dr., Pittsburgh 15237; 412-367-3880) **Compensation:** fee + commission

Linda Jepson, Ch.F.C., C.L.U. (Lillis, McKibben & Jepson, 333 Marine Bank Bldg., Erie 16501; 814-452-4085) **Compensation:** fee + commission. **Specialties:** estate planning and business owners

Dorothy Lebeau, C.F.P., M.B.A. (Lebeau Financial Advisory, 737 Suffolk Rd., Jenkintown 19046; 215-572-7414) **Compensation:** fee only. **Specialties:** professionals and retirement planning

William Marshall, C.F.P., Registry (Marshall Financial Management, 33 W. Court St., Doylestown 18901; 215-348-9393) **Compensation:** fee + commission

Carole Phillips, Ch.F.C. (C.C. Phillips, 340 S. 16th St., Philadelphia 19102; 215-732-2577) **Compensation:** fee only

Kenneth Rudzinski, C.F.P., Ch.F.C., C.L.U. (Financial Advisory Network, 5 Radnor Corporate Center, Radnor 19087; 215-688-6002) **Compensation:** fee + commission

Rhode Island

Malcolm Makin, C.F.P. (Professional Planning Group, 307 Washington Trust Bldg., Westerly 02891; 401-596-2800) **Compensation:** fee + commission. **Specialty:** retirement planning

Charles O'Hara, Registry (Investment Brokers of America, 25 College Park Court, Warwick 02886; 401-823-7770) **Compensation:** commission only. **Specialties:** tax planning and limited partnerships

South Carolina

H. Jack Free, C.F.P., Registry, C.L.U. (H. Jack Free Advisory, 128 E. Richardson Ave., Summerville 29483; 803-871-4384) **Compensation:** fee + commission

Arthur Hogan, C.F.P. (Arthur J. Hogan & Associates, 123 Meeting St., Charleston 29401; 803-577-2884) **Compensation:** fee only

James Edmunds Wilson, C.F.P. (James Edmunds Wilson & Co., 1522 Lady St., Columbia 29201; 803-799-9203) **Compensation:** fee only. **Client income:** $150,000

South Dakota

Harlan Peterson, C.F.P., C.P.A. (121 Third Ave. S.W., Aberdeen 57401; 605-225-6654) **Compensation:** fee only. **Specialty:** small-business owners

Tennessee

P. Kemp Fain, C.F.P., Ch.F.C., C.L.U. (Asset Planning Corp., 238 Peters Rd., Knoxville 37923; 615-690-1231) **Compensation:** fee + commission

Hank Parks, C.F.P. (Lifetime Planning, 1010 June Rd., Memphis 38119; 901-763-4100) **Compensation:** fee + commission. **Client income:** $150,000

Gerald Pierce, C.F.P., C.L.U. (5394 Estate Office Dr., Memphis 38119; 901-682-4073) **Compensation:** fee only. **Client income:** $250,000

Texas

Mark Bass, C.F.P., Registry, C.P.A. (Pennington/Bass Cos., 1001 Main St., Lubbock 79401; 806-765-7471) **Compensation:** fee + commission

Martin Cohen, C.F.P. (Martin Cohen Investments, P.O. Box 9005, Rockwall 75087; 214-475-8662) **Compensation:** fee + commission

David Diesslin, C.F.P., Registry, M.B.A. (Diesslin & Williams Financial Consulting & Money Management, 810 Houston St., Fort Worth 76102; 817-429-8855) **Compensation:** fee only

Paul Ferraresi, C.F.P., Registry, M.B.A. (Founders Group, 11 Greenway Plaza, Houston 77046; 713-871-1404) **Compensation:** fee + commission. **Specialty:** investments

Jim Herridge, C.F.P., Registry, C.L.U. (J.W.H. Advisory Services, 4715 Fredericksburg Rd., San Antonio 78229; 512-377-3420) **Compensation:** fee + commission

Bernard Lauterbach, C.F.P., C.P.A. (Lauterbach Borschow & Co., 715 N. Oregon, El Paso 79902; 915-544-6950) **Compensation:** fee only. **Specialties:** corporate executives and small-business owners

Gary Morris, C.F.P., C.L.U., M.B.A. (Howland & Morris, 6116 N. Central Expressway, Dallas 75206; 214-363-4900) **Compensation:** fee + commission

Kathleen Muldoon, C.F.P., Registry (Carter Financial Management, 5956 Sherry Lane, Dallas 75225; 214-363-4200) **Compensation:** fee + commission

Tom Pazera, C.F.P., C.P.A. (Pazera Capital Management, 4615 Southwest Freeway, Houston 77027; 713-850-9575) **Compensation:** fee + commission. **Specialty:** retirement planning

Katherine Sandberg, C.F.P., Registry, C.F.A., M.B.A. (Sandberg Financial Services, 820 Gessner, Houston 77024; 713-984-1832) **Compensation:** fee + commission. **Specialty:** estate planning

Arv Vilutis, C.F.P., Ch.F.C., C.L.U., M.B.A. (Smith Barney, 1100 Milam, Houston 77002; 713-658-8191) **Compensation:** commission only. **Specialty:** retirement planning

Peggy Wallace (Wallace-Simons Financial Consultants, 1100 N.E. Loop 410, San Antonio 78213; 512-341-2855) **Compensation:** fee + commission. **Specialty:** estate planning. **Client income:** $150,000

Don Ward, C.F.P., Registry (Houston Asset Management, 1800 W. Loop South, Houston 77027; 713-629-1534) **Compensation:** fee + commission

Utah

Henry Brock, Ch.F.C., Registry, C.L.U., C.P.A., M.B.A. (H.S. Brock & Associates, 310 E. 4500 South, Salt Lake City 84107; 801-263-3636) **Compensation:** fee + commission

Terrence Hansen, C.F.P., Registry (The Center for Financial Planning, 2063 E. 3900 South, Salt Lake City 84124; 801-272-8212) **Compensation:** fee + commission

Vermont

David Boardman, C.F.P., C.L.U. (Associates in Financial Planning, P.O. Box 729, Burlington 05402; 802-658-3500) **Compensation:** fee + commission

Amy Leavitt, C.F.P., Registry (Leavitt Associates, Jedediah Strong House, Clubhouse at Deweys Mills Rd., Quechee 05059; 802-295-1206) **Compensation:** fee + commission. **Specialty:** small-business owners. **Client income:** $150,000+

Charles Lyman, C.F.P., C.L.U. (Lyman Financial Services, 168 Battery St., Burlington 05401; 802-863-5695) **Compensation:** fee + commission

Virginia

John Cecil, C.F.P., Registry (Cecil & Saunders, 1004 N. Thompson St., Richmond 23230; 804-358-7151 **Compensation:** fee + commission. **Specialty:** retirement planning

David Dondero, C.F.P., Registry (Dondero & Associates, 665 S. Washington St., Alexandria 22314; 703-549-7331) **Compensation:** fee + commission

Malcolm Fries, C.F.P., Registry, M.B.A. (Malcolm G. Fries & Associates, 749 Thimble Shoals Blvd., Newport News 23606; 804-873-0800) **Compensation:** fee + commission

Lynn Hopewell, C.F.P., Registry, M.B.A. (Hopewell Rembert Advisors, 7647 Leesburg Pike, Falls Church 22043; 703-821-6655) **Compensation:** fee only

Morris Sahr, C.F.P., Registry (Cardinal Financial Planning, 10855 Lee Hwy., Fairfax 22030; 703-385-8040) **Compensation:** fee + commission

Joseph Schopen, C.F.P., Registry (J.J. Schopen & Associates, 4356-3 Bonney Rd., Virginia Beach 23452; 804-463-9800) **Compensation:** fee + commission

Washington

Dick Knight, C.F.P. (Quality Financial Plans, 110 110th N.E. Ave., Bellevue 98004; 206-455-3849) **Compensation:** fee + commission

Diane Schaak, C.F.P., Registry (Schaak Financial Services, 10800 N.E. Eighth St., Bellevue 98004; 206-455-5964) **Compensation:** fee + commission

Houston Scrudder, C.F.P. (Quantum Planning & Investment Group, 4407 Division, Spokane 99207; 509-487-2744) **Compensation:** fee + commission

Muriel Van Housen, C.F.P. (Robert Loring Sheppard & Associates, 414 Olive Way, Seattle 98101; 206-292-9985) **Compensation:** fee + commission

West Virginia

David Lanham, C.F.P., Registry, C.L.U. (Lanham O'Dell Constantino, 3981 Teays Valley Rd., Hurricane 25526; 304-757-8131) **Compensation:** fee + commission. **Specialties:** retirement planning and small-business owners. **Client income:** $200,000+

Wisconsin

Edward Celnicker, C.F.P.(Anchor Investment Advisors, 110 E. Main St., Madison 53703; 608-251-7772) **Compensation:** fee + commission. **Specialty:** ethical investing

Michele Cody, C.F.P. (CRB Financial Services, 245 Main St., Racine 53403; 414-764-2252) **Compensation:** fee + commission

Martin Kummer, J.D. (Kummer Associates, 5150 N. Port Washington Rd., Milwaukee 53217; 414-332-7990) **Compensation:** fee only. **Specialties:** tax and estate planning

Mary Merrill, C.F.P., Registry, M.B.A. (First Wisconsin National Bank—Madison, 1 S. Pinkney St., Madison 53707; 608-252-4403) **Compensation:** fee only

Larry Peters, Ch.F.C., C.L.U. (Coordinated Capital Advisory, 6033 Monona Dr., Madison 53716; 608-221-9050) **Compensation:** fee + commission. **Client income:** $200,000+

J. Gerard Weidmann, Ch.F.C., C.L.U., M.S.F.S. (Megarian Financial Services, 777 E. Wisconsin Ave., Milwaukee 53202; 414-273-5030) **Compensation:** fee + commission. **Client income:** $150,000+

John Windsor, C.F.P., C.F.A., M.B.A. (Oak Financial Advisors, 5150 N. Port Washington Rd., Milwaukee 53217; 414-964-2777) **Compensation:** fee + commission. **Specialty:** retirement planning

Mutual Fund Rankings

On the following pages, you can check up on your own funds or look for new ones to consider from among the 723 tracked by *Money*. To qualify for the list, a fund must be available to the general public in at least 25 states. It must also have $25 million in assets, be at least a year old, and accept a minimum initial investment of $10,000 or less.

Results are provided by Lipper Analytical Services and are net of management fees (including 12b-1 charges, if any) but not of sales charges. The figures assume reinvestment of all dividends. The rankings cover fund performance to October 1, 1987.

A few notes of explanation will help you make greater use of the rankings. In the top-performers tables, the **volatility** rating indicates a fund's relative stability within its broad investment category: funds that hold stocks, those that invest in taxable bonds, and those that buy tax-exempts. To get a rough idea of how much you might earn or lose in one of the top funds in a particularly hot or cold three-month period, note the **maximum quarterly gain (and loss) since October 1, 1982.**

For a look at how various funds did under the same adverse market conditions, see the column headed **% gain (or loss) in last down cycle**—a period defined by Lipper Analytical Services as June 23, 1983, to July 26, 1984. (Tax-exempt funds' down market performance covers the period June 30, 1983, to July 31, 1984.) If you are shopping for a new fund, compare your candidate's performance in the last down cycle to that of the appropriate benchmark—the Standard & Poor's 500-stock index is the most widely used standard for stocks and the Salomon Brothers bond index, for bonds. These are noted in the listings of top-performing funds and on page 204.

If you are searching for a fund that pays out high income, note the column headed **% current yield**, indicating the dividends and interest from securities that a fund passes on to shareholders.

If you are among those who think that smaller funds tend to be nimbler than larger ones, look at the **assets as of August 31, 1987.** The **% gain (or loss) in assets** over the past year will let you know whether the artful ballerina you bought has become a potentially slow-footed behemoth.

The **% maximum initial sales charge** tells you how much load you would have to pay to get into a fund, while the **% annual expense ratio** lets you know how much it costs to stay there. The average expense ratio for stock funds is 1.1%; for bond funds, 0.9%. (If your fund's expense ratio exceeds the average—and its performance consistently lags behind the S&P 500—you might consider switching to another fund.) Most funds accept a **minimum initial investment** of $250 to $1,000, but in many cases you can get in for less if you invest through an Individual Retirement Account or Keogh plan. To track down IRA information and find out more about a fund and its holdings, be sure to ask for the prospectus and latest annual report before investing.

In the alphabetical listings, the column headed **type** indicates the general objectives of the fund—for example, maximum capital gains, long-term growth, or current income. The column for **three-year rating** enables you to compare your fund's results with others of its type since October 1, 1984. A grade of *good* signifies that a fund's three-year performance was in the top 20% for its category; *poor* means it fell in the bottom 20%; and *fair* denotes the three-fifths in between. An excellent 10-year record indicates that the fund is a solid performer over the long term.

The Top-Performing Stock Funds

RANKED BY THREE-YEAR PERFORMANCE	VOLATILITY	% GAIN (OR LOSS) TO OCT. 1, 1987				% COMPOUND ANNUAL RETURN (FIVE YEARS TO OCT. 1)	MAXIMUM QUARTERLY GAIN (AND LOSS) SINCE OCT. 1, 1982		% GAIN (OR LOSS) IN LAST DOWN CYCLE	% CURRENT YIELD
		YEAR TO DATE	ONE YEAR	THREE YEARS	10 YEARS		BEST	WORST		
MAXIMUM CAPITAL GAINS										
1 Twentieth Century Growth	High	55.6	65.3	149.2	1,222.5	25.1	32.0	(14.7)	(27.9)	0.4
2 Hartwell Growth	High	61.9	76.1	135.4	756.5	26.0	38.2	(11.4)	(33.4)	—
3 Weingarten Equity	High	40.3	49.0	135.3	1,000.5	27.0	27.7	(14.1)	(28.4)	0.7
4 Putnam Voyager	High	38.9	50.2	132.3	617.6	24.4	31.8	(14.8)	(28.7)	0.3
5 Constellation Growth	High	40.8	55.4	128.3	816.7	25.6	40.7	(17.0)	(41.2)	—
6 Hartwell Leverage	High	50.9	63.1	126.7	581.5	18.2	46.4	(20.8)	(52.0)	—
7 Shearson Agg. Growth	High	41.3	52.1	125.3	—	—	34.9	(14.5)	—	—
8 Neuberger & Berman Manhattan	Average	35.6	43.0	124.6	607.2	26.4	21.5	(8.7)	(9.4)	0.8
9 Fidelity Freedom**	Average	46.3	49.5	121.5	—	—	29.3	(8.2)	(14.7)	0.7
10 Dreyfus Leverage	Low	36.9	43.7	120.6	563.2	23.6	16.2	(4.4)	(4.0)	2.3
GROWTH										
1 Loomis-Sayles Cap. Dev.*	High	50.3	53.1	187.5	1,199.4	28.8	37.5	(9.1)	(28.2)	0.3
2 Fidelity Magellan	Average	34.2	40.5	144.6	2,043.8	30.8	31.0	(9.1)	(18.4)	0.6
3 New England Growth	High	50.4	55.7	143.4	1,016.6	24.9	33.8	(10.0)	(26.9)	0.4
4 Twentieth Century Select	High	37.6	44.2	125.6	1,133.1	25.6	29.6	(12.1)	(24.6)	0.9
5 Northeast Inv. Growth	Average	28.6	34.2	125.6	—	21.6	19.8	(10.7)	(13.0)	0.2
6 SoGen International	Low	33.2	38.5	125.1	618.8	24.5	21.3	(2.8)	(5.6)	—
7 Thomson McKinnon Growth	Average	36.7	41.8	124.8	—	—	23.0	(3.3)	—	1.0
8 Fidelity Destiny I	Average	39.7	46.1	122.0	822.1	28.5	28.1	(8.6)	(12.9)	1.6
9 T. Rowe Price Growth Stock	Average	31.8	36.0	121.6	295.0	21.5	19.2	(9.7)	(18.8)	1.3
10 IAI Regional	Average	25.4	31.1	121.1	—	23.0	30.2	(10.7)	(16.8)	1.8
GROWTH AND INCOME										
1 New England Retirement Equity	High	40.1	47.5	142.0	589.4	22.6	23.2	(8.6)	(13.9)	0.9
2 Fundamental Investors	Average	33.3	42.5	126.9	463.6	25.3	20.9	(6.1)	(9.1)	2.2
3 Investment Co. of America	Average	29.7	36.4	119.9	518.1	24.1	19.7	(4.4)	(7.3)	2.6
4 Oppenheimer Total Return	Average	32.1	36.3	119.5	287.0	21.9	30.8	(7.8)	(25.5)	4.4
5 Nationwide Fund	Average	30.7	39.4	114.6	315.6	22.4	19.4	(8.7)	(6.1)	2.1
6 Vanguard Index Trust	Average	35.5	42.9	113.7	409.6	23.9	21.2	(7.1)	(7.9)	2.8
7 Lord Abbett Affiliated	Average	29.4	37.9	113.1	473.7	24.2	18.8	(4.8)	(3.9)	3.9
8 IDS Equity Plus	Average	37.3	42.8	112.2	402.9	21.2	24.9	(8.5)	(21.8)	1.9
9 Eaton Vance Total Return Trust	High	6.5	8.8	111.2	—	21.1	26.8	(7.5)	4.8	5.8
10 Washington Mutual Investors	Average	25.2	32.4	110.2	525.7	24.5	18.1	(4.4)	(3.2)	3.5
EQUITY INCOME										
1 United Income	Average	20.8	28.1	109.6	382.6	24.3	22.6	(7.5)	(6.1)	2.9
2 Decatur I	Average	27.4	34.5	105.1	472.6	22.6	16.5	(4.9)	(1.2)	3.8
3 Vanguard High Yield Stock*††	Low	13.4	18.9	98.3	597.3	25.4	17.6	(3.8)	7.9	7.3
4 Oppenheimer Equity Income	Low	25.0	29.8	97.7	478.7	24.4	25.2	(5.7)	(12.1)	4.7
5 Financial Industrial Income	Low	26.4	28.6	96.7	403.8	22.3	17.8	(6.2)	(3.8)	3.8
6 Dreyfus Conv. Securities	Low	22.1	24.7	93.0	307.1	20.7	12.7	(4.3)	0.7	4.5
7 Safeco Income	Low	16.4	21.4	92.5	419.7	22.7	16.0	(3.0)	1.0	4.5
8 Fidelity Puritan	Low	15.1	19.8	87.1	418.6	21.6	15.0	(2.7)	0.8	5.6
9 Fidelity Equity-Income	Low	20.0	24.6	85.8	640.8	22.6	19.6	(3.0)	(4.2)	5.2
10 Evergreen Total Return	Low	6.6	8.5	82.0	—	22.5	34.1	(3.0)	3.1	5.6
S&P 500-stock index	—	35.9	43.4	116.5	435.5	24.4	—	—	(5.8)‡	2.7
Dow Jones industrial average	—	40.1	51.6	142.5	416.5	26.4	—	—	(3.8)	2.7

*Currently closed to new investors   **Open to retirement plans only   †† Formerly called Qualified Dividend Port. I   ‡ Covers period from June 30, 1983 to July 31, 1984

FUND MANAGER, AGE (YEARS MANAGING FUND)	ASSETS AS OF AUG. 31, 1987 (IN MILLIONS)	% GAIN (OR LOSS) IN ASSETS 8/86 - 8/87	% MAXIMUM INITIAL SALES CHARGE	% ANNUAL EXPENSE RATIO (INCLUDES 12B-1 CHARGES, IF ANY)	MINIMUM INITIAL INVESTMENT	TELEPHONE TOLL-FREE (800)	TELEPHONE IN STATE
Committee management	$1,669.2	62.0	None	1.01	None	345-2021	—
William C. Miller IV, 50 (2)	39.7	207.8	None	2.90	$1,000	645-6405	212-308-3355 (N.Y.)
Harry Hutzler, 64 (18)	349.7	51.1	4¾	1.00	1,000	231-0803	800-392-9681 (Texas)
Matthew A. Weatherbie, N.A.	653.5	63.5	8½	0.89	500	225-1581	—
Harry Hutzler, 64 (11)	148.7	22.8	4¾	1.10	1,000	231-0803	800-392-9681 (Texas)
John M. Hartwell, 71 (19)	47.2	22.9	None	2.00	2,000	645-6405	212-308-3355 (N.Y.)
Richard Freeman, 54 (4)	142.1	23.4	5	1.10	500	—	212-321-7155
Irwin Lainoff, 56 (8)	629.1	114.3	None	1.10	500	237-1413	—
Michael Kassen, 34 (2)	1,632.6	75.9	None	1.07	500	544-6666	617-523-1919 (Mass.)
Stanley Druckenmiller, 34 (2)	659.2	20.1	4½	1.01	2,500	645-6561	718-895-1206 (N.Y.)
G. Kenneth Heebner, 47 (11)	308.3	33.6	None	0.74	250	345-4048	617-578-4200 (Mass.)
Peter Lynch, 43 (10)	11,914.0	58.4	3	1.08	1,000	544-6666	617-523-1919 (Mass.)
G. Kenneth Heebner, 47 (11)	528.3	66.4	6½	0.84	250	343-7104	—
Committee management	3,308.3	62.3	None	1.01	None	345-2021	—
William A. Oates Jr., 45 (7)	33.9	68.7	None	1.60	1,000	225-6704	617-523-3588 (Mass.)
Jean-Marie Eveillard, 47 (8)	114.0	88.7	4¼	1.47	1,000	334-2143	212-832-3073 (N.Y.)
Irwin Smith, 48 (1)	475.6	130.0	None†	1.70	1,000	628-1237	212-482-5894 (N.Y.)
George VanderHeiden, N.A. (7)	1,620.6	39.5	9	0.60	25	225-5270	617-328-5000 (Mass.)
M. David Testa, 43 (3)	1,694.7	22.5	None	0.59	1,000	638-5660	301-547-2308 (Md.)
Bing Carlin, 51 (7)	104.6	15.5	None	0.80	2,500	—	612-371-2884
G. Kenneth Heebner, 47 (11)	168.9	59.9	6½	0.90	250	343-7104	—
Committee management	802.7	50.7	8½	0.62	250	421-9900	213-486-9651 (Calif.)
Committee management	5,001.2	33.4	8½	0.41	250	421-9900	213-486-9651 (Calif.)
Diane Jarmusz, 35 (3)	314.3	23.4	8½	0.89	1,000	525-7048	800-356-3556 (Colo.)
Charles Bath, 32 (3)	508.3	38.3	7½	0.62	250	848-0920	800-282-1440 (Ohio)
Unmanaged index fund	1,124.4	119.0	None	0.28	1,500	662-7447	—
John M. McCarthy, 60 (15)	4,349.6	34.4	7¼	0.32	250	223-4224	212-425-8720 (N.Y.)
Joe Barsky, 38 (4)	501.7	23.7	5	0.51	2,000	328-8300	612-372-3733 (Minn.)
Edwin W. Bragdon, 65 (6)	715.1	10.0	4¾	1.65	1,000	225-6265	617-482-8260 (Mass.)
Committee management	3,199.5	91.6	8½	0.54	250	421-9900	213-486-9651 (Calif.)
Russell B. Thompson, 47 (8)	1,129.7	33.1	8½	0.62	500	—	816-842-1075
Kenneth F. Herlihy, 58 (16)	1,778.9	59.5	8½	0.63	25	523-4640	215-988-1333 (Pa.)
John Neff, 56 (12)	199.0	8.7	None	0.52	3,000	622-7447	—
Diane Jarmusz, 35 (5)	807.4	94.2	8½	1.03	1,000	525-7048	800-356-3556 (Colo.)
John Kaweske, 45 (3)	489.9	35.5	None	0.71	250	525-8085	800-525-9769 (Colo.)
Jeffrey Friedman, 42 (6)	295.0	75.7	None	0.85	2,500	645-6561	718-895-1206 (N.Y.)
Arley N. Hudson, 53 (9)	321.7	210.5	None	0.95	1,000	426-6730	800-562-6810 (Wash.)
Richard Fentin, N.A./Margaret Eagle, N.A. (5 months)	5,176.6	112.9	2	0.63	1,000	544-6666	617-523-1919 (Mass.)
C. Bruce Johnstone, 46 (15)	4,477.0	38.2	2	0.65	1,000	544-6666	617-523-1919 (Mass.)
Nola M. Falcone, 49 (8)/Stephen A. Lieber, 62 (16)	1,757.9	129.6	None	1.02	2,000	235-0064	—

† Fund may impose back-end load or exit fee   N.A.(Not available)

RANKED BY THREE-YEAR PERFORMANCE	VOLATILITY	% GAIN (OR LOSS) TO OCT. 1, 1987				% COMPOUND ANNUAL RETURN (FIVE YEARS TO OCT. 1)	MAXIMUM QUARTERLY GAIN (AND LOSS) SINCE OCT. 1, 1982		% GAIN (OR LOSS) IN LAST DOWN CYCLE	% CURRENT YIELD
		YEAR TO DATE	ONE YEAR	THREE YEARS	10 YEARS		BEST	WORST		
BALANCED										
1 **Loomis-Sayles Mutual**	Average	32.8	39.1	139.1	411.5	23.1	19.6	(5.9)	(10.3)	2.8
2 **Axe-Houghton Fund B**	Low	18.4	25.4	101.7	306.8	19.6	16.6	(4.9)	(11.4)	5.1
3 **Phoenix Balanced Series**	Low	20.3	23.4	97.8	410.9	21.8	15.4	(2.9)	3.5	3.9
4 **Mass. Fin. Total Return Trust**	Low	20.5	27.4	96.0	325.1	21.0	16.4	(4.7)	(4.5)	4.7
5 **Alliance Balanced**	Low	13.4	15.9	92.5	293.2	20.4	15.9	(2.4)	1.8	3.7
6 **Kemper Total Return**	Average	27.1	31.6	92.3	493.8	20.3	19.7	(5.9)	(16.6)	3.0
OPTION INCOME										
1 **Pru-Bache Option Growth**	Average	25.2	27.6	87.4	—	—	15.3	(6.8)	(17.6)	1.9
2 **Putnam Option Income**	Low	24.0	30.3	73.2	274.6	17.0	13.6	(3.7)	(8.2)	1.0
3 **Franklin Option**	Low	19.3	26.1	59.5	338.6	16.6	13.7	(8.0)	(7.5)	1.9
4 **Colonial Diversified Income**	Average	24.0	29.2	58.8	236.9	15.7	16.4	(5.1)	(3.4)	1.7
5 **Oppenheimer Premium Income**	Average	29.6	38.1	56.8	—	15.1	19.4	(5.0)	2.0	3.1
6 **First Investors Option**	Low	24.9	28.8	52.8	234.3	12.3	13.7	(3.7)	(4.5)	1.8
SMALL-COMPANY GROWTH										
1 **Putnam OTC Emerging Growth**	High	36.2	44.5	128.1	—	—	32.5	(16.9)	(14.9)	—
2 **Acorn Fund**	Average	31.9	36.8	105.8	604.4	23.9	20.5	(6.7)	(12.7)	1.1
3 **Nicholas II**	Average	29.5	31.4	98.2	—	—	22.6	(8.6)	—	2.0
4 **Kemper Summit**	Average	30.9	39.4	89.5	649.8	21.6	31.0	(9.9)	(23.7)	—
5 **Babson Enterprise**	Average	26.5	28.5	88.6	—	—	21.9	(9.5)	—	0.4
6 **Fairfield Fund**	High	28.1	38.1	85.4	378.3	17.2	34.1	(16.8)	(39.1)	0.9
SECTORS										
1 **Fidelity Select—Leisure**	High	41.0	39.9	168.5	—	—	24.1	(15.7)	—	—
2 **Fidelity Select—Health**	High	38.9	45.4	166.8	—	27.2	31.2	(16.9)	(31.4)	—
3 **Vanguard Sp. Port—Health**	Average	33.7	36.8	150.0	—	—	23.7	(6.5)	—	1.0
4 **Seligman Comm. & Info.**	High	45.8	53.2	128.6	—	—	29.7	(15.8)	—	—
5 **Putnam Health Sciences Trust**	High	36.2	44.7	126.9	—	18.3	25.9	(18.5)	(32.9)	0.8
6 **Alliance Technology**	High	55.8	70.7	117.5	—	28.5	61.3	(15.8)	(36.5)	—
GOLD AND PRECIOUS METALS										
1 **Lexington Goldfund**	High	76.5	81.0	123.4	—	19.4	42.7	(15.5)	(23.5)	0.4
2 **Vanguard Sp. Port.—Gold**	High	79.3	91.8	113.4	—	—	52.9	(16.4)	—	1.2
3 **Bull & Bear Golconda Inv.**	High	73.0	74.9	108.3	447.8	14.9	44.5	(13.0)	(29.7)	—
4 **Keystone Precious Metals**	High	89.8	101.5	99.0	685.9	18.0	52.4	(16.8)	(27.6)	1.0
5 **United Svcs. Prospector***	High	83.1	91.2	97.0	—	—	57.8	(18.1)	—	—
6 **International Investors**	High	72.1	72.4	93.6	1,050.7	20.6	52.9	(14.4)	(23.5)	2.0
GLOBAL										
1 **Paine Webber Atlas**	Low	38.9	46.7	222.3	—	—	20.1	(9.9)	—	4.5
2 **Putnam Intl. Equities**	Average	32.3	40.0	206.5	699.5	32.6	23.5	(8.7)	(5.3)	0.5
3 **Pru-Bache Global**	Average	39.4	41.0	193.8	—	—	24.4	1.1	—	—
4 **Oppenheimer Global**	Average	41.9	52.6	186.6	797.2	28.0	26.4	(14.4)	(26.6)	0.3
5 **Shearson Global Opp.**	Average	26.0	34.7	145.3	—	—	22.0	(0.9)	—	0.3
6 **New Perspective**	Low	38.5	50.1	140.1	635.7	25.9	20.3	(8.2)	(8.3)	1.6
INTERNATIONAL										
1 **Merrill Lynch Pacific Basin**	High	53.5	60.6	306.7	1,032.1	40.3	29.6	(16.4)	6.4	0.4
2 **Financial Strategic—Pacific**	Average	51.2	62.3	216.6	—	—	23.1	(15.4)	—	0.2
3 **Vanguard World—Intl. Growth**	Average	29.2	39.5	214.4	—	35.7	25.9	(11.5)	(1.5)	—
4 **T. Rowe Price Intl. Stock**	Average	30.5	42.2	208.3	—	31.1	22.6	(13.3)	(2.7)	0.6
5 **Alliance International**	Average	24.8	28.4	199.5	—	30.2	25.9	(14.7)	—	0.3
6 **Transatlantic Growth**	Average	33.9	40.7	198.8	480.1	29.2	24.5	(18.2)	(11.5)	—
S&P 500-stock index	—	40.1	43.4	116.5	435.5	24.4	—	—	(5.8)‡	2.7
Dow Jones industrial average	—	35.9	51.6	142.5	416.5	26.4	—	—	(3.8)	2.7

*Currently closed to new investors   ‡ Covers period from June 30, 1983 to July 31, 1984

FUND MANAGER, AGE (YEARS MANAGING FUND)	ASSETS AS OF AUG. 31, 1987 (IN MILLIONS)	% GAIN (OR LOSS) IN ASSETS 8/86 - 9/87	% MAXIMUM INITIAL SALES CHARGE	% ANNUAL EXPENSE RATIO (INCLUDES 12B-1 CHARGES, IF ANY)	MINIMUM INITIAL INVESTMENT	TELEPHONE TOLL-FREE (800)	TELEPHONE IN STATE
G. Kenneth Heebner, 47 (11)	$358.3	87.5	None	0.84	$250	345-4048	617-578-4200 (Mass.)
Committee management	214.0	11.8	None	0.98	1,000	431-1030	914-631-8131 (N.Y.)
Patricia Bannan, 27 (2)	390.4	153.3	8½	0.75	1,000	243-4361	800-243-1574 (Conn.)
Richard Dahlberg, 47 (3)	537.1	63.8	7¼	0.66	250	—	617-423-3500
J. Andrew Richey, 38 (1)	130.6	58.1	5½	0.99	250	221-5672	—
Gordon P. Wilson, 46 (15)/Jerry Castellini, N.A. (2)	1,401.8	122.3	8½	0.72	1,000	621-1048	—
Theresa Hamacher, 27 (3)	94.3	24.9	None†	1.55	1,000	872-7787	212-214-1234 (N.Y.)
Robert S. Stephenson, N.A.	1,307.6	11.4	8½	0.73	500	225-1581	—
Martin Wesskemann, 60 (15)	44.4	81.2	4	0.85	100	632-2180	—
Committee management	1,051.5	(16.8)	6¾	0.98	250	426-3750	—
Milton Berg, 37 (3)	372.1	(8.3)	8½	0.89	1,000	525-7048	800-356-3556 (Colo.)
Denise Moretti Burns, 28 (3)	236.3	14.9	7¼	1.00	200	423-4026	—
Matthew A. Weatherbie, N.A.	175.6	314.2	6¾	1.46	500	225-1581	—
Ralph Wanger, 53 (17)	563.6	33.5	None	0.79	4,000	—	312-621-0630
Albert O. Nicholas, 56 (4)	446.8	35.9	None	0.79	1,000	—	414-272-6133
Albert W. Gustafson, 44 (2)	385.3	13.5	8½	0.48	1,000	621-1048	—
Peter C. Schliemann, 42 (2)	57.9	8.8	None	1.37	1,000	422-2766	816-471-5200 (Mo.)
Robert Steers, 34 (5)	55.6	7.5	8½	1.20	500	223-7757	212-661-3000 (N.Y.)
Karen Firestone, N.A. (1)	173.0	(18.4)	2†	1.55	1,000	544-6666	617-523-1919 (Mass.)
William J. Hayes, N.A.	398.8	4.6	2†	1.39	1,000	544-6666	617-523-1919 (Mass.)
Edward P. Owens, 41 (3)	78.6	43.4	None	0.61	1,500	662-7447	—
Calvert Dooman, 60 (4)	55.6	15.6	4¾	1.68	None	221-7844	800-522-6869 (N.Y.)
Cheryl D. Alexander, N.A.	347.3	20.0	8½	1.00	500	225-1581	—
Richard S. Coons, 40 (3)	234.2	67.0	5½	1.13	250	221-5672	—
Caesar M. P. Bryan, 32 (1)	110.2	498.9	None	1.50	1,000	526-0057	—
David J. Hutchins, 27 (2)	227.2	524.2	None	0.59	1,500	662-7447	—
Robert W. Radsch, 44 (5)	·79.7	213.8	None	2.46	1,000	847-4200	—
Frederick G. P. Thorne, 52 (13)/Malcolm Pirnie, 41 (18)	309.1	393.0	None†	2.66	250	225-2618	617-338-3400 (Mass.)
Brad L. Heaston, 33 (2)	85.0	26.9	None†	2.90	100	824-4653	—
John Van Eck, 72 (32)	1,319.1	65.8	8½	0.86	1,000	221-2220	212-687-5200 (N.Y.)
Ellen R. Harris, 41 (2)	364.5	51.2	8½	1.52	1,000	544-9300	—
Bart Nuboer, N.A./Brooks A. Cobb, N.A.	708.6	84.1	8½	1.19	500	225-1581	—
Wallace Wormley, 39 (3)	910.3	126.1	None†	2.01	1,000	872-7787	212-214-1234 (N.Y.)
Kenneth Oberman, 57 (6)	587.6	47.3	8½	1.60	1,000	525-7048	800-356-3556 (Colo.)
D. Mark Tapley, 41 (3)	283.9	(0.9)	5	1.60	500	—	212-321-7155
Committee management	1,229.7	34.9	8½	0.66	250	421-9900	213-486-9651 (Calif.)
Stephen J. Silverman, 37 (4)	511.1	6.0	6½	0.98	250	—	609-282-2800
William R. Kiethler, 35 (1)	76.8	460.6	None	1.47	250	525-8085	800-525-9769 (Colo.)
Richard R. Foulkes, 41 (6)	605.0	34.1	None	0.78	1,500	662-7447	—
Martin G. Wade, 44 (7)	1,063.2	30.1	None	1.10	1,000	638-5660	301-547-2308 (Md.)
Glen Wellman, 39 (3)	188.4	7.3	5½	1.30	250	221-5672	—
Henry deVismes, 45 (17)	97.5	(5.4)	None	1.49	1,000	233-9164	212-687-2515 (N.Y.)

† Fund may impose back-end load or exit fee   N.A. (Not available)

The Top-Performing Bond Funds

RANKED BY THREE-YEAR PERFORMANCE	VOLATILITY	% GAIN (OR LOSS) TO OCT. 1, 1987				% COMPOUND ANNUAL RETURN (FIVE YEARS TO OCT. 1)	MAXIMUM QUARTERLY GAIN (AND LOSS) SINCE OCT. 1, 1982		% GAIN (OR LOSS) IN LAST DOWN CYCLE	% CURRENT YIELD
		YEAR TO DATE	ONE YEAR	THREE YEARS	10 YEARS		BEST	WORST		
HIGH-YIELD CORPORATES										
1 Kemper High Yield	Average	6.9	12.1	62.5	—	16.4	10.6	(2.2)	5.4	11.3
2 Financial Bond Shares–Hi. Yld.	Average	3.6	4.1	58.3	—	—	9.5	(1.8)	—	11.8
3 Fidelity High Income	Average	1.9	5.6	56.8	—	15.9	10.2	(2.5)	4.6	11.7
4 Delchester Bond	Average	3.2	6.9	56.4	168.2	14.3	10.4	(4.8)	(0.1)	12.7
5 Investment Port.–High Yld.	Average	4.9	9.4	56.3	—	—	7.8	(1.4)	—	10.0
6 Eaton Vance High Yield	Average	4.6	8.7	55.6	157.2	14.5	10.9	(2.7)	3.8	11.7
HIGH-GRADE CORPORATES										
1 Axe-Houghton Income	High	(1.7)	3.3	57.8	174.1	13.3	12.0	(4.1)	0.3	9.7
2 Sigma Income Shares	High	(1.6)	1.4	53.5	145.0	13.6	11.8	(4.0)	0.8	8.3
3 United Bond	High	(0.6)	3.9	53.0	143.7	13.8	10.2	(4.1)	1.9	8.9
4 American Capital Corp.	Average	3.7	7.5	52.4	133.8	13.6	10.9	(3.3)	0.7	11.7
5 Bond Fund of America	High	(3.0)	1.8	49.7	168.0	12.9	9.1	(3.8)	3.7	10.8
6 Alliance Bond–Monthly Inc.	High	(1.5)	3.6	49.4	130.5	13.8	13.2	(3.7)	0.6	9.3
U.S. GOVERNMENT BONDS										
1 Lord Abbett U.S. Gov. Sec.	Average	(5.0)	(1.8)	43.7	161.4	12.1	10.6	(3.8)	1.5	12.1
2 Value Line U.S. Gov. Sec.	Average	(2.2)	0.6	42.2	—	11.0	10.1	(4.1)	2.8	10.6
3 Carnegie Gov. Sec.–Hi. Yld.	Average	(2.0)	0.5	41.7	—	—	9.2	(2.2)	5.6	7.9
4 AMEV U.S. Gov. Securities	Average	(1.8)	0.6	40.9	141.4	10.4	8.7	(2.0)	(2.9)	9.9
5 John Hancock–U.S. Gov. Sec.	Average	(4.7)	(1.5)	40.3	135.4	10.5	7.8	(2.9)	6.4	8.5
6 Pru-Bache Gov.–Intermed. Term	Average	(2.0)	0.7	39.2	—	10.2	7.3	(1.5)	6.6	8.9
MORTGAGE-BACKED SECURITIES										
1 Kemper U.S. Gov. Sec.	High	(2.1)	1.4	47.1	121.8	12.1	8.6	(3.0)	7.3	11.1
2 Franklin U.S. Gov. Series	Low	(0.3)	2.6	41.8	102.6	12.0	10.3	(3.5)	4.3	10.5
3 Vanguard Fixed Inc.–GNMA	Average	(4.3)	(0.7)	39.2	—	10.9	8.9	(4.0)	5.9	10.0
4 Van Kampen Merritt U.S. Gov.	Average	(5.8)	(2.0)	39.0	—	—	8.2	(4.5)	—	11.8
5 Alliance Mortgage Sec.	Low	(1.7)	1.5	39.0	—	—	7.9	(2.6)	—	11.4
6 Putnam U.S. Gov. Guar. Sec.	Low	(0.3)	2.9	38.0	—	—	7.8	(4.0)	—	10.6
HIGH-YIELD TAX-EXEMPTS #										
1 IDS High-Yield Tax-Exempt	Average	(4.6)	0.0	46.4	—	12.1	10.6	(4.9)	6.9	8.3
2 Stein Roe High-Yield Muni	Average	(3.6)	0.3	46.2	—	—	9.1	(4.3)	—	7.9
3 Merrill Lynch Muni–High Yield	Average	(4.6)	(0.9)	43.4	—	11.6	9.6	(4.4)	8.5	8.2
4 Fidelity High-Yield Muni	High	(6.1)	(2.7)	42.6	—	11.3	9.4	(5.9)	7.6	7.9
5 Vanguard Muni Bond–High Yield	High	(6.7)	(2.5)	42.4	—	11.0	9.8	(5.9)	6.8	8.3
6 GIT Tax-Free–High Yield	Average	(2.9)	0.9	42.2	—	—	10.6	(4.1)	5.2	7.9
HIGH-GRADE TAX-EXEMPTS #										
1 Stein Roe Managed Muni	High	(4.9)	(1.3)	50.9	98.3	13.1	12.2	(4.6)	8.0	7.4
2 DMC Tax-Free Inc.–USA	Average	(6.2)	(0.9)	49.2	—	—	10.4	(6.2)	—	8.3
3 Kemper Municipal	Average	(2.1)	1.8	49.1	92.4	12.7	9.1	(3.7)	7.8	7.9
4 United Municipal Bond	High	(7.7)	(3.5)	48.3	55.2	11.7	11.3	(6.5)	5.2	7.7
5 Mutual of Omaha Tax-Free Income	High	(7.5)	(0.9)	48.0	61.1	11.1	10.4	(6.0)	4.6	7.8
6 Seligman Tax-Exempt–National	Average	(6.2)	(2.4)	47.0	—	—	10.8	(5.7)	—	7.9
INTERMEDIATE-TERM TAX-EXEMPTS #										
1 Vanguard Muni Bond–Intermediate	Average	(3.2)	0.1	37.2	58.3	9.7	7.4	(3.6)	6.2	7.3
2 Dreyfus Intermediate Tax-Exempt	Low	(1.4)	2.6	36.8	—	—	6.7	(2.8)	—	7.4
3 Fidelity Limited Term Muni	Average	(3.1)	(0.3)	35.5	75.2	10.0	7.4	(3.6)	7.6	6.6
4 Scudder Tax-Free Target–1993	Low	(0.9)	2.1	32.9	—	—	6.2	(2.1)	8.3	6.0
5 USAA Tax Exempt–Intermediate	Average	(2.5)	0.0	32.4	—	9.2	6.5	(2.8)	5.0	7.3
6 Limited Term Muni	Low	1.7	3.8	30.1	—	—	4.7	(0.7)	—	6.5
Salomon Bros. investment-grade bond index§	—	(3.0)	0.2	47.2	—	13.0	—	—	8.7	9.2

§ Corporate and government bonds and mortgage-backed securities   # Maximum quarterly gain (or loss) figure does not include the calendar quarter that ended Sept. 30, 1987

FUND MANAGER, AGE (YEARS MANAGING FUND)	ASSETS AS OF AUG. 31, 1987 (IN MILLIONS)	% GAIN (OR LOSS) IN ASSETS 8/86 - 8/87	% MAXIMUM INITIAL SALES CHARGE	% ANNUAL EXPENSE RATIO (INCLUDES 12B-1 CHARGES, IF ANY)	MINIMUM INITIAL INVESTMENT	TELEPHONE TOLL-FREE (800)	TELEPHONE IN STATE
William R. Buecking, 53 (N.A)/Ken Urbaszewski, 40 (7)	$468.1	42.8	5½	0.68	$1,000	621-1048	—
William W. Veronda, 41 (4)	44.6	1.4	None	0.76	250	525-8085	800-525-9769 (Colo.)
William Pike, N.A. (6)	1,791.2	24.4	None	0.80	2,500	544-6666	617-523-1919 (Mass.)
J. Michael Pokorny, 48 (6)	406.9	142.3	6¾	0.84	25	523-4640	215-988-1333 (Pa.)
Ken Urbaszewski, 40 (3)	323.8	91.0	None†	2.19	250	621-1048	—
Hooker Talcott Jr., 55 (1)	36.1	16.5	4¾	0.93	1,000	225-6265	617-482-8260 (Mass.)
Committee management	52.4	14.7	None	1.37	1,000	431-1030	914-631-8131 (N.Y.)
Richard V. King, 68 (13)	33.9	3.7	8½	0.82	None	441-9490	302-652-3091 (Del.)
Robert Alley, 39 (3)	314.3	(9.3)	8½	0.64	500	—	816-842-1075
David Troth, 53 (7)	154.4	25.8	4¾	0.72	500	847-5636	—
Committee management	808.1	37.7	4¾	0.58	1,000	421-9900	213-486-9651 (Calif.)
Wayne D. Lyski, 46 (6 months)	40.1	(10.9)	5½	1.27	250	221-5672	—
Robert S. Dow, 42 (2)	710.2	167.9	4¾	0.82	500	223-4224	212-425-8720 (N.Y.)
Milton C. Schlein, 55 (1)	219.4	97.5	None	0.73	1,000	223-0818	—
John Shriver, 31 (1)	49.4	116.7	4½	1.30	1,000	321-2322	216-781-4440 (Ohio)
Dennis Ott, 42 (2)	106.3	92.9	4½	1.00	500	872-2638	800-328-1001 (Minn.)
David Turner, 41 (3)	208.0	15.4	8½	0.90	500	225-5291	617-572-4120 (Mass.)
Jeffrey Pantages, 33 (2)	824.5	23.2	None	0.75	1,000	872-7787	212-214-1234 (N.Y.)
Patrick Beimford, N.A.	4,386.3	92.6	4½	0.48	1,000	621-1048	—
Jack Lemein, 43 (3)	13,786.9	(2.8)	4	0.53	100	632-2180	—
Paul Sullivan, 44 (7)	2,236.0	24.4	None	0.38	3,000	662-7447	—
John Doyle, 53 (3)/Robert Davidson, 41 (2)	5,096.5	52.3	4.9	0.59	1,500	225-2222	—
Worth Bruntjen, 50 (3)	733.7	(0.9)	5½	1.00	250	221-5672	—
Jaclyn S. Conrad, N.A.	1,262.6	31.1	4¾	0.56	500	225-1581	—
Kurt A. Larson, 48 (8)	3,881.4	13.4	5	0.60	2,000	328-8300	612-372-3733 (Minn.)
Thomas Conlin, 33 (10)	214.9	17.9	None	0.72	1,000	338-2550	—
Vincent R. Giordano, 43 (8)	1,781.2	16.8	4	0.56	1,000	—	609-282-2800
Guy Wickwire, 40 (6)	1,883.2	(11.3)	None	0.57	2,500	544-6666	617-523-1919 (Mass.)
Ian A. MacKinnon, 39 (6)	793.4	(0.1)	None	0.33	3,000	662-7447	—
Rick Gunn, 39 (2)	48.9	6.5	None	1.16	1,000	336-3063	800-572-2050 (Va.)
David Snowbeck, 45 (11)	492.3	2.6	None	0.64	1,000	338-2550	—
J. Michael Pokorny, 48 (3)	372.5	47.3	4¾	0.80	1,000	523-4640	215-988-1333 (Pa.)
Patrick Beimford, N.A.	1,242.3	39.3	4½	0.52	1,000	621-1048	—
John M. Holliday, 53 (7)	445.1	10.5	4	0.61	500	—	816-842-1075
Mark L. Winter, 36 (1)	308.1	36.6	8	0.61	1,000	228-9596	800-642-8112 (Neb.)
Thomas Moles, 45 (4)	142.1	33.7	4¾	0.76	None	221-7844	800-522-6869 (N.Y.)
Ian A. MacKinnon, 39 (6)	921.2	13.5	None	0.33	3,000	662-7447	—
Monica Wieboldt, 37 (3)	1,169.0	11.0	None	0.73	2,500	645-6561	718-895-1206 (N.Y.)
John F. Haley Jr., N.A. (3)	524.4	15.4	None	0.68	2,500	544-6666	617-523-1919 (Mass.)
Donald C. Carleton, 53 (4)	143.8	55.6	None	0.81	1,000	225-2470	—
Kenneth E. Willmann, 41 (5)	354.9	32.8	None	0.60	3,000	531-8000	—
Brian J. McMahon, 32 (3)	131.5	90.0	2¾	1.00	2,500	847-0200	505-984-0200 (N.M.)

† Fund may impose back-end load or exit fee   N.A. (Not available)

Alphabetical Guide to Mutual Funds

ABBREVIATIONS

Bal Balanced; **Eql** Equity income; **G&I** Growth and income; **Glo** Global; **Gold** Gold and metals; **Gro** Growth; **HGC** High-grade corporates; **HGT** High-grade tax-exempts; **HYC** High-yield corporates.; **HYT** High-yield tax-exempts; **Intl** International; **ITT** Intermediate-term tax-exempts; **Max** Maximum capital gains; **MBS** Mortgage-backed securities; **OpInc** Option income; **SCG** Small-company growth; **Sec** Sector; **USG** U.S. Government bonds

BENCHMARKS FOR INVESTORS

	% GAIN (OR LOSS) TO OCT. 1, 1987			% GAIN (OR LOSS) IN LAST DOWN CYCLE (6/83-7/84)	% CURRENT YIELD
	YEAR TO DATE	THREE YEARS	10 YEARS		
S&P 500-stock index	40.1	116.5	435.5	(5.8)‡	2.7
Dow Jones industrial average	35.9	142.5	416.5	(3.8)	2.7
Lipper growth fund index	28.4	96.8	402.9	(17.9)	—
Lipper growth and income fund index	29.2	95.4	405.3	(10.1)	—
Salomon Bros. investment-grade bond index	(3.0)	47.2	—	8.7	9.2
Lipper muni bond fund index	(10.7)	9.7	—	(4.0)	—

FUND NAME	TYPE	% GAIN (OR LOSS) TO OCT. 1, 1987			THREE-YEAR RATING (WITHIN CATEGORY)	% GAIN (OR LOSS) IN LAST DOWN CYCLE	% CURRENT YIELD	% ANNUAL EXPENSE RATIO (INCLUDES 12B-1 CHARGES, IF ANY)	TELEPHONE TOLL-FREE (800)	TELEPHONE IN STATE
		YEAR TO DATE	THREE YEARS	10 YEARS						
ABT Emerging Growth	Max	13.7	82.8	—	Fair	(26.6)	—	1.65	354-0436	800-582-7396 (Ohio)
ABT Growth & Income Trust	G&I	31.0	107.4	365.4	Fair	(21.7)	2.5	1.35	354-0436	800-582-7396 (Ohio)
ABT Utility Income	Sec	0.3	58.4	—	Fair	(10.3)	6.9	1.36	354-0436	800-582-7396 (Ohio)
Acorn Fund	SCG	31.9	105.8	604.4	Good	(12.7)	1.1	0.79	—	312-621-0630
AIM Convertible Sec.	Eql	8.9	39.7	—	Poor	(16.3)	5.5	1.50	231-0803	800-392-9681 (Texas)
AIM High-Yield Sec.	HYC	3.7	36.9	163.4	Poor	3.4	12.3	1.06	231-0803	800-392-9681 (Texas)
AIM Summit Investors	Gro	33.0	92.8	—	Fair	(27.0)	0.5	1.16	231-0803	800-392-9681 (Texas)
Alliance Balanced	Bal	13.4	92.5	293.2	Fair	1.8	3.7	0.99	221-5672	—
Alliance Bond—High Yield Port.	HYC	1.7	—	—	—	—	13.1	1.18	221-5672	—
Alliance Bond—Monthly Income	HGC	(1.5)	49.4	130.5	Good	0.6	9.3	1.27	221-5672	—
Alliance Bond—U.S. Gov. Port.	USG	0.1	—	—	—	—	11.2	1.07	221-5672	—
Alliance Canadian	Intl	35.5	63.5	277.5	Poor	(11.6)	0.9	1.19	221-5672	—
Alliance Convertible	Eql	13.9	—	—	—	—	5.1	1.25	221-5672	—
Alliance Counterpoint	G&I	29.4	—	—	—	—	1.8	1.55	221-5672	—
Alliance Dividend Shares	G&I	26.6	108.3	373.9	Fair	(5.1)	2.9	0.81	221-5672	—
Alliance Fund	Gro	37.2	100.1	357.2	Fair	(20.7)	1.0	0.61	221-5672	—
Alliance International	Intl	24.8	199.5	—	Fair	—	0.3	1.30	221-5672	—
Alliance Mortgage Sec.	MBS	(1.7)	39.0	—	Fair	—	11.4	1.00	221-5672	—
Alliance Surveyor	Gro	31.2	82.6	379.5	Fair	(30.1)	0.3	1.22	221-5672	—
Alliance Technology	Sec	55.8	117.5	—	Good	(36.5)	—	1.13	221-5672	—
AMA Growth—Classic Growth Port.	Gro	28.3	82.3	283.0	Fair	(17.0)	1.1	1.34	262-3863	—
AMA Income	HGC	(3.4)	35.7	115.0	Poor	(0.9)	6.8	1.65	262-3863	—
AMCAP Fund	Gro	36.3	95.2	726.7	Fair	(13.0)	1.4	0.51	421-9900	213-486-9651 (Calif.)
American Balanced	Bal	16.4	81.4	301.6	Fair	(2.7)	5.3	0.67	421-9900	213-486-9651 (Calif.)
American Capital Comstock	Max	37.8	88.6	706.9	Fair	(6.2)	1.9	0.60	847-5636	—
American Capital Corp.	HGC	3.7	52.4	133.8	Good	0.7	11.7	0.72	847-5636	—
American Capital Enterprise	Gro	36.4	92.8	628.5	Fair	(22.0)	1.3	0.60	847-5636	—
American Capital Fed. Mort.	MBS	(5.8)	—	—	—	—	7.0	0.98	847-5636	—
American Capital Gov. Sec.	USG	(6.1)	27.9	—	Poor	—	8.5	0.60	847-5636	—
American Capital Harbor	Eql	20.9	73.4	417.7	Fair	(10.3)	5.4	0.64	847-5636	—
American Capital High Yield	HYC	5.8	46.8	—	Fair	1.6	12.9	0.66	847-5636	—
American Capital Muni	HGT	(9.8)	35.9	60.4	Poor	6.6	8.6	0.68	847-5636	—

‡ Covers period from June 30, 1983 to July 31, 1984

FUND NAME	TYPE	% GAIN (OR LOSS) TO OCT. 1, 1987			THREE-YEAR RATING (WITHIN CATEGORY)	% GAIN (OR LOSS) IN LAST DOWN CYCLE	% CURRENT YIELD	% ANNUAL EXPENSE RATIO (INCLUDES 12B-1 CHARGES, IF ANY)	TELEPHONE	
		YEAR TO DATE	THREE YEARS	10 YEARS					TOLL-FREE (800)	IN STATE
American Capital OTC Sec.	SCG	21.8	29.3	—	Poor	—	0.1	1.14	847-5636	—
American Capital Pace	Max	37.8	90.3	1,053.2	Fair	(7.3)	1.9	0.60	847-5636	—
American Capital Tax-Ex.–High Yld.	HYT	(4.6)	—	—	—	—	8.9	0.50	847-5636	—
American Capital Tax-Ex.–Insured	HGT	(11.2)	—	—	—	—	7.4	0.58	847-5636	—
American Capital Venture	Max	30.6	49.5	626.3	Poor	(19.7)	1.2	0.71	847-5636	—
American Growth	Gro	31.4	62.6	400.2	Poor	(6.7)	1.0	1.28	525-2406	303-623-6137 (Colo.)
American Investors Growth	Gro	39.4	53.1	139.4	Poor	(41.5)	—	1.40	243-5353	203-531-5000 (Conn.)
American Leaders	G&I	22.7	86.4	391.6	Fair	4.0	2.9	1.00	541-6133	—
American Mutual	G&I	20.2	94.9	506.4	Fair	(4.9)	3.6	0.45	421-9900	213-486-9651 (Calif.)
American National Growth	Gro	43.7	109.9	520.7	Fair	(33.1)	0.9	1.00	231-4639	800-392-9753 (Texas)
American National Income	EqI	27.7	71.2	441.8	Fair	(6.2)	2.7	0.96	231-4639	800-392-9753 (Texas)
AMEV Capital	G&I	26.2	103.1	689.9	Fair	(20.1)	0.6	1.06	872-2638	800-328-1001 (Minn.)
AMEV Growth	Max	31.1	104.5	905.8	Fair	(26.5)	0.2	1.00	872-2638	800-328-1001 (Minn.)
AMEV U.S. Gov. Securities	USG	(1.8)	40.9	141.4	Fair	(2.9)	9.9	1.00	872-2638	800-328-1001 (Minn.)
Axe-Houghton Fund B	Bal	18.4	101.7	306.8	Good	(11.4)	5.1	0.98	431-1030	914-631-8131 (N.Y.)
Axe-Houghton Income	HGC	(1.7)	57.8	174.1	Good	0.3	9.7	1.37	431-1030	914-631-8131 (N.Y.)
Axe-Houghton Stock	Gro	47.2	112.4	401.3	Good	(39.0)	—	1.28	431-1030	914-631-8131 (N.Y.)
Babson Bond Trust	HGC	(3.2)	41.3	138.3	Fair	4.8	9.6	0.97	422-2766	816-471-5200 (Mo.)
Babson Enterprise	SCG	26.5	88.6	—	Good	—	0.4	1.37	422-2766	816-471-5200 (Mo.)
Babson Growth	Gro	32.9	108.5	323.8	Fair	(14.8)	1.8	0.74	422-2766	816-471-5200 (Mo.)
Bartlett Basic Value	G&I	20.5	76.9	—	Poor	4.4	3.5	1.28	543-0863	800-327-4363 (Ohio)
Benham Gov.–GNMA Inc.	MBS	(3.5)	—	—	—	—	9.2	0.74	472-3389	800-982-6150 (Calif.)
Blanchard Strategic Growth	Max	31.6	—	—	—	—	3.0	3.01	922-7771	212-750-0555 (N.Y.)
Bond Fund of America	HGC	(3.0)	49.7	168.0	Good	3.7	10.8	0.58	421-9900	213-486-9651 (Calif.)
Boston Co. Cap. Appreciation	Gro	25.0	114.6	417.7	Good	(7.5)	3.8	0.95	225-5267	—
Boston Co. Managed Income	HYC	2.7	52.5	—	Fair	5.8	10.5	0.88	225-5267	—
Boston Co. Special Growth	Gro	27.4	78.7	—	Fair	(25.9)	1.5	1.32	225-5267	
Bull & Bear Capital Growth	Gro	32.8	77.0	382.0	Fair	(23.4)	—	2.25	847-4200	
Bull & Bear Golconda Investors	Gold	73.0	108.3	447.8	Good	(29.7)	—	2.46	847-4200	—
Bull & Bear High Yield	HYC	0.4	33.3	—	Poor	—	13.4	1.50	847-4200	—
Bull & Bear U.S. Gov. Guar. Sec.	USG	0.6	—	—	—	—	10.2	2.06	847-4200	—
Calamos Convertible Income	EqI	13.1	—	—	—	—	4.4	1.30	323-9943	312-571-7115 (Ill.)
Calvert Social Inv. Man. Gro.	G&I	18.2	85.2	—	Fair	(9.7)	2.9	1.30	368-2748	301-951-4820 (Md.)
Calvert Tax-Free Res.–Limited	ITT	2.7	22.9	—	Fair	6.1	5.7	0.81	368-2748	301-951-4820 (Md.)
Calvert Tax-Free Res.–Long Term	HGT	(6.4)	36.1	—	Poor	—	7.5	0.85	368-2748	301-951-4820 (Md.)
Capital Pres. Treasury Note	USG	(6.7)	35.0	—	Fair	8.6	7.2	0.93	472-3389	800-982-6150 (Calif.)
Cardinal Fund	G&I	21.9	97.2	473.8	Fair	(5.4)	2.4	0.75	848-7734	800-282-9446 (Ohio)
Cardinal Gov. Guar.	USG	(1.3)	—	—	—	—	10.4	0.70	848-7734	800-282-9446 (Ohio)
Carnegie Cappiello–Growth	Gro	18.6	77.7	—	Fair	—	1.0	1.58	321-2322	216-781-4440 (Ohio)
Carnegie Gov. Sec.–High Yield	USG	(2.0)	41.7	—	Good	5.6	7.9	1.30	321-2322	216-781-4440 (Ohio)
Carnegie Total Return	G&I	10.5	—	—	—	—	4.2	1.75	321-2322	216-781-4440 (Ohio)
Century Shares Trust	Sec	12.3	93.9	368.0	Fair	(6.8)	2.5	0.77	321-1928	617-482-3060 (Mass.)
Charter Fund	G&I	36.4	104.0	618.8	Fair	(23.0)	1.6	1.21	231-0803	800-392-9681 (Texas)
Cigna Growth	Gro	35.1	94.0	397.8	Fair	(15.2)	0.6	0.85	562-4462	—
Cigna High Yield	HYC	2.3	53.4	—	Good	3.2	12.1	0.92	562-4462	—
Cigna Income	EqI	(5.2)	46.8	141.5	Fair	1.1	9.2	0.82	562-4462	—
Cigna Municipal Bond	HGT	(7.9)	42.6	65.5	Fair	4.9	7.1	0.78	562-4462	—
Cigna Value	G&I	30.4	73.7	—	Poor	—	1.0	1.04	562-4462	—
Colonial Adv. Strategies Gold	Gold	86.1	—	—	—	—	0.5	1.67	426-3750	—
Colonial Diversified Income	OpInc	24.0	58.8	236.9	Fair	(3.4)	1.7	0.98	426-3750	—
Colonial Fund	G&I	18.4	91.6	339.5	Fair	(0.8)	4.6	1.02	426-3750	—
Colonial Gov. Mortgage	MBS	(6.5)	—	—	—	—	7.5	1.61	426-3750	—

FUND NAME	TYPE	% GAIN (OR LOSS) TO OCT. 1, 1987			THREE-YEAR RATING (WITHIN CATEGORY)	% GAIN (OR LOSS) IN LAST DOWN CYCLE	% CURRENT YIELD	% ANNUAL EXPENSE RATIO (INCLUDES 12B-1 CHARGES, IF ANY)	TELEPHONE	
		YEAR TO DATE	THREE YEARS	10 YEARS					TOLL-FREE (800)	IN STATE
Colonial Gov. Sec. Plus	USG	(6.9)	34.7	—	Fair	—	7.5	1.10	426-3750	—
Colonial Growth Shares	Gro	31.1	97.7	435.6	Fair	(16.8)	0.8	1.34	426-3750	—
Colonial High Yield Sec.	HYC	4.3	53.4	192.1	Fair	4.4	11.4	1.11	426-3750	—
Colonial Income	EqI	(0.6)	43.9	134.6	Poor	2.4	11.6	1.11	426-3750	—
Colonial Income Plus	OpInc	17.2	46.2	—	Poor	—	2.5	1.04	426-3750	—
Colonial Small Stock Index	SCG	28.6	—	—	—	—	0.3	1.35	426-3750	—
Colonial Tax-Exempt High Yield	HYT	(2.7)	42.1	—	Fair	5.0	8.1	1.10	426-3750	—
Colonial Tax-Exempt Insured	HGT	(6.7)	—	—	—	—	7.1	1.10	426-3750	—
Colonial U.S. Equity Index	Gro	33.1	—	—	—	—	0.6	1.25	426-3750	—
Columbia Fixed Income Sec.	HGC	(4.2)	37.8	—	Poor	6.7	9.3	0.79	547-1037	800-452-4512 (Ore.)
Columbia Growth	Gro	37.9	98.8	590.9	Fair	(23.8)	0.8	1.00	547-1037	800-452-4512 (Ore.)
Columbia Special	Max	43.6	—	—	—	—		1.54	547-1037	800-452-4512 (Ore.)
Constellation Growth	Max	40.8	128.3	816.7	Good	(41.2)	—	1.10	231-0803	800-392-9681 (Texas)
Continental U.S. Gov. Plus	USG	(3.0)	—	—	—	—	10.2	2.27	626-3863	212-440-3863 (N.Y.)
Copley Fund	G&I	4.3	66.8	238.9	Poor	3.1	—	1.42	—	617-674-8459
Criterion Commerce Inc. Shares	EqI	20.9	73.9	288.3	Fair	(9.3)	2.3	1.21	231-4645	800-392-7802 (Texas)
Criterion Insured Qlty. Tax-Free	HGT	(9.1)	33.5	—	Poor	9.8	7.1	1.29	231-4645	800-392-7802 (Texas)
Criterion Invst. Qlty. Interest	HGC	(4.4)	43.9	—	Fair	3.0	11.5	1.01	231-4645	800-392-7802 (Texas)
Criterion Pilot	Max	42.4	86.8	388.3	Fair	(27.1)	0.8	1.22	231-4645	800-392-7802 (Texas)
Criterion Sunbelt Growth	Gro	28.2	70.1	—	Poor	(25.0)	0.1	1.54	231-4645	800-392-7802 (Texas)
Criterion U.S. Gov. Hi. Yld.	USG	(2.2)	—	—	—	—	7.8	1.03	231-4645	800-392-7802 (Texas)
DBL Tax-Free—Limited	ITT	2.9	14.5	—	Poor	5.5	3.8	0.74	272-2700	212-482-1623 (N.Y.)
Dean Witter American Value	Gro	24.9	91.7	—	Fair	(25.7)	1.5	1.39	221-2685	212-938-4554 (N.Y.)
Dean Witter Convertible Sec.	EqI	18.5	—	—	—	—	3.9	1.72	221-2685	212-938-4554 (N.Y.)
Dean Witter Developing Growth	SCG	23.2	41.9	—	Poor	(28.0)	0.1	1.80	221-2685	212-938-4554 (N.Y.)
Dean Witter Dividend Growth	G&I	20.5	96.9	—	Fair	(2.8)	2.4	1.52	221-2685	212-938-4554 (N.Y.)
Dean Witter High Yield Sec.	HYC	3.3	50.7	—	Fair	(2.0)	13.6	0.60	221-2685	212-938-4554 (N.Y.)
Dean Witter Nat. Resources	Sec	40.7	68.9	—	Fair	(23.6)	1.3	1.74	221-2685	212-938-4554 (N.Y.)
Dean Witter Option Income	OpInc	11.4	—	—	—	—	5.7	1.90	221-2685	212-938-4554 (N.Y.)
Dean Witter Tax-Exempt Sec.	HGT	(6.4)	42.9	—	Fair	6.1	8.3	0.56	221-2685	212-938-4554 (N.Y.)
Dean Witter U.S. Gov. Sec.	MBS	(0.7)	29.2	—	Poor	—	10.1	1.20	221-2685	212-938-4554 (N.Y.)
Dean Witter World Wide	Glo	26.6	129.1	—	Fair	—	0.6	2.10	221-2685	212-938-4554 (N.Y.)
Decatur I	EqI	27.4	105.1	472.6	Good	(1.2)	3.8	0.63	523-4640	215-988-1333 (Pa.)
Delaware Fund	G&I	29.0	98.7	478.5	Fair	(19.8)	1.7	0.69	523-4640	215-988-1333 (Pa.)
Delaware—GNMA Series	MBS	(1.3)	—	—	—	—	10.5	0.95	523-4640	215-988-1333 (Pa.)
Delaware—U.S. Gov. Series	USG	(4.2)	—	—	—	—	10.2	0.95	523-4640	215-988-1333 (Pa.)
Delcap Fund I	Max	41.1	—	—	—	—	1.1	0.74	523-4640	215-988-1333 (Pa.)
Delchester Bond	HYC	3.2	56.4	168.2	Good	(0.1)	12.7	0.84	523-4640	215-988-1333 (Pa.)
Delta Trend	Max	34.1	74.0	479.2	Poor	(37.5)	—	1.20	523-4640	215-988-1333 (Pa.)
DMC Tax Free Inc.—USA	HGT	(6.2)	49.2	—	Good	—	8.3	0.80	523-4640	215-988-1333 (Pa.)

FUND NAME	TYPE	% GAIN (OR LOSS) TO OCT. 1, 1987 YEAR TO DATE	THREE YEARS	10 YEARS	THREE-YEAR RATING (WITHIN CATEGORY)	% GAIN (OR LOSS) IN LAST DOWN CYCLE	% CURRENT YIELD	% ANNUAL EXPENSE RATIO (INCLUDES 12B-1 CHARGES, IF ANY)	TELEPHONE TOLL-FREE (800)	IN STATE
Drexel Burnham	G&I	20.9	99.9	432.3	Fair	(6.0)	3.3	1.10	272-2700	212-482-1623 (N.Y.)
Drexel Series—Convertible	EqI	16.1	—	—	—	—	2.9	2.12	272-2700	212-482-1623 (N.Y.)
Drexel Series—Emerging Growth	SCG	21.8	—	—	—	—	—	2.35	272-2700	212-482-1623 (N.Y.)
Drexel Series—Gov. Sec.	USG	(8.7)	—	—	—	—	7.6	1.87	272-2700	212-482-1623 (N.Y.)
Drexel Series—Growth	Gro	30.8	—	—	—	—	1.4	2.28	272-2700	212-482-1623 (N.Y.)
Drexel Series—Option Inc.	OpInc	19.9	—	—	—	—	2.2	2.26	272-2700	212-482-1623 (N.Y.)
Dreyfus A Bond Plus	HGC	(6.4)	40.6	147.1	Fair	1.6	9.6	0.84	645-6561	718-895-1206 (N.Y.)
Dreyfus Capital Value	Max	37.6	—	—	—	—	0.2	1.01	645-6561	718-895-1206 (N.Y.)
Dreyfus Convertible Sec.	EqI	22.1	93.0	307.1	Good	0.7	4.5	0.85	645-6561	718-895-1206 (N.Y.)
Dreyfus Fund	G&I	26.3	86.0	414.4	Fair	(6.9)	3.3	0.74	645-6561	718-895-1206 (N.Y.)
Dreyfus Gen. Agg. Growth	Max	38.8	119.7	—	Good	—	0.2	1.50	645-6561	718-895-1206 (N.Y.)
Dreyfus GNMA	MBS	(2.2)	—	—	—	—	9.4	1.01	645-6561	718-895-1206 (N.Y.)
Dreyfus Growth Opportunity	Gro	39.0	102.4	526.6	Fair	(15.7)	1.3	0.95	645-6561	718-895-1206 (N.Y.)
Dreyfus Insured Tax-Exempt	HGT	(6.3)	—	—	—	—	7.5	0.84	645-6561	718-895-1206 (N.Y.)
Dreyfus Intermed. Tax-Ex.	ITT	(1.4)	36.8	—	Good	—	7.4	0.73	645-6561	718-895-1206 (N.Y.)
Dreyfus Leverage	Max	36.9	120.6	563.2	Good	(4.0)	2.3	1.01	645-6561	718-895-1206 (N.Y.)
Dreyfus New Leaders	SCG	32.3	—	—	—	—	0.3	1.30	645-6561	718-895-1206 (N.Y.)
Dreyfus Tax-Exempt Bond	HGT	(6.2)	37.9	62.7	Poor	6.8	8.1	0.68	645-6561	718-895-1206 (N.Y.)
Dreyfus Third Century	Gro	26.9	75.2	428.4	Poor	(13.5)	2.9	0.99	645-6561	718-895-1206 (N.Y.)
Eaton & Howard Stock	G&I	23.3	93.7	332.8	Fair	(2.5)	3.1	0.86	225-6265	617-482-8260 (Mass.)
Eaton Vance Gov. Obligations	USG	0.1	34.8	—	Fair	—	10.2	1.46	225-6265	617-482-8260 (Mass.)
Eaton Vance Growth	Gro	39.9	99.9	525.1	Fair	(12.9)	0.7	0.91	225-6265	617-482-8260 (Mass.)
Eaton Vance High Yield	HYC	4.6	55.6	157.2	Good	3.8	11.7	0.93	225-6265	617-482-8260 (Mass.)
Eaton Vance High Yield Muni Trust	HYT	(5.8)	—	—	—	—	8.5	0.63	225-6265	617-482-8260 (Mass.)
Eaton Vance Inc. of Boston	EqI	6.0	61.5	207.8	Fair	1.6	10.3	1.16	225-6265	617-482-8260 (Mass.)
Eaton Vance Investors	Bal	20.5	71.0	327.3	Poor	(3.4)	4.2	0.86	225-6265	617-482-8260 (Mass.)
Eaton Vance Muni Bond	HGT	(5.2)	43.5	—	Fair	6.6	8.0	0.81	225-6265	617-482-8260 (Mass.)
Eaton Vance Special Equities	Gro	25.6	47.9	417.0	Poor	(19.4)	0.4	0.99	225-6265	617-482-8260 (Mass.)
Eaton Vance Total Return Trust	G&I	6.5	111.2	—	Good	4.8	5.8	1.65	225-6265	617-482-8260 (Mass.)
Enterprise Growth Port.	Gro	37.4	95.1	500.7	Fair	(15.4)	0.6	1.50	443-3521	404-521-6250 (Ga.)
Equitec Siebel Aggr. Growth	Max	24.7	—	—	—	—	5.4	2.30	826-7194	—
Equitec Siebel Total Return	G&I	20.6	—	—	—	—	3.6	2.13	826-7194	—
Equitec Siebel U.S. Gov.	USG	2.2	—	—	—	—	9.1	2.26	826-7194	—
EuroPacific Growth	Intl	33.1	150.1	—	Poor	—	0.7	1.27	421-9900	213-486-9651 (Calif.)
Evergreen Fund	Gro	23.6	92.1	864.1	Fair	(16.8)	0.9	1.04	235-0064	—
Evergreen Total Return	EqI	6.6	82.0	—	Fair	3.1	5.6	1.02	235-0064	—
Fairfield Fund	SCG	28.1	85.4	378.3	Fair	(39.1)	0.9	1.20	223-7757	212-661-3000 (N.Y.)
Fairmont Fund	Max	24.5	92.6	—	Fair	(4.8)	0.5	1.17	262-9936	502-636-5633 (Ky.)
Farm Bureau Growth	G&I	17.7	62.0	240.1	Poor	(15.8)	5.4	1.04	247-4170	800-422-3175 (Iowa)
Fenimore International	Intl	35.8	—	—	—	—	—	2.26	272-2700	212-482-1623 (N.Y.)
Fidelity Aggressive Tax Free	HYT	(0.2)	—	—	—	—	8.3	0.65	544-6666	617-523-1919 (Mass.)
Fidelity Contrafund	Gro	37.8	101.6	374.7	Fair	(23.1)	0.9	0.88	544-6666	617-523-1919 (Mass.)
Fidelity Destiny I	Gro	39.7	122.0	822.1	Good	(12.9)	1.6	0.60	225-5270	617-328-5000 (Mass.)
Fidelity Destiny II	Gro	42.4	—	—	—	—	—	1.50	225-5270	617-328-5000 (Mass.)
Fidelity Equity-Income	EqI	20.0	85.8	640.8	Fair	(4.2)	5.2	0.65	544-6666	617-523-1919 (Mass.)
Fidelity Flexible Bond	HGC	(4.9)	38.9	120.8	Fair	1.3	9.9	0.69	544-6666	617-523-1919 (Mass.)
Fidelity Freedom**	Max	46.3	121.5	—	Good	(14.7)	0.7	1.07	544-6666	617-523-1919 (Mass.)
Fidelity Fund	G&I	33.6	104.2	460.9	Fair	(13.1)	3.0	0.60	544-6666	617-523-1919 (Mass.)
Fidelity GNMA Port.	MBS	(4.1)	—	—	—	—	9.0	0.75	544-6666	617-523-1919 (Mass.)
Fidelity Gov. Securities	USG	(3.1)	38.7	—	Fair	4.2	8.9	0.84	544-6666	617-523-1919 (Mass.)
Fidelity Growth & Income	G&I	34.3	—	—	—	—	1.9	1.21	544-6666	617-523-1919 (Mass.)
Fidelity Growth Co.	Gro	29.3	104.7	—	Fair	(25.7)	—	1.10	544-6666	617-523-1919 (Mass.)

**Open to retirement plans only

FUND NAME	TYPE	% GAIN (OR LOSS) TO OCT. 1, 1987			THREE-YEAR RATING (WITHIN CATEGORY)	% GAIN (OR LOSS) IN LAST DOWN CYCLE	% CURRENT YIELD	% ANNUAL EXPENSE RATIO (INCLUDES 12B-1 CHARGES, IF ANY)	TELEPHONE	
		YEAR TO DATE	THREE YEARS	10 YEARS					TOLL-FREE (800)	IN STATE
Fidelity High Income	HYC	1.9	56.8	—	Good	4.6	11.7	0.80	544-6666	617-523-1919 (Mass.)
Fidelity High-Yield Muni	HYT	(6.1)	42.6	—	Fair	7.6	7.9	0.57	544-6666	617-523-1919 (Mass.)
Fidelity Insured Tax Free	HGT	(8.0)	—	—	—	—	7.2	0.60	544-6666	617-523-1919 (Mass.)
Fidelity Intermediate Bond	HGC	(2.3)	42.7	182.5	Fair	4.2	13.8	0.75	544-6666	617-523-1919 (Mass.)
Fidelity Limited Term Muni	ITT	(3.1)	35.5	75.2	Good	7.6	6.6	0.68	544-6666	617-523-1919 (Mass.)
Fidelity Magellan	Gro	34.2	144.6	2,043.8	Good	(18.4)	0.6	1.08	544-6666	617-523-1919 (Mass.)
Fidelity Mortgage Sec.	MBS	(2.4)	—	—	—	—	9.4	0.75	544-6666	617-523-1919 (Mass.)
Fidelity Municipal Bond	HGT	(6.4)	40.5	52.2	Fair	5.3	7.4	0.51	544-6666	617-523-1919 (Mass.)
Fidelity OTC	SCG	37.6	—	—	—	—	0.1	1.31	544-6666	617-523-1919 (Mass.)
Fidelity Overseas	Intl	43.3	—	—	—	—	—	1.57	544-6666	617-523-1919 (Mass.)
Fidelity Puritan	EqI	15.1	87.1	418.6	Fair	0.8	5.6	0.63	544-6666	617-523-1919 (Mass.)
Fidelity Select—American Gold	Gold	76.3	—	—	—	—	—	1.21	544-6666	617-523-1919 (Mass.)
Fidelity Select—Biotechnology	Sec	36.3	—	—	—	—	—	1.38	544-6666	617-523-1919 (Mass.)
Fidelity Select—Chemical	Sec	52.8	—	—	—	—	—	1.52	544-6666	617-523-1919 (Mass.)
Fidelity Select—Computer	Sec	45.3	—	—	—	—	—	1.58	544-6666	617-523-1919 (Mass.)
Fidelity Select—Energy	Sec	30.0	49.5	—	Poor	(6.8)	—	1.50	544-6666	617-523-1919 (Mass.)
Fidelity Select—Energy Service	Sec	43.0	—	—	—	—	—	1.49	544-6666	617-523-1919 (Mass.)
Fidelity Select—Financial Services	Sec	9.4	96.7	—	Fair	(1.9)	—	1.57	544-6666	617-523-1919 (Mass.)
Fidelity Select—Health Care	Sec	38.9	166.8	—	Good	(31.4)	—	1.39	544-6666	617-523-1919 (Mass.)
Fidelity Select—Leisure	Sec	41.0	168.5	—	Good	—	—	1.55	544-6666	617-523-1919 (Mass.)
Fidelity Select—Paper & For. Prods.	Sec	36.8	—	—	—	—	—	1.29	544-6666	617-523-1919 (Mass.)
Fidelity Select—Precious Metals	Gold	78.8	77.6	—	Fair	(29.5)	—	1.50	544-6666	617-523-1919 (Mass.)
Fidelity Select—Retailing	Sec	29.2	—	—	—	—	—	1.54	544-6666	617-523-1919 (Mass.)
Fidelity Select—Software	Sec	43.4	—	—	—	—	—	1.51	544-6666	617-523-1919 (Mass.)
Fidelity Select—Technology	Sec	36.7	34.9	—	Poor	(31.9)	—	1.44	544-6666	617-523-1919 (Mass.)
Fidelity Select—Telecommuni.	Sec	41.1	—	—	—	—	—	1.52	544-6666	617-523-1919 (Mass.)
Fidelity Select—Utilities	Sec	(1.0)	76.4	—	Fair	10.7	—	1.45	544-6666	617-523-1919 (Mass.)
Fidelity Special Situations	Max	18.0	109.3	—	Fair	—	0.5	1.50	544-6666	617-523-1919 (Mass.)
Fidelity Trend	Gro	30.6	93.5	354.7	Fair	(15.4)	1.2	0.52	544-6666	617-523-1919 (Mass.)
Fidelity Value	Max	24.4	76.2	—	Poor	(23.4)	0.5	1.07	544-6666	617-523-1919 (Mass.)
Fiduciary Capital Growth	SCG	22.7	52.6	—	Fair	(17.6)	4.3	1.20	—	414-271-6666
Fin. Bond Shares—High Yield	HYC	3.6	58.3	—	Good	—	11.8	0.76	525-8085	800-525-9769 (Colo.)
Financial Dynamics	Max	46.0	94.2	404.3	Fair	(32.3)	0.2	0.90	525-8085	800-525-9769 (Colo.)
Financial Independence—Growth	Gro	39.0	111.3	—	Fair	(11.4)	—	1.78	543-8721	800-582-7396 (Ohio)
Financial Independence—U.S. Gov. Sec.	MBS	(4.6)	33.0	—	Fair	—	8.9	1.25	543-8721	800-582-7396 (Ohio)
Financial Industrial	G&I	32.7	92.4	365.8	Fair	(20.0)	1.5	0.74	525-8085	800-525-9769 (Colo.)
Financial Industrial Income	EqI	26.4	96.7	403.8	Good	(3.8)	3.8	0.71	525-8085	800-525-9769 (Colo.)
Financial Strategic—Gold	Gold	75.4	87.5	—	Fair	—	0.8	1.50	525-8085	800-525-9769 (Colo.)
Financial Strategic—Pacific Basin	Intl	51.2	216.6	—	Good	—	0.2	1.47	525-8085	800-525-9769 (Colo.)
Financial Strategic—Technology	Sec	38.7	105.5	—	Fair	—	—	1.50	525-8085	800-525-9769 (Colo.)
Financial Tax-Free Inc. Shares	HGT	(8.4)	44.3	—	Fair	5.1	7.9	0.70	525-8085	800-525-9769 (Colo.)
First Investors Bond Appreciation	HYC	10.0	49.5	—	Fair	(5.7)	10.2	1.10	423-4026	—
First Investors Discovery	SCG	25.0	6.2	221.0	Poor	(38.0)	—	1.36	423-4026	—
First Investors Fund for Growth	Gro	30.4	15.5	192.3	Poor	(35.8)	—	1.08	423-4026	—
First Investors Fund for Inc.	HYC	1.0	36.8	132.7	Poor	(3.6)	12.2	1.13	423-4026	—
First Investors Government	MBS	(7.7)	29.4	—	Poor	—	8.9	1.30	423-4026	—
First Investors International	Glo	58.8	123.7	—	Fair	(13.7)	0.2	1.70	423-4026	—
First Investors Nat. Resources	Sec	55.7	4.5	7.5	Poor	(35.1)	0.7	1.55	423-4026	—
First Investors Option	OpInc	24.9	52.8	234.3	Fair	(4.5)	1.8	1.00	423-4026	—
First Investors Tax-Exempt	HGT	3.1	38.4	85.2	Fair	7.2	8.1	1.16	423-4026	—
Flexfund Retirement Growth	Max	26.5	60.0	—	Poor	(3.7)	0.5	1.44	325-3539	614-766-7000 (Ohio)
Fortress High Quality Stock	G&I	26.4	—	—	—	—	1.4	1.25	541-6133	—

FUND NAME	TYPE	% GAIN (OR LOSS) TO OCT. 1, 1987			THREE-YEAR RATING (WITHIN CATEGORY)	% GAIN (OR LOSS) IN LAST DOWN CYCLE	% CURRENT YIELD	% ANNUAL EXPENSE RATIO (INCLUDES 12B-1 CHARGES, IF ANY)	TELEPHONE	
		YEAR TO DATE	THREE YEARS	10 YEARS					TOLL-FREE (800)	IN STATE
Founders Growth	Gro	37.5	115.0	564.0	Good	(24.6)	3.4	1.15	525-2440	800-874-6301 (Colo.)
Founders Mutual	G&I	29.4	104.4	333.7	Fair	(7.8)	2.6	0.79	525-2440	800-874-6301 (Colo.)
Founders Special	Max	37.1	85.0	512.9	Fair	(32.2)	0.7	1.03	525-2440	800-874-6301 (Colo.)
FPA Capital	Gro	45.9	110.7	320.0	Fair	(17.6)	1.9	0.89	421-4374	—
FPA Paramount*	G&I	45.2	88.5	524.2	Fair	0.2	2.0	1.02	421-4374	—
FPA Perennial	G&I	17.9	62.4	—	Poor	—	3.0	1.14	421-4374	—
Franklin AGE High Income	HYC	1.5	43.4	160.9	Fair	2.0	13.0	0.57	632-2180	—
Franklin DynaTech Series	Sec	43.1	51.7	427.2	Poor	(21.3)	0.5	0.89	632-2180	—
Franklin Equity	Gro	34.1	118.8	515.4	Good	(8.0)	1.2	0.82	632-2180	—
Franklin Federal Tax-Free Income	HGT	(7.8)	40.0	—	Fair	—	9.0	0.54	632-2180	—
Franklin Gold	Gold	96.1	92.7	965.2	Fair	(26.2)	2.1	1.01	632-2180	—
Franklin Growth Series	Gro	32.6	103.4	383.0	Fair	(14.8)	1.4	0.79	632-2180	—
Franklin Income Series	EqI	5.5	61.6	361.6	Fair	0.5	9.0	0.64	632-2180	—
Franklin Insured Tax-Free Income	HGT	(9.2)	—	—	—	—	8.4	0.72	632-2180	—
Franklin Option	OpInc	19.3	59.5	338.6	Fair	(7.5)	1.9	0.85	632-2180	—
Franklin U.S. Gov. Series	MBS	(0.3)	41.8	102.6	Good	4.3	10.5	0.53	632-2180	—
Franklin Utilities Series	Sec	(0.6)	66.1	267.5	Fair	5.2	7.3	0.64	632-2180	—
Freedom Global	Glo	55.3	—	—	—	—	—	2.38	225-6258	800-392-6037 (Mass.)
Freedom Gold & Government	Gold	4.4	42.5	—	Poor	—	5.7	1.68	225-6258	800-392-6037 (Mass.)
Freedom Government Plus	USG	(6.3)	—	—	—	—	9.7	1.26	225-6258	800-392-6037 (Mass.)

*Currently closed to new investors

Money Notes

Blanchard Strategic Growth charges a one-time $125 start-up fee which translates into a 4.16% load on the minimum investment of $3,000. The fund has four separate portfolio managers who specialize in U.S. stocks, foreign stocks, bonds, and precious metals. A fifth manager serves as the mixmaster, deciding the weighting of each in the main fund.

Calvin Bullock investors should review holdings in the **Calvin Bullock** group, which merged with **Alliance Capital Management** last year. Some Bullock funds were combined with Alliance funds while other funds have new portfolio managers.

If you use **dollar-cost averaging** to accumulate shares, you should also sell off your portfolio over a complete market cycle, usually four to five years. This prevents you from cashing in at a market bottom.

Dreyfus and **T. Rowe Price** are arranging to sell funds that are comparable to their no-load offerings through banks—with sales charges of up to 4%.

Evergreen Total Return places equal emphasis on income and capital appreciation.

At **Fidelity**, fund switching may cost you $25 a switch, depending on the fund; at the two other major sector fund families, **Vanguard** and **Financial Programs**, switches are free.

Fidelity Overseas usually favors stocks of companies selling below their breakup value.

John Butler, president of Denver's 19-fund **Financial Programs** family, advises investors to minimize hassles by avoiding peak telephone-inquiry times such as Monday and Friday between 8 a.m. and 10 a.m.

FUND NAME	TYPE	% GAIN (OR LOSS) TO OCT. 1, 1987			THREE-YEAR RATING (WITHIN CATEGORY)	% GAIN (OR LOSS) IN LAST DOWN CYCLE	% CURRENT YIELD	% ANNUAL EXPENSE RATIO (INCLUDES 12B-1 CHARGES, IF ANY)	TELEPHONE	
		YEAR TO DATE	THREE YEARS	10 YEARS					TOLL-FREE (800)	IN STATE
Freedom Regional Bank	Sec	21.3	—	—	—	—	1.2	1.48	225-6258	800-392-6037 (Mass.)
F.S. Gov. Sec. Income‡	USG	(2.8)	21.7	—	Poor	(0.2)	9.7	1.17	845-8406	212-309-8400 (N.Y.)
Fundamental Investors	G&I	33.3	126.9	463.6	Good	(9.1)	2.2	0.62	421-9900	213-486-9651 (Calif.)
Fund for U.S. Gov. Sec.	MBS	1.3	36.2	121.4	Fair	5.4	9.4	0.95	541-6133	—
Fund of America	G&I	47.8	82.5	590.4	Fair	(0.9)	1.4	0.76	847-5636	—
Gateway Option Income	OpInc	12.9	52.1	—	Fair	(2.6)	2.3	1.49	354-6339	513-248-2700 (Ohio)
Gintel Capital Appreciation	Max	14.7	—	—	—	—	1.1	1.90	243-5808	203-622-6400 (Conn.)
GIT Tax-Free–High Yield	HYT	(2.9)	42.2	—	Fair	5.2	7.6	1.16	336-3063	800-572-2050 (Va.)
Gradison Established Growth	Gro	30.1	113.4	—	Good	—	1.9	1.61	543-1818	800-582-7062 (Ohio)
Growth Fund of America	Gro	32.9	99.4	753.2	Fair	(17.9)	2.6	0.66	421-9900	213-486-9651 (Calif.)
Growth Industry Shares	Gro	28.5	65.3	469.1	Poor	(22.4)	1.2	0.90	635-2886	800-635-2840 (Mass.)
G.T. Pacific Growth	Intl	33.6	154.4	456.6	Fair	(2.8)	—	1.50	824-1580	—
Guardian Park Avenue	Gro	29.6	110.8	637.2	Fair	(6.8)	1.1	0.72	221-3253	800-522-7800 (N.Y.)
Hancock (John) Bond	HGC	(3.6)	45.2	118.8	Fair	3.7	10.2	0.72	225-5291	617-572-4120 (Mass.)
Hancock (John) Global Trust	Glo	31.8	—	—	—	—	—	1.50	225-5291	617-572-4120 (Mass.)
Hancock (John) Growth	Gro	33.7	97.6	456.9	Fair	(17.1)	0.7	1.03	225-5291	617-572-4120 (Mass.)
Hancock (John) Tax-Ex. Inc. Trust	HGT	(4.8)	46.1	49.1	Good	5.0	7.3	0.71	225-5291	617-572-4120 (Mass.)
Hancock (John)–U.S. Gov. Sec.	USG	(4.7)	40.3	135.4	Fair	6.4	8.5	0.90	225-5291	617-572-4120 (Mass.)
Hancock (John)–U.S. Gov. Guar. Mort.	MBS	(3.8)	—	—	—	—	9.8	0.91	225-5291	617-572-4120 (Mass.)
Hartwell Growth	Max	61.9	135.4	756.5	Good	(33.4)	—	2.90	645-6405	212-308-3355 (N.Y.)
Hartwell Leverage	Max	50.9	126.7	581.5	Good	(52.0)	—	2.00	645-6405	212-308-3355 (N.Y.)
Heartland Value	Max	27.2	—	—	—	—	2.5	1.70	558-1015	800-242-1001 (Wis.)
Heritage Capital Appreciation	Max	18.3	—	—	—	—	0.7	2.00	—	813-578-3800
Hutton Inv. Series–Basic Value	Gro	24.2	—	—	—	—	1.8	1.47	334-2626	—
Hutton Inv. Series–Bond & Inc.	HGC	(11.5)	43.5	—	Fair	2.2	10.9	1.62	334-2626	—
Hutton Inv. Series–Gov. Sec.	USG	(7.6)	30.9	—	Fair	—	11.3	1.56	334-2626	—
Hutton Inv. Series–Growth	Gro	28.6	88.7	—	Fair	(13.0)	1.2	1.61	334-2626	—
Hutton Inv. Series–Option Inc.	OpInc	28.2	49.6	—	Fair	—	2.2	2.64	334-2626	—
Hutton Inv. Series–Pr. Metals	Gold	78.9	—	—	—	—	0.8	2.53	334-2626	—
Hutton National Muni Bond	HGT	(8.0)	43.8	—	Fair	—	8.3	0.66	334-2626	—
Hutton Special Equities	SCG	24.7	79.0	—	Fair	(30.7)	—	2.12	334-2626	—
IAI Apollo	Max	42.2	61.5	—	Poor	—	1.2	1.00	—	612-371-2884
IAI Bond	HGC	(3.1)	41.2	147.3	Fair	2.9	10.9	0.70	—	612-371-2884
IAI Regional	Gro	25.4	121.1	—	Good	(16.8)	1.8	0.80	—	612-371-2884
IAI Reserve	USG	7.8	—	—	—	—	6.8	0.80	—	612-371-2884
IAI Stock	Max	39.5	97.9	438.9	Fair	(9.2)	1.0	0.80	—	612-371-2884
IDS Bond	HYC	(3.6)	47.8	168.3	Fair	2.2	9.5	0.62	328-8300	612-372-3733 (Minn.)
IDS Discovery	SCG	14.9	50.9	—	Fair	(34.6)	0.8	0.67	328-8300	612-372-3733 (Minn.)
IDS Equity Plus	G&I	37.3	112.2	402.9	Good	(21.8)	1.9	0.51	328-8300	612-372-3733 (Minn.)
IDS Extra Income	HYC	1.5	48.1	—	Fair	—	10.9	0.84	328-8300	612-372-3733 (Minn.)
IDS Federal Income	USG	(3.3)	—	—	—	—	8.4	0.86	328-8300	612-372-3733 (Minn.)
IDS Growth	Gro	30.9	100.5	778.4	Fair	(37.2)	0.6	0.67	328-8300	612-372-3733 (Minn.)
IDS High-Yield Tax-Exempt	HYT	(4.6)	46.4	—	Good	6.9	8.3	0.60	328-8300	612-372-3733 (Minn.)
IDS International	Intl	32.9	—	—	—	—	0.3	1.13	328-8300	612-372-3733 (Minn.)
IDS Managed Retirement	G&I	36.6	—	—	—	—	1.4	0.99	328-8300	612-372-3733 (Minn.)
IDS Mutual	Bal	18.2	88.7	307.5	Fair	0.2	5.5	0.59	328-8300	612-372-3733 (Minn.)
IDS New Dimensions	Gro	35.1	114.4	701.9	Good	(22.8)	1.4	0.63	328-8300	612-372-3733 (Minn.)
IDS Precious Metals	Gold	95.9	—	—	—	—	0.3	1.28	328-8300	612-372-3733 (Minn.)
IDS Progressive	Max	33.6	88.5	484.8	Fair	(8.0)	2.5	0.71	328-8300	612-372-3733 (Minn.)
IDS Selective	HGC	(4.3)	45.2	161.4	Fair	3.6	9.3	0.66	328-8300	612-372-3733 (Minn.)
IDS Stock	G&I	32.2	95.4	333.3	Fair	(10.8)	2.3	0.53	328-8300	612-372-3733 (Minn.)
IDS Strategy–Agg. Equity Port.	Max	24.3	116.6	—	Fair	—	—	1.64	328-8300	612-372-3733 (Minn.)

‡ Performance data cover period to Sept. 1, 1987

FUND NAME	TYPE	% GAIN (OR LOSS) TO OCT. 1, 1987 YEAR TO DATE	THREE YEARS	10 YEARS	THREE-YEAR RATING (WITHIN CATEGORY)	% GAIN (OR LOSS) IN LAST DOWN CYCLE	% CURRENT YIELD	% ANNUAL EXPENSE RATIO (INCLUDES 12B-1 CHARGES, IF ANY)	TELEPHONE TOLL-FREE (800)	IN STATE
IDS Strategy—Equity Portfolio	G&I	18.5	82.1	—	Fair	—	1.9	1.67	328-8300	612-372-3733 (Minn.)
IDS Strategy—Income Portfolio	HGC	(3.6)	46.6	—	Good	—	8.0	1.64	328-8300	612-372-3733 (Minn.)
IDS Tax-Exempt Bond	HGT	(7.1)	42.5	65.3	Fair	5.6	7.8	0.60	328-8300	612-372-3733 (Minn.)
Income Fund of America	EqI	9.1	69.7	313.4	Fair	2.4	7.1	0.54	421-9900	213-486-9651 (Calif.)
Industrial—Option Income	OpInc	19.7	—	—	—	—	8.4	1.02	222-2274	800-824-6067 (Fla.)
International Investors	Gold	72.1	93.6	1,050.7	Fair	(23.5)	2.0	0.86	221-2220	212-687-5200 (N.Y.)
Investment Co. of America	G&I	29.7	119.9	518.1	Good	(7.3)	2.6	0.41	421-9900	213-486-9651 (Calif.)
Investment Portfolio—Equity	Gro	36.7	71.1	—	Poor	—	0.4	2.23	621-1048	—
Investment Portfolio—Gov. Plus	USG	(3.2)	—	—	—	—	10.5	2.02	621-1048	—
Investment Portfolio—High Yield	HYC	4.9	56.3	—	Good	—	10.0	2.19	621-1048	—
Investment Portfolio—Option Inc.	OpInc	14.2	—	—	—	—	13.3	2.18	621-1048	—
Investment Trust of Boston	G&I	24.9	87.5	284.8	Fair	(21.1)	2.5	1.24	451-0502	617-542-0213 (Mass.)
Investors Research	Max	34.6	105.9	655.8	Fair	(26.0)	0.4	0.81	—	213-595-7711
ISI Trust	G&I	16.7	39.8	179.0	Poor	—	4.4	1.21	441-9490	302-652-3091 (Del.)
Ivy Growth	Gro	24.1	97.8	589.8	Fair	(1.8)	3.8	1.29	235-3322	617-749-1422 (Mass.)
Janus Fund	Max	24.6	72.8	658.1	Poor	(14.0)	4.6	1.00	525-3713	303-333-3863 (Colo.)
Janus Venture	SCG	26.5	—	—	—	—	4.3	1.44	525-3713	303-333-3863 (Colo.)
JP Growth	Gro	26.7	85.3	388.8	Fair	(9.0)	2.1	0.89	—	919-378-2448
Kemper Growth	Gro	37.6	94.8	561.6	Fair	(17.3)	0.7	0.78	621-1048	—
Kemper High Yield	HYC	6.9	62.5	—	Good	5.4	11.3	0.68	621-1048	—
Kemper Income & Capital Pres.	HGC	(1.0)	46.1	147.4	Fair	6.0	10.9	0.69	621-1048	—
Kemper International	Intl	26.7	177.8	—	Fair	(8.4)	1.0	1.23	621-1048	—
Kemper Municipal	HGT	(2.1)	49.1	92.4	Good	7.8	7.9	0.52	621-1048	—
Kemper Option Income	OpInc	18.5	42.2	221.6	Poor	(0.3)	12.3	0.85	621-1048	—
Kemper Summit	SCG	30.9	89.5	649.8	Good	(23.7)	—	0.48	621-1048	—
Kemper Technology	Sec	43.1	104.4	513.3	Fair	(17.6)	0.8	0.60	621-1048	—
Kemper Total Return	Bal	27.1	92.3	493.8	Fair	(16.6)	3.0	0.72	621-1048	—
Kemper U.S. Gov. Securities	MBS	(2.1)	47.1	121.8	Good	7.3	11.1	0.48	621-1048	—
Keystone B-1	HGC	(7.1)	37.1	139.2	Poor	(1.8)	9.2	2.25	225-2618	617-338-3400 (Mass.)
Keystone B-2	HYC	(1.1)	43.2	173.4	Poor	(4.7)	10.0	1.68	225-2618	617-338-3400 (Mass.)
Keystone B-4*	HYC	2.0	37.9	178.6	Poor	(2.5)	12.1	1.65	225-2618	617-338-3400 (Mass.)
Keystone International	Intl	33.2	171.4	421.7	Fair	(19.1)	0.6	2.73	225-2618	617-338-3400 (Mass.)
Keystone K-1	EqI	17.5	77.1	274.2	Fair	(5.5)	5.2	1.93	225-2618	617-338-3400 (Mass.)
Keystone K-2	Gro	31.2	109.7	369.1	Fair	(21.0)	1.3	1.99	225-2618	617-338-3400 (Mass.)
Keystone Precious Metals	Gold	89.8	99.0	685.9	Fair	(27.6)	1.0	2.66	225-2618	617-338-3400 (Mass.)
Keystone S-1	G&I	38.2	104.6	295.8	Fair	(14.1)	1.5	2.21	225-2618	617-338-3400 (Mass.)
Keystone S-3	Gro	34.2	87.6	414.1	Fair	(21.9)	0.9	2.05	225-2618	617-338-3400 (Mass.)
Keystone S-4	Gro	32.2	73.1	385.5	Poor	(41.1)	—	1.19	225-2618	617-338-3400 (Mass.)
Keystone Tax-Free Trust*	HGT	(4.8)	41.1	—	Fair	5.0	8.2	2.08	225-2618	617-338-3400 (Mass.)
Kidder Peabody Equity Income	EqI	23.5	—	—	—	—	2.2	1.13	—	212-510-5552
Kidder Peabody Gov. Income	USG	(1.9)	—	—	—	—	7.9	0.86	—	212-510-5552
Kidder Peabody Special Growth	Gro	32.4	23.2	—	Poor	—	—	1.39	—	212-510-5552
Legg Mason Special Invest.	SCG	24.3	—	—	—	—	—	2.50	822-5544	800-638-1107 (Md.)
Legg Mason Total Return Trust	Gro	21.3	—	—	—	—	1.5	2.40	822-5544	800-638-1107 (Md.)
Legg Mason Value Trust	Gro	23.1	89.8	—	Fair	1.1	1.2	2.00	822-5544	800-638-1107 (Md.)
Lehman Capital	Max	40.1	94.3	1,009.7	Fair	(14.6)	0.5	1.13	221-5350	212-668-8578 (N.Y.)
Lehman Investors	G&I	31.1	92.0	472.6	Fair	(12.4)	2.3	0.45	221-5350	212-668-8578 (N.Y.)
Lehman Opportunity	Max	29.6	92.5	—	Fair	(0.8)	2.0	1.60	221-5350	212-668-8578 (N.Y.)
Lepercq-Istel Fund	G&I	22.6	53.4	259.1	Poor	(14.1)	2.2	1.67	548-7878	212-702-0174 (N.Y.)
Leverage Fund of Boston	Max	46.7	91.7	351.9	Fair	(32.3)	—	2.76	225-6265	617-482-8260 (Mass.)
Lexington GNMA Income	MBS	(4.3)	34.2	94.2	Fair	4.3	9.3	0.86	526-0057	—
Lexington Goldfund	Gold	76.5	123.4	—	Good	(23.5)	0.4	1.50	526-0057	—

*Currently closed to new investors

FUND NAME	TYPE	% GAIN (OR LOSS) TO OCT. 1, 1987			THREE-YEAR RATING (WITHIN CATEGORY)	% GAIN (OR LOSS) IN LAST DOWN CYCLE	% CURRENT YIELD	% ANNUAL EXPENSE RATIO (INCLUDES 12B-1 CHARGES, IF ANY)	TELEPHONE	
		YEAR TO DATE	THREE YEARS	10 YEARS					TOLL-FREE (800)	IN STATE
Lexington Growth	Gro	32.1	103.1	352.0	Fair	(35.2)	1.4	1.32	526-0057	—
Lexington Research	Gro	26.2	92.3	391.3	Fair	(16.8)	3.4	0.95	526-0057	—
Liberty High Income Sec.	HYC	0.2	43.9	—	Fair	5.0	12.8	1.02	541-6133	—
Liberty Tax-Free Income	HGT	(5.3)	43.2	55.8	Fair	0.4	7.6	0.95	541-6133	—
Limited Term Muni–National	ITT	1.7	30.1	—	Fair	—	6.5	1.00	847-0200	505-984-0200 (N.M.)
Lindner Dividend*	EqI	3.1	53.4	577.9	Fair	11.9	7.7	1.00	—	314-727-5305
Lindner Fund*	Gro	30.1	84.1	878.9	Fair	3.6	3.2	0.89	—	314-727-5305
LMH Fund	G&I	7.2	51.7	—	Poor	—	—	1.29	422-2564	800-522-2564 (Conn.)
Loomis-Sayles Cap. Development*	Gro	50.3	187.5	1,199.4	Good	(28.2)	0.3	0.74	345-4048	617-578-4200 (Mass.)
Loomis-Sayles Mutual	Bal	32.8	139.1	411.5	Good	(10.3)	2.8	0.84	345-4048	617-578-4200 (Mass.)
Lord Abbett Affiliated	G&I	29.4	113.1	473.7	Good	(3.9)	3.9	0.32	223-4224	212-425-8720 (N.Y.)
Lord Abbett Bond-Debenture	HYC	7.0	46.2	189.7	Fair	(5.5)	11.2	0.61	223-4224	212-425-8720 (N.Y.)
Lord Abbett Dev. Growth	SCG	27.8	41.0	410.0	Poor	(35.7)	—	0.90	223-4224	212-425-8720 (N.Y.)
Lord Abbett Tax-Free Inc.–Nat.	HGT	(5.5)	43.7	—	Fair	—	8.1	0.60	223-4224	212-425-8720 (N.Y.)
Lord Abbett U.S. Gov. Sec.	USG	(5.0)	43.7	161.4	Good	1.5	12.1	0.82	223-4224	212-425-8720 (N.Y.)
Lord Abbett Value App.	Gro	25.0	104.8	—	Fair	—	2.3	0.89	223-4224	212-425-8720 (N.Y.)
Lowry Market Timing	Max	28.4	41.0	—	Poor	—	3.2	1.46	231-4645	800-392-7802 (Texas)
Mass. Capital Development	Gro	37.3	84.7	798.9	Fair	(24.4)	1.1	0.71	—	617-423-3500
Mass. Financial Bond	HGC	(5.9)	44.3	145.6	Fair	3.2	9.4	0.68	—	617-423-3500
Mass. Fin. Development	G&I	37.9	105.6	505.8	Fair	(24.1)	1.3	0.78	—	617-423-3500

*Currently closed to new investors

Money Notes

The largest brokerage house government bond fund, **Hutton Investment Series—Government Securities**, with some $6.6 billion in assets, posted the worst record of all brokerage house funds for the year that ended April 30, 1987— a 1.9% total return.

California and Tennessee prohibit mutual funds from selling shares to residents if management expenses exceed a certain percentage of the fund's assets. California, therefore, prohibits the sale of shares of **Ivy Growth**, which has assets of $186 million and an expense ratio of 1.29%, compared with 1% for the average stock fund.

If you are nervous about the market, consider moving into a money-market fund. If you are a little braver, turn toward funds that will try to time the market for you, such as **Janus** or **Strong Total Return**.

The argument against buying a load bond fund is especially convincing. Investors who pay a front-end sales charge that can be as high as 8.5% effectively give up their first year's profits. Nonetheless, **Kemper High Yield**, with a 5.5% load, managed the best performance of *any* bond fund for the past three, five, six, and seven years.

Lehman Opportunity manager Irving Brilliant likes medium-size, well-established companies whose cash flow is high in relation to their stock prices.

G. Kenneth Heebner of Boston's **Loomis-Sayles & Co.** runs five funds, four of which cracked *Money's* Top 40 in May 1987. Heebner looks for companies with the potential for sizable, unexpected earnings that will propel the stock ahead 50 percentage points faster than the market average.

FUND NAME	TYPE	% GAIN (OR LOSS) TO OCT. 1, 1987			THREE-YEAR RATING (WITHIN CATEGORY)	% GAIN (OR LOSS) IN LAST DOWN CYCLE	% CURRENT YIELD	% ANNUAL EXPENSE RATIO (INCLUDES 12B-1 CHARGES, IF ANY)	TELEPHONE TOLL-FREE (800)	TELEPHONE IN STATE
		YEAR TO DATE	THREE YEARS	10 YEARS						
Mass. Fin. Emerging Growth	SCG	27.7	78.8	—	Fair	(27.7)	—	1.39	—	617-423-3500
Mass. Fin. Gov. Guaranteed	MBS	(3.1)	31.1	—	Fair	—	9.7	1.18	—	617-423-3500
Mass. Fin. Gov. Sec. High Yield	USG	(8.2)	—	—	—	—	8.7	1.31	—	617-423-3500
Mass. Fin. High Inc. Trust	HYC	3.6	44.8	—	Fair	0.4	13.5	0.71	—	617-423-3500
Mass. Fin. Intl. Trust–Bond	Glo	5.9	82.8	—	Poor	(1.4)	7.0	1.17	—	617-423-3500
Mass. Fin. Man. Hi. Yd. Muni Bond*	HYT	(0.1)	34.8	—	Poor	—	9.1	1.00	—	617-423-3500
Mass. Fin. Managed Muni Bond	HGT	(3.5)	43.8	136.1	Fair	8.1	7.4	0.64	—	617-423-3500
Mass. Fin. Special	Max	39.6	104.4	—	Fair	(21.0)	0.3	1.31	—	617-423-3500
Mass. Fin. Total Return Trust	Bal	20.5	96.0	325.1	Good	(4.5)	4.7	0.66	—	617-423-3500
Mass. Investors Growth Stock	Gro	37.9	94.3	429.9	Fair	(20.1)	1.5	0.50	—	617-423-3500
Mass. Investors Trust	G&I	39.8	108.7	396.3	Good	(10.5)	2.4	0.49	—	617-423-3500
Mathers Fund	Gro	30.7	94.3	498.1	Fair	(18.2)	2.0	0.77	—	312-236-8215
Medical Technology	Sec	29.4	105.2	—	Fair	(39.7)	—	1.90	262-3863	—
Merrill Lynch Basic Value	G&I	27.5	106.2	536.6	Fair	(3.4)	3.0	0.61	—	609-282-2800
Merrill Lynch Capital	G&I	24.4	104.6	515.1	Fair	(5.4)	1.5	0.62	—	609-282-2800
Merrill Lynch Corp.–High Inc.	HYC	5.0	50.0	—	Fair	2.8	11.8	0.71	—	609-282-2800
Merrill Lynch Corp.–High Qual.	HGC	(5.3)	42.5	—	Fair	2.8	9.3	0.85	—	609-282-2800
Merrill Lynch Corp.–Intermed. Bond	HGC	(4.2)	41.5	—	Fair	4.1	8.7	0.62	—	609-282-2800
Merrill Lynch Fed. Sec.	MBS	(3.1)	37.2	—	Fair	—	8.9	0.75	—	609-282-2800
Merrill Lynch Fund for Tomorrow	Gro	23.3	84.9	—	Fair	—	0.5	1.87	—	609-282-2800
Merrill Lynch International	Glo	25.5	121.9	—	Fair	—	1.4	1.78	—	609-282-2800
Merrill Lynch Muni–High Yield	HYT	(4.6)	43.4	—	Fair	8.5	8.2	0.56	—	609-282-2800
Merrill Lynch Muni–Insured	HGT	(4.9)	38.6	—	Fair	7.3	7.8	0.60	—	609-282-2800
Merrill Lynch Muni–Ltd. Mat.	ITT	1.6	19.3	—	Fair	6.2	5.3	0.42	—	609-282-2800
Merrill Lynch Natural Resources*	Sec	61.4	—	—	—	—	2.5	1.96	—	609-282-2800
Merrill Lynch Pacific	Intl	53.5	306.7	1,032.1	Good	6.4	0.4	0.98	—	609-282-2800
Merrill Lynch Phoenix	G&I	24.0	96.8	—	Fair	2.9	3.6	1.18	—	609-282-2800
Merrill Lynch Retirement Income	MBS	(3.7)	—	—	—	—	8.4	1.42	—	609-282-2800
Merrill Lynch Sci.-Tech.	Sec	34.2	85.9	—	Fair	(14.7)	0.4	1.44	—	609-282-2800
Merrill Lynch Special Value	Gro	11.6	44.1	—	Poor	(24.7)	0.4	1.19	—	609-282-2800
MidAmerica Mutual	Gro	29.4	89.3	361.2	Fair	(12.0)	2.8	0.93	553-4287	800-342-4490 (Iowa)
Midwest Inc.–Inter. Term Gov.	USG	(1.6)	32.5	—	Fair	5.5	7.7	1.10	543-8721	800-582-7396 (Ohio)
Midwest Tax-Free–Limited Term	ITT	(0.5)	19.0	—	Poor	5.4	5.5	1.10	543-8721	800-582-7396 (Ohio)
Monitrend Value	Max	1.4	—	—	—	—	1.4	2.50	251-1970	201-886-2300 (N.J.)
Mutual of Omaha America	USG	(5.1)	28.1	114.4	Poor	6.5	8.7	0.98	228-9596	800-642-8112 (Neb.)
Mutual of Omaha Growth	Gro	29.1	91.8	277.4	Fair	(20.5)	1.0	1.11	228-9596	800-642-8112 (Neb.)
Mutual of Omaha Income	EqI	10.7	56.5	173.0	Fair	2.0	8.0	0.77	228-9596	800-642-8112 (Neb.)
Mutual of Omaha Tax-Free Inc.	HGT	(7.5)	48.0	61.1	Good	4.6	7.8	0.61	228-9596	800-642-8112 (Neb.)
Mutual Qualified Income	G&I	28.5	97.1	—	Fair	15.7	4.4	0.67	553-3014	—
Mutual Shares Corp.	G&I	26.8	92.5	671.2	Fair	13.4	3.3	0.70	553-3014	—
National Aviation & Tech.	Sec	21.4	74.4	364.6	Fair	(25.7)	5.6	1.23	654-0001	—
National Bond	HYC	(1.9)	34.9	117.6	Poor	0.4	16.9	0.96	223-7757	212-661-3000 (N.Y.)
National Federal Sec. Trust	USG	(11.4)	—	—	—	—	12.0	0.84	223-7757	212-661-3000 (N.Y.)
National Growth	Gro	13.4	55.3	187.8	Poor	(29.5)	1.9	1.11	223-7757	212-661-3000 (N.Y.)
National Industries	G&I	27.8	56.9	206.4	Poor	(11.8)	0.9	1.68	367-7814	303-220-8500 (Colo.)
National Sec. Tax-Exempt	HGT	(5.6)	45.1	62.7	Fair	6.4	7.9	0.79	223-7757	212-661-3000 (N.Y.)
National Stock	G&I	24.6	92.9	345.4	Fair	(6.9)	4.5	0.98	223-7757	212-661-3000 (N.Y.)
National Telecomm. & Tech.	Sec	36.9	65.3	—	Fair	(24.4)	0.7	1.75	654-0001	—
National Total Income	EqI	11.0	79.6	353.5	Fair	2.0	5.3	1.04	223-7757	212-661-3000 (N.Y.)
National Total Return	EqI	15.7	78.8	406.6	Fair	(2.9)	4.6	0.97	223-7757	212-661-3000 (N.Y.)
Nationwide Bond	HGC	(5.4)	36.5	—	Poor	4.1	9.6	0.68	848-0920	800-282-1440 (Ohio)
Nationwide Fund	G&I	30.7	114.6	315.6	Good	(6.1)	2.1	0.62	848-0920	800-282-1440 (Ohio)

*Currently closed to new investors

FUND NAME	TYPE	% GAIN (OR LOSS) TO OCT. 1, 1987			THREE-YEAR RATING (WITHIN CATEGORY)	% GAIN (OR LOSS) IN LAST DOWN CYCLE	% CURRENT YIELD	% ANNUAL EXPENSE RATIO (INCLUDES 12B-1 CHARGES, IF ANY)	TELEPHONE	
		YEAR TO DATE	THREE YEARS	10 YEARS					TOLL-FREE (800)	IN STATE
Nationwide Growth	Gro	27.8	105.2	515.9	Fair	(2.5)	2.7	0.65	848-0920	800-282-1440 (Ohio)
Nationwide Tax-Free Income	HGT	(8.5)	—	—	—	—	7.3	0.99	848-0920	800-282-1440 (Ohio)
Neuberger & Berman Energy	Sec	29.4	72.6	360.1	Fair	(5.0)	2.1	0.88	237-1413	—
Neuberger & Berman Guardian Mutual	G&I	29.1	90.0	495.5	Fair	(8.3)	3.1	0.73	237-1413	—
Neuberger & Berman Manhattan	Max	35.6	124.6	607.2	Good	(9.4)	0.8	1.10	237-1413	—
Neuberger & Berman Partners	Gro	26.9	97.4	657.8	Fair	(3.9)	2.0	0.86	237-1413	—
Neuwirth Fund	Gro	23.8	81.2	349.3	Fair	(35.8)	—	1.78	225-8011	816-283-1700 (Mo.)
New Economy	Gro	30.8	115.9	—	Good	—	1.9	0.68	421-9900	213-486-9651 (Calif.)
New England Bond Income	EqI	(2.8)	41.5	110.5	Poor	3.5	9.0	1.02	343-7104	—
New England Equity Income	G&I	26.1	97.9	425.5	Fair	(9.3)	2.3	1.19	343-7104	—
New England Growth	Gro	50.4	143.4	1,016.6	Good	(26.9)	0.4	0.84	343-7104	
New England Retirement Equity	G&I	40.1	142.0	589.4	Good	(13.9)	0.9	0.90	343-7104	
New England Tax-Exempt	HGT	(9.2)	42.5	67.6	Fair	4.9	7.2	0.85	343-7104	—
New Perspective	Glo	38.5	140.1	635.7	Fair	(8.3)	1.6	0.66	421-9900	213-486-9651 (Calif.)
Newton Growth	Gro	37.0	91.8	505.2	Fair	(27.1)	1.2	1.23	247-7039	800-242-7229 (Wis.)
New York Venture	Gro	20.7	111.5	727.7	Fair	(10.6)	0.9	0.93	545-2098	505-983-4335 (N.M.)
Nicholas Fund	Gro	19.1	76.2	726.1	Poor	(9.5)	2.9	0.86	—	414-272-6133
Nicholas Income	EqI	1.4	45.8	123.1	Poor	4.7	9.7	0.96	—	414-272-6133
Nicholas II	SCG	29.5	98.2	—	Good	—	2.0	0.79	—	414-272-6133
Nomura Pacific Basin	Intl	45.8	—	—	—	—	—	1.45	833-0018	—
Northeast Investors Growth	Gro	28.6	125.6	—	Good	(13.0)	0.2	1.60	225-6704	617-523-3588 (Mass.)
Northeast Investors Trust	EqI	1.9	64.8	176.5	Fair	(0.9)	11.3	0.75	225-6704	617-523-3588 (Mass.)
Nova Fund	Sec	36.2	81.7	—	Fair	(21.0)	—	1.70	572-0006	617-439-9683 (Mass.)
Nuveen Municipal Bond	HGT	(4.0)	44.1	79.6	Fair	4.6	7.3	0.71	621-7210	312-917-7844 (Ill.)
Omega Growth Portfolio	Max	34.3	110.1	307.5	Fair	(24.2)	1.3	1.47	237-5047	—
Oppenheimer Directors	Max	31.1	70.5	—	Poor	(38.6)	1.9	1.04	525-7048	800-356-3556 (Colo.)
Oppenheimer Equity Income	EqI	25.0	97.7	478.7	Good	(12.1)	4.7	1.03	525-7048	800-356-3556 (Colo.)
Oppenheimer Fund	Gro	30.6	75.4	285.7	Poor	(29.0)	0.2	1.01	525-7048	800-356-3556 (Colo.)
Oppenheimer Global	Glo	41.9	186.6	797.2	Fair	(26.6)	0.3	1.60	525-7048	800-356-3556 (Colo.)
Oppenheimer Gold & Sp. Min.	Gold	52.3	83.8	—	Fair	—	1.2	1.61	525-7048	800-356-3556 (Colo.)
Oppenheimer High Yield	HYC	9.8	45.2	—	Fair	(1.6)	12.9	0.89	525-7048	800-356-3556 (Colo.)
Oppenheimer Premium Income	OpInc	29.6	56.8	—	Fair	2.0	3.1	0.89	525-7048	800-356-3556 (Colo.)
Oppenheimer Regency**	Max	28.9	72.7	—	Poor	(30.8)	1.5	1.11	525-7048	800-356-3556 (Colo.)
Oppenheimer Special	Gro	7.0	44.9	423.0	Poor	(17.3)	4.5	0.95	525-7048	800-356-3556 (Colo.)
Oppenheimer Target	Max	20.1	63.2	—	Poor	(32.3)	0.5	1.16	525-7048	800-356-3556 (Colo.)
Oppenheimer Tax-Free Bond	HGT	(4.4)	46.7	81.5	Good	11.3	7.6	0.78	525-7048	800-356-3556 (Colo.)
Oppenheimer Time	Max	34.5	117.5	687.4	Fair	(27.4)	0.6	0.96	525-7048	800-356-3556 (Colo.)
Oppenheimer Total Return	G&I	32.1	119.5	287.0	Good	(25.5)	4.4	0.89	525-7048	800-356-3556 (Colo.)
Over-the-Counter Securities	SCG	21.1	71.5	634.3	Fair	(14.1)	1.1	0.85	523-2578	215-643-2510 (Pa.)
Pacific Horizon Agg. Growth	Max	40.1	119.5	—	Good	—	0.1	1.20	645-3515	—
Pacific Horizon High Yield	HYC	2.6	53.1	—	Fair	—	11.8	1.16	645-3515	—
Paine Webber America	G&I	19.7	71.7	—	Poor	—	5.1	1.15	544-9300	—
Paine Webber Atlas	Glo	38.9	222.3	—	Good	—	4.5	1.52	544-9300	—
Paine Webber Fixed Inc.—GNMA	MBS	(5.2)	33.3	—	Fair	—	10.9	0.66	544-9300	—
Paine Webber High Yield	HYC	3.6	52.2	—	Fair	—	13.5	0.69	544-9300	—
Paine Webber Inv. Grade Bond	HGC	(7.4)	37.9	—	Fair	—	12.2	0.68	544-9300	—
Paine Webber Master Growth	Gro	27.5	—	—	—	—	0.6	2.13	544-9300	—
Paine Webber Master Income	EqI	(8.2)	—	—	—	—	9.8	1.54	544-9300	—
Paine Webber Olympus	Gro	39.4	—	—	—	—	1.3	1.23	544-9300	—
Paine Webber Tax-Ex. Inc.—Nat.	HGT	(3.6)	—	—	—	—	7.5	0.72	544-9300	—
Pax World	Bal	18.5	69.0	269.2	Poor	(4.7)	3.4	1.20	343-0529	603-431-8022 (N.H.)
PBHG Growth	Max	41.7	—	—	—	—	0.3	1.31	262-6686	—

**Open to retirement plans only

FUND NAME	TYPE	% GAIN (OR LOSS) TO OCT. 1, 1987			THREE-YEAR RATING (WITHIN CATEGORY)	% GAIN (OR LOSS) IN LAST DOWN CYCLE	% CURRENT YIELD	% ANNUAL EXPENSE RATIO (INCLUDES 12B-1 CHARGES, IF ANY)	TELEPHONE	
		YEAR TO DATE	THREE YEARS	10 YEARS					TOLL-FREE (800)	IN STATE
Penn Square Mutual	G&I	30.4	88.5	378.0	Fair	(7.8)	3.3	0.80	523-8440	800-222-7506 (Pa.)
Permanent Portfolio	Sec	17.1	42.3	—	Poor	(17.0)	—	1.17	531-5142	512-453-7558 (Texas)
Philadelphia Fund	G&I	26.8	66.3	349.8	Poor	(12.5)	1.9	0.83	221-5588	212-668-8111 (N.Y.)
Phoenix Balanced Series	Bal	20.3	97.8	410.9	Good	3.5	3.9	0.75	243-4361	800-243-1574 (Conn.)
Phoenix Convertible	EqI	20.4	75.6	424.2	Fair	(1.9)	4.3	0.80	243-4361	800-243-1574 (Conn.)
Phoenix Growth Series	Gro	27.8	109.3	767.8	Fair	(0.3)	1.0	0.78	243-4361	800-243-1574 (Conn.)
Phoenix High Yield Series	HYC	2.0	49.3	—	Fair	2.3	13.0	0.79	243-4361	800-243-1574 (Conn.)
Phoenix Stock Series	Max	30.8	102.3	906.7	Fair	(7.4)	1.2	0.85	243-4361	800-243-1574 (Conn.)
Pilgrim GNMA	MBS	(3.8)	23.4	—	Poor	—	10.2	1.00	334-3444	800-341-1080 (Calif.)
Pilgrim High Yield	HYC	5.6	43.4	162.1	Fair	(0.5)	12.4	1.50	334-3444	800-341-1080 (Calif.)
Pilgrim MagnaCap	Gro	28.9	114.9	483.7	Good	2.1	1.5	1.40	334-3444	800-341-1080 (Calif.)
Pine Street	G&I	21.8	87.3	334.2	Fair	(10.4)	2.4	1.14	225-8011	816-283-1700 (Mo.)
Pioneer Bond	HGC	(2.1)	37.5	—	Poor	4.7	9.2	1.00	225-6292	617-742-7825 (Mass.)
Pioneer Fund	G&I	35.9	93.3	410.7	Fair	(13.7)	2.1	0.68	225-6292	617-742-7825 (Mass.)
Pioneer Three	G&I	23.2	67.0	—	Poor	(5.0)	1.9	0.71	225-6292	617-742-7825 (Mass.)
Pioneer II	G&I	34.2	103.0	596.9	Fair	(15.6)	2.0	0.72	225-6292	617-742-7825 (Mass.)
Principal Pres. Gov. Plus	USG	(3.8)	—	—	—	—	8.0	0.70	826-4600	—
Principal Pres. Hedged Tax-Ex.	ITT	2.6	16.5	—	Poor	—	7.0	1.10	826-4600	—
Princor Capital Accum.	Max	37.7	118.6	482.5	Fair	(0.5)	1.3	0.98	—	515-247-5711
Princor Gov. Sec. Income	USG	(5.6)	—	—	—	—	8.8	0.92	—	515-247-5711

Money Notes

At most, money managers usually suggest that investors limit their **metals** investments to 5% to 15% of their portfolios because of the high risks and volatility.

Mutual Shares, a conservative growth fund, buys shares in undervalued or out-of-favor companies.

Stanley Egener, president of **Neuberger & Berman Management**, says, "In the final analysis, total return is the most important figure to a bond fund investor."

New Alternatives, a natural resources fund, invests in solar, hydroelectric, natural gas, and geothermal energy producers, but holds no oil stocks. "It reduces our status as a potential hostage to changing OPEC politics," explains co-manager David Schoenwald.

Among funds that have performed well in down markets are **Nicholas Fund, Neuberger & Berman Partners,** and **Neuberger & Berman Manhattan.**

Permanent Portfolio calls itself a no-load, but there is a $35 one-time start-up charge ($40 for IRAs) and an $18 annual maintenance fee (plus $8 extra for IRAs). The fund sticks to fixed percentages split six ways: U.S. Government bonds (35%), gold (20%), natural resources and real estate (15%), U.S. stocks (15%), Swiss francs (10%), and silver (5%).

Phoenix Balanced is required by its charter to keep at least 25% of the portfolio in bonds.

Selected American and **Lehman Opportunity** are among the funds best for buy-and-hold investors.

FUND NAME	TYPE	% GAIN (OR LOSS) TO OCT. 1, 1987			THREE-YEAR RATING (WITHIN CATEGORY)	% GAIN (OR LOSS) IN LAST DOWN CYCLE	% CURRENT YIELD	% ANNUAL EXPENSE RATIO (INCLUDES 12B-1 CHARGES, IF ANY)	TELEPHONE	
		YEAR TO DATE	THREE YEARS	10 YEARS					TOLL-FREE (800)	IN STATE
Princor Growth	Gro	36.8	108.8	419.0	Fair	(18.9)	0.8	1.01	—	515-247-5711
Provident Fund for Income	EqI	25.5	69.6	317.3	Fair	1.8	5.5	0.76	847-5636	—
Pru-Bache Equity	Gro	32.2	105.1	—	Fair	(10.1)	0.8	1.52	872-7787	212-214-1234 (N.Y.)
Pru-Bache Global	Glo	39.4	193.8	—	Good	—	—	2.01	872-7787	212-214-1234 (N.Y.)
Pru-Bache GNMA	MBS	(3.9)	33.7	—	Fair	5.4	8.0	1.39	872-7787	212-214-1234 (N.Y.)
Pru-Bache Gov.–Intermed. Term	USG	(2.0)	39.2	—	Fair	6.6	8.9	0.75	872-7787	212-214-1234 (N.Y.)
Pru-Bache Gov. Plus	MBS	(5.3)	—	—	—	—	7.1	1.53	872-7787	212-214-1234 (N.Y.)
Pru-Bache Growth Opportunity	Gro	26.1	74.7	—	Poor	(31.6)	—	1.40	872-7787	212-214-1234 (N.Y.)
Pru-Bache High Yield	HYC	2.2	47.9	—	Fair	4.2	11.7	1.19	872-7787	212-214-1234 (N.Y.)
Pru-Bache IncomeVertible Plus	Sec	15.3	—	—	—	—	5.3	1.99	872-7787	212-214-1234 (N.Y.)
Pru-Bache National Muni	HGT	(6.6)	41.4	—	Fair	8.4	7.3	0.90	872-7787	212-214-1234 (N.Y.)
Pru-Bache Option Growth	OpInc	25.2	87.4	—	Good	(17.6)	1.9	1.55	872-7787	212-214-1234 (N.Y.)
Pru-Bache Research	Gro	34.8	120.3	—	Good	(15.5)	0.6	1.94	872-7787	212-214-1234 (N.Y.)
Pru-Bache Utility	Sec	2.3	96.3	—	Fair	7.0	6.0	1.42	872-7787	212-214-1234 (N.Y.)
Putnam Convertible Inc. & Gro.	EqI	17.2	76.8	440.7	Fair	(9.7)	5.3	0.83	225-1581	—
Putnam Energy Resources	Sec	38.0	43.4	—	Poor	(12.4)	3.1	1.77	225-1581	—
Putnam Fund for Gro. & Inc.	G&I	27.6	108.5	494.6	Good	(6.7)	4.1	0.53	225-1581	—
Putnam (George) Fund of Boston	Bal	20.1	91.8	339.3	Fair	(13.8)	5.0	0.58	225-1581	—
Putnam GNMA Plus	MBS	(6.6)	—	—	—	—	12.8	0.55	225-1581	—
Putnam Health Sciences Trust	Sec	36.2	126.9	—	Good	(32.9)	0.8	1.00	225-1581	—
Putnam High Inc. Gov.	USG	(8.0)	—	—	—	—	9.0	0.82	225-1581	—
Putnam High Yield*	HYC	4.3	47.6	—	Fair	(2.1)	12.9	0.57	225-1581	—
Putnam High Yield II	HYC	4.5	—	—	—	—	11.8	0.85	225-1581	—
Putnam Income	HGC	(3.5)	40.3	144.6	Fair	3.9	12.0	0.73	225-1581	—
Putnam Information Sciences	Sec	50.6	94.0	—	Fair	—	0.1	1.14	225-1581	—
Putnam Intl. Equities	Glo	32.3	206.5	699.5	Good	(5.3)	0.5	1.19	225-1581	—
Putnam Investors	Gro	32.9	102.3	446.4	Fair	(20.6)	1.6	0.49	225-1581	—
Putnam Option Income	OpInc	24.0	73.2	274.6	Good	(8.2)	1.0	0.73	225-1581	—
Putnam Option Income II	OpInc	17.8	—	—	—	—	2.4	0.82	225-1581	—
Putnam OTC Emerging Growth	SCG	36.2	128.1	—	Good	(14.9)	—	1.46	225-1581	—
Putnam Tax-Exempt Income	HGT	(7.5)	44.7	113.9	Fair	5.5	7.9	0.53	225-1581	—
Putnam U.S. Gov. Guar. Sec.	MBS	(0.3)	38.0	—	Fair	—	10.6	0.56	225-1581	—
Putnam Vista Basic Value	Max	34.8	108.8	639.1	Fair	(25.4)	1.9	1.02	225-1581	—
Putnam Voyager	Max	38.9	132.3	617.6	Good	(28.7)	0.3	0.89	225-1581	—
Quasar Associates*	Gro	29.1	108.6	973.6	Fair	(29.8)	—	1.18	221-5672	—
Quest for Value	Max	24.0	82.4	—	Fair	(4.0)	0.9	2.17	862-7778	212-667-7587 (N.Y.)
Rea-Graham Fund	Bal	5.1	60.2	—	Poor	(9.2)	3.2	1.48	433-1998	213-471-1917 (Calif.)
Reich & Tang Equity	Gro	28.1	—	—	—	—	1.7	1.16	221-3079	212-370-1240 (N.Y.)
Royce Value	SCG	22.9	66.9	—	Fair	(4.9)	0.5	1.98	221-4268	212-355-7311 (N.Y.)
Safeco Equity	G&I	30.0	100.6	400.3	Fair	(11.7)	1.8	0.88	426-6730	800-562-6810 (Wash.)
Safeco Growth	Gro	30.3	66.5	414.8	Poor	(17.0)	1.3	0.85	426-6730	800-562-6810 (Wash.)
Safeco Income	EqI	16.4	92.5	419.7	Good	1.0	4.5	0.95	426-6730	800-562-6810 (Wash.)
Safeco Municipal	HGT	(4.6)	43.7	—	Fair	6.4	7.8	0.59	426-6730	800-562-6810 (Wash.)
Scudder Capital Growth	Gro	30.9	112.5	584.1	Good	(14.3)	1.1	0.84	225-2470	—
Scudder Development	SCG	27.4	62.9	509.9	Fair	(25.2)	—	1.25	225-2470	—
Scudder Global	Glo	34.5	—	—	—	—	0.2	1.68	225-2470	—
Scudder Gov. Mortgage Sec.	MBS	(3.1)	—	—	—	—	9.0	1.02	225-2470	—
Scudder Growth & Income	G&I	25.0	108.5	365.7	Fair	(22.1)	3.8	0.83	225-2470	—
Scudder Income	EqI	(4.2)	43.2	134.3	Poor	1.8	9.3	0.88	225-2470	—
Scudder International	Intl	31.4	193.0	603.9	Fair	(1.6)	0.9	1.09	225-2470	—
Scudder Managed Muni Bond	HGT	(4.2)	38.9	74.4	Fair	5.0	7.6	0.58	225-2470	—
Scudder Tax-Free Target–1987*	ITT	2.7	21.3	—	Fair	6.0	4.8	0.94	225-2470	—

*Currently closed to new investors

FUND NAME	TYPE	YEAR TO DATE	THREE YEARS	10 YEARS	THREE-YEAR RATING (WITHIN CATEGORY)	% GAIN (OR LOSS) IN LAST DOWN CYCLE	% CURRENT YIELD	% ANNUAL EXPENSE RATIO (INCLUDES 12B-1 CHARGES, IF ANY)	TOLL-FREE (800)	IN STATE
Scudder Tax-Free Target–1990	ITT	1.1	28.6	—	Fair	6.5	5.6	0.82	225-2470	—
Scudder Tax-Free Target–1993	ITT	(0.9)	32.9	—	Fair	8.3	6.0	0.81	225-2470	—
Scudder Tax-Free Target–1996	ITT	(2.7)	—	—	—	—	6.3	1.00	225-2470	—
Security Action	Max	26.4	81.5	—	Poor	(22.7)	2.7	0.80	255-2461	—
Security Equity	Gro	34.2	100.9	452.8	Fair	(23.3)	2.0	0.67	255-2461	—
Security Income–Corp. Bond	HGC	(0.2)	42.2	136.3	Fair	4.1	11.1	1.04	255-2461	—
Security Investment	G&I	22.0	59.3	262.1	Poor	(21.1)	4.8	0.78	255-2461	—
Security Ultra	Max	22.8	69.1	540.4	Poor	(22.2)	4.2	0.78	255-2461	—
Selected American Shares	G&I	23.9	100.3	359.5	Fair	9.3	2.7	0.85	621-7321	800-572-4437 (Ill.)
Selected Special Shares	Gro	34.4	79.4	278.5	Fair	(16.2)	2.1	1.08	621-7321	800-572-4437 (Ill.)
Seligman Capital	Max	31.7	98.6	622.4	Fair	(35.1)	—	0.78	221-7844	800-522-6869 (N.Y.)
Seligman Common Stock	G&I	25.2	109.6	463.6	Good	(11.1)	2.9	0.55	221-7844	800-522-6869 (N.Y.)
Seligman Commun. & Info.	Sec	45.8	128.6	—	Good	—	—	1.68	221-7844	800-522-6869 (N.Y.)
Seligman Growth	Gro	32.4	102.0	358.7	Fair	(26.4)	1.4	0.57	221-7844	800-522-6869 (N.Y.)
Seligman Hi. Inc.–Hi. Yield Bond	HYC	(1.1)	—	—	—	—	11.7	1.08	221-7844	800-522-6869 (N.Y.)
Seligman Hi. Inc.–Sec. Mort. Inc.	MBS	(4.1)	—	—	—	—	9.2	1.06	221-7844	800-522-6869 (N.Y.)
Seligman Hi. Inc.–U.S. Gov. Guar.	USG	(10.1)	—	—	—	—	8.1	1.10	221-7844	800-522-6869 (N.Y.)
Seligman Income	EqI	(1.2)	57.5	231.7	Fair	(0.5)	8.4	0.73	221-7844	800-522-6869 (N.Y.)
Seligman Tax-Exempt–National	HGT	(6.2)	47.0	—	Good	—	7.9	0.76	221-7844	800-522-6869 (N.Y.)
Sentinel Balanced	Bal	13.6	83.2	300.2	Fair	2.5	5.7	0.68	233-4332	802-229-3900 (Vt.)
Sentinel Common Stock	G&I	25.5	110.0	469.6	Good	0.4	3.3	0.64	233-4332	802-229-3900 (Vt.)
Sentinel Growth	Gro	37.4	120.0	551.6	Good	(28.0)	1.7	0.77	233-4332	802-229-3900 (Vt.)
Sentry Fund	Gro	23.5	92.6	403.3	Fair	(23.9)	1.9	0.72	826-0266	800-472-0280 (Wis.)
Sequoia Fund*	Gro	19.4	79.6	614.7	Fair	15.0	3.4	1.00	—	212-245-4500
Shearson Aggressive Growth	Max	41.3	125.3	—	Good	—	—	1.10	—	212-321-7155
Shearson Appreciation	Gro	32.6	118.7	741.7	Good	(9.6)	1.2	1.00	—	212-321-7155
Shearson Fundamental Value	Gro	32.5	71.0	—	Poor	(1.1)	3.8	1.10	—	212-321-7155
Shearson Global Opp.	Glo	26.0	145.3	—	Fair	—	0.3	1.60	—	212-321-7155
Shearson High Yield	HYC	6.4	47.7	—	Fair	1.9	11.6	0.75	—	212-321-7155
Shearson Lehman–Intermed. Term	USG	(1.4)	—	—	—	—	6.1	1.60	—	212-321-7155
Shearson Lehman–Intl. Equity	Intl	26.6	—	—	—	—	—	2.65	—	212-321-7155
Shearson Lehman–L.G. Gov. Sec.	USG	(6.5)	—	—	—	—	7.2	1.46	—	212-321-7155
Shearson Lehman–Spl. Equity Plus	Max	25.0	—	—	—	—	0.9	2.50	—	212-321-7155
Shearson Lehman–Spl. Growth	Gro	21.0	—	—	—	—	1.5	2.00	—	212-321-7155
Shearson Managed Governments	MBS	(2.1)	34.0	—	Fair	—	8.8	0.77	—	212-321-7155
Shearson Managed Muni	HGT	(4.3)	44.2	—	Fair	6.9	8.1	0.59	—	212-321-7155
Sigma Capital Shares	Max	25.0	94.0	566.5	Fair	(9.5)	1.4	0.91	441-9490	302-652-3091 (Del.)
Sigma Income Shares	HGC	(1.6)	53.5	145.0	Good	0.8	8.3	0.82	441-9490	302-652-3091 (Del.)
Sigma Investment Shares	G&I	24.7	108.4	411.5	Fair	(3.2)	1.9	0.92	441-9490	302-652-3091 (Del.)
Sigma Trust Shares	Bal	9.5	71.7	258.8	Fair	(0.6)	4.8	0.99	441-9490	302-652-3091 (Del.)
Sigma Venture Shares	SCG	19.1	66.9	520.1	Fair	(28.4)	—	0.96	441-9490	302-652-3091 (Del.)
Smith Barney Equity	Gro	32.5	100.0	462.5	Fair	(16.5)	2.2	0.85	221-8806	212-356-2631 (N.Y.)
Smith Barney Inc. & Growth	G&I	17.5	87.3	451.9	Fair	(4.2)	5.4	0.56	221-8806	212-356-2631 (N.Y.)
Smith Barney U.S. Gov. Sec.	MBS	(3.3)	—	—	—	—	10.9	0.35	221-8806	212-356-2631 (N.Y.)
SoGen International	Gro	33.2	125.1	618.8	Good	(5.6)	—	1.47	334-2143	212-832-3073 (N.Y.)
Sovereign Investors	G&I	17.0	96.9	380.8	Fair	(2.3)	4.1	0.70	—	215-254-0703
Stein Roe & Farnham Cap. Opp.	Gro	44.7	103.8	584.9	Fair	(40.5)	0.1	0.92	338-2550	—
Stein Roe & Farnham Stock	Gro	42.9	112.3	430.7	Fair	(33.9)	1.1	0.64	338-2550	—
Stein Roe Discovery	SCG	32.8	79.0	—	Fair	—	0.1	1.36	338-2550	—
Stein Roe High-Yield Bond	HYC	(0.6)	—	—	—	—	10.6	0.96	338-2550	—
Stein Roe High-Yield Muni	HYT	(3.6)	46.2	—	Good	—	7.9	0.72	338-2550	—
Stein Roe Managed Bond	HGC	(5.3)	44.9	—	Fair	1.9	8.5	0.65	338-2550	—

*Currently closed to new investors

| FUND NAME | TYPE | % GAIN (OR LOSS) TO OCT. 1, 1987 | | | THREE-YEAR RATING (WITHIN CATEGORY) | % GAIN (OR LOSS) IN LAST DOWN CYCLE | % CURRENT YIELD | % ANNUAL EXPENSE RATIO (INCLUDES 12B-1 CHARGES, IF ANY) | TELEPHONE | |
		YEAR TO DATE	THREE YEARS	10 YEARS					TOLL-FREE (800)	IN STATE
Stein Roe Managed Muni	HGT	(4.9)	50.9	98.3	Good	8.0	7.4	0.64	338-2550	—
Stein Roe Special	Max	29.6	96.9	682.9	Fair	(15.1)	1.7	0.93	338-2550	—
Stein Roe Total Return	Bal	14.0	75.4	243.4	Fair	(9.7)	5.7	0.76	338-2550	—
Stein Roe Universe	Max	34.6	91.2	—	Fair	(35.7)	1.1	1.20	338-2550	—
Strategic Investments	Gold	56.6	13.9	516.7	Poor	(33.2)	5.3	1.46	527-5027	214-484-1326 (Texas)
Strategic Silver	Gold	56.7	—	—	—	—	—	1.54	527-5027	214-484-1326 (Texas)
Stratton Monthly Div. Shares	Sec	(1.6)	68.3	190.3	Fair	(1.0)	8.5	1.24	634-5726	—
Strong Income	EqI	4.5	—	—	—	—	12.7	1.00	368-3863	—
Strong Investment	Bal	6.4	55.8	—	Poor	4.9	7.1	1.10	368-3863	—
Strong Opportunity	Max	39.1	—	—	—	—	0.5	1.70	368-3863	—
Strong Total Return	Max	20.9	88.7	—	Fair	2.6	5.0	1.10	368-3863	—
Tax-Exempt Bond of America	HGT	(5.6)	42.0	—	Fair	5.6	7.4	0.59	421-9900	213-486-9651 (Calif.)
Templeton Foreign	Intl	49.9	148.5	—	Poor	0.2	1.6	0.79	237-0738	800-282-0106 (Fla.)
Templeton Global I*	Glo	20.1	88.4	—	Poor	(6.3)	2.2	0.66	237-0738	800-282-0106 (Fla.)
Templeton Global II	Glo	20.1	76.0	—	Poor	—	2.1	0.76	237-0738	800-282-0106 (Fla.)
Templeton Growth	Glo	32.6	105.8	522.8	Fair	(4.8)	1.1	0.73	237-0738	800-282-0106 (Fla.)
Templeton World	Glo	28.2	101.2	—	Fair	(2.6)	2.3	0.67	237-0738	800-282-0106 (Fla.)
Thomson McKinnon—Growth	Gro	36.7	124.8	—	Good	—	1.0	1.70	628-1237	212-482-5894 (N.Y.)
Thomson McKinnon—Inc.	EqI	2.4	39.8	—	Poor	—	10.2	1.60	628-1237	212-482-5894 (N.Y.)
Thomson McKinnon—Opp.	Max	34.8	82.5	—	Fair	—		1.80	628-1237	212-482-5894 (N.Y.)

*Currently closed to new investors

Money Notes

Avoid **stock funds** with expense ratios, including 12b-1 charges, greater than 2%, and bond funds that hit you for more than 1.1% annually.

T. Rowe Price funds will lower minimums to $50 from $1,000 for investors who state an intention to establish their own dollar-cost averaging plan.

In general, **total-return funds** can be subdivided into three groups: growth and income funds, which buy stocks with above-average yields and moderate capital-gains possibilities; equity income funds, which favor high-yield stocks; and balanced funds, which hold a mixed portfolio of stocks and bonds.

Treasury bond funds are the place to be if you figure interest rates will fall.

USAA Cornerstone divvies its holdings virtually equally among five investment areas: U.S. stocks, foreign stocks, real estate, government bonds, and non-South African gold. "We're not trying to outguess the market. In an up market we look to stay close to the S&P, and in down markets we won't fall as much as the index," says chief portfolio manager Harry Miller.

Vanguard Index Trust, a growth and income fund, has the lowest expense ratio among the 526 stock funds tracked for *Money* by Lipper Analytical Services, only .28%.

A variation on the asset allocation theme is **Vanguard STAR**, which places 60% to 70% of its cash in other Vanguard stock funds and 30% to 40% in Vanguard bond funds.

FUND NAME	TYPE	% GAIN (OR LOSS) TO OCT. 1, 1987			THREE-YEAR RATING (WITHIN CATEGORY)	% GAIN (OR LOSS) IN LAST DOWN CYCLE	% CURRENT YIELD	% ANNUAL EXPENSE RATIO (INCLUDES 12B-1 CHARGES, IF ANY)	TELEPHONE	
		YEAR TO DATE	THREE YEARS	10 YEARS					TOLL-FREE (800)	IN STATE
Thomson McKinnon—Tax Exempt	HGT	(6.7)	—	—	—	—	6.4	1.80	628-1237	212-482-5894 (N.Y.)
Thomson McKinnon—U.S. Gov.	USG	(4.8)	—	—	—	—	9.7	1.70	628-1237	212-482-5894 (N.Y.)
Transatlantic Growth	Intl	33.9	198.8	480.1	Fair	(11.5)	—	1.49	233-9164	212-687-2515 (N.Y.)
T. Rowe Price Cap. Appreciation	Max	17.3	—	—	—	—	1.1	1.20	638-5660	301-547-2308 (Md.)
T. Rowe Price Equity Inc.	EqI	20.2	—	—	—	—	4.4	1.00	638-5660	301-547-2308 (Md.)
T. Rowe Price Growth & Income	G&I	20.8	60.0	—	Poor	(9.2)	5.4	0.96	638-5660	301-547-2308 (Md.)
T. Rowe Price Growth Stock	Gro	31.8	121.6	295.0	Good	(18.8)	1.3	0.59	638-5660	301-547-2308 (Md.)
T. Rowe Price High Yield	HYC	4.7	—	—	—	—	12.2	0.99	638-5660	301-547-2308 (Md.)
T. Rowe Price International Stock	Intl	30.5	208.3	—	Fair	(2.7)	0.6	1.10	638-5660	301-547-2308 (Md.)
T. Rowe Price New America Growth	Gro	19.7	—	—	—	—	0.4	1.00	638-5660	301-547-2308 (Md.)
T. Rowe Price New Era	Sec	46.7	112.4	550.7	Fair	(8.0)	1.5	0.73	638-5660	301-547-2308 (Md.)
T. Rowe Price New Horizons	SCG	25.6	50.8	428.7	Fair	(28.1)	0.1	0.73	638-5660	301-547-2308 (Md.)
T. Rowe Price New Income	HGC	(3.2)	36.0	147.1	Poor	7.4	9.0	0.65	638-5660	301-547-2308 (Md.)
T. Rowe Price Short Term Bond	HGC	1.4	30.4	—	Poor	—	7.5	0.94	638-5660	301-547-2308 (Md.)
T. Rowe Price Tax-Free—High Yld.	HYT	(2.2)	—	—	—	—	7.7	0.98	638-5660	301-547-2308 (Md.)
T. Rowe Price Tax-Free Income	HGT	(7.1)	34.5	83.1	Poor	2.8	7.1	0.61	638-5660	301-547-2308 (Md.)
T. Rowe Price Tax-Free Short Int.	ITT	0.0	22.7	—	Fair	—	5.4	0.73	638-5660	301-547-2308 (Md.)
Tudor Fund	Max	38.0	108.2	795.7	Fair	(28.7)	—	1.01	223-3332	212-908-9582 (N.Y.)
Twentieth Century Growth	Max	55.6	149.2	1,222.5	Good	(27.9)	0.4	1.01	345-2021	—
Twentieth Century Select	Gro	37.6	125.6	1,133.1	Good	(24.6)	0.9	1.01	345-2021	—
Twentieth Century Ultra	Max	45.5	97.5	—	Fair	(40.8)	0.1	1.01	345-2021	—
Twentieth Century U.S. Gov.	USG	(0.1)	30.8	—	Poor	7.5	8.3	1.01	345-2021	—
Twentieth Century Vista	Max	43.7	111.9	—	Fair	—	—	1.01	345-2021	—
Unified Growth	Gro	17.0	72.9	420.0	Poor	(14.6)	1.3	1.01	862-7283	—
United Accumulative	Gro	24.3	92.0	460.4	Fair	(9.0)	1.3	0.60	—	816-842-1075
United Bond	HGC	(0.6)	53.0	143.7	Good	1.9	8.9	0.64	—	816-842-1075
United Continental Income	Bal	10.8	90.5	354.6	Fair	(3.1)	4.3	0.79	—	816-842-1075
United Gold & Government	Gold	77.7	—	—	—	—	0.9	1.48	—	816-842-1075
United Gov. Securities	USG	(8.6)	38.5	—	Fair	—	9.1	0.72	—	816-842-1075
United High Income*	HYC	3.1	53.2	—	Fair	1.0	12.8	0.76	—	816-842-1075
United High Income II	HYC	3.3	—	—	—	—	11.5	0.77	—	816-842-1075
United Income	EqI	20.8	109.6	382.6	Good	(6.1)	2.9	0.62	—	816-842-1075
United International Growth	Intl	36.8	151.4	640.7	Fair	(6.0)	0.2	1.07	—	816-842-1075
United Municipal Bond	HGT	(7.7)	48.3	55.2	Good	5.2	7.7	0.61	—	816-842-1075
United Municipal High Income	HYT	(0.4)	—	—	—	—	8.7	0.75	—	816-842-1075
United New Concepts	SCG	28.0	81.9	—	Fair	(5.0)	0.4	1.19	—	816-842-1075
United Science & Energy	Sec	37.0	101.7	428.2	Fair	(10.7)	0.6	0.83	—	816-842-1075
United Services Gold Shares	Gold	58.9	31.4	643.0	Poor	(30.5)	4.9	1.32	824-4653	—
United Services Good & Bad Times	G&I	28.7	80.5	—	Poor	(10.5)	1.6	1.35	824-4653	—
United Services New Prospector	Gold	85.5	—	—	—	—	0.4	1.47	824-4653	—
United Services Prospector*	Gold	83.1	97.0	—	Fair	—	—	2.90	824-4653	—
United Vanguard	Gro	32.7	97.2	781.5	Fair	(17.9)	1.9	0.98	—	816-842-1075
USAA Cornerstone	Sec	32.5	113.6	—	Good	—	1.5	1.50	531-8000	—
USAA Gold	Gold	84.9	91.9	—	Fair	—	0.6	1.50	531-8000	—
USAA Growth	Gro	33.0	78.3	287.9	Fair	(29.3)	1.0	1.09	531-8000	—
USAA Income	EqI	(2.8)	40.0	146.0	Poor	6.4	11.4	0.65	531-8000	—
USAA Sunbelt Era	SCG	27.4	59.0	—	Fair	(37.4)	0.3	1.05	531-8000	—
USAA Tax Exempt—High Yield	HGT	(6.5)	38.0	—	Poor	6.3	8.3	0.49	531-8000	—
USAA Tax Ex.—Intermed. Term	ITT	(2.5)	32.4	—	Fair	5.0	7.3	0.60	531-8000	—
USAA Tax Ex.—Short Term	ITT	0.7	22.3	—	Fair	6.5	5.8	0.57	531-8000	—
U.S. Gov. Guar. Securities	USG	(5.0)	—	—	—	—	10.2	1.00	421-9900	213-486-9651 (Calif.)
U.S. Trend	Gro	36.7	91.4	579.8	Fair	(24.0)	2.2	1.01	262-6686	—

*Currently closed to new investors

| FUND NAME | TYPE | % GAIN (OR LOSS) TO OCT. 1, 1987 | | | THREE-YEAR RATING (WITHIN CATEGORY) | % GAIN (OR LOSS) IN LAST DOWN CYCLE | % CURRENT YIELD | % ANNUAL EXPENSE RATIO (INCLUDES 12B-1 CHARGES, IF ANY) | TELEPHONE | |
		YEAR TO DATE	THREE YEARS	10 YEARS					TOLL-FREE (800)	IN STATE
UST Master Int.-Term Tax-Ex.	ITT	(0.5)	—	—	—	—	6.3	0.81	223-1136	—
Value Line Aggressive Income	HYC	4.1	—	—	—	—	13.1	1.23	223-0818	—
Value Line Convertible	EqI	14.6	—	—	—	—	4.5	1.04	223-0818	—
Value Line Fund	G&I	29.8	108.5	483.9	Good	(35.0)	1.3	0.69	223-0818	—
Value Line Income	EqI	16.0	74.0	401.8	Fair	(17.4)	6.4	0.74	223-0818	—
Value Line Leveraged Growth	Max	34.7	117.6	667.1	Fair	(28.7)	0.5	0.99	223-0818	—
Value Line Special Situations	Gro	24.7	50.0	366.3	Poor	(39.0)	0.3	1.00	223-0818	—
Value Line Tax Ex. High Yield	HYT	(2.8)	39.9	—	Poor	—	8.4	0.68	223-0818	—
Value Line U.S. Gov. Sec.	USG	(2.2)	42.2	—	Good	2.8	10.6	0.73	223-0818	—
Van Eck Gold Resources	Gold	103.8	—	—	—	—	0.1	1.52	221-2220	212-687-5200 (N.Y.)
Van Eck World Trends	Glo	23.4	—	—	—	—	1.7	1.46	221-2220	212-687-5200 (N.Y.)
Van Kampen Merr. Ins. Tax Fr. Inc.	HGT	(4.8)	—	—	—	—	7.6	0.76	225-2222	—
Van Kampen Merr. Tax Fr. Hi. Inc.	HYT	0.1	—	—	—	—	8.2	0.67	225-2222	—
Van Kampen Merritt U.S. Gov.	MBS	(5.8)	39.0	—	Fair	—	11.8	0.59	225-2222	—
Vance Sanders Special	Gro	21.9	25.7	323.1	Poor	(19.8)	0.3	0.97	225-6265	617-482-8260 (Mass.)
Vanguard Convertible	EqI	7.6	—	—	—	—	5.1	0.80	662-7447	—
Vanguard Explorer*	Sec	26.0	30.2	460.6	Poor	(30.4)	0.1	0.76	662-7447	—
Vanguard Explorer II	SCG	29.2	—	—	—	—	0.2	1.17	662-7447	—
Vanguard Fixed Inc.—GNMA	MBS	(4.3)	39.2	—	Good	5.9	10.0	0.38	662-7447	—
Vanguard Fixed Inc.—High Yield	HYC	1.0	51.1	—	Fair	2.0	12.0	0.45	662-7447	—
Vanguard Fixed Inc.—Invest. Grade	HGC	(6.9)	38.7	134.8	Fair	1.3	10.4	0.41	662-7447	—
Vanguard Fixed Inc.—Short Term	HGC	1.2	38.1	—	Fair	7.7	7.4	0.38	662-7447	—
Vanguard Fixed Inc.—U.S. Treasury	USG	(10.2)	—	—	—	—	9.1	0.35	662-7447	—
Vanguard High Yld. Stock*††	EqI	13.4	98.3	597.3	Good	7.9	7.3	0.52	662-7447	—
Vanguard Index Trust	G&I	35.5	113.7	409.6	Good	(7.9)	2.8	0.28	662-7447	—
Vanguard Muni Bond—High Yield	HYT	(6.7)	42.4	—	Fair	6.8	8.3	0.33	662-7447	—
Vanguard Muni Bond—Ins. Long	HGT	(4.7)	37.8	—	Poor	—	7.9	0.33	662-7447	—
Vanguard Muni Bond—Intermed.	ITT	(3.2)	37.2	58.3	Good	6.2	7.3	0.33	662-7447	—
Vanguard Muni Bond—Long Term	HGT	(6.6)	41.0	51.6	Fair	6.1	8.1	0.33	662-7447	—
Vanguard Muni Bond—Short Term	ITT	2.3	20.0	78.0	Fair	6.0	5.1	0.33	662-7447	—
Vanguard Naess & Thomas Spec.	SCG	34.5	50.7	350.9	Poor	(38.7)	—	0.92	662-7447	—
Vanguard Preferred Stock†††	EqI	(7.6)	59.1	142.9	Fair	(5.6)	9.3	0.58	662-7447	—
Vanguard Sp. Port.—Gold & PM	Gold	79.3	113.4	—	Good	—	1.2	0.59	662-7447	—
Vanguard Sp. Port.—Health	Sec	33.7	150.0	—	Good	—	1.0	0.61	662-7447	—
Vanguard Sp. Port.—Serv. Econ.	Sec	17.5	91.0	—	Fair	—	1.9	0.48	662-7447	—
Vanguard Sp. Port.—Technology	Sec	31.1	53.8	—	Fair	—	0.3	0.65	662-7447	—
Vanguard STAR	Bal	14.1	—	—	—	—	5.1	—	662-7447	—
Vanguard Wellesley Income	EqI	(0.3)	60.3	242.0	Fair	5.1	8.6	0.58	662-7447	—
Vanguard Wellington	Bal	16.7	86.2	356.8	Fair	(1.6)	5.2	0.53	662-7447	—
Vanguard Windsor*	G&I	24.4	102.7	610.4	Fair	2.6	5.0	0.52	662-7447	—
Vanguard Windsor II	G&I	23.8	—	—	—	—	2.8	0.65	662-7447	—
Vanguard W.L. Morgan Growth	Sec	38.4	98.6	458.9	Fair	(20.2)	1.3	0.54	662-7447	—
Vanguard World—Int. Growth	Intl	29.2	214.4	—	Good	(1.5)	—	0.78	662-7447	—
Vanguard World—U.S. Growth	Gro	20.8	76.3	395.2	Poor	(15.7)	—	0.80	662-7447	—
Venture Income Plus	HYC	9.6	44.6	—	Fair	3.6	14.4	1.14	545-2098	505-983-4335 (N.M.)
Venture Muni Plus	HGT	(2.6)	16.1	—	Poor	9.3	9.3	2.69	545-2098	505-983-4335 (N.M.)
Venture Ret. Plan of Am.—Bond	HYC	(5.3)	25.9	—	Poor	5.2	9.7	2.39	545-2098	505-983-4335 (N.M.)
Washington Mutual Investors	G&I	25.2	110.2	525.7	Good	(3.2)	3.5	0.54	421-9900	213-486-9651 (Calif.)
Weingarten Equity	Max	40.3	135.3	1,000.5	Good	(28.4)	0.7	1.00	231-0803	800-392-9681 (Texas)
Winthrop Focus Growth	Gro	26.5	—	—	—	(22.3)	—	1.43	225-8011	816-283-1700 (Mo.)
WPG Fund	Max	36.2	106.7	—	Fair	(19.5)	—	1.23	223-3332	212-908-9582 (N.Y.)

*Currently closed to new investors   †† Formerly called Qualified Dividend Port. I   ††† Formerly called Qualified Dividend Port. II

Index